# Canoeing to
## Western Pennsylvania
### and
# Northern West Virginia

## Eighth Edition - 1991

Compiled and edited by

## Roy R. Weil
## Mary M. Shaw

Published by the Pittsburgh Council
American Youth Hostels, Inc.
6300 Fifth Avenue
Pittsburgh, Penn. 15232
(412) 362-8181

# Eighth Edition

Printed in the United States of America


Text Copyright © 1991, 1983, 1975, 1973, 1971, 1969
Pittsburgh Council, American Youth Hostels
6300 Fifth Avenue
Pittsburgh, Pennsylvania 15232

Appendix F Copyright © 1991 by Mary Shaw
Photographs Copyright © 1991 by Mary Shaw
        1983 by Mary Shaw and Jim Roberts

Photographs by Mary Shaw, Roy Weil,
Jim Roberts

Cartography by Don Hoecker

Hydrology by Mary Shaw


ISBN 1-879724-00-6

# Table of Contents

# On Judgement and Personal Responsibility

We have compiled this guide as an aid to pleasure canoeists. We have tried to present accurate descriptions of these rivers and creeks. However, we are human, and rivers change with time. The suggestions in this guide can be invalidated by water and weather conditions, by the skill of your paddling party, and by changes in the rivers themselves. Therefore we can not take responsibility for errors, omissions, changes in the rivers, or for other problems encountered through the use of this guide. Each paddler who sets forth on a river assumes personal responsibility, not only for his or her own safety, but also for the safety of others on the trip. Ultimately, your safety depends mostly on your own common sense and good judgement.

# Acknowledgements

Throughout its 30-year history this guide has been the product of volunteer effort. Many individuals have contributed to the development of this guide. The editors wish to recognize especially the following people who have made major contributions to this guide throughout its development: Rich Bartoo, Bob Buck, Gordon Bugby, Bob Burrell, Carol Davis, Lloyd Geertz, Ed Gertler, Ray Gerard, Jim Gogots, Don Hoecker, Ed Holloway, Tom Irwin, John Mahaffey, Walt Pilewski, Tom Reilly, Harvey Shapiro, Katherine Spindt, and John Sweet.

We also want to thank the following for their contributions to this, the eighth edition: Tom Irwin, Ed Gertler for bagging and writing up a host of new streams. Edward Link and Don Frew for fresh write-ups on a variety of rivers. Frank Bruns for custom printing the photographs. Bob Buck, Gordon Bugby, Don Hoecker, Karen Lukas, Ray Yutzy, Jane Swanson, Rick Tomlinson, and others who gave up Tuesday evenings to edit and revise the text. Bill Salesky of the US Army Corps of Engineers and Joe Lescinsky of the US Geological Survey for providing information enabling us to do a much better job on the gauge readings. Marian Hrubovcak of Pennsylvania DER for an update to the Scenic Rivers Section. Terry Palmo of Laurel Highlands River Tours for a much needed correlation chart.

This guide is revised periodically. Any canoeist who sends in new information that is used in the next edition will receive a complimentary copy of that edition when it is published.

Happy Canoeing

Roy Weil

Mary Shaw

February 1991

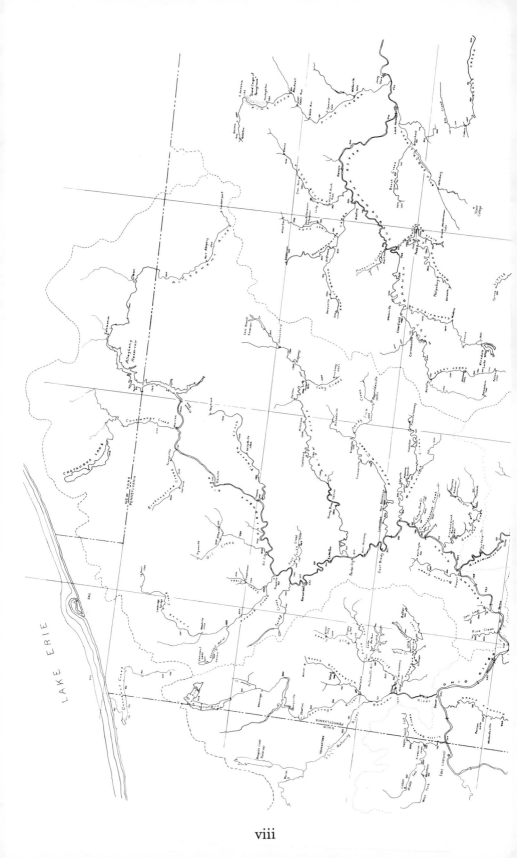

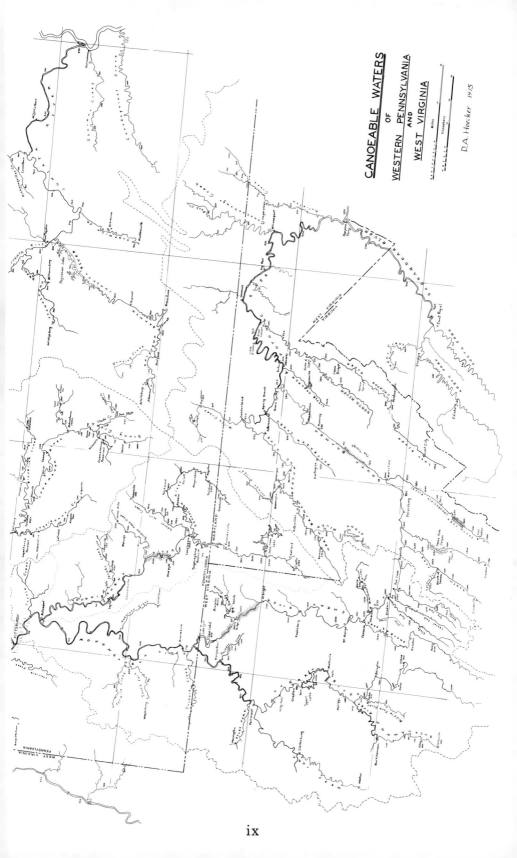

CANOEABLE WATERS
OF
WESTERN PENNSYLVANIA
AND
WEST VIRGINIA

D.A. Hoecker 1975

# Introduction

Western Pennsylvania offers many types of canoeing. From the exuberant whitewater of the mountains, to the flowing rivers of the valleys, to the lakes nestled in the rolling hills, the region abounds with canoeing opportunities suited to almost every taste. Most of the recreational canoeing activity in Western Pennsylvania is on moving-water rivers. The rivers range from narrow creeks that are canoeable only after a heavy rain to major rivers with year-round flow. They cover the complete spectrum from still through swift, from pristine through industrial, and from easy through difficult.

## Coverage

The geographic area covered by this guide includes all streams whose waters drain into the Ohio River within Pennsylvania and the northern panhandle of West Virginia or into Lake Erie from Pennsylvania. The southern portion of this range is well-covered by Davidson, Eister, and Davidson's excellent *Wildwater West Virginia* (see Appendix D); we therefore describe only the most significant runs in this region of overlapping coverage. Trip descriptions and gauge information are also included for some of the popular streams around the periphery of this area (e.g., Pine Creek, the West Branch of the Susquehanna, and a few streams in the Potomac River basin). Streams in northeastern West Virginia that drain into the Potomac, though popular with Western Pennsylvania canoeists, are not included in this guide since they are adequately covered by other guides which are described in Appendix D.

This guide emphasizes open-canoe paddling on easy to intermediate whitewater, although included are major rivers, flat streams of scenic interest, and more difficult creeks of interest to closed boaters (kayakers). The coverage in the guide is of many canoeable streams rather than extensive description of a few.

Canoeists should be aware of certain hazards that are intrinsic to the sport. General precautions are described in the sections on "Canoeing Safety" and "Organizing Canoe Trips". Specific difficulties for individual rivers are described in the trip write-ups.

1

## History of this Guide

This is the eighth edition of a guide originally compiled in 1960, based mainly on the canoeing experiences of members of the Pittsburgh Council, American Youth Hostels. Subsequent editions have incorporated trip reports submitted by canoeists from AYH and other groups, most notably the Three Rivers Paddling Club. Thus, this guide has become a creation of the Western Pennsylvania canoeing community, rather than of a single canoeing group.

The guide has evolved over 30 years from a mimeographed pamphlet of 11 pages with 20 trips covering 350 miles of streams to its present size of 480 pages with 270 trips covering 3039 miles of streams. The major revisions in this edition include completely revised hydrology (more usable stream size, gauges, and normal wet period), addition of over 50 new streams, and revisions of almost all of the write-ups. The average age of the write-ups was decreased from nearly 8 years in the seventh edition to about 3 years at the end of canoeing season 1990. A rewrite of the shuttles into a more usable, consistent format was initiated.

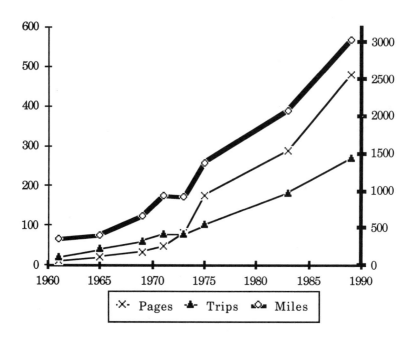

# Canoeing in Western Pennsylvania

The varied terrain of Western Pennsylvania offers
unparalleled canoeing opportunities. Whitewater rivers
spilling west from the mountain ridges challenge canoeists,
kayakers, and rafters. Gentle gradients attract open
canoeists, who may choose between paddle and pole for
controlling their craft. The many lakes offer opportunities
for placid paddling on calm water or for canoe sailing.

## Varieties of Paddling Opportunities

### River Canoeing

The major focus of this canoe guide is on the rivers of
Western Pennsylvania. Several kinds of watercraft are
commonly used on Western Pennsylvania rivers. The most
common, as well as the most versatile, is the classic "open"
canoe, pointed at both ends, paddled by one or two people,
and undecked for most of its length. Open canoes in the
hands of trained paddlers are suitable for easy to intermediate rivers as well as for lakes. With extra flotation
experts can use them on difficult rivers.

Most paddlers who run intermediate to difficult rivers use
rafts or "closed boats". Closed boats are completely decked to
prevent waves from swamping the boat; even the paddler's
cockpit is covered with a flexible "spray skirt". In the closed
canoe (C1) the paddler kneels and uses a single-bladed
paddle whereas in a kayak (K1) the paddler is seated and
uses a double-bladed paddle. Rafts are more stable, though
less maneuverable, than either open or closed boats. They
make it possible for less experienced paddlers to enjoy trips
on more difficult rivers.

### Canoe Poling

Local canoeists have discovered the sport of canoe poling. A
solo canoeist stands in the center of the boat and uses a
12-foot aluminum pole to control the boat by pushing the pole
against the bottom of the stream. A poling stream should be
shallow, with a gravel or firm dirt bottom. Rivers up to
Class III in difficulty can be run both upstream and

3

downstream. Good poling can be found on Wolf Creek, Little Connoquenessing Creek, the lower sections of Slippery Rock Creek, Cowanshannock Creek, Crooked Creek, and many similar small streams.

## Lake Canoeing

Canoeing on the numerous local lakes is another popular activity. Many of the lakes in this area were constructed by the Army Corps of Engineers and have excellent facilities. The length of the trip can be suited to your desires, and if you take account of the wind direction, you can make the return trip easier than the outbound trip. Some of the lakes have motorboat horsepower restrictions, making them more pleasant for the non-motorized canoe. Maps of the lakes maintained by the Army Corps of Engineers are available from the Pittsburgh District Office, Federal Building, Pittsburgh, Pennsylvania, 15222. Maps of lakes controlled by the Pennsylvania Fish Commission are available from them at PO Box 1673, Harrisburg, Pennsylvania, 17120. The maps show the lake area, surrounding highways and local roads, and developed recreation sites, such as launching sites and picnic areas. The maps also give technical information about the dams. A favorite lake is Lake Arthur in Moraine State Park. A State Park map is available at the park headquarters, or at some of the bulletin boards on the park grounds. A chart of lakes in Western Pennsylvania that permit canoeing is included in Appendix A. Many of these lakes are suitable for canoe sailing.

## Sea Kayaking

Another type of canoeing is sea kayaking. Sea kayaking typically involves large bodies of water, where wind and waves make a difference. Lake Erie and our famous three rivers can provide Western Pennsylvania sea kayakers with sea-like conditions without the rocks of a New England shore. The sea kayak is at home on any flatwater. It can be used on many of the Class I rivers and lakes that abound in Western Pennsylvania. It is an ideal craft for solo boat camping along many of these streams.

The sea kayak is generally either plastic or fiberglass. Compared to the river kayak, it is longer (17 feet or more), with more "V" to the hull and a lot more cargo space.

Because of the hull shape, it does not turn as easily. Many sea kayaks feature rudders. A skeg, a six-to-ten-inch fin sticking out of the bottom of the boat, may also be used.

### Canoe Sailing

A canoe can be outfitted for sailing by rigging it with a sail and leeboards. Because of its light weight and generally large sail area, a sailing canoe will give an exciting ride.

### Swamp Canoeing

Swamp canoeing is a different type of canoeing from running whitewater streams or paddling open lakes. In this type of canoeing, many twisting channels and exploration of backwaters make the straight-line distance traveled very small. Much time is spent looking at the wildlife and wildflowers, and exploring back channels and side streams. Depending on the time of year, it is some-times necessary to push your way through lilypads and marsh grasses as well as over logs and around beaver dams.

Poling in a swamp requires a pole whose end does not sink into the soft bottom muck. In the picture below the left pole is a new river pole, the second from left is a well used river pole, and the right two are swamp poles constructed with a tennis ball and a small plumber's helper.

# The Pennsylvania Scenic Rivers Program

The Pennsylvania Scenic Rivers Act of 1972 authorizes the establishment of a state system of wild, scenic, pastoral, recreational, and modified recreational rivers and streams. It specifies procedures by which waterways of outstanding aesthetic and recreational value may become a part of this system. Once included in the system, a stream is protected from adverse actions by state agencies.

State designation does not provide absolute protection from Federal projects, such as Army Corps of Engineers dams, but such projects must consider the fact that a stream is a part of the state system. Since the state system neither buys land nor enforces land-use controls on private land owners, compliance with the goals of the system on other than state land is purely voluntary. The program cannot halt every threat to a waterway, but it can be used to recognize and encourage protection of the aesthetic value of a stream. It is the only state program for this purpose available at the present time, so we should make the best use of it we can.

In order for a stream to be designated:

• It must have priority 1-A status.

• It must be recommended by the State Scenic Rivers Task Force.

• Public Informational Meetings must be held.

• A study must be done to determine river eligibility.

• Legislation must be passed by the General Assembly.

• Legislation must be signed by the Governor.

In order for this complex designation procedure to be accomplished successfully, several favorable conditions must exist. The most important is the presence of an organized local group which will lobby for the stream and head off any opposition at the local level. No stream has been, or probably ever will be, designated in the absence of such a favorable local group or in the presence of organized local opposition.

Streams that have been designated (as of February 1990) as part of the Pennsylvania Scenic Rivers Program are:

- Schuylkill River from Port Clinton to Fairmount Dam. (124.8 miles Recreational)

- Stony Creek in Dauphin and Lebanon Counties. (16.0 miles Wild)

- Lehigh River from Francis E. Walter Dam to Jim Thorpe. (64.0 miles Scenic). A number of its tributaries are in both the Wild and the Scenic categories.

- French Creek and tributaries in Chester and Berks Counties. (42.8 miles Scenic)

- Lick Run in Clinton County. (23.0 miles Wild)

- Octoraro Creek in Lancaster and Chester Counties. (36.5 miles Scenic, Pastoral)

- Letort Spring Run in Cumberland County. (7.6 miles Pastoral, Modified Recreational)

- Bear Run in Fayette County. (4.3 miles Scenic)

- Tucquan Creek in Lancaster County. (8.1 miles Wild, Scenic)

- Lower Brandywine in Chester and Delaware Counties. (65.9 miles Scenic, Pastoral)

In addition, the Pine Creek (Grand Canyon of Pennsylvania) has been submitted to the Legislature, the Tulpehocken Creek is being prepared for Legislative submission, and studies are officially under way on the Loyalsock Creek and Yellow Breeches Creek.

If your favorite stream has not received the recognition it deserves, you should go about creating the necessary local support, and then bring it to the attention of the Scenic River Task Force.

To find out more about the system, several publications are available.

- *Pennsylvania Scenic River Program: Brochure with Map* - this map shows the designated and candidate rivers state wide.

- *Pennsylvania Scenic Rivers Inventory* - contains a detailed list of potential scenic river candidates.

- *The Pennsylvania Scenic Rivers Program: Questions and Answers* - gives responses to the most frequently asked questions about the program.

- *Pennsylvania Scenic Rivers Program: Program Guidelines* - contains a general overview including eligibility and classification criteria.

- *Citizen Participation Guidelines* includes guidelines for citizens to write their own detailed waterway study.

These publications are available from the Pennsylvania Scenic Rivers Program, Dept. of Environmental Resources, Box 8761, Harrisburg, Pennsylvania 17105-8761. If you would like to provide information, services, make comments or suggestions, or ask for information and assistance, contact the Program Director at the above address. Copies of letters are circulated to the Task Force, which has members representing such river-oriented groups as the American Canoe Association, the Sierra Club, and Trout Unlimited.

## Legal Matters

Not all lakes and streams in Western Pennsylvania can be
canoed at will. Many access points are on private land, and
special restrictions apply to some bodies of water. In
general, assume that you are a guest or a trespasser on
private land. When you put in, take out, eat lunch, or camp
along the river, ask permission. Be considerate of local
residents by avoiding noise and road congestion. Carry out
your trash. Thoughtless encounters with landowners or
local inhabitants can result in the denial of river access or
camp sites to all canoeists. Fishermen deserve
consideration as well. Steer your boat as wide of them and
their fishing spot as possible. Do not run trips on popular
fishing streams during the first few days of the fishing
season. Do not insist on spoiling their fun while having
yours.

### Canoeing and the Law

One attorney has rendered these opinions:

"The streams of Pennsylvania are classed as either
navigable (public) or unnavigable (private). The
determination of whether a section of a stream is navigable
or not rests with the court and each case must stand on its
own merit."

"On navigable streams the public has the right to use the
banks from the high-water mark on one side to the high-
water mark on the other side, including the bottom of the
river, and to navigate the river."

"On unnavigable streams the banks and the bottom thereof
belong to the riparian owners but the river itself can be used
for navigation. On such rivers a canoeist would be
trespassing if he waded in the stream or landed on the
banks."

"'Navigable' is not restricted to the sense of use by
commercial vessels. Sometimes "navigable" and
"canoeable" are taken as being synonymous. Rapids, falls,
occasional portages, and low summer water levels do not
necessarily make a river unnavigable".

## *State Permits and Fees*

**Pennsylvania:** As of January 1991 it was not necessary to register a boat in Pennsylvania unless it was motor powered. However, if a boat is to be used in a Pennsylvania State Park Lake, it must have a State Park Launching Permit. The rules also require you to launch at an official launching area. These permits cost $5.00 (summer 1990) and may be obtained during normal operating hours and seasons at the launching areas and/or at park offices in parks with launching areas. A permit may also be obtained by sending the required fee to Commonwealth of Pennsylvania, Department of Environmental Resources, Bureau of State Parks, PO Box 1467, Harrisburg, Pennsylvania 17120.

**Ohio:** As of January 1991, all boats on the waters of Ohio must be registered with the state. The registration fee for a non-motor powered boat is $10.00. You must place the registration number in three-inch high numbers on the boat. You may register a boat at the State Parks during normal operating hours and seasons. You may also register your boat by sending the correct fee to Ohio Department of Natural Resources, Fountain Square, Columbus, Ohio 43229.

# Canoe Safety

Whitewater canoeing has become a very popular sport. It is enjoyable when you do not overreach your ability, but it can become dangerous if you disregard common safety precautions. This section discusses whitewater hazards and ways for your trips to be both safe and enjoyable. Each season brings some canoeing fatalities. Most of these accidents involve the situations described below and disregard of safety rules or common sense. Please read this section carefully and exercise your best judgement in handling the challenge of each trip that you plan.

## Whitewater Hazards to Life

A few basic situations account for essentially all serious or fatal whitewater canoeing accidents. Some of these situations can be avoided by taking simple precautions, but others are intrinsic to the sport. Moderate whitewater can overpower even a very strong swimmer. The awesome force of moving water creates special hazards when a canoeist shares the river with floating objects such as debris or canoes. Common sense can help you avoid these dangers:

• Drowning through failure to wear a life jacket (PFD) that fits properly and is fastened securely.

• Being pinned and crushed between a rock (or other obstruction) and the 2000 pound force of a pinned canoe.

• Cold water, which can sap your strength very quickly if you fall in without adequate protection. After 5-10 minutes you will not be able to hold onto a canoe or a safety line. Cold water, combined with the failure to wear a life jacket (PFD), is one of the most common causes of whitewater canoeing deaths.

• Obstructions, such as fallen trees and narrow chutes between rocks, permit passage of water but can trap people and equipment. The force of the moving water drives the victim beneath the surface.

• Large hydraulics, such as the backwash of a dam, can trap a person for a long time and can cause death, especially when the water is cold.

12

- Submerged objects, such as a rock crevice or a log with branches, that can catch and trap a canoeist's foot. Even submerged objects close to the surface can be dangerous in a fast current which prevents you from standing or even sitting slightly upright.

- Long distances from shore on Lake Erie or similar large bodies of water can be dangerous. If the weather changes unexpectedly, waves can become quite large and swamp a boat.

## High Water Hazards

As the water level in a river rises, the flow rate increases even more rapidly. Thus water formations and rapids in the river change radically from low to high water. High water levels can be determined from the tables in this guide or by simply looking at the river and its banks. See the next section for how to recognize high water. High water generally means:

- The river becomes swifter and more powerful.

- If you spill, it takes longer to get out of the water, increasing the danger of exposure.

- Faster reactions are needed to avoid obstacles because the river is carrying you toward them faster.

- The banks may be submerged and disappear into the trees, forcing you to paddle through the trees and underbrush or making it impossible to get out of the river easily or safely.

- Eddies are often washed out or become whirlpools with very sharp lines between the opposing currents. Although eddies are good places to stop for a rest in low water, at high water they can be very turbulent.

- Hydraulics, or places where the water backwashes over a rock or ledge (as in the case of a low head dam), become large enough to stop and hold a swimmer, a canoe or even a raft.

- Trees, logs and other floating objects can damage a boat or injure a swimming person.

Effects of changing water levels on the Youghiogheny River just above Ohiopyle Falls. The upper picture was taken at normal water level (3 feet on Confluence gauge), the lower picture at near-flood levels (9 feet on Confluence gauge). Note that the person in the upper picture is standing next to the only rock showing in the lower picture.

## Checking Water Levels

Recommended procedures for checking water levels:

• Have a general knowledge of recent weather conditions. Heavy widespread rains and extended dry periods have predictable effects on local rivers. However, after localized thunderstorms, one creek may be in flood while another is nearly dry.

• Get a government gauge reading and check it against the tables in this guide for acceptability of level. In general, you should seek a pertinent gauge reading taken not more than one day prior to your trip. A heavy rain will change water levels drastically 12 to 36 hours after the rain. See Appendix E for sources of gauge information.

• Get an auxiliary reading whenever possible before you put in on any river. These are listed in the write-up for some rivers. They may be painted gauges, the number of bricks showing on a bridge abutment, or some "natural" feature. Getting such a reading usually involves going to the river with the understanding that you may not be able to run that section of river that day. Check the guide for alternate trips if one section is too high or too low.

• Look at the river bank and decide whether the river is too high before you put in or run the car shuttle. Some indicators to help you determine this include:
  - water significantly out of its normal channel, i.e. water in the trees or grass growing out of the water and being pushed over.
  - brown, swirling, and angrily boiling water.
  - riverside gauge that is under water.
  - floating trash.
  - apparent size of the river is significantly larger than its volume rating.

It takes two to pin a boat, but more to pry it off -- even on a Class I section of the Slippery Rock Creek.

If the river is too high, it can be dangerous. Check this guide for an alternate trip or try again another day.

To illustrate the difference a change in water levels can make, we offer two pair of photographs. Each pair was taken at the same spot on the Youghiogheny River at different levels. See page 14 and page 430.

Take your gauge readings seriously! To give the reader an idea of how rivers fluctuate in this area, a graph is provided in Appendix F of the readings of the Casselman River during 1988. One can see that in late May, the water levels dropped from spring levels to summer levels, but that even in summer a heavy rain can produce water levels that are far beyond what an open canoe can handle. One canoeist submitted a trip report claiming that the difficulty of another stream was not Class C as indicated in the guide but was a much more difficult Class II. Upon checking his report, we discovered that he had ignored the water level recommendations. This small creek was 2 feet higher than the recommended acceptable level. The increase in water substantially changed the character of the stream. Use your judgement and all resources available!

## Hazards of the River Bank

Most of the canoeing in Western Pennsylvania, especially whitewater canoeing, takes place in areas that have not been developed specifically for that purpose. Canoeists should be aware of the natural and man-made hazards found at river access points, on islands, and along the river banks.

### Poison ivy

This probably affects more canoeists each year than all other hazards combined, although it is mostly a nuisance rather than a serious danger. Pennsylvania's fertile hillsides are host to lush stands of poison ivy which appear in forms ranging from ground cover to heavy vines climbing through tree trunks. If you are sensitive, any part of the plant will affect you at any time of the year. Learn to recognize it and avoid it. If you cannot recognize it, just remember the handy rule, "Everything green is poison ivy!"

### Sun exposure

Sunburn also ranks high on the summertime nuisance list. The combination of lack of shade and water surface reflections will start a sunburn faster than you may expect. Be aware, and take the usual precautions.

### Broken glass

Glass and other junk is often a problem at river access points. Watch carefully where you step and renew your tetanus shots if you get a deep cut or puncture wound. Current medical advice is to renew a tetanus shot every ten years or within three days if you receive a deep and/or dirty puncture wound or injury.

### Snakes

Snakes are often regarded as a common river bank hazard. We rarely see snakes and most snakes we do see are not poisonous. Nevertheless, snakes do live along rivers. They particularly like to sun themselves on warm rocks. Make noise as you move among rocks or river banks, and look before you step.  Also, look into cracks in rocks before sticking your hands in.

## Water

River water or local spring water should not be used as drinking water.  A lot of the streams in Western Pennsylvania are polluted with sewage from upstream houses. Most of the remote lakes and springs are infected with giardia, which can make you sick if you drink it.  During hot summer months, you should plan on bringing and drinking one to two quarts of liquid per day.

## Hospital Locations

If you need medical treatment on a river trip, a good way to find the closest hospital is to ask a local resident.  Another good way is dial "911" or "0" (zero) for the operator and say, "I have an emergency".  The operator or the supervisor has readily available the name and address of the hospital closest to any named town.

## Clothing

The choice of clothing is an important factor in determining how pleasant and safe your canoeing experiences will be. In the spring, when whitewater canoeing is at its best, warmth is the major factor to be considered for both safety and comfort.   If you don't canoe (or windsurf or dive) enough to justify the purchase of a wetsuit, wear polypropylene or woolen long johns, shirts, etc.  Wool can keep you warm even when it and you are wet.  Several modern synthetics, such as polypropylene and capilene, are comparable to wool for insulation, and in addition will dry quickly. Wet cotton or denim will actually make you colder than if you removed them.  A pair of wetsuit "booties" is one of the best initial investments in comfort and warmth any canoeist can make.  Get booties with soles, or wear a pair of oversized tennis shoes over the booties to provide better grip and longer life.

Canoeing in water near freezing requires hand protection. Wet suit gloves are best, but plastic-coated mittens with wool or polypropylene liners will do.  For canoeists, 2-3 mm thick nylon-lined wetsuits are standard, although some canoeists prefer thicker suits for warmth at the expense of some freedom of arm and leg motion.  Most canoeists find wetsuits 6 mm or thicker too restrictive.  Another combination that is often seen is a 2-3 mm jacket, along with a 2-3 mm farmer john.  Remember that wetsuits do not protect you very well from wind.  Below 50F (10C), even a 4-5 mm wetsuit or combination should be covered with a windbreaker or other tightly-woven garment.  Wetsuits designed specifically for canoeists are now available from some outfitters.  Wetsuits designed for windsurfers also work fine, but be sure to get neoprene rather than fabric sleeves.  If you buy a wetsuit at a dive shop, tell the salesman to fit you much looser than he would fit a scuba diver.

Paddlers who frequently paddle in temperatures below 40F (5C) often buy drysuits.  They cost more than wetsuits, but they can keep you toasty warm and dry at very cold temperatures, even when ice is on the river.  Drysuits are worn over an appropriate number of insulating layers.

# American Whitewater Affiliation Safety Code

The following pages contain the American Whitewater Affiliation Safety Code. Copies of the code are available in lots of 50 at $5.50; 100 at $10.00; and 200 or more at $9.00 per hundred. AWA, PO Box 85, Phoenicia, New York 12464. Also available (free) is a copy of the bi-monthly AMERICAN WHITEWATER JOURNAL. Send self-addressed number 10 (9 1/2 inch by 4 1/2 inch) envelope with two first class stamps to the above address.

## I. Personal Preparedness and Responsibility

1. Be a competent swimmer, with the ability to handle yourself underwater.

2. Wear a lifejacket. A snugly fitting vest type life preserver offers back and shoulder protection as well as the flotation needed to swim safely in whitewater.

3. Wear a solid, correctly-fitted helmet when upsets are likely. This is essential in kayaks or covered canoes, and recommended for open canoeists using thigh straps and rafters running steep drops.

4. Do not boat out of control. Your skills should he sufficient to stop or reach shore before reaching danger. Do not enter a rapid unless you are reasonably sure that you can run it safely or swim it without injury.

5. Whitewater rivers contain many hazards which are not always easily recognized. The following are the most frequent killers:

A. High Water. The river's speed and power increase tremendously as the flow increases, raising the difficulty of most rapids. Rescue becomes progressively harder as the water rises, adding to the danger. Floating debris and strainers make even an easy rapid quite hazardous. It is often misleading to judge the river level at the put-in, since a small rise in a wide, shallow place will be multiplied many times where the river narrows. Use reliable gauge information whenever possible, and be aware that sun on snowpack, hard rain, and upstream dam releases may greatly increase the flow.

B. Cold. Cold drains your strength, and robs you of the ability to make sound decisions on matters affecting your survival. Cold water immersion, because of the initial shock and the rapid heat loss which follows, is especially dangerous. Dress appropriately for bad weather or sudden immersion in the water. When the water temperature is less than 50 degrees F, a wetsuit or drysuit is essential for protection if you swim. Next best is wool or pile clothing under a waterproof shell. In this case, you should also carry waterproof matches and a change of clothing in a waterproof bag. If, after prolonged exposure, a person experiences uncontrollable shaking, loss of coordination, or difficulty speaking, he or she is hypothermic and needs your assistance.

C. Strainers. Brush, fallen trees, bridge pilings, undercut rocks or anything else which allows river current to sweep through can pin boats and boaters against the obstacle. Water pressure on anything trapped this way can be overwhelming. Rescue is often extremely difficult. Pinning may occur in fast current, with little or no whitewater to warn of the danger.

D.  Dams, Weirs, Ledges, Reversals, Holes and Hydraulics.  When water drops over an obstacle, it curls back on itself, forming a strong upstream current which may be capable of holding a boat or a swimmer. Some holes make for excellent sport; others are proven killers. Paddlers who cannot recognize the differences should avoid all but the smallest holes. Hydraulics around man-made dams must be treated with utmost respect regardless of their height or the level of the river. Despite their seemingly benign appearance, they can create an almost escape proof trap. The swimmer's only exit from the "downing machine" is to dive below the surface where the downstream current is flowing beneath the reversal.

E.  Broaching. When a boat is pushed side ways against a rock by strong current, it may collapse and wrap. This is especially dangerous to kayak and decked canoe paddlers; these boats will collapse and the combination of indestructible hulls and tight outfitting may create a deadly trap. Even without entrapment, releasing pinned boats can be extremely time-consuming and dangerous. To avoid pinning, throw your weight downstream towards the rock. This allows the current to slide harmlessly underneath the hull.

6.  Boating alone is discouraged. The minimum party is three people or two craft.

7.  Have a frank knowledge of your boating ability, and don't attempt rivers or rapids which lie beyond that ability.

A.  Develop the paddling skills and teamwork required to match the river you plan to boat. Most good paddlers develop skills gradually, and attempts to advance too quickly will compromise your safety and enjoyment.

B.  Be in good physical and mental condition, consistent with the difficulties which may be expected. Make adjustments for loss of skills due to age, health, fitness. Any health limitations must be explained to your fellow paddlers prior to starting the trip.

8.  Be practiced in self-rescue, including escape from an overturned craft. The eskimo roll is strongly recommended for decked boaters who run rapids of Class IV or greater, or who paddle in cold environmental conditions.

9.  Be trained in rescue skills, CPR, and first aid with special emphasis on the recognizing and treating hypothermia. It may save your friend's life.

10.  Carry equipment needed for unexpected emergencies, including footwear which will protect your feet when walking out, a throw rope, knife, whistle and waterproof matches. If you wear eyeglasses, tie them on and carry a spare pair on long trips. Bring cloth repair tape on short runs, and a full repair kit on isolated rivers. Do not wear bulky jackets, ponchos, heavy boots, or anything else which could reduce your ability to survive a swim.

11.  Despite the mutually supportive group structure described in this code, individual paddlers are ultimately responsible for their own safety, and must assume sole responsibility for the following decisions:

A.  The decision to participate on any trip. This includes an evaluation of the expected difficulty of the rapids under the conditions existing at the time of the put-in.

B. The selection of appropriate equipment, including a boat design suited to their skills and the appropriate rescue and survival gear.

C. The decision to scout any rapid, and to run or portage according to their best judgement. Other members of the group may offer advice, but paddlers should resist pressure from anyone to paddle beyond their skills. It is also their responsibility to decide whether to pass up any walk out or take out opportunity.

D. All trip participants should constantly evaluate their own and their group's safety, voicing their concerns when appropriate and following what they believe to be the best course of action. Paddlers are encouraged to speak with anyone whose actions on the water are dangerous, whether they are a part of your group or not.

## II. Boat and Equipment Preparedness

1. Test new and different equipment under familiar conditions before relying on it for difficult runs. This is especially true when adopting a new boat design or outfitting system. Low volume craft may present additional hazards to inexperienced or poorly conditioned paddlers.

2. Be sure your boat and gear are in good repair before starting a trip. The more isolated and difficult the run, the more rigorous this inspection should be.

3. Install flotation bags in non-inflatable craft, securely fixed in each end, designed to displace as much water as possible. Inflatable boats should have multiple air chambers and be test inflated before launching.

4. Have strong, properly sized paddles or oars for controlling your craft. Carry sufficient spares for the length and difficulty of the trip.

5. Outfit your boat safely. The ability to exit your boat quickly is an essential component of safety in rapids. It is your responsibility to see that there is absolutely nothing to cause entrapment when coming free of an upset craft. This includes:

A. Spray covers which won't release reliably or which release prematurely.

B. Boat outfitting too tight to allow a fast exit, especially in low volume kayaks or decked canoes. This includes low hung thwarts in canoes lacking adequate clearance for your feet and kayak footbraces which fail or allow your feet to become wedged under them.

C. Inadequately supported decks which collapse on a paddler's legs when a decked boat is pinned by water pressure. Inadequate clearance with the deck because of your size or build.

D. Loose ropes which cause entanglement. Beware of any length of loose line attached to a whitewater boat. All items must be tied tightly and excess line eliminated, painters, throw lines, and safety rope systems must be completely and effectively stored. Do not knot the end of a rope, as it can get caught in cracks between rocks.

6.  Provide ropes which permit you to hold on to your craft so that it may be rescued. The following methods are recommended.

A.  Kayaks and covered canoes should have grab loops of quarter inch rope or equivalent webbing sized to admit a normal sized hand. Stern painters are permissible if properly secured.

B.  Open canoes should have securely anchored bow and stern painters consisting of 8 to 10 feet of line. These must be secured in such a way that they are readily accessible, but cannot come loose accidently. Grab loops are acceptable, but are more difficult to reach after an upset.

C.  Rafts and dories may have taut perimeter lines threaded through the loops provided. Footholds should be designed so that a paddler's feet cannot be forced through them, causing entrapment. Flip lines should be carefully and reliably stowed.

7.  Know your craft's carrying capacity, and how added loads affect boat handling in whitewater. Most rafts have a minimum crew size which can be added to on day trips or in easy rapids. Carrying more than two paddlers in an open canoe when running rapids is not recommended.

8.  Car top racks must be strong and attach positively to the vehicle. Lash your boat to each crossbar, then tie the ends of the boats directly to the bumpers for added security. This arrangement should survive all but the most violent vehicle accident.

## III. Group Preparedness and Responsibility

1.  Organization. River trips should be regarded as common adventures by all participants, except on specially designated instructional or guided trips. The group is collectively responsible for the conduct of the trip, and participants are individually responsible for judging their own capabilities and for their own safety as the trip progresses.

2.  River Conditions. The group should have a reasonable knowledge of the difficulty of the run. Participants should evaluate this information and adjust their plans accordingly. If the run is exploratory or no one is familiar with the river, maps and guidebooks, if available, should be examined. The group should secure accurate flow information; the more difficult the run, the more important this will be. Be aware of possible changes in river level and how this will affect the difficulty of the run. If the trip involves tidal stretches, secure appropriate information on tides.

3.  Group equipment should be suited to the difficulty of the river. The group should always have a throw line available, and one line per boat is recommended on difficult runs. The list may include: carabiners, prusik loops, first aid kit, flashlight, folding saw, fire starter, guidebooks, maps, food, extra clothing, and any other rescue or survival items suggested by conditions. Each item is not required on every run, and this list is not meant to be a substitute for good judgement.

4.  Keep the group compact, but maintain sufficient spacing to avoid collisions. If the group is large, consider dividing into smaller groups or using the "Buddy System" as an additional safeguard. Space yourselves closely enough to permit good communication, but not so close as to interfere with one another in rapids.

A.  The lead paddler sets the pace. When in front, do not get in over your head. Never run drops when you cannot see a clear route to the bottom or, for advanced paddlers, a sure route to the next eddy. When in doubt, stop and scout.

B.  Keep track of all group members. Each boat keeps the one behind it in sight, stopping if necessary. Know how many people are in your group and take head counts regularly. No one should paddle ahead or walk out without first informing the group. Weak paddlers should stay at the center of a group, and not allow themselves to lag behind. If the group is large and contains a wide range of abilities, a designated "Sweep Boat" should bring up the rear.

C.  Courtesy. On heavily used rivers, do not cut in front of a boater running a drop. Always look upstream before leaving eddies to run or play. Never enter a crowded drop or eddy when no room for you exists. Passing other groups in a rapid may be hazardous: it's often safer to wait upstream until the group ahead has passed.

5.  Float plan. If the trip is into a wilderness area or for an extended period, plans should be filed with a responsible person who will contact the authorities if you are overdue. It may be wise to establish checkpoints along the way where civilization could be contacted if necessary. Knowing the location of possible help and preplanning escape routes can speed rescue.

6.  Drugs. The use of alcohol or mind altering drugs before or during river trips is not recommended. It dulls reflexes, reduces decision making ability, and may interfere with important survival reflexes.

7.  Instruction or guided trips. In this format, a person assumes the responsibilities of a trip leader. He or she may pass judgement on a participant's qualifications, check equipment, and assume responsibilities for the conduct of the trip normally taken by the group as a whole.

A.  These trips must be clearly designated as such in advance, as they could expose the leader to legal liability. Trip or personal liability insurance should be considered.

B.  Even on trips with a designated leader, participants must recognize that whitewater rivers have inherent hazards, that each person is still responsible for their decision to participate and their safety on the water.

## IV.  Guidelines for River Rescue

1.  Recover from an upset with an eskimo roll whenever possible. Evacuate your boat immediately if there is imminent danger of being trapped against rocks, brush, or any other kind of strainer.

2.  If you swim, hold on to your boat. It has much flotation and is easy for rescuers to spot. Get to the upstream end so that you cannot be crushed between a rock and your boat by the force of the current. Persons with good balance may be able to climb on top of a swamped kayak or flipped raft and paddle to shore.

3.  Release your craft if this will improve your chances, especially if the water is cold or dangerous rapids lie ahead. Actively attempt self-rescue whenever

possible by swimming for safety. Be prepared to assist others who may come to your aid.

A. When swimming in shallow or obstructed rapids, lie on your back with feet held high and pointed downstream. Do not attempt to stand in fast moving water; if your foot wedges on the bottom, fast water will push you under and keep you there. Get to slow or very shallow water before attempting to stand or walk. Look ahead. Avoid possible pinning situations including undercut rocks, strainers, downed trees, holes, and other dangers by swimming away from them.

B. If the rapids are deep and powerful, roll over onto your stomach and swim aggressively for shore. Watch for eddies and slackwater and use them to get out of the current. Strong swimmers can effect a powerful upstream ferry and get to shore fast. If the shores are obstructed with strainers or undercut rocks, however, it is safer to "ride the rapid out" until a safer escape can be found.

4. If others spill and swim, go after the boaters first. Rescue boats and equipment only if this can be done safely. While participants usually assist one another to the best of their ability, they should do so only if they can, in their judgement, do so safely. The first duty of a rescuer is not to compound the problem by becoming another victim.

5. The use of rescue lines requires training; uninformed use may cause injury. Never tie yourself into either end of a line without a reliable quick-release system. Have a knife handy to deal with unexpected entanglement. Learn to place set lines effectively, to throw accurately, to belay effectively, and to properly handle a rope thrown to you.

6. When reviving a drowning victim, be aware that cold water may greatly extend survival time underwater. Victims of hypothermia may have depressed vital signs so they look and feel dead. Don't give up; continue CPR for as long as possible without compromising safety.

## V. Universal River Signals

**Stop**: Potential hazard ahead. Wait for "all clear" signal before proceeding, or scout ahead. Form a horizontal bar with your outstretched arms. Those seeing the signal should pass it back to others in the party.

**Help/Emergency**: Assist the signaller as quickly as possible.Give three long blasts on a police whistle while waving a paddle, helmet or life vest over your head. If a whistle is not available, use the visual signal alone. A whistle is best carried on a lanyard attached to your life vest.

**All Clear**: Come ahead (in the absence of other directions proceed down the center). Form a vertical bar with your paddle or one arm held high above your head. Paddle blade should be turned flat for maximum visibility. To signal direction or a preferred course through a rapid around obstruction, lower the previously vertical "all clear" by 45 degrees toward the side of the river with the preferred route. Never point toward the obstacle you wish to avoid.

Stop                              Help/Emergency

All Clear                         All Clear
                                  go to your right

This code has been prepared by the American Whitewater Affiliation using the best available information and has been reviewed by a broad cross section of whitewater experts. It was Adopted in 1959 and Revised in 1987 by Charlie Walbridge, Revision Chairman and Pete Skinner, Production Coordinator.

The code, however, is only a collection of guidelines; attempts to minimize risks should be flexible, not constrained by a rigid set of rules. Varying conditions and group goals may combine with unpredictable circumstances to require alternate procedures.

# International Scale of River Difficulty

This is the American version of a rating system used to compare river difficulty throughout the world. This system is not exact; rivers do not always fit easily into one category, and regional or individual interpretations may cause misunderstandings. It is no substitute for a guidebook or accurate first-hand descriptions of a run. Paddlers attempting difficult runs in an unfamiliar area should act cautiously until they get a feel for the way the scale is interpreted locally. River difficulty may change each year due to fluctuations in water level, downed trees, geological disturbances, or bad weather. Stay alert for unexpected problems! As river difficulty increases, the danger to swimming paddlers becomes more severe. As rapids become longer and more continuous, the challenge increases. There is a difference between running an occasional Class IV rapid and dealing with an entire river of this category. Allow an extra margin of safety between skills and river ratings when the water is cold or if the river itself is remote and inaccessible.

**Class I: Easy.** Fast moving water with riffles and small waves. Few obstructions, all obvious and easily missed with little training. Risk to swimmers is slight; self-rescue is easy.

**Class II: Novice.** Straightforward rapids with wide, clear channels which are evident without scouting. Occasional maneuvering may be required, but rocks and medium sized waves are easily missed by trained paddlers. Swimmers are seldom injured and group assistance, while helpful, is seldom needed.

**Class III: Intermediate.** Rapids with moderate, irregular waves which may be difficult to avoid and which can swamp an open canoe. Complex maneuvers in fast current and good boat control in tight passages or around ledges are often required; large waves or strainers may be present but are easily avoided. Strong eddies and powerful current effects can be found, particularly on large-volume rivers. Scouting is advisable for inexperienced parties. Injuries while swimming are rare; self-rescue is usually easy but group assistance may be required to avoid long swims.

**Class IV. Advanced.** Intense, powerful but predictable rapids requiring precise boat handling in turbulent water. Depending on the character of the river, it may feature large, unavoidable waves and holes or constricted passages demanding fast maneuvers under pressure. A fast, reliable eddy turn may be needed to initiate maneuvers, scout rapids, or rest. Rapids may require "must" moves above dangerous hazards. Scouting is necessary the first time down. Risk of injury to swimmers is moderate to high, and water conditions may make self-rescue difficult. Group assistance for rescue is often essential but requires practiced skills. A strong eskimo roll is highly recommended.

**Class V: Expert.** Extremely long, obstructed, or very violent rapids which expose a paddler to above average endangerment. Drops may contain large, unavoidable waves and holes or steep, congested chutes with complex, demanding routes. Rapids may continue for long distances between pools, demanding a high level of fitness. What eddies exist may be small, turbulent, or difficult to reach. At the high end of the scale, several of these factors may be combined. Scouting is mandatory, but often difficult. Swims are dangerous, and rescue is difficult even for experts. A very reliable eskimo roll, proper equipment, extensive experience, and practiced rescue skills are essential for survival.

**Class VI: Extreme.** One grade more difficult than Class V. These runs often exemplify the extremes of difficulty, unpredictability and danger. The consequences of errors are very severe and rescue may be impossible. For teams of experts only, at favorable water levels, after close personal inspection and taking all precautions. This class does not represent drops thought to be unrunnable, but may include rapids which are only occasionally run.

Three additional ratings of A, B, or C are also used in this guide to extend the international scale for smooth water:

**Class A:** Pools, lakes, very slow moving rivers.

**Class B:** Flat flowing rivers with no obstructions and with maximum flow velocity equal to an easy backpaddle.

**Class C:** Flat flowing rivers with velocities above an easy backpaddle. They may have some sharp bends and/or obstructions or a few easy riffles.

## Canoeing Safety Rules

• Know the difficulty of the river you intend to run.

• Check to be sure the water level of the river is okay.

• Acquire and know how to use the equipment in the equipment check lists presented below.

• Wear a life jacket. (Personal Flotation Device).

• Never canoe alone. (Preferred minimum is 3 boats).

• Keep your craft under control. In a rapid, know where your next stopping point is.

• Know your ability and do not allow other trip members to talk you into something that is way beyond your skills.

• Never get ahead of the lead canoe or lag behind the sweep canoe. Keep the canoe behind you in view.

• Do not "ride the tail" of the canoe in front of you, especially in rapids.

• Wear polypropylene, woolen long johns, or a wetsuit when the water is cold.

• Be sure that someone has a safety line (throw rope) and first-aid kit and knows how to use them.

• Be able to swim, but don't expect to overpower the river.

• Avoid large hydraulics. If caught in a hydraulic first try moving to either end. Another technique to try is diving down toward the bottom of the river.

• If spilled, keep upstream of the canoe. Float downstream, feet first and lying on your back. Keep your feet near the surface of the water to fend off rocks and to prevent them from being caught in a rock crevice.

• When canoeing in remote areas, carry topographic maps and a compass, and know how to use them in case you need to walk out.

# Organizing Canoe Trips

Canoeing is intrinsically a group activity. As with any group activity, a little organization can make a big difference in the success of the trip. This section offers some suggestions on equipment, logistics, and leadership.

## Equipment Checklist

The following items are essential:

- Life preserver for each person

- Three paddles per canoe

- Rescue line (Throw rope) 3/8 inch, 60-80 feet long

- First Aid kit (in a waterproof box)

- Painter ropes, 17-20 feet

- Two rubber knee pads per person

- Proper clothing for the weather

- Spare wool sweater and a poncho

- Helmet (for closed boaters and open boaters on Class III or above)

- Flotation for any closed boat or for open boats on Class III or above

- Spray skirt for closed boats

- Heavy plastic or aluminum tape (for patching rips, leaks in canoes)

The following items are highly desirable:

- Waterproof pack

- Cap or hat with brim

- Sun screen

- Sunglasses

- Light string to tie in sponge, and spare paddle (also to tie on glasses, etc.)

- Bailing buckets (plastic) and/or sponges

- Lunch and a canteen

- Camera and film, in waterproof container

- Insect repellant

- Flashlights

- Change of clothing

- Topographic maps

- Matches (in waterproof container)

- Pocket knife

- Whistle

# Favorite AYH Trips for One Day Canoeing

This list is not a substitute for study of the canoe guide, but a summary of rivers often used or suitable for group trips. It is provided as a guide for trip leaders who are responsible for choosing rivers for a particular trip.

Within each group, streams are approximately ordered by difficulty. Higher water levels often increase difficulty by increasing water force. Lower levels often increase difficulty by increasing maneuvering required.

The "old standbys" (favorite trips, run frequently) are marked with an *

| Kind | River | Section |
|------|-------|---------|
| Flat | | |
| | Lake Arthur | |
| | Shenango Lake | |
| | Conneaut Marsh | |
| | Allegheny R | various |
| | Youghiogheny R | Sutersville-Boston ("Bottom Yough") |
| | | |
| Class I | | |
| * | Youghiogheny R | Dawson-Layton |
| | Crooked Ck | Creekside-Shelocta-Girty |
| | Otter Ck | |
| | Slippery Rock Ck | Harris-Ellport |
| * | Red Bank Ck | New Bethlehem-Lawsonham |
| | | |
| Class I-II | | |
| | Sandy Lick Ck | State Game Lands- Port Barnett |
| | Buffalo Ck | W.Winfield-Freeport |
| | Conemaugh R | New Florence-Torrance |
| * | Buffalo Ck | Worthington-West Winfield |
| | Wolf Ck | Courtneys Mills-Sl.Rock |
| | Crooked Ck | Girty-Cochrans Mills |
| | Casselman R | Garrett-Rockwood |
| | Mahoning Ck | Mahoning Dam-Putneyville |
| * | Little Beaver R | Fredericktown-Ohio River |
| | | |
| Class II | | |
| * | Youghiogheny R | Confluence-Ohiopyle ("Middle Yough") |
| | Loyalhanna R | Ligonier-Kingston Dam |
| * | Connoquenessing | Frisco-Ellport ("Connie's Challenge") |

| Kind    River | Section |
|---|---|
| Class II-III | |
| Connoquenessing | Ellport-2nd sewer ("Upper Gorge") |
| Casselman R | Rockwood-Markleton |
| Casselman R | Ft.Hill-Harnedsville |
| * Slippery Rock Ck | Eckert-Harris ("Breakneck-Harris") |
| | |
| Class III | |
| Connoquenessing | 2nd sewer-Beaver River ("Lower Gorge") |
| Laurel Hill Ck | Whipkey Dam-Ursina |
| Casselman R | Markleton-Ft.Hill |
| | |
| Hard Class III | only paddlers in full control on III sections |
| | only with strong safety |
| Slippery Rock Ck | Rose Point-McConnells Mill |
| Slippery Rock Ck | McConnells Mill-Eckert ("The Mile") |

## Leading Canoe Trips

These guidelines were developed for leaders of canoe trips that use equipment from a sponsoring organization. They can also be adapted to trips on which paddlers bring their own gear.

- Before you agree to lead a trip:
  - know the river: difficulty, appropriate water levels, and alternatives in case the river is too low or high.
  - know how to find the put-in, the shuttle, and the take-out.
  - be able to give directions or maps to each of these places. Caravanning is difficult over long distances. If you must caravan, each car should keep the car immediately behind in sight.
  - be sure no other trip plans to use the same equipment.
  - decide on the maximum safe trip size, and stick to it.

- As people sign up, record the following information:
  - names and phone numbers (in case of a change of plans).
  - what equipment they need.
  - whether they can drive, and if so, the number of passengers and the amount of equipment they can handle.
  - their ability and experience. **Important**: keep a balanced trip. Do not be afraid to say, "**No**, all novice slots are filled."

- Before the day of the trip:
  - get a key for access to the equipment.
  - determine exactly how much equipment is available and usable.
  - call to check the gauges or otherwise check water levels.

- At the equipment storage building:
  - delegate responsibility for organizing and loading gear.

- collect money for fees now! This helps to obtain the exact head count.
- be sure you have neither too many cars nor too few.
- instruct drivers on the route.
- make final check for enough equipment.
- recheck to be sure the canoes are securely tied down.
- be sure the storage building door is locked before leaving.

- At the river's edge:
  - based on water level and the skills in your group, decide whether to run this river or try another; if someone should not make the trip, this is the time to decide.
  - assign partners if necessary.
  - decide which car(s) will be left at the take-out and have trippers put dry clothes in it.
  - get the shuttle started.
  - get novices on the river to practice while the shuttle is being run.
  - appoint lead and sweep canoes.

- On the river:
  - be sure the trip does not string out.
  - alert the trippers to possible hazards in the river.
  - decide who should not run a rapid.
  - do not let other members of the trip encourage a tripper to try something far beyond his ability.
  - pick a good spot for lunch and be sure it gets cleaned up.
  - check on weak trippers, reassign partners, or appoint instructors as necessary.

- At the take-out:
  - get the shuttle moving as soon as possible.
  - check to make sure you have all the gear.
  - arrange for the return of the equipment, particularly if part of the group stops for dinner.

- Back at the equipment storage building:
  - delegate responsibility for unloading and storing gear.
  - verify that all the gear is returned and properly stowed.
  - if equipment is damaged, report it to the canoeing chairman and to the leader of the next trip.
  - fill out the trip report and send it to the proper location.
  - return the building key to the agreed-upon spot.
  - make sure the storage building door is locked.

- As soon after the trip as possible:
  - write notes on the trip, including date and gauge readings.
  - if information is not in this guide, send a copy to the editor.

## Shuttle Logistics

River trips are usually planned to travel downstream from one point on a river (the "put-in") to another point on that river (the "take-out"). This requires some sort of arrangement (a "shuttle") for reuniting the people and equipment at the take-out with the cars left at the put-in. It is easiest to arrange a shuttle with two or more cars; one or more cars are positioned at the take-out before the trip starts, and one or more cars remain at the put-in. Shuttles can be arranged ("run") in many variations. The particular choice depends on parking, amount of equipment, and location of roads.

One of the common choices is for all cars to go to the put-in and unload all of the equipment. All cars then go to the take-out. Using just one car, the drivers return to the put-in and join the rest of the party to run the river. At the end of the run, one car, its driver, and the upstream car's driver return to the put-in to retrieve the shuttle car.

# How to Use This Guide

The bulk of this guide is devoted to write-ups of individual river trips. The organization is by watershed, with larger streams listed first, followed by their tributaries, then by the tributaries of the tributaries, and so forth.

This information is given in two forms: Trip Tables and River Descriptions. The Trip Tables immediately after this text present information in a tabular form for a quick reference. The River Descriptions which follow give a general description of each river. They are intended to give the flavor of the streams. Your best guide to a river is someone who has run it many times before.

We have compiled this guide as an aid to pleasure canoeists. We have tried to present accurate descriptions of these rivers and creeks. However we are human, and rivers change with time. The suggestions in this guide can be invalidated by water and weather conditions, by the skill of your paddling party, and by changes in the rivers themselves. Therefore we can not take responsibility for errors, omissions, changes in the rivers, or for other problems encountered through the use of this guide. Each paddler who sets forth on a river assumes personal responsibility, not only for his or her own safety, but also for the safety of others on the trip. Ultimately, your safety depends mostly on your own common sense and good judgement.

The character of moving and whitewater rivers can change drastically in the distance of a few miles. A stream that is boisterous whitewater as it races down the side of a mountain can be flat and gently-flowing when it reaches the plain. Consequently each stream has been divided into various sections. Whenever possible, sections have been separated where the character of the stream changes. Additional section breaks have been inserted to correspond to put-ins and take-outs that are typically used on one-day trips.

## Kinds of Information in this Guide

For each section of the river, the guide contains the following information:

* An idea of the **difficulty** of the stream is provided by the Class, Gradient, and Volume section.

* An idea of the **aesthetic** quality of the stream is provided by the Scenery and Pollution section.

* A general idea of the seasons **when the stream is canoeable** is provided by the Volume, Drainage Area, Acceptable Water Levels, Gauge, and Normal Wet period section.

* A narrative **description** of the river and any **unusual problems** that may exist on the stream is provided by the Description and Difficulties section. It is strongly recommended that you read the section on Whitewater Safety in this book.

* The route that is typically used to run **shuttles** for the stream is provided by the Shuttles and Maps section.

## Detailed Description of Guide Entries

*River Name:*

This is the name of the river. In case of multiple spellings, or name confusion, we use the information provided by the *Pennsylvania Gazetteer*

*Section:*

Each section is identified by its starting and stopping points.

*Distance:*

The length of each section as measured along the river is given. This distance is expressed to the nearest tenth of a mile.

*Class:*

The class of the river is based on the International Scale of River Difficulties. This scale classifies rivers on a scale from I to VI (one to six) based on characteristics related to the difficulty of the stream. Class I denotes moving water with few or no obstructions, while Class VI involves risk of life. Three additional ratings of A, B, or C are also used in this guide to extend the international scale for smooth water. See Section V of the AWA Safety Code (page 28-29) for a more detailed description of each class, with skill levels suggested for running a river of a particular class. This standard is used by almost all canoeists, although some closed boaters often improperly shift the scale to downrate a river. The use of a mixed rating such as II-III means that the river is intermediate in difficulty between Class II and Class III, either because it is mostly Class II with a few Class III rapids or because it shifts from Class II to Class III depending on water level.

*Gradient:*

Two numbers are given for the gradient. The first number is the mean (average) elevation drop for the stream section. It is expressed in feet of drop per mile of river. It is obtained by subtracting the elevation at the end of the section from the elevation at the beginning of the section and dividing by the distance along the river in miles. The second number given for gradient is the maximum drop per mile. It is also expressed in feet of drop per mile of river. It is arbitrarily computed from the appropriate topographic map, as the contour interval (vertical distance between adjacent contour lines) divided by the distance between the two closest contour lines crossing the stream section. Where contour lines are less than a 0.25 miles apart, the computation uses two or three contour intervals to obtain a more reasonable value. If the section of river is a lake with no current, then the gradient is reported as Lake. If the section of river is almost a lake but there is some current flow then the gradient is reported as Pool.

## Size:

We describe the size of a river in terms of its drainage basin area (the area of land that supplies water to the river) and the river's volume (the average amount of water flowing). We divide streams into five sizes based on their drainage area in square miles, or their volume in cfs (cubic feet per second) (if known).

| Size | Area (sq mi) | Mean Volume (cfs) |
|------|-------------|-------------------|
| Tiny | less than 60 | less than 100 |
| Small | 60 to 180 | 100 to 300 |
| Medium | 180 to 1,200 | 300 to 2,000 |
| Large | 1,200 to 6,000 | 2,000 to 10,000 |
| Huge | more then 6,000 | more than 10,000 |

## Drainage areas:

This is the land area drained by a river section at a specific point on the river. The drainage area gives a feeling for how fast the stream will fall after widespread rain (faster for smaller areas), for how long it takes upstream rain to affect downstream sections (longer for larger areas), and for how sensitive the stream is to localized thunderstorms (more for smaller areas). This number is extremely well-correlated with its mean annual flow. Information about drainage area is available for many more streams than flow information. When flow information is not available, the size of a river is classified on the basis of its drainage area.

## *Volume:*

This is the mean (average) annual rate of discharge, expressed in cubic feet per second (cfs). When a specific number is not given, the river is designated tiny, small, medium, or large according to its watershed area.

Also be aware that certain conditions (such as spring thaw or rainstorms) can change water levels quickly and drastically. Although only a rough indicator, the volume does suggest the size of the river bed and the force of the water when it is at a canoeable level.

## *Scenery:*

The scenic value rating is based on the following scale:

**A** Natural state; very few signs of human developments and possessing appealing natural features.

**B** Basically natural state but lacking appealing natural features, often of a rural character with scattered summer homes.

**C** Light strip mining, and/or moderate population (small villages or numerous summer homes), no industry.

**D** Heavy population, industry, and/or strip mining.

## *Pollution:*

The pollution rating is based on the following scale:

**A**: None to very little. Good swimming.

**B**: Moderate but not offensive. No odor.

**C**: Foul.

## *Level:*

These two numbers when available give the lowest and highest water levels for safe and pleasurable canoeing. readings summarize experience with gauge levels that have been reported to us. Gauge readings are usually expressed as depth of river in feet from an arbitrary zero point. For Corps of Engineers gauges, which are the ones most widely

used, the zero point is chosen so that the gauge reading will
not go negative.

It must be remembered that there is a considerable amount
of subjectivity in these numbers. For example, a canoeist
with limited ability at maneuvering among rocks may find a
certain low level exasperating, if not impossible, whereas a
more advanced canoeist may find the same level interesting
and a challenge to his canoeing ability. An effort was made
in this guide to take this factor into account. Thus, data for
a stream rated Class I should be pertinent to a Class I
canoeist. Canoeists with more skill might expand the range
of readings labeled "O.K.".

Keep in mind that rafts require more water than canoes and
kayaks. Rafts flex and sink deeper into the water at the
spots where people sit (no matter how hard the rafts are
inflated). Thus a water level that is comfortable for canoes
and kayaks may be marginal or unacceptable for rafts.
Also, rafts tend to suffer more damage from scrapes over
rocks than do plastic or metal boats. Good quality rafts are
very expensive these days. For these reasons it is advisable
to revise the gauge readings upward for trips that include
rafts. In general, the minimum "comfortable" level should
be increased by about 0.2 foot.

### *Topographic maps:*

The maps named are the standard US Geological Survey 7.5
minute topographic maps (scale 1:24,000 or 2,000 feet to the
inch) that cover the particular stream section. For the maps
not in Pennsylvania, the state name will be included. These
maps are particularly useful for locating back roads for put-
ins and take-outs. They should be considered absolutely
essential on any whitewater trip where the possibility of
having to walk out exists. See Appendix D for sources.
However, bear in mind that these maps are not revised very
often, roads may have been created and/or destroyed since
the last map revision. The USGS is now offering
topographic county maps. These maps are made from
mosaics of the 7.5 minute maps, reduced to the scale of
1:50,000. A booklet of reduced size topographic maps is also
available at many outdoor stores. Note that the State Route
numbers in the second edition of this booklet are old

numbers. The third edition (1990) has been updated to match the road signs.

## County maps:

Another good map to have for running shuttle is the local county road map. These are generally available free at the local courthouse. A booklet of county road maps is available (1989) for $11.90 from County Maps, Puetz Place, Lyndon Station, Wisconsin 53944. Telephone (608) 666-3331. Order the *Pennsylvania County Maps*.

As noted above, the USGS now offers county maps based on the standard 7.5 minute quads.

## Other maps:

Several other agencies publish maps of selected areas or streams. When other good maps are available, they are described in this section.

## Description:

A narrative description of the river tells you what to expect. This section may give some general description of the stream, its geology, history, type of whitewater or just some unusual feature that is worth noting. With the description is a date enclosed in brackets [ ]. A "Reported" date is the date that someone initially gave us a written report on the stream. Generally it would have been canoed that season. A "Checked" date is the date that someone canoed the stream, and either verified or updated the current description in the guide.

## Difficulties:

This section includes any unusual hazards and/or difficulties that were known at the time of the report.

*Note:* The usual sort of difficulties that one may normally expect when canoeing rivers of the indicated class and size are generally not included in this section. Furthermore, of all the information in this guide, the "difficulty" is the most likely to change. It is strongly recommended that you read the section on Whitewater Safety. Water levels, weather conditions, the skill of the canoeists all play a part in the difficulty of a river. Ultimately, your safety depends mostly on your own common sense and good judgement.

### Shuttle:

This section includes a brief description of the usual shuttle routes. First it describes the put-in, then the route between the put-in and take-out, and then finally it may describe intermediate access points. All state route numbers mentioned are Pennsylvania State Route numbers unless otherwise noted. Pennsylvania has recently (Summer 1986) renumbered all state maintained roads. They used to be labeled with Legislative Route (LR) numbers that changed at the county borders. They are now labeled with State Route numbers that do not change at the county border. These numbers appear on signs at the side of the road that are about 12 inches high and vary in width from between 18 to 24 inches. They contain the letters S R, followed by the State Route number. Underneath is a distance measurement from some point. They are placed about every 1000 feet along the side of the road. Many of the state route numbers that appear in this book come from the maps with no check with what is actual in the field. If the shuttle has a checked date then it was field checked. If no checked date appears with the shuttle be a little cautious.

Maps are good supplements to shuttle instructions. See the sections above on maps.

### Gauge:

The gauge listed for each trip is the one picked as best-suited to report the river level in the area of the trip. The values are feet above some arbitrary zero point. See Appendix F for a more detailed description of gauge information.

### Normal wet period:

This data gives an idea of how late in the year a given stream can be run. Needless to say, this will depend very much on rainfall, the amount of snow the previous winter, etc. Where data is available a percent/level value is given. This percent represents the percentage of the year that the stream is higher or lower than the given level. This statistic and the knowledge of recent rainfall or snowmelt can suggest whether a particular stream is likely to be runnable. See Appendix F if you would like to know more about how these numbers were determined.

- Tiny rivers are runnable only during snowmelt or after a heavy rain. They may be briefly too high after a heavy rain, and they are usually too low.

- Small rivers are runnable about 20 percent of the year. They may be too high for a day or two after a rain, and are too low about 80 percent of the year.

- Medium rivers may be too high about 10 percent of the year, and too low about 50-60 percent of the year.

- Large rivers are rarely too low.

- Huge rivers are always high enough to run and often are too high.

*Page:*

This entry in the Trip Tables gives the page number for the detailed description of the stream.

| Stream/Section | Dist (mi) | Class | Sc/Pol | Grad Mean/Max | Area (sq mi) | Vol (cfs) | Size |
|---|---|---|---|---|---|---|---|
| Allegheny Portage Ck | | | | | | page | 292 |
| Wrights-mouth | 5.5 | I-II | B/A | 16/20 | 61 | 102 | Sm |
| Allegheny R | | | | | | page | 140 |
| A: Coudersport-Salamanca | 78.0 | A | AB/AB | 3/11 | 248 | 464 | Med |
| B: Salamanca-Kinzua Dam | 33.0 | A | AB/AB | lake | 1,608 | 2,777 | Lg |
| C: Kinzua Dam-West Monterey | 120.0 | B | AB/AB | 3/3 | 5,982 | 10,550 | Lg |
| D: West Monterey-Pittsburgh | 79.0 | A | BD/BC | pool | 11,410 | 19,670 | Huge |
| Bear Ck (Elk Co) | | | | | | page | 250 |
| FS 339-Clarion R | 9.0 | I | A/A | 20/26 | 41 | 68 | Tiny |
| Bear Ck (Garrett Co, Md) | | | | | | page | 344 |
| SR 219-Friendsville | 6.7 | III-IV | AB/A | 75/120 | | | - |
| Bear Ck, South Branch | | | | | | page | 346 |
| Accident-Bear Ck | 5.9 | III-IV | A/A | 107/154 | | | - |
| Beaver R | | | | | | page | 90 |
| A: New Castle-Wampum | 6.5 | A-B | BC/C | 3/3 | 2,235 | 2,494 | Lg |
| B: Wampum-Ohio R | 16.5 | A-B | D/C | pool | 3,106 | 3,758 | Lg |
| Bens Ck | | | | | | page | 194 |
| North Fork Bens Ck-Stony Ck | 3.0 | II | B/B | 35/55 | 49 | 82 | Tiny |
| Big Sandy Ck | | | | | | page | 369 |
| A: Bruceton Mills-Rockville | 5.8 | III-IV | A/A | 28/47 | 200 | 422 | Med |
| B: Rockville-Jenkinsburg Br | 5.1 | V | A/A | 81/107 | 200 | 422 | Med |
| Black Fk | | | | | | page | 378 |
| Hendricks-Parsons | 3.7 | II | B/AB | 16/26 | 475 | 792 | Med |
| Blacklick Ck | | | | | | page | 170 |
| A: Wehrum-Heshbon | 12.0 | I-II | CD/C | 18/20 | 150 | 250 | Sm |
| B: Heshbon-Josephine | 6.2 | III-IV | CD/C | 26/66 | 195 | 370 | Med |
| C: Josephine-Conemaugh L | 11.0 | B | CD/C | 5/15 | 390 | 671 | Med |
| Blacklick Ck, North Br | | | | | | page | 183 |
| Below SR 271-Vintondale | 10.0 | II-III | B/C | 36/50 | 69 | 115 | Sm |
| Blacklick Ck, South Br | | | | | | page | 182 |
| Nanty Glo-Vintondale | 7.1 | II-III | B/B | 42/105 | 47 | 78 | Tiny |
| Blackwater R | | | | | | page | 378 |
| North Fork Jct-Hendricks | 7.0 | V-VI | A/B | 96/120 | 86 | 199 | Sm |
| Brokenstraw Ck | | | | | | page | 290 |
| Garland-Youngsville | 12.0 | C-I | A/A | 8/14 | 321 | 587 | Med |
| Brush Ck | | | | | | page | 302 |
| Manor-Trafford | 11.8 | I | C/B | 15/20 | 58 | 97 | Tiny |
| Buffalo Ck (Armstrong Co) | | | | | | page | 152 |
| A: Worthington-W Winfield | 8.5 | I-II | AB/AB | 12/22 | 90 | 150 | Sm |
| B: W Winfield-Freeport | 11.0 | I | B/B | 10/10 | 137 | 194 | Sm |
| Buffalo Ck (Washington Co) | | | | | | page | 72 |
| A: Taylorstown Sta-Bethany | 21.8 | I-II | B/AB | 11/15 | 114 | 190 | Sm |
| B: Bethany-Wellsburg | 13.0 | I | B/B | 10/16 | 150 | 250 | Sm |
| Canadaway | | | | | | page | 396 |
| Hamlet/Cassadaga Rd-Laona | 9.0 | III-IV | A/A | 67/100 | | | - |

| Stream/Gauge | Levels Low Hi | Aux Gauge | Levels Low Hi | Normally Runnable | Nonrunnable Low Hi |
|---|---|---|---|---|---|
| **Allegheny Portage Ck**------------------------------------------------page 292 | | | | | |
| - | | Port Allegany | | | |
| **Allegheny R** ------------------------------------------------page 140 | | | | | |
| Port Allegheny | 3.0 | Eldred | 4.6 | | |
| Salamanca | 4.0 | | | | |
| Franklin | 1.7 4.9 | Kinzua | 7.5 8.5 | | 1% 38% |
| Natrona | | | | | |
| **Bear Ck (Elk Co)** ------------------------------------------------page 250 | | | | | |
| - | | Ridgway | 7.0 | | |
| **Bear Ck (Garrett Co, Md)** ------------------------------------------------page 344 | | | | | |
| - | | | | | |
| **Bear Ck, South Branch**------------------------------------------------page 346 | | | | | |
| - | | Friendsville | 4.3 5.0 | | |
| **Beaver R**------------------------------------------------ page 90 | | | | | |
| Wampum | 3.5 | Beaver Falls | 4.0 | EDec-MJun | 40% |
| Beaver Falls | 3.9 | | | | 40% |
| **Bens Ck**------------------------------------------------page 194 | | | | | |
| - | | Ferndale | 4.0 | | |
| **Big Sandy Ck**------------------------------------------------page 369 | | | | | |
| Rockville | 5.8 7.0 | | | MFeb-MApr | |
| Rockville | 5.8 6.5 | | | MFeb-MApr | |
| **Black Fk**------------------------------------------------page 378 | | | | | |
| Parsons | 4.0 6.0 | | | | |
| **Blacklick Ck**------------------------------------------------page 170 | | | | | |
| Josephine | 4.1 | | | | 31% |
| Josephine | 3.8 4.6 | | | | 60% 10% |
| Josephine | | | | | |
| **Blacklick Ck, North Br** ------------------------------------------------page 183 | | | | | |
| - | | Josephine | | | |
| **Blacklick Ck, South Br**------------------------------------------------page 182 | | | | | |
| - | | Josephine | 5.5 | | |
| **Blackwater R**------------------------------------------------page 378 | | | | | |
| Davis | 2.5 3.5 | Parsons | 4.0 5.5 | | |
| **Brokenstraw Ck** ------------------------------------------------page 290 | | | | | |
| Youngsville | | | | | |
| **Brush Ck** ------------------------------------------------page 302 | | | | | |
| - | | | | | |
| **Buffalo Ck (Armstrong Co)**------------------------------------------------page 152 | | | | | |
| Freeport | 1.6 2.6 | | | EJan-MMay | 55% 8% |
| Freeport | 1.7 2.8 | | | EJan-MMay | 60% 6% |
| **Buffalo Ck (Washington Co)** ------------------------------------------ page 72 | | | | | |
| - | | | | | |
| **Canadaway**------------------------------------------------page 396 | | | | | |
| - | | | | | |

| *Stream*/*Section* | *Dist* (mi) | *Class* | *Sc/Pol* | *Grad* Mean/Max | *Area* (sq mi) | *Vol* (cfs) | *Size* |
|---|---|---|---|---|---|---|---|
| **Casselman R** ---------------------------------------------------------- **page 330** | | | | | | | |
| A: Grantsville-Salisbury | 6.7 | I | B/A | 15/23 | 63 | 119 | Sm |
| B: Salisbury-Garrett | 15.0 | I | B/A | 6/7 | 125 | 208 | Sm |
| C: Garrett-Rockwood | 7.5 | I-II | A/A | 15/20 | 250 | 417 | Med |
| D: Rockwood-Markleton | 7.0 | II-III | A/A | 20/38 | 325 | 542 | Med |
| E: Markleton-Ft Hill | 6.0 | III | A/A | 29/36 | 382 | 661 | Med |
| F: Ft Hill-Harnedsville | 5.7 | II-III | A/B | 24/33 | 425 | 708 | Med |
| G: Harnedsville-Confluence | 3.5 | I | AB/B | 7/10 | 590 | 983 | Med |
| **Cattaraugus Ck** ---------------------------------------------------- **page 398** | | | | | | | |
| A: NY39-Otto Rd Br | 19.0 | I-II | | | | | - |
| B: Otto Rd Br-Gowanda | 8.8 | III-IV | A/B | 20/40 | | | - |
| **Cattaraugus Ck, South Branch** ---------------------------- **page 400** | | | | | | | |
| Otto-main stem | 12.0 | III-IV | A/A | 33/56 | | | - |
| **Chartiers Ck** ---------------------------------------------------------- **page 133** | | | | | | | |
| A: Washington-Van Emman | 13.7 | | BD/C | 7/13 | 60 | 100 | Sm |
| B: Van Emman-Kirwan Hts | 15.0 | I-II | BC/C | 8/11 | 200 | 333 | Med |
| C: Kirwan Hts-McKees Rocks | 12.5 | | BC/C | 6/10 | 257 | 292 | Med |
| **Chautauqua Ck** ---------------------------------------------------- **page 395** | | | | | | | |
| Lyons Rd-L Erie | 13.1 | III-IV | A/A | 63/90 | | | - |
| **Cheat R** ------------------------------------------------------------------ **page 361** | | | | | | | |
| A: Parsons-Rowlesburg | 36.0 | C-I | AB/AB | 7/8 | 718 | 1,697 | Med |
| B: Rowlesburg-Lick Run | 5.2 | III | A-B/A-B | 19/23 | 972 | 2,284 | Med |
| C: Lick Run-Albright | 6.3 | I | /C | 8/8 | 1,000 | 1,667 | Med |
| D: Albright-Jenkins Br | 11.4 | IV-V | A/B | 25/43 | 1,300 | 2,167 | Lg |
| E: Jenkins Br-L Lynn | 9.0 | III | A/B | 12/20 | 1,400 | 2,333 | Lg |
| **Clarion R** ---------------------------------------------------------------- **page 236** | | | | | | | |
| A: Johnsonburg-Ridgway | 8.5 | C-I | B/B | 8/11 | 204 | 385 | Med |
| B: Ridgway-Cooksburg | 44.0 | C-I | A/B | 6/10 | 303 | 591 | Med |
| C: Cooksburg-Mill Ck | 11.8 | C-I | A/B | 6/20 | 807 | 1,462 | Med |
| D: Mill Ck-Callensburg | 21.0 | C-I | B/B | 6/10 | 951 | 1,787 | Med |
| E: Callensburg-Parker | 17.0 | B | AB/B | 6/6 | 1,246 | 2,252 | Lg |
| **Clarion R, East Branch** -------------------------------------- **page 257** | | | | | | | |
| Glen Hazel-Johnsonburg | 6.2 | I | A/B | 11/15 | 73 | 138 | Sm |
| **Clarion R, West Branch** -------------------------------------- **page 256** | | | | | | | |
| Rocky Run-Johnsonburg | 9.9 | I | B/B | 13/18 | 63 | 126 | Sm |
| **Clear Shade Ck** -------------------------------------------------- **page 198** | | | | | | | |
| Ashtola Rd-Shade Ck | 5.5 | IV | A/A | 45/90 | 31 | 52 | Tiny |
| **Conemaugh R** ---------------------------------------------------- **page 166** | | | | | | | |
| A: Johnstown-New Florence | 12.9 | II | A/BC | 7/11 | 715 | 1,281 | Med |
| B: New Florence-Torrance | 13.0 | I-III | AB/B | 10/13 | 715 | 1,281 | Med |
| C: Torrance-Conemaugh Dam | 17.0 | A | D/C | flat | 890 | 1,483 | Med |
| D: Conemaugh Dam-Saltsburg | 6.9 | C | B/B | 6/6 | 1,358 | 2,882 | Lg |
| **Conneaut Ck** ---------------------------------------------------------- **page 391** | | | | | | | |
| Cherry Hill-Conneaut | 26.5 | I | B/A | 9/15 | 152 | 253 | Sm |
| **Conneaut Outlet Marsh** ------------------------------------ **page 272** | | | | | | | |
| A: Geneva Dike area | 5.5 | A | A/A | marsh | 75 | 125 | Sm |
| B: Interstate 79 area | 3.7 | A | A/A | marsh | 90 | 150 | Sm |
| C: Interstate 79-French Ck | 6.0 | B | B/A | 1/1 | 101 | 168 | Sm |

| Stream/Gauge | Levels Low | Hi | Aux Gauge | Levels Low | Hi | Normally Runnable | Nonrunnable Low | Hi |
|---|---|---|---|---|---|---|---|---|
| **Casselman R**----------------------------------------------------------------page **330** | | | | | | | | |
| Grantsville | | | Markleton | 2.8 | | EMar-MApr | | |
| Grantsville | | | Markleton | 2.7 | | LDec-LMay | | |
| Markleton | 2.2 | 3.6 | | | | EDec-LMay | 57% | 7% |
| Markleton | 2.1 | 3.5 | | | | EDec-EJun | 52% | 8% |
| Markleton | 2.0 | 3.5 | [Ft Hill Br (brks)] | 10 | 3 | EDec-EJun | 48% | 8% |
| Markleton | 2.0 | 4.0 | [Ft Hill Br (brks)] | 10 | | EDec-EJun | 48% | 5% |
| Markleton | 2.0 | 4.0 | | | | EDec-EJun | 48% | 5% |
| **Cattaraugus Ck**--------------------------------------------------------page **398** | | | | | | | | |
| - | | | [Otto Br] | | 3.5 | | | |
| - | | | [Otto Br] | | 3.5 | | | |
| **Cattaraugus Ck, South Branch** ------------------------------------page **400** | | | | | | | | |
| - | | | [Otto Br] | | 3.5 | | | |
| **Chartiers Ck** ---------------------------------------------------------page **133** | | | | | | | | |
| Washington | | | | | | | | |
| - | | | | | | | | |
| Carnegie | | | | | | | | |
| **Chautauqua Ck** ------------------------------------------------------page **395** | | | | | | | | |
| - | | | | | | | | |
| **Cheat R**--------------------------------------------------------------page **361** | | | | | | | | |
| Parsons | 2.9 | 5.0 | [Albright Br] | 3.0 | 4.5 | | | |
| Rowlesburg | | | [Albright Br] | 0.5 | 4.0 | | | |
| - | | | [Albright Br] | 0.5 | 4.0 | | | |
| [Albright Bridge] | -0.5 | 5.0 | Parsons | 1.9 | 6.1 | | | |
| [Albright Bridge] | 0.0 | 4.0 | Parsons | 2.3 | 5.3 | | | |
| **Clarion R**-----------------------------------------------------------page **236** | | | | | | | | |
| Johnsonburg | 2.2 | | Ridgway | 4.0 | | | 68% | |
| Ridgway | 3.0 | | Cooksburg | 2.8 | 5.0 | | 40% | |
| Cooksburg | 2.3 | | | | | | 20% | |
| Piney Dam | | | | | | | | |
| Piney Dam | | | | | | | | |
| **Clarion R, East Branch** ---------------------------------------------page **257** | | | | | | | | |
| EBr Clarion Dam | 2.0 | | Ridgway | 4.5 | | | 40% | |
| **Clarion R, West Branch** ---------------------------------------------page **256** | | | | | | | | |
| Wilcox | 2.0 | 3.0 | Ridgway | 4.5 | | | 70% | 4% |
| **Clear Shade Ck**-----------------------------------------------------page **198** | | | | | | | | |
| - | | | Ferndale | | | | | |
| **Conemaugh R**-------------------------------------------------------page **166** | | | | | | | | |
| Seward | 3.0 | | | | | LFeb-LMay | 65% | |
| Seward | 2.4 | 4.0 | | | | MNov-EJul | 23% | 10% |
| - | | | | | | | | |
| Tunnelton | 3.0 | 6.7 | | | | MNov-LJun | | |
| **Conneaut Ck**-------------------------------------------------------page **391** | | | | | | | | |
| - | | | | | | | | |
| **Conneaut Outlet Marsh** ------------------------------------------page **272** | | | | | | | | |
| - | | | | | | | | |
| - | | | | | | | | |
| - | | | | | | | | |

| Stream/Section | Dist (mi) | Class | Sc/Pol | Grad Mean/Max | Area (sq mi) | Vol (cfs) | Size |
|---|---|---|---|---|---|---|---|
| **Connoquenessing Ck** ---------------------------------------------------------- page **92** | | | | | | | |
| A: Zelienople-Country Club | 11.0 | I | C/B | 4/4 | 356 | 466 | Med |
| B: Country Club-Frisco | 2.0 | I | B/C | 6/10 | 400 | 667 | Med |
| C: Frisco-Ellport Pk | 2.0 | II | C/C | 17/20 | 829 | 1,382 | Med |
| D: Ellport Pk-Ellwood City | 3.0 | II-III | C/C | 11/12 | 832 | 1,387 | Med |
| E: Ellwood City-Beaver R | 1.5 | III | C/C | 20/33 | 838 | 1,397 | Med |
| **Cowanshannock Ck** ----------------------------------------------------------page **207** | | | | | | | |
| A: Greendale-St Rt 66 | 8.0 | II | AB/A | 18/26 | 40 | 67 | Tiny |
| B: St Rt 66-Allegheny R | 3.6 | IV | B/A | 36/80 | 63 | 105 | Sm |
| **Coxes Ck** -------------------------------------------------------------------page **343** | | | | | | | |
| Somerset-Rockwood | 10.5 | III | B/B | 29/55 | 55 | 92 | Tiny |
| **Crabtree Ck** ---------------------------------------------------------------page **162** | | | | | | | |
| Crabtree-New Alexandria | 4.0 | II | B/B | 9/25 | 19 | 32 | Tiny |
| **Crooked Ck (Armstrong Co)** -------------------------------------------------page **201** | | | | | | | |
| A: SR 119-Creekside | 6.5 | I | AB/B | 8/8 | 50 | 83 | Tiny |
| B: Creekside-Shelocta | 8.1 | I | AB/B | 5/5 | 90 | 150 | Sm |
| C: Shelocta-Girty | 10.5 | I | B/B | 4/6 | 175 | 295 | Sm |
| D: Girty-Cochrans Mill | 7.2 | I-II | B/B | 9/11 | 200 | 333 | Med |
| E: Cochrans Ml-Crooked Ck Dam | 8.0 | A | B/B | lake | 278 | 423 | Med |
| F: Crooked Ck Dam-Rosston | 7.0 | B | B/B | 5/5 | 292 | 487 | Med |
| **Crooked Ck (Mercer Co)** ---------------------------------------------------page **126** | | | | | | | |
| Hartstown-Osgood | 12.0 | I-II | AB/A | 5/6 | 46 | 77 | Tiny |
| **Cross Ck** ------------------------------------------------------------------ page **75** | | | | | | | |
| A: Haynan Ck-Avella | 2.3 | I-II | C/C | 13/13 | 30 | 50 | Tiny |
| B: Avella-Pa state line | 5.8 | I-II | B/C | 20/29 | 63 | 105 | Sm |
| C: Pa state line-Ohio R | 7.0 | II | B/C | 24/28 | 63 | 105 | Sm |
| **Cussewago Ck** -------------------------------------------------------------page **276** | | | | | | | |
| Crossingville-Meadville | 28.5 | C | AB/A | 2/2 | 90 | 130 | Sm |
| **Dark Shade Ck** ------------------------------------------------------------page **199** | | | | | | | |
| Cairnbrook-Clear Shade Ck | 1.9 | IV-V | A/B | 60/160 | 36 | 60 | Tiny |
| **Deer Ck** -------------------------------------------------------------------page **151** | | | | | | | |
| SR 910-L Deer Ck | 8.0 | I | C/BC | 9/26 | 51 | 85 | Tiny |
| **Dry Fk** --------------------------------------------------------------------page **379** | | | | | | | |
| A: Harman-Jenningston | 7.0 | III | B/A | 36/40 | | | - |
| B: Jenningston-Hendricks | 13.4 | III-IV | A/A | 24/31 | 345 | 832 | Med |
| **Dunbar Ck** ----------------------------------------------------------------page **324** | | | | | | | |
| Dunbar-Connellsville | 6.4 | III-IV | B/A | 59/112 | 38 | 63 | Tiny |
| **Dunkard Ck** ---------------------------------------------------------------page **360** | | | | | | | |
| SR 2019-Monongahela R | 8.0 | I | C/ | 6/7 | 229 | 276 | Med |
| **Dunlap Ck** ----------------------------------------------------------------page **350** | | | | | | | |
| Allison-Brownsville | 6.2 | II | BC/C | 26/40 | 33 | 43 | Tiny |
| **East Sandy Ck** ------------------------------------------------------------page **261** | | | | | | | |
| Van-Allegheny R | 10.5 | II | A/A | 21/25 | 103 | 172 | Sm |
| **Elk Ck** --------------------------------------------------------------------page **254** | | | | | | | |
| Daguscahonda-Ridgway | 6.4 | I-III | BC/B | 15/25 | 64 | 107 | Sm |
| **Fike Run/L Sandy Ck (Fayette Co)** -----------------------------------------page **375** | | | | | | | |
| Five Forks-Gibbon Glade | 4.5 | IV | A/A | 93/180 | 28 | 47 | Tiny |
| **Fourmile Run** -------------------------------------------------------------page **163** | | | | | | | |
| SR 130-Darlington | 10.0 | III-IV,I-II | B/A | 28/80 | 39 | 65 | Tiny |

| Stream/Gauge | Levels Low | Hi | Aux Gauge | Levels Low | Hi | Normally Runnable | Nonrunnable Low | Hi |
|---|---|---|---|---|---|---|---|---|
| **Connoquenessing Ck** ---------------------------------------------------- page **92** | | | | | | | | |
| Zelienople | 1.8 | 3.5 | McConnells Mill | 0.0 | 2.5 | MNov-MJun | 45% | 10% |
| Zelienople | 1.7 | 3.5 | McConnells Mill | 0.0 | 2.5 | MNov-MJun | 42% | 10% |
| Zelienople | 1.6 | 3.0 | McConnells Mill | 0.0 | 1.7 | LNov-EJun | 38% | 15% |
| Zelienople | 1.6 | 3.0 | McConnells Mill | 0.0 | 1.7 | LNov-EJun | 38% | 15% |
| Zelienople | 1.6 | | McConnells Mill | 0.0 | 1.7 | MNov-LJun | 38% | |
| **Cowanshannock Ck** --------------------------------------------------page **207** | | | | | | | | |
| [SR 85 Br (brks)] | 6.0 | | | | | | | |
| - | | | | | | | | |
| **Coxes Ck** --------------------------------------------------------------page **343** | | | | | | | | |
| - | | | | | | | | |
| **Crabtree Ck** ------------------------------------------------------------page **162** | | | | | | | | |
| - | | | Kingston | 4.5 | | | | |
| **Crooked Ck (Armstrong Co)** ----------------------------------------page **201** | | | | | | | | |
| Idaho | | | Creekside | | | | | |
| Idaho | 2.7 | 5.0 | | | | EJan-MMay | 41% | 3% |
| Idaho | 3.0 | 4.5 | | | | EJan-MMay | 60% | 5% |
| Idaho | 2.7 | 4.0 | | | | LDec-LMay | 41% | 8% |
| Crooked Ck Dam | | | | | | | | |
| Crooked Ck Dam | | | | | | | | |
| **Crooked Ck (Mercer Co)** -------------------------------------------page **126** | | | | | | | | |
| - | | | Greenville | 2.0 | | | | |
| **Cross Ck** ----------------------------------------------------------- page **75** | | | | | | | | |
| - | | | | | | | | |
| - | | | | | | | | |
| - | | | | | | | | |
| **Cussewago Ck** --------------------------------------------------------page **276** | | | | | | | | |
| Meadville | | | Union City Dam | 4.6 | | | | |
| **Dark Shade Ck** ----------------------------------------------------page **199** | | | | | | | | |
| - | | | Ferndale | 3.6 | | | | |
| **Deer Ck** -------------------------------------------------------------page **151** | | | | | | | | |
| - | | | | | | | | |
| **Dry Fk** -----------------------------------------------------------------page **379** | | | | | | | | |
| Hendricks | 3.0 | | Parsons | 4.5 | | | | |
| Hendricks | 3.0 | | Parsons | 4.5 | | | | |
| **Dunbar Ck** --------------------------------------------------------------page **324** | | | | | | | | |
| - | | | | | | | | |
| **Dunkard Ck** ------------------------------------------------------------page **360** | | | | | | | | |
| Shannopin | | | | | | | | |
| **Dunlap Ck** --------------------------------------------------------------page **350** | | | | | | | | |
| Allison | | | | | | | | |
| **East Sandy Ck** ------------------------------------------------------page **261** | | | | | | | | |
| [Van Br] | IV | | Rouseville | 3.5 | | | | |
| **Elk Ck** ----------------------------------------------------------------page **254** | | | | | | | | |
| - | | | Wilcox | 4.3 | | | | |
| **Fike Run/L Sandy Ck (Fayette Co)** -----------------------------page **375** | | | | | | | | |
| - | | | Rockville | 8.6 | | | | |
| **Fourmile Run** --------------------------------------------------------page **163** | | | | | | | | |
| - | | | Kingston | 4.5 | 6.0 | | | |

| Stream/Section | Dist (mi) | Class | Sc/Pol | Grad Mean/Max | Area (sq mi) | Vol (cfs) | Size |
|---|---|---|---|---|---|---|---|
| **French Ck** --------------------------------------------------------------page 262 | | | | | | | |
| A: Pa St line-Union City Dam | 15.3 | I | A/A | 10/20 | 92 | 153 | Sm |
| B: Union City Dam-Cambr Spr | 27.0 | B | A/A | 4/10 | 222 | 439 | Med |
| C: Cambridge Spr-Seagertown | 15.0 | I | B/B | 2/4 | 597 | 1,064 | Med |
| D: Seagertown-Cochranton | 20.0 | B | | 4/6 | 629 | 1,056 | Med |
| E: Cochranton-Utica | 8.8 | C | BC/B | 3/3 | 998 | 1,722 | Med |
| F: Utica-Franklin | 7.0 | C-I | BC/B | 6/6 | 1,028 | 1,837 | Med |
| **Georges Ck**----------------------------------------------------------page 359 | | | | | | | |
| US 119-New Geneva | 8.0 | II | /C | 18/20 | 16 | 18 | Tiny |
| **Glady Fk**--------------------------------------------------------------page 380 | | | | | | | |
| Evenwood-Panther Camp Run | 10.4 | II-III | A/A | 26/38 | | | - |
| **Indian Ck**------------------------------------------------------------page 326 | | | | | | | |
| A: Jones Mill-Indianhead L | 16.0 | I-II | A/A | 13/20 | 33 | 55 | Tiny |
| B: Indianhead L-Youghiogheny R | 4.9 | V-VI | A/A | 57/80 | 125 | 208 | Sm |
| **Jacobs Ck** ------------------------------------------------------------page 319 | | | | | | | |
| A: Acme-Laurelville | 4.5 | IV | AB/A | 125/164 | 30 | 50 | Tiny |
| B: Laurelville-Scottdale | 10.0 | I | AB/AB | 12/76 | 60 | 100 | Sm |
| C: Scottdale-Chaintown | 5.0 | B | C/B | 4/4 | 80 | 133 | Sm |
| D: Chaintown-Jacobs Ck | 7.1 | II-III | B/B | 32/41 | 95 | 158 | Sm |
| **Kinzua Ck**------------------------------------------------------------page 291 | | | | | | | |
| Westline-FS 150 | 5.5 | I | A/A | 18/29 | 46 | 78 | Tiny |
| **Kiskiminetas R**------------------------------------------------------page 155 | | | | | | | |
| A: Saltsburg-Salina | 6.7 | B | B/B | 6/6 | 1,723 | 2,872 | Lg |
| B: Salina-Freeport | 21.0 | B | C/B | 3/3 | 1,825 | 3,106 | Lg |
| **Lake Erie** -----------------------------------------------------------page 387 | | | | | | | |
| A: Conneaut-Walnut Ck | 18.5 | A | B/A | lake | | | - |
| B: Walnut Ck-Erie pub dock | 15.0 | A | A/A | lake | | | - |
| C: Erie pub dock-Ripley NY | 21.0 | A | B/C | lake | | | - |
| **Laurel Fk**------------------------------------------------------------page 380 | | | | | | | |
| US 33-Jenningston | 13.0 | III-IV | A/A | 54/72 | | | Sm |
| **Laurel Hill Ck**------------------------------------------------------page 340 | | | | | | | |
| A: Laurel Hill SP-Whipkey Dam | 8.2 | III | A/A | 31/50 | 60 | 100 | Sm |
| B: Whipkey Dam-Ursina | 8.0 | III | A/A | 40/70 | 121 | 266 | Sm |
| **Little Beaver Ck** ------------------------------------------------ page 78 | | | | | | | |
| A: Beaver Ck SP-Fredericktown | 6.5 | I | A/B | 10/11 | 450 | 750 | Med |
| B: Fredericktown-Ohio R | 7.8 | I-II | A/B | 11/12 | 493 | 514 | Med |
| **Little Beaver Ck, M Fk**---------------------------------------- page 84 | | | | | | | |
| Coleman-Beaver Ck SP | 20.5 | I | C/C | 7/11 | 149 | 248 | Sm |
| **Little Beaver Ck, North Fk** ------------------------------------ page 81 | | | | | | | |
| Negley-Fredericktown | 7.0 | I-II | B/B | 9/15 | 193 | 322 | Med |
| **Little Beaver Ck, West Fk** ----------------------------------- page 82 | | | | | | | |
| West Point-Beaver Ck SP | 8.5 | I | B/B | 10/15 | 100 | 167 | Sm |
| **Little Conemaugh R**------------------------------------------------page 186 | | | | | | | |
| A: Lilly-Portage | 5.6 | III-IV | CD/C | 53/100 | 60 | 100 | Sm |
| B: Portage-South Fork | 10.4 | I | C/C | 12/20 | 100 | 167 | Sm |
| C: South Fork-Johnstown | 10.2 | II-III | B/BC | 23/30 | 183 | 328 | Med |

| Stream/Gauge | Levels Low Hi | Aux Gauge | Levels Low Hi | Normally Runnable | Nonrunnable Low Hi |
|---|---|---|---|---|---|
| **French Ck** ----------------------------------------------------------------------------------page **262** | | | | | |
| Wattsburg | | | | | |
| Union City Dam | 2.3 5.0 | | | | 25% 7% |
| Meadville | 2.0 | [Seagertown Br] | 4.5 | | |
| Meadville | 2.0 | [Seagertown Br] | 4.5 | | |
| Utica | 1.6 5.5 | | | | 15% 12% |
| Utica | 1.6 5.5 | | | | 15% 12% |
| **Georges Ck** ---------------------------------------------------------page **359** | | | | | |
| Smithfield | | | | | |
| **Glady Fk** -----------------------------------------------------------page **380** | | | | | |
| Hendricks(DryFk) | 3.7 | Parsons | 5.0 | | |
| **Indian Ck** --------------------------------------------------------page **326** | | | | | |
| White Bridge | | Ursina | 2.0 | | |
| White Bridge | | Ursina | 2.0 | | |
| **Jacobs Ck** -------------------------------------------------------page **319** | | | | | |
| [Freemans Falls] | 34" 24" | | | | |
| - | | | | | |
| - | | | | | |
| [Staff at take-out] | 2.2 | Connellsville | 4.7 6.9 | | |
| **Kinzua Ck** -------------------------------------------------------page **291** | | | | | |
| Guffey | 3.0 | | | | 85% |
| **Kiskiminetas R** --------------------------------------------page **155** | | | | | |
| Vandergrift | 3.5 8.0 | Tunnelton | 3.0 6.7 | ENov-MAug | 23% 11% |
| Vandergrift | | Tunnelton | 3.0 6.7 | | |
| **Lake Erie** ---------------------------------------------------page **387** | | | | | |
| - | | | | | |
| - | | | | | |
| **Laurel Fk** --------------------------------------------------page **380** | | | | | |
| Hendricks(DryFk) | 3.7 | Parsons | 5.0 | | |
| **Laurel Hill Ck** ---------------------------------------------page **340** | | | | | |
| Ursina | 2.1 | | | none | 88% |
| Ursina | 1.9 3.1 | | | EMar-MApr | 80% 1% |
| **Little Beaver Ck** ------------------------------------ page **78** | | | | | |
| E Liverpool | 2.9 4.7 | | | | |
| E Liverpool | 2.8 4.6 | | | LNov-LJun | |
| **Little Beaver Ck, M Fk** --------------------------- page **84** | | | | | |
| - | | E Liverpool | 4.3 | | |
| **Little Beaver Ck, North Fk** --------------------- page **81** | | | | | |
| - | | | | | |
| **Little Beaver Ck, West Fk** -------------------- page **82** | | | | | |
| - | | E Liverpool | 4.3 | | |
| **Little Conemaugh R** ------------------------------page **186** | | | | | |
| - | | | | | |
| - | | | | | |
| East Conemaugh | | Seward | 2.7 4.0 | | |

| Stream/Section | Dist (mi) | Class | Sc/Pol | Grad Mean/Max | Area (sq mi) | Vol (cfs) | Size |
|---|---|---|---|---|---|---|---|
| **Little Conemaugh R, South Fk** | | | | | | page | 189 |
| Beaverdale-South Fork | 7.3 | III | C/C | 58/100 | 64 | 107 | Sm |
| **Little Connoquenessing Ck** | | | | | | page | 112 |
| A: SR 3007-SR 528 | 6.3 | II | B/AB | 16/36 | 45 | 75 | Tiny |
| B: SR 528-w SR 3025 | 5.0 | C-I | B/AB | 7/10 | 65 | 108 | Sm |
| **Little Mahoning Ck** | | | | | | page | 219 |
| A: Nashville-Rochester Mills | 6.0 | II | A/A | 25/40 | 20 | 33 | Tiny |
| B: Rochester Mills-SR 119 | 4.0 | C-I | AB/A | 14/22 | 60 | 100 | Sm |
| C: SR 119-SR 210 | 5.0 | C | AB/A | 6/6 | 70 | 117 | Sm |
| D: SR 210-McCormick | 4.0 | B | AB/A | 4/4 | 80 | 133 | Sm |
| E: McCormick-Smicksburg | 5.0 | C-I | AB/A | 6/6 | 87 | 153 | Sm |
| F: Smicksburg-Mahoning Ck | 5.0 | C | AB/A | 5/5 | 113 | 188 | Sm |
| **Little Sandy Ck (Jefferson Co)** | | | | | | page | 229 |
| Worthville-Mayport | 8.0 | I | AB/A | 15/30 | 73 | 122 | Sm |
| **Little Sandy Ck (Preston Co, WVa)** | | | | | | page | 372 |
| A: Hazelton-Brandonville Pk | 8.5 | II-III | | 31/80 | | | - |
| B: Brandonville Pk-W VA 26 | 2.5 | | | 18/35 | | | - |
| C: W VA 26-Big Sandy Ck | 2.8 | III-IV | A/A- | 32/80 | | | - |
| **Little Shenango R** | | | | | | page | 125 |
| Osgood-Greenville | 3.2 | I | AB/A | 9/20 | 104 | 142 | Sm |
| **Little Toby Ck (Elk Co)** | | | | | | page | 251 |
| Brockway-Clarion R | 11.0 | I | AB/AB | 10/14 | 91 | 152 | Sm |
| **Loyalhanna Ck** | | | | | | page | 157 |
| A: Rector-Ligonier | 4.9 | II | B/A | 8/20 | 70 | 117 | Sm |
| B: Ligonier-Kingston Dam | 6.9 | II | C/A | 18/50 | 120 | 200 | Sm |
| C: Kingston Dam-Latrobe | 4.6 | I-II | B/A | 9/15 | 172 | 303 | Sm |
| D: Latrobe-New Alexandria | 12.0 | B-I | C/D | 3/8 | 265 | 439 | Med |
| E: Loyalhanna Dam-Saltsburg | 4.0 | B-I | B/B | 10/15 | 292 | 481 | Med |
| **Mahoning Ck** | | | | | | page | 212 |
| A: Big Run-Punxsutawney | 10.9 | C | BC/B | 7/11 | 158 | 277 | Sm |
| B: Punxsutawney-Valier | 9.5 | B | B/AB | 3/3 | 158 | 269 | Sm |
| C: Valier-SR 839 | 17.1 | C | B/B | 7/9 | 200 | 333 | Med |
| D: SR 839-Mahoning Dam | 6.0 | A | | lake | 321 | 561 | Med |
| E: Mahoning Dam-Putneyville | 6.5 | I-II | AB/A | 12/13 | 344 | 601 | Med |
| F: Putneyville-Allegheny R | 16.5 | I | AB/A | 7/13 | 425 | 708 | Med |
| **Mahoning R** | | | | | | page | 128 |
| Alliance-New Castle | 120 | A-I | D/C | 3/ | 1,140 | 1,900 | Med |
| **Meadow Run** | | | | | | page | 328 |
| A: SR 381-SR 2011 | 5.0 | II-III | A/A | 53/90 | 30 | 50 | Tiny |
| B: SR2011-Youghiogheny R | 3.0 | IV-V | A/A | 88/135 | 41 | 68 | Tiny |
| **Middle Fork Tygart R** | | | | | | page | 384 |
| A: Laurel Fk-Audra SP | 5.0 | III | A/B | 26/40 | | | - |
| B: Audra SP- Tygart R | 6.0 | IV-V | A/A | 65/120 | | | - |
| **Mill Ck (Clarion Co)** | | | | | | page | 243 |
| below SR 949-Clarion L | 10.5 | II | A/A | 23/52 | 59 | 98 | Tiny |
| **Mill Ck (Elk Co)** | | | | | | page | 252 |
| A: SR 948-Ridgway Res | 9.0 | III | A/A | 25/28 | 25 | 42 | Tiny |
| B: Ridgway Res-Clarion R | 2.2 | III | A/A | 32/33 | 32 | 53 | Tiny |

| Stream/Gauge | Levels Low Hi | Aux Gauge | Levels Low Hi | Normally Runnable | Nonrunnable Low Hi |
|---|---|---|---|---|---|
| **Little Conemaugh R, South Fk** ----------------------------------------page 189 | | | | | |
| - | | | | | |
| **Little Connoquenessing Ck** ----------------------------------------page 112 | | | | | |
| [SR3205 br] | 2.0 | | | | |
| [SR3205 br] | 1.5 | Zelienople | 3.0 | | |
| **Little Mahoning Ck** ----------------------------------------page 219 | | | | | |
| McCormick | | | | | |
| McCormick | | | | | |
| McCormick | 3.0 | | | 72% | |
| McCormick | 3.0 | | | 72% | |
| McCormick | 3.0 | | | 72% | |
| McCormick | 3.0 | | | 72% | |
| **Little Sandy Ck (Jefferson Co)** ----------------------------------------page 229 | | | | | |
| - | | St Charles | 6.3 | | |
| **Little Sandy Ck (Preston, WVa)** ----------------------------------------page 372 | | | | | |
| - | | Bruceton | 2.0 | | |
| - | | | | | |
| [Rt 26 Br] | 0.5 2.0 | | | | |
| **Little Shenango R** ----------------------------------------page 125 | | | | | |
| Greenville | 2.0 | | | | |
| **Little Toby Ck (Elk Co)** ----------------------------------------page 251 | | | | | |
| - | | Wilcox | 2.0 | | |
| **Loyalhanna Ck** ----------------------------------------page 157 | | | | | |
| Kingston | 4.5 5.3 | | | none | 95% 2% |
| Kingston | 3.2 5.3 | | | LDec-LMay | 72% 2% |
| Kingston | 3.4 5.0 | | | LDec-LMay | 77% 3% |
| Kingston | | | | | |
| Loyalhanna Dam | | | | | |
| **Mahoning Ck** ----------------------------------------page 212 | | | | | |
| Punxsutawney | | | | | |
| Punxsutawney | | | | | |
| - | | McCormick | 1.9 2.6 | | |
| - | | | | | |
| Mahoning Dam | 2.8 3.9 | | | EDec-LMay | 55% 15% |
| Mahoning Dam | 3.0 | | | EJan-LMay | 65% |
| **Mahoning R** ----------------------------------------page 128 | | | | | |
| - | | | | | |
| **Meadow Run** ----------------------------------------page 328 | | | | | |
| - | | Ursina | 2.1 | | |
| - | | Ursina | 2.1 | | |
| **Middle Fork Tygart R** ----------------------------------------page 384 | | | | | |
| Audra St Pk | 3.5 6.0 | Belington | 4.0 | | |
| Audra St Pk | 3.5 5.0 | Belington | 4.0 | | |
| **Mill Ck (Clarion Co)** ----------------------------------------page 243 | | | | | |
| - | | Cooksburg | 6.5 | | |
| **Mill Ck (Elk Co)** ----------------------------------------page 252 | | | | | |
| - | | Wilcox | 4.3 | | |
| - | | Wilcox | 4.3 | | |

| Stream/Section | Dist (mi) | Class | Sc/Pol | Grad Mean/Max | Area (sq mi) | Vol (cfs) | Size |
|---|---|---|---|---|---|---|---|
| **Mill Ck (Jefferson Co)** ----------page 234 | | | | | | | |
| Allen Mills-Port Barnett | 9.0 | II | A/B | 35/52 | 53 | 88 | Tiny |
| **Mill Ck (Westmoreland Co)** ----------page 165 | | | | | | | |
| Waterford-Ligonier | 5.0 | II | C/A | 30/55 | 33 | 55 | Tiny |
| **Millstone Ck, East Branch** ----------page 246 | | | | | | | |
| A: Gurgling Run-Loleta Rec Area | 5.7 | III+ | A/A | 42/112 | 26 | 43 | Tiny |
| B: Loleta Rec Area - Clarion R | 4.0 | II-III | A/A | 35/52 | 54 | 90 | Tiny |
| **Millstone Ck, West Branch** ----------page 245 | | | | | | | |
| FS 130-Clarion R | 12.2 | I-II | A/A | 34/47 | 24 | 40 | Tiny |
| **Monongahela R** ----------page 296 | | | | | | | |
| Fairmont WVa-Pittsburgh | 128.0 | A | D/C | pool | 7,337 | 12,500 | Huge |
| **Montour Run** ----------page 131 | | | | | | | |
| Enlow-Groveton | 11.0 | II-III | C/B | 22/33 | 29 | 48 | Tiny |
| **Neshannock Ck** ----------page 122 | | | | | | | |
| A: Neshannock Fl-Lakewood Pk | 7.0 | II | AB/A | 27/60 | 228 | 243 | Med |
| B: Lakewood Pk-New Castle | 4.3 | I-II | AB/AB | 18/26 | 244 | 407 | Med |
| **Ohio R** ----------page 68 | | | | | | | |
| Pittsburgh-Pa state line | 40.0 | A | D/C | pool | 19,500 | 33,040 | Huge |
| **Oil Ck** ----------page 277 | | | | | | | |
| A: Centerville-Titusville | 12.0 | I | B/A | 7/10 | 250 | 417 | Med |
| B: Titusville-Rouseville | 12.0 | I | B/AB | 10/12 | 300 | 538 | Med |
| **Otter Ck** ----------page 124 | | | | | | | |
| US 19-Mercer | 7.0 | I | AB/AB | 18/22 | 49 | 82 | Tiny |
| **Paint Ck** ----------page 195 | | | | | | | |
| Windber-Stony Ck | 2.7 | V+ | C/C | 130/200 | 37 | 62 | Tiny |
| **Peters Ck** ----------page 348 | | | | | | | |
| Snowden-USX Clairton Works | 7.0 | I | C/B | 14/20 | 51 | 85 | Tiny |
| **Pine Ck (Allegheny Co)** ----------page 149 | | | | | | | |
| A: North Pk-Allison Pk | 6.6 | C-I | C/BC | 7/26 | 45 | 75 | Tiny |
| B: Allison Pk-Etna | 6.5 | I-II | D/C | 5/16 | 67 | 112 | Sm |
| **Pine Ck (Armstrong Co)** ----------page 209 | | | | | | | |
| A: Echo-Pine Furnace | 7.0 | I-II | AB/B | 20/30 | 20 | 33 | Tiny |
| B: Pine Furnace-St Rt 28/66 | 1.5 | | B/B | 26/28 | 30 | 50 | Tiny |
| C: St Rt 28/66-Allegheny R | 3.0 | II-III | B/B | 39/100 | 38 | 63 | Tiny |
| **Pine Ck (Pa Grand Canyon)** ----------page 402 | | | | | | | |
| Ansonia-Slate Run | 29.1 | II | A/A | 15/27 | 604 | 816 | Med |
| **Pithole Ck** ----------page 279 | | | | | | | |
| Pithole-Oleopolis | 6.5 | III | AB/A | 44/70 | 42 | 70 | Tiny |
| **Potomac R** ----------page 408 | | | | | | | |
| Harpers Fy-Sandy Hook Md | 3.0 | II | A/B | 14/14 | | | - |
| **Potomac R, North Branch** ----------page 410 | | | | | | | |
| Gormania WVa-Kitzmiller Md | 15.0 | IV | B/C | 47/66 | 225 | 452 | Med |
| **Presque Isle** ----------page 390 | | | | | | | |
| Graveyard Pond & return | 4.0 | A | A/A | lake | | | - |
| **Quemahoning Ck** ----------page 200 | | | | | | | |
| Boswell-Reservoir | 3.4 | III | A/B | 50/65 | 98 | 163 | Sm |

| Stream/Gauge | Levels Low Hi | Aux Gauge | Levels Low Hi | Normally Runnable | Nonrunnable Low Hi |
|---|---|---|---|---|---|
| **Mill Ck (Jefferson Co)** ----------------------------------------------page 234 | | | | | |
| Brookville | | St Charles | 7.0 | | |
| **Mill Ck (Westmoreland Co)** ----------------------------------page 165 | | | | | |
| - | | Kingston | 4.5 6.0 | | |
| **Millstone Ck, East Branch**------------------------------------page 246 | | | | | |
| - | | Ridgway | 8.0 | | |
| - | | Ridgway | 6.0 | | |
| **Millstone Ck, West Branch** --------------------------------page 245 | | | | | |
| - | | Ridgway | 8.5 9.5 | | |
| **Monongahela R**------------------------------------------------page 296 | | | | | |
| - | | | | all year | |
| **Montour Run** ------------------------------------------------page 131 | | | | | |
| [Beaver Gr Rd Br]0.0 2.0 | | | | | |
| **Neshannock Ck**------------------------------------------------page 122 | | | | | |
| - | | | | | |
| - | | | | | |
| **Ohio R**------------------------------------------------------ page 68 | | | | | |
| Dashields L&D | | | | | |
| **Oil Ck** ------------------------------------------------------page 277 | | | | | |
| Rouseville | 3.0 5.0 | | | | 72% 4% |
| Rouseville | 2.5 5.0 | | | | 55% 4% |
| **Otter Ck** ----------------------------------------------------page 124 | | | | | |
| - | | | | | |
| **Paint Ck**----------------------------------------------------page 195 | | | | | |
| - | | Ferndale | | | |
| **Peters Ck**----------------------------------------------------page 348 | | | | | |
| - | | | | | |
| **Pine Ck (Allegheny Co)**----------------------------------page 149 | | | | | |
| - | | | | | |
| - | | | | | |
| **Pine Ck (Armstrong Co)** --------------------------------page 209 | | | | | |
| - | | | | | |
| - | | | | | |
| - | | | | | |
| **Pine Ck (Pa Grand Canyon)**--------------------------------page 402 | | | | | |
| Cedar Run | 2.0 3.5 | | | | |
| **Pithole Ck** --------------------------------------------------page 279 | | | | | |
| - | | Rouseville | 4.0 5.0 | | |
| **Potomac R** --------------------------------------------------page 408 | | | | | |
| Hancock | 2.0 4.0 | | | | |
| **Potomac R, North Branch** --------------------------------page 410 | | | | | |
| Kitzmiller | 4.0 6.0 | | | | |
| **Presque Isle** ------------------------------------------------page 390 | | | | | |
| - | | | | | |
| **Quemahoning Ck**--------------------------------------------page 200 | | | | | |
| - | | | | | |

| Stream/Section | Dist (mi) | Class | Sc/Pol | Grad Mean/Max | Area (sq mi) | Vol (cfs) | Size |
|---|---|---|---|---|---|---|---|
| **Raccoon Ck** ------------------------------------------------------------- page 86 | | | | | | | |
| A: Raccoon-Murdocksville | 12.0 | I | B/C | 10/20 | 75 | 125 | Sm |
| B: Murdocksville-SR 151 | 11.0 | C-I | B/BC | 6/10 | 125 | 208 | Sm |
| C: SR 151-SR 18 | 13.0 | I | C/B | 8/14 | 178 | 193 | Sm |
| **Red Bank Ck** ------------------------------------------------------------ page 225 | | | | | | | |
| A: Brookville-Summerville | 10.5 | C-I | B/B | 6/10 | 220 | 367 | Med |
| B: Summerville-New Bethlehem | 16.5 | C-I | B/B | 6/11 | 350 | 583 | Med |
| C: New Bethlehem-Rimer | 27.8 | I | A/B | 9/29 | 528 | 873 | Med |
| **Red Bank Ck, North Fk** ------------------------------------------------- page 231 | | | | | | | |
| Richardsville-Brookville | 10.0 | I | A/A | 13/17 | 98 | 163 | Sm |
| **Redstone Ck** ----------------------------------------------------------- page 349 | | | | | | | |
| Smock-Albany | 8.5 | II | C/C | 15/20 | 74 | 101 | Sm |
| **Salmon Ck** ------------------------------------------------------------- page 285 | | | | | | | |
| A: FS 128-FS 145 | 6.8 | III | A/A | 43/89 | 40 | 67 | Tiny |
| B: FS 145-Kellettville | 7.1 | II | A/A | 25/42 | 55 | 92 | Tiny |
| **Sandy Ck** -------------------------------------------------------------- page 258 | | | | | | | |
| A: Goddard SP-Raymilton | 9.0 | C | AB/AB | 8/13 | 100 | 167 | Sm |
| B: Raymilton-Pecan | 8.5 | I-II | AB/B | 14/14 | 161 | 268 | Sm |
| **Sandy Lick Ck** --------------------------------------------------------- page 233 | | | | | | | |
| Reynoldsville-Brookville | 20.0 | I-II | B/B | 8/19 | 114 | 190 | Sm |
| **Sewickley Ck** ---------------------------------------------------------- page 318 | | | | | | | |
| Yukon-Youghiogheny R | 12.0 | III | C/C | 13/33 | 165 | 275 | Sm |
| **Shade Ck** -------------------------------------------------------------- page 196 | | | | | | | |
| Dark Shade Ck-Stony Ck | 9.8 | III | A/A | 56/75 | 97 | 162 | Sm |
| **Shavers Fk** ------------------------------------------------------------ page 377 | | | | | | | |
| A: Bemis-US 33 Br | 14.0 | II-IV | A/A | 40/65 | 150 | 250 | Sm |
| B: US 33-Parsons | 22.0 | I-II | AB/AB | 19/19 | 214 | 553 | Med |
| **Shenandoah R** ---------------------------------------------------------- page 406 | | | | | | | |
| Millville WVa-Sandy Hook Md | 7.0 | II-III | A/B | 10/20 | 3,040 | 2,698 | Lg |
| **Shenango R** ------------------------------------------------------------ page 116 | | | | | | | |
| A: Pymatuning Dam-Greenville | 8.5 | A-B | A/A | 4/6 | 167 | 208 | Sm |
| B: Greenville-New Hamburg | 9.5 | A | B/B | 2/2 | 337 | 481 | Med |
| C: N Hamburg-Sharpsville Dam | 16.5 | A | B/A | lake | 400 | 667 | Med |
| D: Sharpsville Dam-W Middlesex | 12.0 | C-I | D/B | 5/6 | 584 | 761 | Med |
| E: W Middlesex-Harbor Br | 13.8 | B | B/B | 2/2 | 700 | 1,167 | Med |
| F: Harbor Br-Wampum | 14.5 | B-I | C/C | 3/3 | 792 | 871 | Med |
| **Slippery Rock Ck** ------------------------------------------------------ page 98 | | | | | | | |
| A: Rock Falls-Moores Cor | 9.0 | C | A/B | 4/10 | 150 | 250 | Sm |
| B: Moores Cor-Kennedy Mill | 8.5 | C | BC/B | 5/6 | 260 | 433 | Med |
| C: Kennedy Mill-Rose Point | 1.5 | II | AB/B | 11/11 | 300 | 500 | Med |
| D: Rose Point-Breakneck | 2.5 | III-IV | A/A | 30/40 | 360 | 600 | Med |
| E: Breakneck-Harris Br | 3.2 | II-III | A/A | 23/27 | 380 | 633 | Med |
| F: Harris Br-Ellport Pk | 6.0 | I | AB/AB | 12/13 | 398 | 572 | Med |
| **South Sandy Ck** -------------------------------------------------------- page 260 | | | | | | | |
| Game Lands #39-Pecan | 8.5 | I-II | A/A | 23/28 | 31 | 52 | Tiny |
| **Spring Ck** ------------------------------------------------------------- page 248 | | | | | | | |
| Duhring-Hallton | 10.5 | I | A/A | 15/25 | 88 | 147 | Sm |
| **Spring Ck, East Branch** ------------------------------------------------ page 249 | | | | | | | |
| Pigs Ear-Duhring | 5.5 | II | A/A | 11/30 | 24 | 40 | Tiny |

| Stream/Gauge | Levels Low Hi | Aux Gauge | Levels Low Hi | Normally Runnable | Nonrunnable Low Hi |
|---|---|---|---|---|---|
| **Raccoon Ck** --------------------------------------------------------- | | | | | **page 86** |
| Moffatts Mills | 2.5 | | | MMar-LMar | 82% |
| Moffatts Mills | 2.4 | | | LFeb-EMay | 80% |
| Moffatts Mills | 2.4 | | | LFeb-EMay | 80% |
| **Red Bank Ck** ------------------------------------------------------- | | | | | **page 225** |
| Brookville | | St Charles | 3.8 | | |
| St Charles | 3.8 5.5 | | | EDec-LMay | 60% 15% |
| St Charles | 3.6 6.9 | | | LNov-LMay | 55% 5% |
| **Red Bank Ck, North Fk** ------------------------------------- | | | | | **page 231** |
| Brookville | | St Charles | 4.5 8.0 | | |
| **Redstone Ck** ------------------------------------------------------- | | | | | **page 349** |
| Waltersburg | 0.8 | | | | 60% |
| **Salmon Ck** --------------------------------------------------------- | | | | | **page 285** |
| - | | Cooksburg | 8.0 | | |
| - | | Cooksburg | 8.0 | | |
| **Sandy Ck** ----------------------------------------------------------- | | | | | **page 258** |
| - | | Rouseville | 4.0 | | |
| SR 965 br (blks) | 8.0 5.5 | Rouseville | 3.0 | | |
| **Sandy Lick Ck** ----------------------------------------------------- | | | | | **page 233** |
| Brookville | | St Charles | 4.3 6.0 | | |
| **Sewickley Ck** ------------------------------------------------------- | | | | | **page 318** |
| - | | | | | |
| **Shade Ck** ----------------------------------------------------------- | | | | | **page 196** |
| [Hillsboro (brks)] | 12.0 9.0 | Ferndale | 3.6 4.6 | | |
| **Shavers Fk** --------------------------------------------------------- | | | | | **page 377** |
| Parsons(ShvrsFk) | | [CR33/8 Br] | 1.5 2.5 | | |
| Parsons(ShvrsFk) | | [CR33/8 Br] | 1.0 2.5 | | |
| **Shenandoah R** ----------------------------------------------------- | | | | | **page 406** |
| Millville | 2.0 4.0 | | | | |
| **Shenango R** -------------------------------------------------------- | | | | | **page 116** |
| Pymatuning Dam | 4.6 5.6 | | | | 28% 10% |
| Transfer | 2.5 | | | | 10% |
| Transfer | 2.5 | | | | 10% |
| Sharpsville | 2.6 | | | | 40% |
| Sharpsville | 2.6 | | | | 40% |
| New Castle | | Sharpsville | 2.6 | | |
| **Slippery Rock Ck** ------------------------------------------------- | | | | | **page 98** |
| Wurtemburg | 2.3 | McConnells Mill | 2.0 3.0 | EMar-LMar | 81% |
| Wurtemburg | 1.9 | McConnells Mill | | LFeb-MApr | 72% |
| Wurtemburg | 1.5 | McConnells Mill | | EJan-LMay | 61% |
| Wurtemburg | 1.0 2.0 | McConnells Mill | -0.3 1.0 | MNov-LJun | 43% 36% |
| Wurtemburg | 1.0 2.5 | McConnells Mill | -0.3 1.5 | ENov-EJul | 43% 17% |
| Wurtemburg | 1.3 3.0 | McConnells Mill | 0.2 2.0 | EJan-LMay | 53% 12% |
| **South Sandy Ck** --------------------------------------------------- | | | | | **page 260** |
| - | | Rouseville | 4.5 6.5 | | |
| **Spring Ck** ----------------------------------------------------------- | | | | | **page 248** |
| - | | Wilcox | 2.5 | | |
| **Spring Ck, East Branch** --------------------------------------- | | | | | **page 249** |
| - | | Ridgway | 7.0 | | |

60                                                                    River tables

| Stream/Section | Dist (mi) | Class | Sc/Pol | Grad Mean/Max | Area (sq mi) | Vol (cfs) | Size |
|---|---|---|---|---|---|---|---|
| **Stony Ck** | | | | | | page | 190 |
| A: Shanksville-Kantner | 7.0 | IV | A/A | 61/80 | 85 | 142 | Sm |
| B: Kantner-Hollsopple | 12.0 | I-II | CD/C | 19/30 | 244 | 407 | Med |
| C: Hollsopple-Kring | 8.5 | IV | AB/BC | 34/66 | 375 | 625 | Med |
| D: Kring-Johnstown | 7.0 | B-I | D/C | 11/20 | 451 | 771 | Med |
| **Stony R** | | | | | | page | 412 |
| VEPCO Dam-N Br Potomac R | 13.6 | IV-V | A/B | 75/150 | | | - |
| **Sugar Ck** | | | | | | page | 269 |
| Cooperstown-Sugar Ck | 7.5 | I-II | B/A | 16/27 | 166 | 267 | Sm |
| **Sugar Ck, East Branch** | | | | | | page | 271 |
| Wallaceville-Cooperstown | 7.0 | I-II | B/A | 12/20 | 49 | 82 | Tiny |
| **Susquehanna R, West Branch** | | | | | | page | 404 |
| Shawville-Keating | 54.0 | I | A/B | 6/12 | 1,462 | 2,447 | Lg |
| **Ten Mile Ck** | | | | | | page | 352 |
| A: Ten Mile-Marianna | 6.3 | I | B/A | 7/7 | 100 | 167 | Sm |
| B: Marianna-Clarksville | 9.0 | I-II | B/A | 11/23 | 150 | 250 | Sm |
| C: Clarksville-Monongahela R | 2.5 | A | D/B | pool | 388 | 647 | Med |
| **Ten Mile Ck, South Fk** | | | | | | page | 355 |
| A: Waynesburg-Jefferson | 7.0 | C-I | B/AB | 7/8 | 180 | 201 | Med |
| B: Jefferson-Clarksville | 9.0 | I-II | BC/AB | 10/17 | 199 | 332 | Med |
| **Tionesta Ck** | | | | | | page | 281 |
| A: Sheffield-Lynch | 9.0 | I | A/A | 7/8 | 233 | 426 | Med |
| B: Lynch-Kellettville | 15.0 | C-I | A/A | 5/8 | 307 | 594 | Med |
| C: Kellettville-Nebraska Br | 11.4 | C-I | AB/A | 7/7 | 469 | 824 | Med |
| D: Tionesta Res below Nebr Br | 5.5 | A | | lake | 479 | 891 | Med |
| **Tionesta Ck, South Branch** | | | | | | page | 289 |
| Brookston-Barnes | 5.3 | I-II | C/B | 14/22 | 85 | 156 | Sm |
| **Tionesta Ck, West Branch** | | | | | | page | 288 |
| Weldbank-Sheffield | 6.0 | C-I | B/B | 7/9 | 128 | 248 | Sm |
| **Toby Ck (Clarion Co)** | | | | | | page | 241 |
| A: SR 1013-Game Lands #72 | 7.0 | I | A/B | 23/47 | 25 | 42 | Tiny |
| B: Game Lands #72-Clarion L | 2.1 | III | A/A | 29/60 | 35 | 58 | Tiny |
| **Tubmill Ck** | | | | | | page | 185 |
| SR 711-Bolivar | 5.6 | I-II | B/B | 20/40 | 54 | 90 | Tiny |
| **Turtle Ck** | | | | | | page | 299 |
| A: W Export-Abers Ck | 4.1 | I | C/C | 22/40 | 45 | 75 | Tiny |
| B: Abers Ck-Trafford | 5.0 | I | BC/C | 6/22 | 56 | 76 | Tiny |
| C: Trafford-Monongahela R | 7.5 | I | D/B | 7/9 | 148 | 247 | Sm |
| **Twentymile Ck** | | | | | | page | 393 |
| above Ripley NY-L Erie | 10.6 | IV | | 47/100 | 36 | 60 | Tiny |
| **Two Lick Ck** | | | | | | page | 173 |
| A: Wandin-Clymer | 5.4 | I | AB/BC | 15/20 | 70 | 117 | Sm |
| B: Clymer-Two Lick Res | 4.5 | C | BC/BC | 12/14 | 80 | 133 | Sm |
| C: Indiana Waterwks-Homer City | 7.0 | I-II | A/BC | 13/17 | 100 | 167 | Sm |
| D: Homer City-Blacklick Br | 7.0 | C-II | BC/BC | 7/8 | 171 | 284 | Sm |

# River tables 61

| Stream/Gauge | Levels Low Hi | Aux Gauge | Levels Low Hi | Normally Runnable | Nonrunnable Low Hi |
|---|---|---|---|---|---|
| **Stony Ck** | | | | | page 190 |
| - | | | | | |
| [Hollsopple] | 3.0 5.0 | | | | |
| Ferndale | 3.4 3.9 | Hollsopple | 1.5 3.5 | | 65% 25% |
| Ferndale | | | | | |
| **Stony R** | | | | | page 412 |
| | | Kitzmiller | 4.0 6.5 | | |
| **Sugar Ck** | | | | | page 269 |
| Sugar Creek | | Rouseville | 3.7 5.0 | | |
| **Sugar Ck, East Branch** | | | | | page 271 |
| - | | Rouseville | 4.5 | | |
| **Susquehanna R, West Branch** | | | | | page 404 |
| Karthaus | 2.0 | | | | |
| **Ten Mile Ck** | | | | | page 352 |
| Marianna | 2.2 | | | | |
| Marianna | 2.0 | | | | |
| - | | | | | |
| **Ten Mile Ck, South Fk** | | | | | page 355 |
| Jefferson | 2.0 | | | LDec-LApr | 70% |
| Jefferson | 2.0 | | | LDec-LApr | 70% |
| **Tionesta Ck** | | | | | page 281 |
| Lynch | 2.8 | | | | 88% |
| Sheffield | 2.1 | Lynch | | | |
| Sheffield | 2.1 | Lynch | | | |
| Tionesta Outflow | | | | | |
| **Tionesta Ck, South Branch** | | | | | page 289 |
| - | | Lynch | 3.0 | | |
| **Tionesta Ck, West Branch** | | | | | page 288 |
| - | | Lynch | 3.0 | | |
| **Toby Ck (Clarion Co)** | | | | | page 241 |
| - | | Cooksburg | 7.0 | | |
| - | | Cooksburg | 6.5 | | |
| **Tubmill Ck** | | | | | page 185 |
| - | | | | | |
| **Turtle Ck** | | | | | page 299 |
| - | | | | | |
| - | | | | | |
| - | | | | | |
| **Twentymile Ck** | | | | | page 393 |
| - | | | | | |
| **Two Lick Ck** | | | | | page 173 |
| - | | | | | |
| - | | | | | |
| ["gates open"] | 0.3 1.0 | Graceton | 2.5 | | |
| Graceton | 2.5 | | | | 53% |

| Stream/Section | Dist (mi) | Class | Sc/Pol | Grad Mean/Max | Area (sq mi) | Vol (cfs) | Size |
|---|---|---|---|---|---|---|---|
| **Tygart Valley R** |  |  |  |  |  | page | **381** |
| Norton-Junior | 6.5 | III-IV | C/B | 25/36 |  |  | Med |
| Belington-Buckhannon | 11.0 | IV-V | A/B | 37/65 | 408 | 814 | Med |
| above Arden-Big Cove Run | 8.0 | V | C/B | 27/39 | 916 | 1,926 | Med |
| "Valley Falls" | 0.5 | VI | A/A | 40/40 |  |  | Lg |
| **Wheeling Ck** |  |  |  |  |  | page | **71** |
| Majorsville-Wheeling | 29.5 | I-II | AB/B | 7/10 | 282 | 333 | Med |
| **Whiteley Ck** |  |  |  |  |  | page | **358** |
| SR 2011-SR 88 | 2.5 | III | B/B | 18/25 | 54 | 90 | Tiny |
| **Whites Ck** |  |  |  |  |  | page | **342** |
| Unamis-Harnedsville | 7.0 | III | A/A | 80/100 | 36 | 60 | Tiny |
| **Wolf Ck** |  |  |  |  |  | page | **107** |
| A: above Grove City | 4.0 | A | A/A | swamp | 13 | 22 | Tiny |
| B: Grove City-Courtneys Mill | 4.5 | C-I | AB/A | 9/10 | 87 | 133 | Sm |
| C: Courtneys Mill-Slip'y Rk Ck | 7.0 | I-II | A/A | 11/20 | 100 | 167 | Sm |
| **Yellow Ck (Butler Co)** |  |  |  |  |  | page | **115** |
| M Lancaster-L Connie | 5.0 | C-I | BC/B | 15/15 | 17 | 28 | Tiny |
| **Yellow Ck (Indiana Co)** |  |  |  |  |  | page | **178** |
| A: Yellow Ck SP-Ferrier Run Rd | 3.0 | I-II | A/A | 24/29 | 40 | 67 | Tiny |
| B: Ferrier Run Rd-SR 954 Br | 2.5 | I-II | A/AB | 32/46 | 55 | 92 | Tiny |
| C: SR 954 Br-SR 56 Br | 3.5 | I-II | AC/AC | 23/80 | 57 | 107 | Tiny |
| **Youghiogheny R** |  |  |  |  |  | page | **303** |
| A: Swallow Falls SP-Sang Run | 5.7 | V-VI | A/A | 42/130 | 200 | 333 | Med |
| B: Sang Run-Friendsville | 9.3 | V-VI | A/A | 56/100 | 295 | 646 | Med |
| C: Friendsville-Confluence | 5.0 | A | A/A | lake | 436 | 878 | Med |
| D: Confluence-Ohiopyle | 11.0 | I-II | AB/A | 9/20 | 1,029 | 2,005 | Med |
| E: Ohiopyle-Bruner Run | 10.1 | III-IV | A/A | 17/45 | 1,200 | 2,000 | Lg |
| F: Bruner Run-S. Connellsville | 9.0 | II-III | AB/A | 10/17 | 1,300 | 2,167 | Lg |
| G: S Connellsville-Dawson | 5.7 | C-I | A/B | 5/6 | 1,350 | 2,580 | Lg |
| H: Dawson-Whitsett | 9.7 | C-I | BC/B | 6/8 | 1,400 | 2,333 | Lg |
| I: Whitsett-McKeesport | 28.8 | C | C/B | 1/1 | 1,700 | 3,043 | Lg |

| Stream/Gauge | Levels Low Hi | Aux Gauge | Levels Low Hi | Normally Runnable | Nonrunnable Low Hi |
|---|---|---|---|---|---|
| **Tygart Valley R** ----------------------------------------------------------- page 381 | | | | | |
| Belington | 4.0 5.0 | | | | |
| Belington | 2.5 6.8 | | | | |
| Philippi | 2.5 4.5 | | | | |
| - | | | | | |
| **Wheeling Ck** -------------------------------------------------------- page 71 | | | | | |
| Elm Grove | | | | | |
| **Whiteley Ck** ------------------------------------------------------- page 358 | | | | | |
| - | | | | | |
| **Whites Ck** ---------------------------------------------------------- page 342 | | | | | |
| - | | Markleton | 5.0 | | |
| **Wolf Ck** ------------------------------------------------------------ page 107 | | | | | |
| - | | | | | |
| Wurtemburg | 1.6 4.6 | McConnells Mill | 1.0 5.0 | | 64% 3% |
| Wurtemburg | 1.6 4.6 | McConnells Mill | 1.0 5.0 | | 64% 3% |
| **Yellow Ck (Butler Co)** --------------------------------------- page 115 | | | | | |
| - | | Zelienople | 3.0 | | |
| **Yellow Ck (Indiana Co)** ------------------------------------- page 178 | | | | | |
| - | | | | | |
| Homer City | 2.3 | [Water works dam] | 3.5 4.5 | | |
| Homer City | 2.3 | | | | |
| **Youghiogheny R** ------------------------------------------------ page 303 | | | | | |
| Sang Run | .8 2.7 | | | | |
| Sang Run | 1.8 2.8 | | | | |
| Yough Dam | | | | | |
| Confluence | 1.8 3.5 | Ohiopyle | 1.3 3.5 | dam controlled | 8% 28% |
| Confluence | 1.9 3.5 | Ohiopyle | 1.4 3.5 | dam controlled | 15% 28% |
| Confluence | 2.4 | Connellsville | 2.7 | MNov-LSep | 38% |
| Connellsville | 2.1 4.5 | | | dam controlled | 19% 15% |
| Connellsville | 2.1 4.5 | | | dam controlled | 19% 15% |
| Sutersville | | Connellsville | 2.0 4.5 | | |

# Ohio Watershed

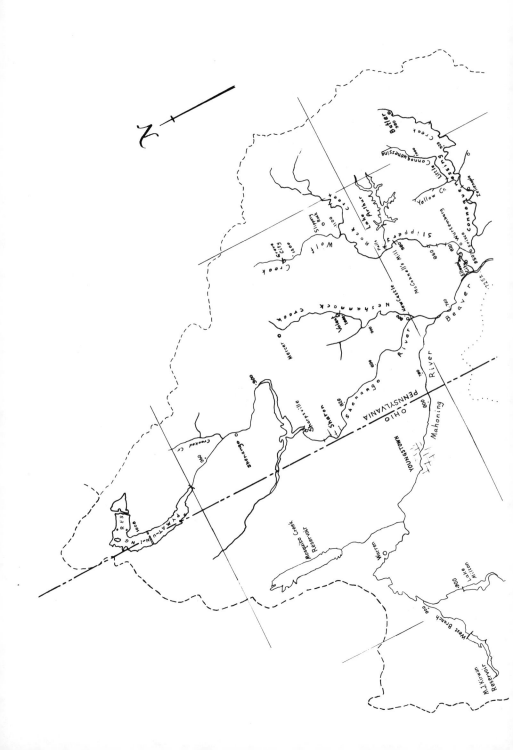

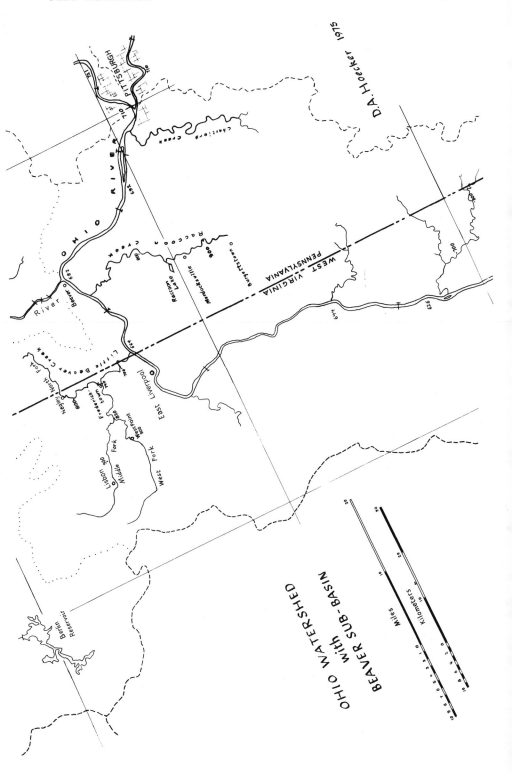

OHIO WATERSHED
with
BEAVER SUB-BASIN

D.A. Hoecker 1975

# Ohio River

## Pittsburgh to Pennsylvania/Ohio border        40 miles

| Class | Grad | Size (Area/Volume) | Scene/Poll | Level |
|---|---|---|---|---|
| A | Pool | Huge (19,500/33,040) | D/C | |
| | | Sewickley | | Dashields |
| | | Huge (23,487/ ) Pa State Line | | |

*Topographic Maps:* Pittsburgh West, Emsworth, Ambridge, Baden, Beaver, Midland, East Liverpool North

*County Maps:* Allegheny, Beaver

*Other Maps:* A set of detailed navigation charts is available for $6.00 from the District Engineer, Pittsburgh District Corps of Engineers, Federal Building, 1000 Liberty Ave., Pittsburgh, Pennsylvania 15222.

*Description:* This is a wide, turbulent, commercial waterway. Any section of this river is an industrial trip with ship building, steel mills, railroad operations, and large structures of many types along the banks of the river. Towns and cities are continuously interspersed between the industries. Records show that the Ohio River is the busiest inland body of water of its size in the world. Large boats and barges run almost continuously. The Ohio is badly polluted and smells foul in places. It is best not to go ashore where the water forms a stagnant pool, but to seek a better spot. [Reported 1989]

*Difficulties:* The Ohio is for experts of a different type. A knowledge of seamanship and how to handle a canoe in heavy waves is important here. This river may be too turbulent to cross during the day in open canoes. Thermal winds and large boats combine to create ocean-like swells which do not look formidable from shore but can swamp a canoe if not expected, or handled improperly. The river is calmer in the mornings or evenings.

Barges are moving faster than they look, sometimes almost silently. Keep clear of large boats. They need lots of room to maneuver. Stay clear not only of the physical barge itself, but also of the very turbulent wake created by the push-boat.

These boats not only make wake out the back, but some also have additional propellers pointed sideways, so that the wake may come straight out the side. Not only are barges hard to maneuver, they are slow to turn and stop. This means that by the time a barge captain sees a canoe, it'is too late to stop. In addition the barges themselves block the captain's line of sight far in front of the boat.

Stay well away from the dams because strong currents near the dams pick up speed without notice. Plan to be on the same side of the river as the lock. Cross at the earliest time that it is safe and convenient. Use a bicycle flag to make the canoe more visible to the thousands of power boats.

There are three locks and dams in the Pennsylvania section of the river. These locks are double passage locks. Each has two locking chambers, with one chamber smaller than the other. Small craft are usually put through the smaller lock, which is between the large lock on shore and the dam.

To pass through a lock you will need to have a 75-foot rope, minimum of 3/8 inch thick available for each boat. Follow the lockmaster's instructions. He may have you tie up to another boat already going through, or he may have you pull your canoe up onto one of the barges, or he may have you paddle into the lock and hang onto a line that is already in place, or he may loop your line over one of his tie-down points and expect you to hang on that way. Remember that the water level will drop and you should not tie anything to this line or the sides of the lock.

*Shuttle:* Use a road map. The locks on the Ohio are named unlike the Allegheny and Monongahela locks which are just numbered. Going downstream, the locks and access areas are as follows:

| Access point | River Mile Mark |
|---|---|
| Pittsburgh | 0.0 |
| Emsworth Lock and Dam | 6.2 Right |
| Sewickley | 11.7 Right |
| Dashields Lock and Dam | 13.3 Left |
| Leetsdale | 15.0 Right |
| Rochester | 25.1 Right |
| Beaver River | 25.4 Right |
| New Brighton 2 mile upstream on Beaver River | |
| Montgomery Lock and Dam | 31.7 Left |
| Little Beaver Creek | 39.5 Right |
| State Line (No access) | 40.0 |
| Chester, West Virginia | 43.0 Left |
| East Liverpool, Ohio | 43.5 Right |

*Gauges:*   Since this is a huge river, it should be runnable all year but is often too high. It will be too high whenever the river is reported as too high for recreational boating.

*Normal Wet Period:* No available statistics on seasons. In the spring it will often be too high. In late summer, the lockmaster may make you wait until there is a collection of pleasure boats at the lock to save water. Further, at the lock, commercial traffic takes precedence over pleasure traffic.

# Wheeling Creek

## Majorsville to Wheeling    29.5 miles

| Class | Grad | Size (Area/Volume) | Scene/Poll | Level |
|-------|------|--------------------|------------|-------|
| I-II | 7/10 | Medium (282/333) | A-B/B | |
| | | Elm Grove | | Elm Grove |

*Topographic Maps:* Majorsville, Moundsville, Wheeling (all West Virginia)

*County Maps:* Marshall (West Virginia), Ohio County (West Virginia)

*Description:* Put in on Enlow Fork at Majorsville, West Virginia. Do not be distressed if the stream seems small, a mile later the Dunkard Fork joins in to form Wheeling Creek. Note there is also a Wheeling Creek in Ohio which enters the Ohio River directly across from this one. [Reported 1980]

*Difficulties:* There is a small dam at Elm Grove, about one to 2 feet high. This is followed by small rapids for the next mile.

*Shuttle:* Use the Elm Grove exit from Interstate 70, then follow the river to Majorsville. In Wheeling the take-out is on the Ohio River at the 16th Street parking garage.

*Gauges:* Elm Grove. We do not have enough information to report runnable levels on this section. A reading of 2.0 on the Elm Grove gauge corresponds to the mean flow of 333 cfs. Since this is a medium-sized river, we speculate that the river will be runnable at 2.0 and may be on the high side of runnable at that level. Note that there is also a Blaine gauge on a Wheeling Creek, but this is a completely different Wheeling Creek just across the Ohio River in Ohio.

*Normal Wet Period:* No available statistics on seasons. Since this section is medium-sized, it should normally be runnable approximately December through May.

# Buffalo Creek
# (Washington County)

## A. South of Taylorstown Station                21.8 miles
## to Bethany (W. Va. Route 88 Bridge)

| Class | Grad | Size (Area/Volume) | Scene/Poll | Level |
|-------|------|--------------------|--------------|-------|
| I-II | 11/15 | Small (114/190) | B/A-B | |
| | | Pa-WVa State Line | | |

*Topographic Maps:* West Middletown, Bethany (West Virginia)

*County Maps:* Washington, Brooke (West Virginia)

*Description:* This pastoral stream burbles gently through rural Washington County. It winds through lovely farms, villages, and patches of wooded hillside. Wildlife abounds; a March trip encountered wood ducks, redwing blackbirds, a couple of great blue herons, kingfishers, a fox, several groundhogs, signs of beaver, a variety of domestic waterfowl, the usual dogs and cats, and two vest-pocket swamps with choruses of frogs peeping in all registers. The creek's "B" for scenery reflects the rural character of the stream, not any serious aesthetic deficiency. Except for a bank stabilization program in Taylorstown, apparently sponsored by a home appliance dealer, the stream is fairly clean and free of debris. The stream alternates between flowing water and riffles. The current often pushes the boat into the sheer banks that are being eroded on the bends. This requires some alertness in the part of the paddler who prefers not to be swept into the bank or the snags that protrude from it. Precise boat control is also advisable near the many trees that have fallen into or across the river. There was once a dam near the Bethany College boiler plant. The dam is gone now; nothing remains but the former spillway, standing solitary vigil on the right side of the stream. [Checked 1990]

*Difficulties:* Just below Taylorstown Station, a fence across the river was being constructed in 1989. Plan to encounter several trees down across the stream. Some can be snuck under or around, but others have become brush piles completely blocking the creek. One particularly likely place to find a log jam is at the remains of an old dam just around a right-hand bend, out of sight of the road, about 2 miles below Saw Hill covered bridge (or a mile below the undistinguished bridge downstream from Saw Hill Bridge).

*Shuttle:* State Routes 331, 221, and West Virginia Route 67 run in the same valley as the river, offering a choice of several put-ins and take-outs. Check the topographic or county maps.

*Gauge:* Drive along the section you plan to run. If it looks runnable, it probably is.

*Normal Wet Period:* No available statistics on seasons. Since this section is small, it should normally be runnable approximately January through April.

# B. Bethany to Wellsburg                          13.0 miles

| Class | Grad | Size (Area/Volume) | Scene/Poll | Level |
|-------|------|--------------------|-----------|-------|
| I | 10/16 | Small (150/250) estimated | B/B | |

*Topographic Maps:* Bethany (West Virginia), Steubenville East (Ohio)

*County Maps:* Brooke (West Virginia)

*Description:* Both larger and more remote than the section above Bethany, the stream wanders through farms and woods, alternating riffles and flowing pools. Slack water backs up from the Ohio River about a mile above the take-out. Many and varied wildflowers line the banks. [Checked 1989]

*Difficulties:* There is a Class I plus rapid just above the truss bridge on West Virginia Route 67. There is a 2-foot rock dam near the end of the run.

*Shuttle:* The put-in is just south of Bethany, where West Virginia State Route 88 crosses the stream. The put-in is at the site of the old bridge, behind the Bethany College Leadership Center. To reach the take-out, head up the hill towards Bethany. At the top, turn left/west on West Virginia Route 67. Proceed to the Corps of Engineers boat launch area just within sight of the Ohio River, south of Wellsburg.

*Gauges:* Along West Virginia Route 67, about 0.5 miles north of the intersection with West Virginia Route 30, a low water bridge crosses the creek. There should be enough water at the low point in the middle to make it without scraping.

*Normal Wet Period:* No available statistics on seasons. Since this section is small, it should normally be runnable approximately January through April.

# Cross Creek

## A. From mouth of Haynan Creek          2.3 miles
## to Avella

| Class | Grad | Size (Area/Volume) | Scene/Poll | Level |
|-------|------|--------------------|------------|-------|
| I-II  | 13/13 | Tiny (30/50) estimated | C/C | |

*Topographic Maps:* Avella

*County Maps:* Washington

*Description:* There is a lot of trash dumped on both banks of this creek, but the creek is only lightly polluted chemically. The town of Avella seems to be one large trash heap. This is a shallow creek with a gravel bottom making it suitable for poling, even though there is a smooth rock bottom at several ledges. [Reported 1977]

*Difficulties:* There are half a dozen large ledges that make nice rapids, above Avella and in the town. One is just upstream of the main highway bridge in the center of town. All are difficult to run without scraping, unless water levels are very high, in which case they could have powerful cross-currents. A dam alongside a railroad bridge appears to be unrunnable. Portage on left or right with equal difficulty.

*Shuttle:* Put in by the bridge off State Route 50 on the road going up Haynan Creek. By starting here you must portage around a 6-foot dam, 0.25 miles downstream. There is an alternative put-in below the dam near the State Route 50 bridge, 0.5 miles further down (0.5 miles above Avella). Proceed to the take-out along State Route 50 into Avella, then follow the signs for Meadowcroft, to the last bridge in town. Pull off before the mine dump. Access for the take-out is under the railroad bridge at the State Route 231 crossing just west of Avella.

*Gauges:* None available.

*Normal Wet Period:* No available statistics on seasons. Since this section is tiny, it should normally be runnable only after a heavy rain or during spring snowmelt.

# B. Avella to Pennsylvania State Line          5.8 miles

| Class | Grad | Size (Area / Volume) | Scene / Poll | Level |
|-------|------|----------------------|--------------|-------|
| I-II  | 20/29 | Small (63/105) | B/C | |
|       |       | Penowa | | |

*Topographic Maps:* Avella, Steubenville East (Ohio)

*County Maps:* Washington

*Description:* There is a lot of trash on both banks of the creek, but this diminishes and the scenery gradually improves with distance from Avella. The banks are mostly wooded, with many large cliffs and rocks. This is a fast-moving, shallow, challenging stream when runnable, suitable for poling. [Reported 1977]

*Difficulties:* Two Class II rapids. Both are artificial channels caused by the railroad embankment taking bends out of the creek. The first is 1 mile below Avella. The second is 3 miles down (0.25 miles above the bridge near Meadowcroft).

*Shuttle:* Put in under the railroad bridge at the northwest edge of Avella. An alternate access would be at the highway bridge near Meadowcroft. Take out at the bridge near the mouth of Coal Hollow, which is the end of the paved road, and adjacent to the Pennsylvania and West Virginia state line. Follow the county road west of Avella, taking the right-hand fork near the top of the hill 1 mile out of town. This road continues past the entrance to Meadowcroft Village (near "Jefferson" on topographic maps) and follows the creek to the state line, 0.5 miles past the railroad crossing and railroad tunnel. The first mile of this road in West Virginia is nearly impassable.

*Gauges:* None available. Can be judged by shallows at the highway bridge near Meadowcroft Village.

*Normal Wet Period:* No available statistics on seasons. Since this section is small, it should normally be runnable approximately January through April.

# C. Pennsylvania State Line to Ohio River    7.0 miles

| Class | Grad | Size (Area/Volume) | Scene/Poll | Level |
|-------|------|--------------------|-----------|-------|
| II | 24/28 | Small (63/105) | B/C | |
| | | Penowa | | |

*Topographic Maps:* Steubenville East (Ohio)

*County Maps:* Brooke (West Virginia)

*Description:* There is slightly less trash on stream banks than in the upper sections, and the scenery improves (large cliffs, farms, partly wooded banks). This is a fast moving, interesting canoe trip. Good for poling. [Reported 1977]

*Difficulties:* There is a Class II-III rapid just below Scott Run, where the railroad has made an artificial channel for the stream by removing a bend. It is easily scouted from the left bank, just below a small island. Other rapids are Class I. Watch for downed trees, and log jams in the lower part. The backwater from the Ohio River does not start until 0.25 miles from the take-out.

*Shuttle:* Put in at the last bridge in Pennsylvania or, for a longer trip, at the bridge near Meadowcroft Village. Take out at the old highway abutments, 0.25 miles up Cross Creek Road from West Virginia Route 2, adjacent to the Ohio River. From the put-in at Avella, take State Route 50 to Independence, Pennsylvania, then west on West Virginia Route 27 to Wellsburg, West Virginia, then north on West Virginia Route 2 to Cross Creek Road. Do not attempt the road from the state line put-in directly to Virginville. This was a Class VI road in February 1977.

*Gauges:* None available. Can be judged by the shallows at the highway bridge near Meadowcroft Village.

*Normal Wet Period:* No available statistics on seasons. Since this section is small, it should normally be runnable approximately January through April.

# Little Beaver Creek

## A. Beaver Creek State Park                    6.5 miles
## to Fredericktown

| Class | Grad | Size (Area / Volume) | Scene / Poll | Level |
|-------|------|----------------------|--------------|-------|
| I | 10/11 | Medium (450/750) | A/B | 2.9-4.7 |
| | | estimated | | East Liverpool |

*Topographic Maps:* East Liverpool North (Ohio)

*County Maps:* Columbiana (Ohio)

*Description:* This stream is in Ohio but it is very convenient to Pittsburgh (less than one hour driving time). It is quite scenic and offers a pleasant challenge to those just beginning to learn whitewater. The remains of a number of old locks from the Sandy and Beaver Canal (circa 1840) can be seen. It is excellent for family trips. The stream has bass, and the water quality is high enough for swimming. The gradient is very uniform. The Little Beaver is the only stream in this area to be designated a National Scenic River. [Checked 1990]

*Difficulties:* None unless the trip is extended to the Beaver Creek Livery. There is a ledge at the confluence with the North Fork (shortly beyond the State Route 170 bridge). Run on the far right after scouting. In low water the ledge may be unrunnable.

*Shuttle:* Put in about 100 yards upstream of the bridge in Beaver Creek State Park. There is abundant parking in the State Park parking lots nearby. Shuttle via Calcutta to the take-out just upstream of the State Route 170 bridge on the right bank. The Beaver Creek Canoe Livery is located on the east side of State Route 170 just south of the bridge over the Middle Fork of Little Beaver Creek. The livery rents canoes for $20.00/day (1989) including shuttle and offers shuttle service ($5.00 per driver) with their school bus if they can include you and still serve their canoe-rental customers. They operate on only one section on a given day, either this section or the one below. If you use the livery area you should ask permission before loading or unloading private

canoes. The drive into the livery parking areas is chained
and locked at the end of the day. The preferred take-out for
private trips is just upstream of the State Route 170 bridge,
on the right bank.

*Gauges:* East Liverpool. This gauge should read between
2.9 and 4.7 feet. This corresponds to a flow of 172 cfs to
957 cfs. This stream seems to be runnable at a wide range of
levels. You can check the water level with the Beaver Creek
Canoe Livery (216) 385-8579 or the Park Ranger (216) 385-3091
will be happy to advise canoeists on water levels as well.
Each day the ranger looks at the river and lets his secretary
know if it is runnable or not. They hope to install a gauge in
the State Park, but since it is designated a National Scenic
River one can not do anything within 1000 feet of the shore
line without federal approvals.

*Normal Wet Period:* This section is normally runnable
from late November to late June, except it is normally too
high from mid March to early April.

## B. Fredericktown                                  7.8 miles
## to the Ohio River (Glasgow)

| Class | Grad | Size (Area / Volume) | Scene / Poll | Level |
|---|---|---|---|---|
| I-II | 11/12 | Medium (493/514 ) | A/B | 2.8-4.6 |
| | | Grimms Bridge | | East Liverpool |
| | | Medium(503/838) mouth | | |

*Topographic Maps:* East Liverpool North (Ohio)

*County Maps:* Columbiana (Ohio), Beaver

*Description:* This stream is, for the most part, in Ohio. It
drains into the Ohio River at Glasgow, Pennsylvania, a few
miles west of Midland on State Route 68. The remains of
several locks from the Sandy and Beaver Canal (circa 1840)
can be seen. It is not quite as scenic as either the upstream
section or the Middle Fork of Little Beaver Creek. It is still
very pleasant and very popular. For a pleasant weekend
camping trip, put in on the Middle Fork of Little Beaver and
run down to the Ohio. This gives you up to 30 miles if the
entire section is done, but there are plenty of alternative put-
ins to cut the trip down to any desired size. There is plenty

of time to stop to look at the remains of the old locks and to swim in the pools. Campsites are easy to find, but you should bring your own water, since side-streams are not trustworthy. Except for Beaver Creek State Park, all land is privately owned, mainly by a single party who is interested in protecting the natural values of Little Beaver Creek Valley. Make sure your camping manners demonstrate this same interest. [Checked 1989]

*Difficulties:* If you put in above the State Route 170 bridge, be aware of the ledge below the bridge, described in trip A above.

*Shuttle:* Note that the road from Glasgow to Calcutta is not shown on some road maps. The put-in for this trip is the same as the take-out for trip A above. Also, you can put in just upstream from the State Route 170 bridge on the right/south side of the creek. Shuttle via Calcutta on the Calcutta-Smith Ferry Road to the take-out which is visible from the State Route 68 bridge over the creek at Glasgow (west side of stream, north side of the road). Alternatively, you can take out on the east side of the creek about 0.25 miles north of State Route 68 on a well-maintained gravel road upstream from the barge loading chute. The Beaver Creek Canoe Livery rents canoes and provides shuttle service for this section (1988). An alternative take-out is at Grimms Bridge. Turn west on Grimms Bridge Road off the Calcutta-Smith Ferry Road. This splits the trip in half.

*Gauges:* East Liverpool. This gauge should read between 2.8 and 4.6 feet. This corresponds to a flow of 150 cfs to 898 cfs. Call Beaver Creek Canoe Livery or Beaver Creek State Park. See Section A of the Little Beaver Creek for phone numbers. It is not unusual to run this stream year round except for a few dry spells.

*Normal Wet Period:* This section is normally runnable from late November to late June, except it is normally too high from mid March to early April.

# Little Beaver Creek, North Fork

## Negley to Fredericktown                              7.0 miles

| Class | Grad | Size (Area/Volume) | Scene/Poll | Level |
|-------|------|--------------------|------------|-------|
| I-II  | 9/15 | Small (162/ )      | B/B        |       |
|       |      | Negley             |            |       |
|       |      | Medium (193/322) Fredericktown |  |       |

*Topographic Maps:* East Palestine, East Liverpool North (both Ohio)

*County Maps:* Columbiana (Ohio), Beaver

*Description:* In Fredericktown on river right an octagonal building contains displays concerning the history of the Vodery estate, the canal, and surrounding area. In the vicinity is the foundation of an old mill. This is an easy Class I stream through Ohio farm land. It suddenly changes to Class II just above the take-out. [Checked 1988]

*Difficulties:* The Class I run ends suddenly with a 5-foot falls about 0.25 miles above Fredericktown, with a foot bridge a few yards above the falls. This is known locally as "the Tubs". Carry around the falls and prepare for 300 yards of strong Class II water. The land around the falls is private property belonging to the Vodery estate.

*Shuttle:* The put-in is on State Route 154 where it crosses the Little Beaver Creek. This is about 0.5 miles east of Negley. To reach the take-out, go west on State Route 154 to State Route 170, then south to Fredericktown.

*Gauges:* East Liverpool. This gauge is downstream on the Little Beaver Creek. We do not have enough information to report runnable levels on this section. Call Beaver Creek Canoe Livery or Beaver Creek State Park. See Section A of the Little Beaver Creek for phone numbers.

*Normal Wet Period:* No available statistics on seasons. Since this section is medium-sized, it should normally be runnable approximately December through May.

# Little Beaver Creek, West Fork

## West Point to Beaver Creek State Park        8.5 miles

| Class | Grad | Size (Area / Volume) | Scene / Poll | Level |
|-------|------|----------------------|--------------|-------|
| I | 10/15 | Small (100/167) | B/B | |
| | | West Point | | |

*Topographic Maps:* West Point (Ohio), East Liverpool North (Ohio)

*County Maps:* Columbiana (Ohio)

*Description:* Once past the streamside camps and cottages near Pine Ridge Camp, the stream enters a remote valley. The valley floor is covered with sycamore, and the hillsides to the north and south are sheer. This is a very pretty valley. Combining these sections with the lower section down to the Ohio river would make an ideal canoe-camping trip. There is group camping available at the Gretchen's Lock area of Beaver Creek State Park. [Checked 1989]

*Difficulties:* Three or four bends after a pair of power transmission lines cross the river there is a dam with two slots that can be filled by movable gates. If the gates are not in place and if the slots are not blocked by trees, they can be run. Alternately carry around on the right. As with any small stream, strainers are always a possibility.

*Shuttle:* To get to the put-in, leave State Route 11/30 at West Point. Go south on old State Route 45 less than 0.25 miles to the first left. Follow this road about 0.5 miles and put in at the dead end where it once crossed the creek. To get to the take-out follow US Route 30, either old or new, to Ohio Route 7. Turn north on Ohio Route 7 and go about 2.5 miles to the Beaver Creek State Park. Take-out is at the Gaston's Mill area. The trip can be lengthened by using any of various access areas west of West Point along Ohio Route 518. The Ohio Route 164 crossing in Gavers Village is about 10 miles upstream of West Point.

*Gauges:* East Liverpool. This gauge downstream on Little Beaver Creek will probably read above 4.3. Call Beaver Creek Canoe Livery or Beaver Creek State Park. See Section A of the Little Beaver Creek for phone numbers.

*Normal Wet Period:* No available statistics on seasons. Since this section is small, it should normally be runnable approximately January through April.

# Little Beaver Creek, Middle Fork

## Coleman to Beaver Creek State Park          20.5 miles

| Class | Grad | Size (Area/Volume) | Scene/Poll | Level |
|-------|------|--------------------|------------|-------|
| I | 7/11 | Small (149/248 ) | C/C | |
| | | Rodgers | | |

*Topographic Maps:* Lisbon, Elkton, West Point, East Liverpool North (all Ohio)

*County Maps:* Columbiana (Ohio)

*Description:* The Sandy and Beaver Canal follows this stream from Logtown to the mouth of Beaver Creek at the Ohio. The remnants of locks can be spotted all along the river. The best preserved lock is Lusk Lock in Beaver Creek State Park about 0.25 miles below the confluence with Pine Run. In 1972 a chemical spill of Myrex occurred above Lisbon. It is still leaking into the Middle Fork. The Department of Health has posted the stream from the spill through Lisbon against wading, fishing, or canoeing. The pollution has been moving downstream and the posting may reach the main stem soon. As of the summer of 1989 the State Park Rangers still encourage canoeing below Lisbon, but they discourage fisherfolk from eating their catch. If the posting reaches the State Park they will discourage canoeing. [Reported 1988]

*Difficulties:* There is a low dam just west of Lisbon shortly after the US Route 30 bridge comes into view. Portage the dam on river right. On the other side of Lisbon, just upstream of the US Route 30 bridge, is a broken-out dam. In 1988 it could be run on river left.

*Shuttle:* To get to the put-in from Lisbon, follow the road along the north side of the creek through Logtown to Coleman. The trip can easily be split into two sections of 6 and 14 miles by using an intermediate point of Ohio Route 154. For the small-stream paddler, the trip can be extended about 6 miles upstream by putting in at Franklin Square. See pollution warning above. Beaver Creek State Park and

Beaver Creek State Forest lie along the stream for several miles, and are broken into several access sections by private lands. To get to the take-out, go back to Lisbon. Follow Ohio Route 154 east to Elkton. When Ohio Route 154 turns left, continue straight on Middle Beaver Road. Go to Ohio Route 7, turn right/south on Ohio Route 7. Go about 1.5 miles and turn left on Beaver School Road. Go about 1 mile and turn left on Bell School Road, which crosses the creek in about 1.2 miles.

*Gauges:* East Liverpool. This gauge downstream on Little Beaver Creek will probably read above 4.3. Call Beaver Creek Canoe Livery or Beaver Creek State Park. See Section A of the Little Beaver Creek for phone numbers.

*Normal Wet Period:* No available statistics on seasons. Since this section is small, it should normally be runnable approximately January through April.

# Raccoon Creek

## A. Raccoon to Murdocksville                           12.0 miles

| Class | Grad | Size (Area/Volume) | Scene/Poll | Level |
|-------|------|--------------------|------------|-------|
| I | 10/20 | Small (75/125) | B/C | 2.5-?? |
|   |      | estimated |   | Moffatts Mills |

*Topographic Maps:* Burgettstown, Clinton

*County Maps:* Washington, Beaver

*Description:* The creek descends at a steady gradient through woods and beside 50-100 foot cliffs. Between Raccoon and Bavington there is lots of trash, untreated discharge, and evidence of strip mining. The railroad bridge just below Raccoon is worth a look. It is a very impressive piece of work. From Bavington to Murdocksville, the intrusion of civilization is less evident. [Reported 1989]

*Difficulties:* At about 2 and 3 miles below Raccoon there are low-water crossings for heavy equipment. They were built by placing 6 to 8, 20-foot segments of concrete culvert side-by-side in the stream and piling dirt and roadway on top. Carry around, resisting the temptation to try and paddle through. Numerous downed trees completely span the stream and you must carry over or around. Two log jams in the first couple of miles below Bavington appear to have been there for a while.

*Shuttle:* Put in at the State Route 4012 bridge 0.5 miles west of Raccoon. A dirt road parallels the stream to Murdocksville via Bavington. For a somewhat faster shuttle, follow State Route 4012 west to State Route 18. Turn right/north and go about 0.1 miles to the first light on State Route 4007. Turn right and follow this road to Bavington. Turn right on State Route 4004, immediately crossing the creek. After crossing the creek take an immediate left on a dirt road. You will cross the creek in about 0.1 miles. This is an intermediate access point. Continue about 0.75 miles further. About 700 feet before crossing the creek again, turn left on another dirt road. The turn is hidden behind a hill and is easy to miss. Continue 1.6 miles further and make a very sharp right turn at the crossroads. Continue 0.4 miles

to the intersection with the paved road. Turn left onto State
Route 4002 and continue 2 miles or so to Murdocksville,
where the bridge will be in sight on the left. Look for a place
to park that is out of the way. The more reliable shuttle is to
continue north on State Route 18 for about 8 miles. Just
before Franklin Springs turn right/east towards
Murdocksville and go 4 miles to the river. The bridge just
below Bavington provides a good halfway access point.

*Gauges:* Moffatts Mills. This gauge should read above
2.5 feet. This corresponds to a flow of 310 cfs. If there is
enough water in the rapid just upstream of the
Murdocksville bridge, there should be enough for the whole
run.

*Normal Wet Period:* This section is normally runnable
from mid March to late March. The Moffatts Mill gauge is
above 2.5 feet 18% of the time.

# B. Murdocksville to State Route 151         11.0 miles

| Class | Grad | Size (Area / Volume) | Scene/Poll | Level |
|-------|------|----------------------|------------|-------|
| C-I | 6/10 | Small (125/208) estimated | B/B-C | 2.4-?? Moffatts Mills |

*Topographic Maps:* Clinton, Aliquippa

*County Maps:* Beaver

*Description:* For the first 3 miles below US Route 30 the
stream flows gently through woods and against 20-to-40-foot
shale cliffs topped by hemlock. The river passes through the
wooded gorge of Raccoon Creek State Park. After this the
surroundings are more pastoral. Since this section of
Raccoon Creek is just west of Greater Pittsburgh International Airport, DC-9s and 737s provide bass counterpoint to
the usual twitterings of birds and chirpings of critters.
[Reported 1989]

*Difficulties:* Numerous trees have fallen into the creek.
With careful maneuvering you can sneak past most of them
at reasonable water levels. However, exercise special care
near all fallen trees, when high water brings swift currents.

*Shuttle:* To reach the take-out leave Murdocksville going north on State Route 3044, drive 1.8 miles to US Route 30, make a sharp left/west onto US Route 30, go 3 miles, passing the state park. Turn right on State Route 3023, drive 3.5 miles to State Route 151. Turn right/east and go 1 mile to the creek. There is another bridge a mile or so downstream with a little better river access. To reach it proceed east on State Route 151 for another mile, make a sharp left turn, and go north about 0.5 miles to the creek.

*Gauges:* Moffatts Mills. This gauge should read above 2.4 feet. This corresponds to a flow of 263 cfs.

*Normal Wet Period:* This section is normally runnable from late February to early May. The Moffatts Mill gauge is above 2.4 feet 20% of the time.

# C. State Route 151 to State Route 18          13.0 miles

| Class | Grad | Size (Area / Volume) | Scene / Poll | Level |
|---|---|---|---|---|
| I | 8/14 | Small (178/193) Moffatts Mill | C/B | 2.4-?? Moffatts Mills |
| | | Small (184/ ) mouth of creek | | |

*Topographic Maps:* Aliquippa, Beaver

*County Maps:* Beaver

*Description:* This is a near-to-town stream, with accompanying advantages and disadvantages. Raccoon Creek meanders along through populated countryside most of the time. [Reported 1979, Checked to Green Garden Plaza 1989]

*Difficulties:* As the water level rises, the stream meanders less, and cuts through the trees more. Fallen trees may be a problem in some areas.

*Shuttle:* The put-in is on State Route 151 at the crossing of Raccoon Creek about 3 miles west of Gringo. Take State Route 60 from Gringo to Bellowsville. The take-out is about 1 mile west of Bellowsville. An alternative to the State Route 151 access point is a bridge a mile or so farther downstream. A somewhat better take-out spot than the State Route 18 bridge is a bridge about 1 mile upstream. The trip can be broken roughly in half by using access from the Green Garden Plaza shopping center, just west of State Route 60 at the Aliquippa exit.

*Gauges:* Moffatts Mills. This gauge should read above 2.4 feet. This corresponds to a flow of 263 cfs.

*Normal Wet Period:* This section is normally runnable from late February to early May. The Moffatts Mills gauge is above 2.4 feet 20% of the time.

# Beaver River

## A. New Castle to Wampum                    6.5 miles

| Class | Grad | Size (Area/Volume) | Scene/Poll | Level |
|-------|------|--------------------|------------|-------|
| A-B | 3/3 | Large (2,235/2,494) | B-C/C | 3.5-?? |
| | | Wampum | | Wampum |

*Topographic Maps:*  New Castle South, Bessemer

*County Maps:*  Lawrence

*Description:*  This stream offers little attraction to the canoeist.  The valley is wooded, but broad and muddy, with railroads on both sides.  There are several large industrial installations.  The river has a somewhat foul odor, especially in low water. [Checked 1983]

*Difficulties:* The only hazard is a wing dam, which is a wall extending from the right shore to deflect water toward the intake of a power plant on the left shore.  Keep close to the wall to avoid currents at the water intake on the left.

*Shuttle:*  Put in at the old State Route 18 bridge over the Mahoning, south of New Castle.  To reach the take-out, go south on State Route 18.  Take a sharp left turn onto State Route 482.  The take-out is on the left, just below the bridge in Wampum.  For a longer trip you can put in in New Castle on the Neshannock, but the 2 or 3 miles you gain are Class D scenery.

*Gauges:* Wampum.  This gauge should read above 3.5 feet. This corresponds to a flow of 980 cfs.  The Beaver Falls gauge further downstream will probably read above 4.0.  We do not have enough information to report a high runnable level.  However, a  reading of 4.7 on the Wampum gauge corresponds to the mean flow of 2,494 cfs.  Since this is a large size river, we speculate that the river is too high at that level.

*Normal Wet Period:* This section is normally runnable from early December to mid June.  The Wampum gauge is above 3.5 feet 60% of the time.

# B. Wampum to Ohio River                          16.5 miles

| Class | Grad | Size (Area / Volume) | Scene / Poll | Level |
|-------|------|----------------------|--------------|-------|
| A-B | Pool | Large (3,106/3,758) | D/C | 3.9-?? |
|  |  | Beaver Falls |  | Beaver Falls |

*Topographic Maps:* New Castle South, Beaver Falls, Beaver

*County Maps:* Lawrence, Beaver

*Description:* Beyond the bridge at Wampum, the river flows through a deep valley with wooded mud banks to Beaver Falls. There are a few riffles just below Wampum. Below the mouth of the Connoquenessing is the backwater of the dam at Beaver Falls, in which one encounters many motorboats. [Checked 1987]

*Difficulties:* Three dangerous dams in Beaver Falls. Portage the first on the left by walking around the water company fence to put in below the dam. At the second dam portage on the left. The third is a portage on the right. Be careful on the steep banks.

*Shuttle:* The put-in is where State Route 288 crosses the river. To reach the take-out, go west from the put-in about 0.5 miles to State Route 18. Turn left/south on State Route 18. Take out on the right bank 0.3 miles before the junction with the Ohio River. There is an intermediate take-out at the Rock Point Club. See the write-up on the Connoquenessing Creek, Section E.

*Gauges:* Beaver Falls. This gauge should read 3.9 feet. This corresponds to a flow of 1,430 cfs. We do not have enough information to report a high runnable level. However, a reading of 4.9 on the Beaver Falls gauge corresponds to the mean flow of 3758 cfs. Since this is a large size river, we speculate that the river is too high at that level.

*Normal Wet Period:* The Beaver Falls gauge is above 3.9 feet 60% of the time.

# Connoquenessing Creek

## A. Zelienople                                    11.0 miles
## to Country Club, State Route 65

| Class | Grad | Size (Area/Volume) | Scene/Poll | Level |
|-------|------|--------------------|------------|-------|
| I | 4/4 | Medium (356/466) Zelienople | C/B | 1.8-3.5 Zelienople |

*Topographic Maps:* Zelienople, Beaver Falls

*County Maps:* Butler, Beaver

*Description:* From Zelienople to Camp Silver Lake (about 5 miles) there are a dozen or so easy riffles which can be run by anyone with a bare minimum of whitewater training. The remainder is slow current and pools. [Checked 1990]

*Difficulties:* At certain seasons the residents along the stream raise a collapsible 2-foot dam to form a pool ending just above the Country Club bridge. Scout the dam from either bank if you are continuing down the river.

*Shuttle:* Put in upstream of the State Route 588 bridge just west of Zelienople. Shuttle via State Route 588 to the Country Club bridge. Take out on the right bank above the dam, upstream of the bridge.

*Gauges:* Zelienople. This gauge should read between 1.8 and 3.5 feet. This corresponds to a flow of 170 cfs to 1,080 cfs. The McConnells Mill gauge on nearby Slippery Rock Creek will probably read between 0.0 and 2.5 feet.

*Normal Wet Period:* This section is normally runnable from mid November to mid June, and there is no season when it is normally too high. The Zelienople gauge is above 1.8 feet 55% of the time and above 3.5 feet 10% of the time.

# B. Country Club to Frisco                    2.0 miles

| Class | Grad | Size (Area/Volume) | Scene/Poll | Level |
|-------|------|--------------------|-----------|-------|
| I | 6/10 | Medium (400/667) estimated | B/C | 1.7-3.5 Zelienople |

*Topographic Maps:* Beaver Falls

*County Maps:* Beaver

*Description:* This short section, which flows through wooded and farm lands, is usually run together with the Zelienople to Country Club Section (trip A above), or with the Frisco to Ellport Section (trip C below), depending on the skill levels of the paddlers making the trip. [Checked 1990]

*Difficulties:* At certain seasons the residents along the stream raise a collapsible 2-foot dam to form a pool ending just above the Country Club bridge. Scout the dam from the shore before running. About 2 miles below the put-in at low water there is an S-turn rapid which requires a little maneuvering. At higher levels it washes out.

*Shuttle:* The put-in is just off of State Route 65 where it crosses the creek by the country club. It is on the north/east side just alongside an RV dealer. To reach the take-out, go north on State Route 65 to the intersection of 288. Go straight through the intersection rather than following State Route 65 left across the bridge. The take-out is just past the gas station by the stone piers, under the power lines.

*Gauges:* Zelienople. This gauge should read between 1.7 and 3.5 feet. This corresponds to a flow of 140 cfs to 1,080 cfs. The McConnells Mill gauge on nearby Slippery Rock Creek will probably read between 0.0 and 2.5 feet.

*Normal Wet Period:* This section is normally runnable from mid November to mid June, and there is no season when it is normally too high. The Zelienople gauge is above 1.7 feet 58% of the time and above 3.5 feet 10% of the time.

# C. Frisco to Ellport Park                    2.0 miles

| *Class* | *Grad* | *Volume* | *Scene/Poll.* | *Level* |
|---------|--------|----------|---------------|---------|
| II | 17/20 | Medium (829/1,382) | C/C | 1.6-3.0 |
| | | Ellport Park | | Zelienople |

*Topographic Maps:* Beaver Falls

*County Maps:* Beaver, Lawrence

*Description:* This section is known as "Connie's Challenge" and is often used for teaching intermediates in open canoes. It has mostly continuous Class II rapids with a few pools down to the Wurtemburg bridge. [Checked 1990]

*Difficulties:* Calgon Ledge is a 3-foot drop about 0.5 miles downstream from the Frisco (State Route 65) Bridge. It can be scouted from the road during the shuttle. Run it on the right or the extreme left. The rest is fairly clear-cut except for the rapid just before the Wurtemburg Bridge, which can be scouted from the left bank. It is long and it winds around a bend to the left.

*Shuttle:* The put-in is just north of the intersection of State Route 65 and State Route 288. It is just past the gas station by the stone piers, under the power lines. To reach the take out, follow the river downstream/north. Turn left at the tee and cross the river at Wurtemburg. Take the first right past the bridge and turn right on Third Street to get to the park. Continue through the park to the water treatment plant and park at the top of the hill. Do not block the entrance to the plant. To get cars down to the take-out at the end of the trip, take the sharp U-turn to the right that goes down the hill past the treatment plant.

*Gauges:* Zelienople. This gauge should read between 1.6 and 3.0 feet. This corresponds to a flow of 115 cfs to 778 cfs. The McConnells Mill gauge on nearby Slippery Rock Creek will probably read between 0.0 and 1.7 feet, but it is only a mediocre predictor. For a streamside gauge use the large rock in the middle of Calgon Ledge. If it is underwater, open-boat paddlers would be wise to attempt a different river.

The correlation between McConnells Mill and the Zelienople gauge for 1988 is given by the following graph:

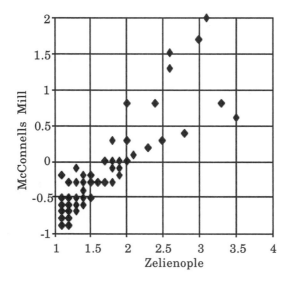

When McConnells Mill is below 0.0 the correlation suffers from the uncertainty in the McConnells Mill reading; when either river is high the correlation is affected by differences in precipitation from one watershed to another.

*Normal Wet Period:* This section is normally runnable from late November to early June, except it is normally too high from early March to mid March. The Zelienople gauge is above 1.6 feet 62% of the time and above 3.0 feet 15% of the time.

# D. Ellport Park                                    3.0 miles
## to Ellwood City Sewer Plant

| Class | Grad | Size (Area/Volume) | Scene/Poll | Level |
|-------|------|--------------------|-----------|-------|
| II-III | 11/12 | Medium (832/1,387) | C/C | 1.6-3.0 |
| | | Ellwood City | | Zelienople |

*Topographic Maps:* Beaver Falls

*County Maps:* Lawrence

*Description:* This is a steep-walled gorge in many places. The river passes through fairly populated areas which, for most of the trip, are out of sight high above the river. The rapids are about as difficult as Connie's Challenge but are longer. Because of the rock structure along the shore, this river is sometimes used for instruction and practice in eddy turns. This section has become quite polluted. Numerous paddlers have reported various infections after being in contact with the "water". [Checked 1990]

*Difficulties:* None.

*Shuttle:* Put in at Ellport Park as described in section C. Take out at the filtration plant on river right about 0.3 miles downstream of the State Route 228 bridge in Ellwood City. This trip is often lengthened upstream by putting in either at Frisco on the Connoquenessing or at Harris Bridge on the Slippery Rock.

*Gauges:* Zelienople. This gauge should read between 1.6 and 3.0 feet. This corresponds to a flow of 115 cfs to 778 cfs. The McConnells Mill gauge on nearby Slippery Rock Creek will probably read between 0.0 and 1.7 feet.

*Normal Wet Period:* This section is normally runnable from late November to early June, except it is normally too high from early March to mid March. The Zelienople gauge is above 1.6 feet 62% of the time and above 3.0 feet 15% of the time.

# E. Ellwood City Sewer Plant          1.5 miles
## to Beaver River

| Class | Grad | Size (Area / Volume) | Scene / Poll | Level |
|-------|------|----------------------|--------------|-------|
| III | 20/33 | Medium (838/1,397) mouth of creek | C/C | 1.6-?? Zelienople |

*Topographic Maps:* Beaver Falls

*County Maps:* Lawrence

*Description:* This final section is a little further from civilization than the earlier sections - vertically if not horizontally. After 0.5 miles of flatwater, you will see a road sign signalling a left turn. This is your cue to scout the first of the rapids in the lower gorge. It is a good whitewater run from here to the take-out. [Checked 1988]

*Difficulties:* In the gorge, the first two rapids should be scouted. The first is under the railroad bridge (run on the right). The second is about 200 yards downstream (run on the left). Be careful about running this trip shortly after a rainstorm because the level rises rapidly in the canyon.

*Shuttle:* This section is generally combined with the previous section. Use the Ellport park put-in. To take out at the junction with the Beaver River, park cars downstream outside the Rock Point Boat Club gates on State Route 288 (north side of the stream). At the end of the run get the caretaker to open the gates and be prepared to pay a charge per car, or carry canoes up to the gate, about 1 mile. Alternatively, one can become a member of Rock Point Boat club and acquire a key. Another alternative is to continue on and paddle 7 miles on the Beaver River to the unrunnable dam in Beaver Falls. Check map for access and shuttles.

*Gauges:* Zelienople. This gauge should read above 1.6 feet. This corresponds to a flow of 115 cfs. The McConnells Mill gauge on nearby Slippery Rock Creek will probably read between 0.0 and 1.7 feet.

*Normal Wet Period:* This section is normally runnable from mid November to late June. The Zelienople gauge is above 1.6 feet 62% of the time.

# Slippery Rock Creek

## A. State Route 173 (Rock Falls Park)          9.0 miles
## to Moores Corners

| Class | Grad | Size (Area / Volume) | Scene / Poll | Level |
|-------|------|----------------------|--------------|-------|
| C | 4/10 | Small (150/250) | A/B | 2.3-?? |
| | | Junction of Wolf Creek | | Wurtemburg |

*Topographic Maps:* Slippery Rock

*County Maps:* Butler

*Description:* This is beautiful country, just south of the glacial moraine. Much wildlife has been reported along this section. Most of the run is mixed pasture and woods. The final mile flows through a small gorge, reminiscent of the McConnells Mill area, but with no whitewater. [Checked 1982]

*Difficulties:* The put-in is immediately below a dam and Class III rapid. There is an unrunnable dam just above the first bridge (Crolls Mills). Use the easy carry on the left.

*Shuttle:* From the put-in in Rock Falls Park, go north on State Route 173 to the town of Slippery Rock, then west on State Route 108. Go 3.5 miles, turn left just past Wolf Creek, go 0.25 miles to the river.

*Gauges:* Wurtemburg. This gauge should read above 2.3 feet. This corresponds to a flow of 850 cfs. The McConnells Mills gauge further downstream will probably read between 2.0 and 3.0 feet.

*Normal Wet Period:* This section is normally runnable from early March to late March. The Wurtemburg gauge is above 2.3 feet 19% of the time.

# B. Moores Corners                                    8.5 miles
# to US Route 19 (Kennedy Mill)

| Class | Grad | Size (Area/Volume) | Scene/Poll | Level |
|-------|------|--------------------|------------|-------|
| C | 5/6 | Medium (260/433) estimated | B-C/B | 1.9-?? Wurtemburg |

*Topographic Maps:* Slippery Rock, Harlansburg, Portersville

*County Maps:* Butler, Lawrence

*Description:* A flat, flowing stream that wanders past farm houses, cornfields and woods. It also passes through a trailer park and several areas of summer homes. [Checked 1978]

*Difficulties:* There is a dam at Kennedy Mill. This dam is at the end of a long pool with summer homes, and has a bridge above it. The portage around this dam is difficult and should be scouted from the bridge before putting on the river. There are currently (1982) landowner problems at Kennedy Mill. The access is blocked by barbed wire and No Trespassing signs. A take-out at US Route 19 is suggested.

*Shuttle:* The put-in is 0.25 miles south of State Route 108 on an unnumbered road 1 mile east of the Interstate 79 exit. From the put-in, go north 0.25 miles to Moores Corners, west on State Route 108 to US Route 19, and south 1 mile to the river crossing.

*Gauges:* Wurtemburg. This gauge should read above 1.9 feet. This corresponds to a flow of 591 cfs.

*Normal Wet Period:* This section is normally runnable from late February to mid April. The Wurtemburg gauge is above 1.9 feet 28% of the time.

## C. US Route 19 (Kennedy Mill)          1.5 miles
## to Rose Point

| Class | Grad | Size (Area / Volume) | Scene / Poll | Level |
|-------|------|----------------------|--------------|-------|
| II | 11/11 | Medium (300/500) estimated | A-B/B | 1.5-?? Wurtemburg |

*Topographic Maps:* Portersville

*County Maps:* Lawrence

*Description:* This short stretch is normally not run because of landowner problems. There is a barbed wire fence and No Trespassing signs at Kennedy Mill. [Checked 1982]

*Difficulties:* Put in below the dam, as it is difficult to portage or run. Immediately below Kennedy Mill dam there are three rapids. The third one has a drop of about 2.5 feet. The next 2 miles to Rose Point are flat and flowing water.

*Shuttle:* The put-in is on US Route 19, 1.5 miles south of the intersection with State Route 108. To get to the take-out, go south on US Route 19 to US Route 422. Turn right/west and go 1 mile to the river. New US Route 422 crosses the creek very high up. The actual take-out is north of the four lane along old route 422 which is down at river level. Take the right turn on either side of the creek within site of the high bridge.

*Gauges:* Wurtemburg. This gauge should read above 1.5 feet. This corresponds to a flow of 375 cfs.

*Normal Wet Period:* This section is normally runnable from early January to late May. The Wurtemburg gauge is above 1.5 feet 39% of the time.

# D. Rose Point                                           2.5 miles
## to Breakneck (Eckert Bridge)

| Class Grad | Size (Area / Volume) | Scene / Poll Level |
|---|---|---|
| III-IV 30/40 | Medium (360/600) estimated | A / A   1.0-2.0 Wurtemburg |

*Topographic Maps:* Portersville

*County Maps:* Lawrence

*Description:* This beautiful stream runs through the gorge cut when an ancient glacial lake (now replaced by Lake Arthur) broke through its wall and rushed madly for the Ohio River. The resulting gorge, seemingly misplaced in the surrounding rolling farmland, is strewn with boulders and lined with hemlock. It is one of the finest places around to see trillium in the spring. It is a drop-and-pool river. The drops are fairly well spaced in the 1.5 miles from Rose Point to McConnells Mill and there are over half a dozen significant drops packed into "The Mile" below the Mill. The stream is runnable most of the year, becoming extremely tight, if less pushy, as the water drops below 0.0 on the gauge at McConnells Mill. A trail from the Mill to Eckert Bridge allows scouting of all but the biggest drop. [Checked 1990]

*Difficulties:* The first 0.5 miles is riffled. The next mile contains several drops, including two tricky S-turn rapids. These have very sharp turns at low water and very strong twisting currents at high levels. The backwater of the unrunnable dam is not very long. Portage is possible on either side of the creek; the park ranger prefers (in 1989) that you use the paths on the left. Below the covered bridge "The Mile" starts. There are several ledges, some with sneak routes, some without. There are small pools below each of the drops in which to recover, at levels below 1.0. The largest drop is hard to scout, either from the river or from the trail. Huge boulders choke the river down to a quarter of its width, and three drops closely follow each other without pause. Small differences in the level at the Mill make big differences in the Triple Drop.

*Shuttle:* To get to the put-in take US Route 422 to where it crosses the river. New US Route 422 crosses the creek very high up.  The actual put-in is north of the four lane along old route 422 which is down at river level.  Take the right turn on either side of the creek within site of the high bridge. Park on New 422 after unloading the boats and gear.  To reach the take-out proceed east on US Route 422 to US Route 19.  Turn right/south and go about 3 miles.  Turn right/west on Cheeseman which is about 0.3 miles north of State Route 488.  Proceed west on Cheeseman until it ends at a tee intersection.  Turn right and proceed to the river down an unmaintained road with its edges falling in, .  Be careful as you descend to the river.  The take-out is actually Eckert Bridge; the location has been called "Breakneck" for years. Breakneck Bridge, now closed, crosses Cheeseman Run, which enters the Slippery Rock just downstream from Eckert Bridge. It is also possible (in 1989) to put in at McConnells Mill.  Unload at the Mill and move the cars to the upper parking lot.  One favorite run combines "the Mile" from McConnells Mill with the next section, taking out at Harris Bridge.

*Gauges:* Wurtemburg. This gauge should read between 1.0 and 2.0 feet. This corresponds to a flow of 185 cfs to 650 cfs. There is a staff gauge at McConnells Mill, located where the water flowing through the mill re-enters the creek. Because of its location and the lack of calibration for levels below zero, this gauge does not give reliable readings below about minus 0.1 ft. The correlation between McConnells Mill and Wurtemburg is given by the following graph:

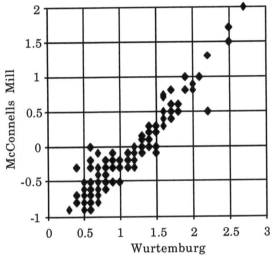

Note that the correlation is poor when the Mill reads below zero. The McConnells Mills gauge on the river side of the mill should read between minus 0.3 and 1.0 (open boats) or 1.5 (closed boats) for the best run. Since the gorge is so steep, the stream gets narrower rather than shallower as the level drops. The painted gauges on Harris Bridge and Eckert Bridge are approximately equal to the McConnells Mill gauge.

*Normal Wet Period:* This section is normally runnable from mid November to late June, except it is normally too high from late January to early May. The Wurtemburg gauge is above 1.0 feet 57% of the time and above 2.0 feet 36% of the time.

# E. Breakneck (Eckert Bridge)                3.2 miles
## to Harris Bridge

| Class | Grad | Size (Area/Volume) | Scene/Poll | Level |
|-------|------|--------------------|-----------|----------|
| II-III | 23/27 | Medium (380/633) estimated | A/A | 1.0-2.5 Wurtemburg |

*Topographic Maps:* Portersville

*County Maps:* Lawrence

*Description:* The valley is still deep, but not as canyon-like through this stretch. The river becomes calmer than it is upstream. However, the rapids in this section will still challenge intermediates. They have the same S-turn character as rapids farther upstream, although they are not as tight. The river is still strewn with immense boulders, some of which are undercut. [Checked 1990]

*Shuttle:* To get to the take-out go back Cheeseman Road to US Route 19. Turn south and go the short distance to State Route 488. Turn right/ west on State Route 488 and proceed for about 3 miles to Mountville Road, State Route 2030. Turn right towards Mt. Hope church. Continue about 3 miles to the river.

*Gauges:* Wurtemburg. This gauge should read between 1.0 and 2.5 feet. This corresponds to a flow of 185 cfs to 990 cfs. The McConnells Mills gauge on the river side of the mill should read between minus 0.3 and 1.5 (open boats) or 2.0 (closed boats) for the best run. The previous section discusses the uncertainty in using McConnells Mill gauge at levels below zero. The painted gauges on Harris Bridge and Eckert Bridge are approximately equal to the McConnells Mill gauge.

*Normal Wet Period:* This section is normally runnable from early November to early July, except it is normally too high from early March to early April. The Wurtemburg gauge is above 1.0 feet 57% of the time and above 2.5 feet 17% of the time.

# F. Harris Bridge to Ellport Park                6.0 miles

| Class | Grad | Size (Area/Volume) | Scene/Poll | Level |
|-------|------|--------------------|-----------|-------|
| I | 12/13 | Medium (398/572) Wurtemburg | A-B/A-B | 1.3-3.0 Wurtemburg |

*Topographic Maps:* Portersville, Zelienople, Beaver Falls

*County Maps:* Lawrence

*Description:* From Harris Bridge to Connoquenessing Creek, the river is essentially flat with a few riffles. [Checked 1989]

*Difficulties:* There are two permanent dams on this section, a runnable broken-out dam, and a movable dam just above the junction with the Connoquenessing. The first dam is immediately below Harris Bridge. Portage on the right. The broken-out dam is at the end of a high concrete retaining wall on the left bank. The dam may be run on the right. The second dam is located at Camp Allegheny just after a foot bridge. It is about 2 feet high and is portaged on the right. The movable dam is just above the junction with the Connoquenessing. If it is up, the portage is on the right.

*Shuttle:* To get to the take-out, go back Mountville Road to State Route 488. Turn right/west. After crossing the creek three times take the first right past the bridge and turn right on Third Street to get to the park. Continue through the park to the water treatment plant and park at the top of the hill. Do not block the entrance to the plant. To get cars down to the take-out at the end of the trip, take the sharp U-turn to the right that goes down the hill past the treatment plant.

*Gauges:* Wurtemburg. This gauge should read between 1.3 and 3.0 feet. This corresponds to a flow of 285 cfs to 1,340 cfs. The McConnells Mills gauge on the river side of the mill should read between 0.2 and 2.0. The painted gauge on Harris Bridge is approximately equal to the McConnells Mill gauge.

*Normal Wet Period:* This section is normally runnable from early January to late May. The Wurtemburg gauge is above 1.3 feet 47% of the time and above 3.0 feet 12% of the time.

# Wolf Creek

## A. Wolf Creek Above Grove City                    4.0 miles

*Class   Grad     Size (Area/Volume)      Scene/Poll  Level*
   A      Swamp        Tiny (13/22)              A/A
                    6 mi north of Grove City

*Topographic Maps:* Grove City

*County Maps:* Mercer

*Description:* A nice poling expedition begins at a put-in on the backwater of the old mill dam, just above the bridge by the old police station in Grove City along State Route 58, two blocks east of McDonalds. First paddle upstream on the backwater past the college campus, and then start poling above the Pine Street bridge, on up to the second low dam at the State Route 208 East bridge. Above the dam, paddle through a short marsh, and start into the very small stream, poling and paddling several miles upstream through beautiful low woodlands until it becomes too narrow. Only a true stump jumper would want to go above Interstate 80. [Reported 1981]

*Difficulties:* None on the river.

*Shuttle:* None if poling.

*Gauges:* None.

*Normal Wet Period:* No available statistics on seasons. Since this section is tiny, it should normally be runnable only after a heavy rain or during spring snowmelt.

# B. Grove City to Courtneys Mills                4.5 miles

| *Class* | *Grad* | *Size (Area/Volume)* | *Scene/Poll* | *Level* |
|---------|--------|----------------------|--------------|---------|
| C-I | 9/10 | Small (87/133) | A-B/A | 1.6-4.6 |
|  |  | Courtneys Mills |  | Wurtemburg |

*Topographic Maps:* Grove City, Slippery Rock

*County Maps:* Mercer

*Description:* A pleasant trip through rural or isolated country.

*Difficulties:* No major problems other than fallen trees. [Checked 1990]

*Shuttle:* Put in on Sewage Plant Road (Greenwood Drive) about 0.25 miles downstream from the unrunnable dam at the old police station. Take State Route 173 south about 3 miles. Take right turn for Linley's Fishing Lake and continue about 0.75 miles to the creek. Ask permission of Mr. Linley to take out on his land next to the bridge. An alternate take-out would be at State Route 258.

*Gauges:* Wurtemburg. This gauge should read between 1.6 and 4.6 feet. This corresponds to a flow of 425 cfs to 2,900 cfs. However, because of the distance to the gauge, Wurtemburg is at best a weak predictor. The shallowest part of the trip is just above the Lake Linley (Courtneys Mills) Bridge. McConnells Mill gauge further downstream will probably read above 1.0.

*Normal Wet Period:* The Wurtemburg gauge is above 1.6 feet 36% of the time and above 4.6 feet 3% of the time.

## C. Courtneys Mills 7.0 miles
## to junction with Slippery Rock Creek

| Class | Grad | Size (Area/Volume) | Scene/Poll | Level |
|-------|------|-------|-------|-------|
| I-II | 11/20 | Small (100/167) | A/A | 1.6-4.6 |
| | | mouth of creek | | Wurtemburg |

*Topographic Maps:* Slippery Rock

*County Maps:* Mercer, Butler

*Description:* This is a pleasant run through fairly remote areas. The stream is usually shallow, flowing over a gravel bed that occasionally changes to large flat rocks. The first few miles of this section are isolated, with the best rapids and the best scenery. The last several miles are much flatter and the shores are heavily populated by summer cottages.

In 1980, the Western Pennsylvania Conservancy acquired 100 acres of virgin timber, wildflowers, and prime fishing waters including the 1 mile section known as Wolf Creek Narrows. It is appropriate for poling. [Checked 1990]

*Difficulties:* When spring thaw or heavy rain brings high water, fallen trees may block the river as potentially lethal strainers. Be very careful at high, fast levels.

*Shuttle:* To find the put-in take State Route 173 north from the town of Slippery Rock. After about 4 miles, take a left turn for Linley's Fishing Lake and continue about 0.75 miles to the creek. Ask permission of Mr. Linley to put in on his land next to the bridge. To find the take-out, return to Slippery Rock. Turn right/east on State Route 108. Go 2.8 miles to where the road crosses Wolf Creek. You may be able to arrange with the landowner to take out here. Wolf Creek enters the Slippery Rock about a tenth of a mile further downstream. Alternatively, continue on State Route 108 for 0.2 miles, turn left/south on State Route 0107 and take out on the Slippery Rock Creek. This will add 0.7 miles of river.

Publicity about the possible inclusion of Wolf Creek in the Pennsylvania Wild and Scenic Rivers program has polarized landowners against stream users, including canoeists.   This makes the use of private land for river access somewhat problematical.   Access points at Linley's Bridge (Courtneys Mills) and the Airport Road are now questionable.   Inquire (politely) before using private property for river access.

*Gauges:*    The shallowest part of the trip is just above the Lake Linley (Courtneys Mills) Bridge.   If the water is sufficient here, the run will probably be okay.   The Wurtemburg gauge on nearby Slippery Rock Creek will probably read between 1.6 and 4.6 feet.   This corresponds to a flow of 650 cfs to 2,900 cfs at Wurtemburg.   However, Wurtemburg is too far downstream to give a good indication of runnability.   The chart below shows that readings below 3.0 (1,300 cfs) have been too low.   McConnells Mill gauge, a little closer, will probably read between 1.0 and 5.0.   This section is a major tributary of the Slippery Rock Creek, so it is probably too low when the Slippery Rock is low or marginal.

From 1976 to 1982 the US Geological Survey operated a gauge at Courtneys Mills bridge.    Runnable levels on the Courtneys Mills gauge were in the range 330-750 cfs.    The correlation between that gauge and Wurtemburg for 1982 is given by the graph below.

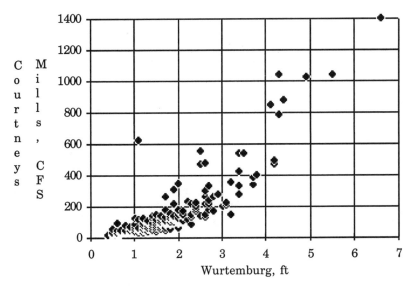

As the graph shows, Wurtemburg is only a fair predictor for Wolf Creek, especially when water levels are rising or falling rapidly.    There is no reason to believe that McConnells Mill is much better.

*Normal Wet Period:*    The Wurtemburg gauge is above 1.6 feet 36% of the time and above 4.6 feet 3% of the time.

# Little Connoquenessing Creek

## A. State Route 3007 to State Route 528          6.3 miles

| Class | Grad  | Size (Area/Volume)      | Scene/Poll | Level           |
|-------|-------|-------------------------|------------|-----------------|
| II    | 16/36 | Tiny (45/75) estimated  | B/A-B      | 2.0-?? Streamside |

*Topographic Maps:* Butler, Evans City

*County Maps:* Butler

*Description:* From the put-in to the junction with Mulligan Run the stream is a tiny Class II. Usually less than 20 feet wide, it is dense with downed trees. Mulligan Run is almost as large as the Little Connoquenessing at the junction, so the stream opens up at that point. [Checked 1977]

*Difficulties:* Trees down through the run, especially in the upper section.

*Shuttle:* The put-in is on State Route 3007, northwest of White Church, which is about 3 miles west of Butler on State Route 68. To reach the take-out, go south on State Route 3007 to State Route 68 and turn right. Go about 2.5 miles, and turn right on State Route 3030, then right again on State Route 528. Take-out is on the left side, downstream at the bridge.

*Gauges:* State Route 3025 crosses the Little Connoquenessing twice. At the eastern crossing, where State Route 3025 turns north away from the stream, there is a government gauge on the downstream side of the center pier. Count on needing at least 2.0 feet for this section.

*Normal Wet Period:* No available statistics on seasons. Since this section is tiny, it should normally be runnable only after a heavy rain or during spring snowmelt.

# B. State Route 528                          5.0 miles
# to western State Route 3025

| *Class* | *Grad* | *Size (Area / Volume)* | *Scene / Poll* | *Level* |
|---------|--------|------------------------|----------------|---------|
| C-I | 7/10 | Small(65/108) | B/A-B | 1.5-?? |
|  |  | mouth of creek |  | Streamside |

*Topographic Maps:* Evans City

*County Maps:* Butler

*Description:* The stream begins as a tiny creek with wooded banks. After a couple of miles it picks up a tributary (Crab Run) and turns into a small stream meandering through farmland and areas of summer houses, with occasional excursions against steep hemlock-covered banks. Ducks and geese can be seen in the spring, as well as an occasional heron. [Checked 1989]

*Difficulties:* About a mile after Crab Run enters, the stream becomes flat. This is the backwater of a 3 foot dam located about a quarter-mile upstream from the bridge with the gauge. In low water you can land on a concrete pad on the left side of the dam and lift over. If you can not clearly identify this pad, take out on the right side and carry around the gazebo. The gazebo is located just upstream of the dam; there is not room to take out below it. In addition to this unrunnable dam, there are numerous runnable rock dams that pool water for homes along the stream.

*Shuttle:* The put-in is on State Route 528 about 4-5 miles north of Evans City. To get to the take-out, go north a quarter of a mile on State Route 528, turn left on Little Creek Road, go 3 miles turn left on State Route 3025, and immediately cross the bridge with the gauge. Then take the left onto a dead-end road just before State Route 3025 crosses the creek again. Park across from the Whiskey Hollow Inn and take out near the embankment that once supported a bridge.

*Gauges:* State Route 3025 crosses the Little Connoquenessing twice. At the eastern crossing, where State Route 3025 turns north away from the stream, there is a government gauge on the downstream side of the center pier. Count on needing at least 1.5 feet for this section. The

Zelienople gauge on nearby Connoquenessing Creek will probably read above 3.0 feet.

*Normal Wet Period:* No available statistics on seasons. Since this section is small, it should normally be runnable approximately January through April.

# Yellow Creek
# (Butler County)

## Middle Lancaster                          5.0 miles
## to Little Connoquenessing

*Class   Grad     Size (Area/Volume)     Scene/Poll   Level*
C-I     15/15        Tiny (17/28)          B-C/B
                  mouth of Yellow Creek

*Topographic Maps:* Evans City

*County Maps:* Butler

*Description:* Yellow Creek runs parallel to Interstate 79 north of Harmony, Pa. and is very, very small. You have to push aside shrubbery to get through. There are fallen trees, and a farmer has put up a fence made of steel cable and oil drums. The Interstate highway is nearby, but usually not offensive. Yellow Creek is short and runs into the Little Connoquenessing which is small. It feels a bit like the Slippery Rock, but is still Class I, flowing with occasional riffles. A good stream for poling. [Reported 1973]

*Shuttle:* The put-in is on the east fork, on the road that crosses under the Interstate to Middle Lancaster. The take-out is shortly before the Little Connoquenessing crosses under Interstate 79.

*Gauges:* Zelienople. This gauge on nearby Connoquenessing Creek will probably read above 3.0. There is a bridge footing at the put-in. If the footing shows about 0.5 inch above water level, Yellow Creek is low, but the Little Connoquenessing is fine.

*Normal Wet Period:* No available statistics on seasons. Since this section is tiny, it should normally be runnable only after a heavy rain or during spring snowmelt.

# Shenango River

## A. Pymatuning Dam to Greenville                8.5 miles

| Class | Grad | Size (Area/Volume) | Scene/Poll | Level |
|-------|------|--------------------|-----------|-------|
| A-B   | 4/6  | Small (167/208)    | A/A       | 4.6-5.6 |
|       |      | Pymatuning Dam     | Pymatuning Dam | |

*Topographic Maps:* Greenville West

*County Maps:* Crawford, Mercer

*Description:* This is a small intimate stream, shallow, slow-flowing, with deep pools. Overhanging tree branches and fallen trees block the channel. [Reported 1983]

*Difficulties:* If the level is high, the tree-blocked channel could be dangerous.

*Shuttle:* Put in at the base of the Pymatuning Dam on the left/east side, of the river, by the gauge station. Follow State Route 3005 to US Route 322. Follow State Route 58 south to State Route 358. Turn right/west on State Route 358 to the Main Street bridge. Take out on the south/east side behind the buildings on the gravel lot.

*Gauges:* Pymatuning Dam. This gauge should read between 4.6 and 5.6 feet. This corresponds to a flow of 66 cfs to 460 cfs.

*Normal Wet Period:* The Pymatuning Dam gauge is above 4.6 feet 72% of the time and above 5.6 feet 10% of the time.

# B. Greenville to New Hamburg                    9.5 miles

| Class | Grad | Size (Area/Volume) | Scene/Poll | Level |
|-------|------|--------------------|------------|-------|
| A | 2/2 | Medium (337/481) | B/B | 2.5-?? |
| | | Transfer | | Transfer |

*Topographic Maps:* Greenville West, Sharpsville, Fredonia

*County Maps:* Mercer

*Description:* This stream traverses through undeveloped farmland with many bends and tree-choked channels. There is a covered bridge at Reynolds Heights. The remains of an old dam just below the New Hamburg bridge is now a good size riffle and nothing more. [Checked 1983]

*Difficulties:* At one point the right-hand channel is impassable due to downed trees, and the channel on the left is a narrow chute. Take the left. If the river is high this section could be dangerous due to the downed trees.

*Shuttle:* To get to the put-in, take State Route 358 to the Main Street bridge in Greenville. Put in on river left behind the buildings on the gravel lot. To get to the take-out go south on State Route 58 towards Mercer, turn right onto State Route 4024. Take out on river left by the old bridge pilings in New Hamburg. It is possible to canoe beyond this point to the Sharpsville Dam.

*Gauges:* Transfer. This gauge should read above 2.5 feet. This corresponds to a flow of 108 cfs.

*Normal Wet Period:* The Transfer gauge is above 2.5 feet 90% of the time.

# C. New Hamburg to Sharpsville Dam            16.5 miles

| Class | Grad | Size (Area/Volume) | Scene/Poll | Level |
|-------|------|--------------------|------------|-------|
| A | Lake | Medium (400/667) estimated | B/A | 2.5-?? Transfer |

*Topographic Maps:* Fredonia, Sharpsville

*County Maps:* Mercer

*Description:* The first 4.3 miles are in the section of Shenango River Lake that fluctuates. The remaining 12 miles are within the summer levels of this Corps of Engineers lake. [Reported 1989]

*Difficulties:* The last 12 miles of the lake have high speed motorboat traffic.

*Shuttle:* The put-in is in New Hamburg, off State Route 4024, by the old bridge pier pilings. To get to the take-out, go west on State Route 4014. At the fork continue on State Route 4007. Turn right/west onto State Route 3022. Turn left/south onto State Route 18. Turn right/west onto State Route 518. Go 3 miles, turn right/north at intersection. Go 2 miles to the dam.

*Gauges:* Transfer. This gauge should read above 2.5 feet. This corresponds to a flow of 108 cfs.

*Normal Wet Period:* The Transfer gauge is above 2.5 feet 90% of the time.

# D. Sharpsville Dam to West Middlesex        12.0 miles

| Class | Grad | Size (Area / Volume) | Scene / Poll | Level |
|-------|------|----------------------|--------------|-------|
| C-I | 5/6 | Medium (584/761) | D/B | 2.6-?? |
| | | Sharpsville Dam | | Sharpsville |

*Topographic Maps:* Sharpsville, Orangeville (Ohio), Sharon
West (Ohio), Sharon East

*County Maps:* Mercer

*Description:* There are Class I rapids above Sharon.
Through Sharon there is a lot of industry along the banks.
Below that the stream banks are reasonably undeveloped.
[Reported 1983]

*Difficulties:* There are two dams and a waterfall in this
section. Portage both dams on the left. The waterfall is
about 20 yards beyond the second dam. Carry far enough
past the dam to bypass the waterfalls and the discharge pipe
on the right bank.

*Shuttle:* Put in on river right near the base of the Sharpsville Dam off of State Route 518. Head east on State Route
518. Turn right/south onto State Route 18. Turn right/west
onto State Route 318. Go 0.1 miles to the bridge. Take-out is
on the left bank under the West Middlesex Bridge.

*Gauges:* Sharpsville. This gauge should read above 2.6 feet.
This corresponds to a flow of 280 cfs. The Sharpsville gauge
reports the outflow from the Shenango River Dam at
Sharpsville.

*Normal Wet Period:* The Sharpsville gauge is above 2.6 feet
60% of the time.

# E. West Middlesex to Harbor Bridge          13.8 miles

| Class | Grad | Size (Area / Volume) | Scene / Poll | Level |
|-------|------|----------------------|--------------|-------|
| B | 2/2 | Medium (700/1,167) estimated | B/B | 2.6-?? Sharpsville |

*Topographic Maps:* Sharon East, Edinburg

*County Maps:* Mercer, Lawrence

*Description:* Pretty much a flatwater trip with some riffles. [Reported 1983]

*Difficulties:* Beware of small rapids at an island about 0.2 miles below Pulaski Road bridge.

*Shuttle:* Put in on the left bank below the bridge on State Route 518 in West Middlesex. Follow State Route 18 south. Bear right/south onto State Route 551. Turn left onto State Route 208. Go 1 mile turn right onto State Route 60. Turn right onto US Business Route 422. Turn right onto State Route 1002. Continue to Harbor Bridge. Take out on the left bank just upstream of the Harbor Road bridge.

*Gauges:* Sharpsville. This gauge should read above 2.6 feet. This corresponds to a flow of 280 cfs. The Sharpsville gauge reports the outflow from the Shenango River Dam at Sharpsville.

*Normal Wet Period:* The Sharpsville gauge is above 2.6 feet 60% of the time.

# F. Harbor Bridge to Wampum          14.5 miles

| Class | Grad | Size (Area/Volume) | Scene/Poll | Level |
|-------|------|-------------------|------------|-------|
| B-I | 3/3 | Medium (792/871) | C/C | |
| | | New Castle | | New Castle |

*Topographic Maps:* Edinburg, New Castle North, New Castle South, Bessemer

*County Maps:* Lawrence

*Description:* Flatwater for the most part, but with a series of rapids downstream of New Castle to the junction with the Mahoning. About half way through the trip, the Shenango and Mahoning come together to form the Beaver River. There is no easy access at this point. See the first section of the Beaver River for the description of the second half of this section river. [Reported 1983]

*Difficulties:* Wing dam at the power plant near West Pittsburg presents no difficulty, however one should stay close to the dam to avoid any current at the intake on the left.

*Shuttle:* Put in just upstream of the bridge in Harbor. Go east on US Route 422. Turn right onto State Route 18. Turn a sharp left onto State Route 288. Take-out is on the left just below the bridge at Wampum.

*Gauges:* New Castle. We do not have enough information to report runnable levels on this section. A reading of 6.9 feet on the New Castle gauge corresponds to the mean flow of 871 cfs. Since this is a medium-sized river, we speculate that the river will be runnable at 6.9 feet and may be on the high side of runnable at that level. The Sharpsville Dam gauge, about 25 miles upstream, will probably read above 2.6 feet.

*Normal Wet Period:* No available statistics on seasons. Since this section is dam controlled we can not even guess the season based on river size.

# Neshannock Creek

## A. Neshannock Falls                        7.0 miles
## to Lakewood Park

| Class | Grad | Size (Area/Volume) | Scene/Poll | Level |
|-------|------|--------------------|-----------|-------|
| II | 27/60 | Medium (228/243) | A-B/A | |
| | | East Brook | | |

*Topographic Maps:* New Castle North

*County Maps:* Lawrence

*Description:* After a brief warm-up in Class I-II riffles, steep banks rise on both sides, homes and fishing camps disappear behind you. The creek swings left and then right, and a twisting S-turn of white froth leads you between two high piers, "the Guardians of the Gorge". This is the first of four Class II-plus rapids which, together with another four easier Class II's, form the 0.8 miles of the Neshannock Gorge. All too soon, you pass out of the gorge, under the Lakewood Road bridge. The remainder of the trip alternates pools with short riffles. [Checked 1990]

*Difficulties:* The paddler has very little warm-up before the gorge, when four hard Class II rapids require solid skill at technical maneuvering.

*Shuttle:* Put in at the State Route 956 bridge, or at the covered bridge on a side road running north about 0.1 miles from the State Route 956 bridge. To get to the take-out, go southeast on State Route 956. Turn right/south on State Route 168. Turn right/west on State Route 1002. The Pennsylvania Fish Commission Neshannock Creek Access Area is just west of the bridge on river right downstream. The trip can be extended 2.5 miles upstream by putting in at Volant. Intermediate access is available at the Lakewood Road and near the mouth of the Little Neshannock Creek.

*Gauges:* We do not have enough information to report runnable levels on this section.

*Normal Wet Period:* No available statistics on seasons. Since this section is medium-sized, it should normally be runnable approximately December through May.

# B. Lakewood Park to New Castle                 4.3 miles

| Class | Grad | Size (Area/Volume) | Scene/Poll | Level |
|-------|------|--------------------|-----------|-------|
| I-II | 18/26 | Medium (228/243) | A-B/A-B | |

East Brook
Medium (244/407) New Castle

*Topographic Maps:* New Castle North

*County Maps:* Lawrence

*Description:* Although this section never enters a true gorge, it usually has high, wooded cliffs on one side or the other. The pace starts out gently, with Class I drops alternating with short pools. It gradually picks up, and the last 2 miles into New Castle are almost continuous Class II rock gardens with maneuvering and standing waves. [Checked 1990]

*Difficulties:* None.

*Shuttle:* Put in at the Pennsylvania Fish Commission Neshannock Creek Access Area, west of Lakewood Park on State Route 1002. The parking lot is downstream river right of the bridge. To reach the take-out, go east on State Route 1002 about 0.4 miles to Lakewood Road, at the top of the first hill. Turn right onto Lakewood Road. Go about a mile, and turn right/south onto State Route 168. Go about 2 miles into New Castle. At the bottom of the hill as you approach town, turn right onto the first bridge, then immediately right again to head upstream on river right. Take out along this road.

*Gauges:* We do not have enough information to report runnable levels on this section.

*Normal Wet Period:* No available statistics on seasons. Since this section is medium-sized, it should normally be runnable approximately December through May.

# Otter Creek

## US Route 19 to Mercer                                7.0 miles

| Class | Grad | Size (Area/Volume) | Scene/Poll | Level |
|-------|------|--------------------|-----------|-------|
| I | 18/22 | Tiny (49/82) | A-B/A-B | |
| | | Mercer | | |

*Topographic Maps:* Jackson Center, Mercer

*County Maps:* Mercer

*Description:* For the first 2.5 miles, this tiny stream twists and turns sharply between eroded silt banks. Overhanging brush is thick in places. Passing under a bridge the creek widens out into a marsh where progress is slow due to thick lilypads. The end of the marsh is marked by three big culverts under the old railroad embankment. From this point to the take-out, about 3 miles, the current picks up a little, but there still is not very much current. [Checked 1984]

*Difficulties:* Downed trees make a nuisance, but not a hazard since the current is negligible.

*Shuttle:* Use US Route 19 north of Mercer. The take-out is on State Route 58, at the eastern edge of Mercer.

*Gauges:* We do not have enough information to report runnable levels on this section.

*Normal Wet Period:* No available statistics on seasons. Since this section is tiny, it should normally be runnable only after a heavy rain or during spring snowmelt.

# Little Shenango River

## Osgood to Greenville                                3.2 miles

| Class | Grad | Size (Area / Volume) | Scene / Pol | Level |
|-------|------|----------------------|-------------|-------|
| I | 9/20 | Small (104/142) | AB/A | 2.0-?? |
|  |  | Greenville |  | Greenville |

*Topographic Maps:* Greenville East, Greenville West

*County Maps:* Mercer

*Description:* Mostly flat with some riffles. Railroad tracks on both banks, but most of the view appears unpopulated in a shallow, wooded gorge. [Reported 1988]

*Difficulties:* None.

*Shuttle:* To get to the put-in, go 0.25 miles south of Osgood on State Route 18. Turn east and the bridge is in sight. To get to the take-out, continue south on State Route 18 into Greenville. Before crossing the Main Street bridge, the take-out is on the south/east side behind the buildings on the gravel lot. It is about 300 yards below the junction of the Little Shenango and the Shenango.

*Gauge:* Greenville. This gauge should read above 2.0 feet.

*Normal Dry Period:* No available statistics on seasons. Since this section is small, it should normally be runnable approximately January through April.

# Crooked Creek
# (Mercer County)

**Hartstown to Osgood**                              12.0 miles

| Class | Grad | Size (Area/Volume) | Scene/Pol | Level |
|-------|------|--------------------|-----------|-------|
| I-II  | 5/6  | Tiny (46/77)       | AB/A      |       |
|       |      | mouth of stream    |           |       |

*Topographic Maps:*  Hartstown, Conneaut Lake, Greenville
East

*County Maps:*  Crawford, Mercer

*Description:*  Only the most dedicated of stream baggers
should consider this nightmare of deadfalls and tornado
devastation. The first few miles run through swamp and
marsh ponds formed by two earthen dikes. Bald eagles live
here. There's no defined channel in the swamp, so pick and
choose. It's very pretty. From the second dike to the first
bridge the creek is tiny and tree-choked with scenery of
woods and farms; it sports some tiny gravel riffles in this
section. From the first bridge to the second the going is
relatively easy. There's a lot of overhanging brush but it's
always passable. From the second bridge to the fourth or
fifth, navigation is essentially impossible because of tornado
destruction. It is, however, a pretty setting in the woods,
sometimes with nice hemlock groves. Below the zone of
tornado destruction and deadfalls progress is much easier.
The final few miles to the mouth are bigger, and obstacles
are few. The scenery is more often pastoral than in the
upper section. [Reported 1988]

*Difficulties:*  Below the second bridge is a zone of what is
probably tornado destruction. You'll drag, push, pull and
curse through this mess as creek navigation is totally out of
the question. Bypassing it is the only sane approach. From
the end of the disaster area to the fourth or fifth bridge are
scores of progress-stopping deadfalls.

*Shuttle:*  Put in at the very head of the stream, at the
Pennsylvania Game Commission access by the trailer park.
This is 0.2 miles east of the intersection of State Route 18 and

US Route 322. To get to the take-out, go south on State Route 18 to Osgood. About 0.25 miles south of Osgood turn left/east and the bridge is in sight. An alternative that gets the benefit of the swamp without the tornado destruction, is to put in and take out at the Game Commission access.

*Gauge:*   Greenville. This gauge on nearby  Little Shenango River will probably read above 2.0 feet.

*Normal Dry Period:*   No available statistics on seasons. Since this section is tiny, it should normally be runnable only after a heavy rain or during spring snowmelt.

# Mahoning River

## Alliance to New Castle                           120 miles

| Class | Grad | Size (Area/Volume) | Scene/Poll ˙Level |
|-------|------|--------------------|--------------------|
| A-I | 3/ | Medium (1,140/1,900) | D/C |
| | | mouth of creek | |

*Topographic Maps:* Alliance (Ohio), Deerfield (Ohio), Lake
   Milton (Ohio), Newton Falls (Ohio), Champion (Ohio),
   Warren (Ohio), Girard (Ohio), Youngstown (Ohio),
   Campbell (Ohio), Edinburg, Bessemer

*County Maps:* Mahoning (Ohio), Stark (Ohio), Portage
   (Ohio), Trumbull (Ohio), Lawrence

*Other Maps:* The Ohio Department of Natural Resources,
   Division of Watercraft "Boating in Ohio Streams #5,
   Northeast Section".

*Description:* The Corps of Engineers advises us (1989) that
the water quality is improving from the report in the
previous guide. The Ohio Department of Natural
Resources, Division of Watercraft has published a series of
pamphlets describing canoeable rivers in Ohio. The
following access points and difficulty locations are taken
from the #5 pamphlet which covers northeast Ohio.

US Route 62 and Brandy Road east of Alliance, roadside
   access river left.

Webb Road bridge in Alliance, roadside access river left.

Ford, pipe and dam below Webb Road bridge in Alliance,
   portage river right.

Gaskill Street off Walnut Street in Alliance, pulloff access
   river right.

Early Hill Park in Alliance off Vine Street, access river
   left.

Greenbower Street bridge at Berlin Lake north of
   Alliance, roadside access river right.

Pine Street bridge at Berlin Lake north of Alliance,
   roadside access river left.

Berlin Lake north of Alliance, roadside access river left and right

Berlin Lake dam at north edge of Berlin Road north of Alliance, portage river left staying near shore as restricted area begins 100 feet above dam.

Shillings Mill bridge (closed) between Lake Berlin and Lake Milton in Shillings Mill, roadside access river right.

City of Youngstown Lake Milton public access off Mahoning Avenue bridge south of Craig Beach, roadside access river right.

Lake Milton Dam on Craig Beach, portage left or right.

Pritchard-Ohltown Road bridge (Mahoning-Trumbull County line) north of Craig Beach, roadside access river right.

West River Road bridge in Newton Falls, roadside access river left.

Dam in Newton Falls on Tickner Avenue bridge between First Street and Ravenna Warren Road, portage river right.

First Street in Newton Falls, roadside pulloff below dam on river left.

Dam above Leavitt Road bridge in Leavittsburg, portage river left.

Canoe City Livery off Leavitt Road bridge in Leavittsburg, access river left with permission.

Leavitt Road bridge in Leavittsburg, roadside pulloff river left.

Packard Park in Warren off Ohio State Route 45 (Mahoning Avenue), access river left.

Dam above Ohio State Route 45 in Warren, portage river left, upstream of dam at Packard Park.

Although there is one more access point below Packard Park, we recommend that the canoeing section stop at Packard Park. Below here the water quality is not as good as above the park, access is not as frequent, and there are several hazardous dams.

Maddel Park off Park Avenue west of Niles, access river left.

Dam north of Liberty Street, James Road in Girard, portage river right.

Dam above the railroad tracks in Worthington and West Federal Streets north of the Ohio State Route 193 bridge in Youngstown, portage river right. Dam is broken, but not runnable.

Broken dam under Marshall Street bridge in Youngstown. There is a chute on the right, but it has strainers and the rest of the dam has a good hydraulic. Portage river right at the railroad tracks.

Dam in steel mill area in Campbell downstream of Center Street bridge, portage river right, but there is no portage path at high water.

Dam above First Street/Washington Street bridge in Lowellville (dangerous), portage river left with difficulty.

[Checked 1988]

*Gauges:* Youngstown, Lowellville (near state line).

*Normal Wet Period:* No available statistics on seasons.

# Montour Run

**Enlow to Groveton**                                    11.0 miles

*Class  Grad     Size (Area / Volume)     Scene / Poll  Level*
II-III  22/33    Tiny (29/48)             C/B         0.0-2.0
                 Coraopolis                           Streamside

*Topographic Maps:* Oakdale, Ambridge

*County Maps:* Allegheny

*Description:* Montour Run is one of the best Allegheny County trips we have found. The gorge deserves a B for scenery, but industry and trash at the beginning and end of the trip make it a C overall. When the creek has enough water to be runnable, it flows continuously, with almost no pools. There are small calm spots along the sides, but few eddies worthy of the name. It is narrow, often too narrow to turn a 17-foot canoe around, and usually less than 3 feet deep. [Checked 1988]

*Difficulties:* Trees down, a pipeline crossing, overhanging branches, and all the usual small-stream hazards. One Class III rapid should be scouted. It is about 0.5 miles below the Beaver Grade Road bridge (the first high bridge after Wickes) and shortly after the railroad crosses the creek from the right bank to the left bank. As the river makes a sharp left-hand bend, a concrete slab dams the river. At the level given above, it could be run on the left by making a left turn through some overhanging shrubbery followed immediately by a tight right turn to put the boat sideways in the hydraulic that slopes down the dam face. This could get too big to handle if the creek has much more water.

*Shuttle:* A Pittsburgh map will help. Put in at any of three bridges in Enlow for the 11 mile trip or at the Wickes parking lot (at the Montour exit from the Parkway) for the 7 mile trip. Take out in Groveton at the Firemans Park next to the State Route 51 bridge; it is on the right side of the river. Shuttle via State Routes 60 and Interstate 79.

*Gauges:* A Randy Carter gauge has been painted on the upstream side of the Beaver Grade Road bridge. At zero, it is a minimum level with some scraping, at 0 to 1 feet it is a good clean swift run, and at 1 to 2 feet it is a fast, sometimes pushy creek.

*Normal Wet Period:* No available statistics on seasons. Since this section is tiny, it should normally be runnable only after a heavy rain or during spring snowmelt.

# Chartiers Creek

## A. Washington, Pa to Van Emman          13.7 miles

| Class | Grad | Size (Area/Volume) | Scene/Poll | Level |
|-------|------|--------------------|-------------|--------|
| | 7/13 | Small (60/100) | B-D/C | |
| | | estimated | | Washington |

*Topographic Maps:* Washington West, Washington East, Canonsburg

*County Maps:* Washington

*Description:* This section has not been run at this time. Beginning west of Washington the creek meanders northeast, paralleling Interstate 79, past the Meadowlands Race Track and through Canonsburg. It appears, from the topographic map, to be a largely industrialized and developed section.

*Difficulties:* There is reported to be a 4-foot dam in Canonsburg, which must be portaged. In some areas the stream bed was relocated during the construction of Interstate 79. There may be various man-made hazards.

*Shuttle:* Put in where Henderson Avenue (State Route 18) crosses the creek south of Washington. Take US Route 19 north from Washington to the Donaldson's Crossroads. Turn left/west at the light onto State Route 1002. Go 0.6 miles and turn left/west when the road bends sharply right continuing on State Route 1002. Go 0.1 miles and cross Little Chartiers Creek just downstream of the Canonsburg Dam. Continue for about 0.2 miles and turn right/north on a side road that immediately crosses the creek. This is a suggested take-out based on the topographic map. Another possibility from the map would be about a mile further upstream where old State Route 51 crosses the creek.

*Gauges:* We do not have enough information to report runnable levels on this section.

*Normal Wet Period:* No available statistics on seasons. Since this section is small, it should normally be runnable approximately January through April.

## B. Van Emman to Kirwan Heights          15.0 miles

| Class | Grad | Size (Area / Volume) | Scene / Poll | Level |
|-------|------|----------------------|--------------|-------|
| I-II  | 8/11 | Med (200/333)        | B-C/C        |       |
|       |      | estimated            |              |       |

*Topographic Maps:* Canonsburg, Bridgeville

*County Maps:* Washington, Allegheny

*Description:* The first 3 miles of this section is rural with farms, countryside and wooded banks. Meandering northward, the stream loops around Mayville State Hospital and around Bridgeville before the take-out at Kirwan Heights. [Checked 1990]

*Difficulties:* In Bridgeville, a section of stream has been channelized with concrete banks and bottom which causes a stretch of large haystacks (standing waves) to form.

After crossing Interstate 79 from east to west above Bridgeville, there is a four foot high dam. A fifteen foot diameter culvert on the right leads to a flood bypass which cuts off 2.5 miles of stream. This bypass is a shear walled trench excavated into rock with several drops and keepers. Do not take it. Because of the walls, once into this section you will be in it for the entire section, whether you are in or out of your canoe.

*Shuttle:* To reach the put-in, use the Canonsburg exit of Interstate 79. Go north on US Route 19 about 2 miles to Donaldson's Crossroads; turn west/left onto State Route 1002. Go 0.5 mile to where the road crosses Little Chartiers Creek just below the Canonsburg Lake. Put in here and paddle the 100 yards to the junction with Chartiers Creek. To reach the take-out go back to Interstate 79 and go north. Take the Bridgeville exit over to State Route 50. At State Route 50 turn right/south and then take the next left (about 0.1 miles) onto Vanadium Road. Proceed 0.3 miles down the hill to the bridge crossing.

*Gauges:* We do not have enough information to report runnable levels on this section.

*Normal Wet Period:* No available statistics on seasons. Since this section is medium-sized, it should normally be runnable approximately December through May.

## C. Kirwan Heights to McKees Rocks          12.5 miles

| Class | Grad | Size (Area/Volume) | Scene/Poll | Level |
|-------|------|--------------------|-----------|-------|
|       | 6/10 | Medium (257/292)   | BC/C      |       |
|       |      | Carnegie           |           | Carnegie |

*Topographic Maps:* Bridgeville, Pittsburgh West

*County Maps:* Allegheny

*Description:* Not run at this time. Heading towards the Ohio, Chartiers Creek goes through Heidelburg, Carnegie, Rosslyn Farms, and Thornburg before heading through the Scully Railroad Yard and ending at McKees Rocks next to Brunot Island.

*Difficulties:* It is reported to be heavily channelized with concrete banks in areas. This is an industrialized area and there may be various man-made hazards.

*Shuttle:* To reach the put-in, take the Bridgeville exit on Interstate 79 over to State Route 50. Turn right/south onto State Route 50. Take the next left (about 0.1 mile) onto Vanadium Road. Proceed 0.3 miles down the hill to the bridge crossing. Since this is an unrun section you will have to find your own take-out in McKees Rocks.

*Gauges:* Carnegie. We do not have enough information to report runnable levels on this section. A reading of 1.6 feet on the Carnegie gauge corresponds to the mean flow of 292 cfs. Since this is a medium-sized river, we speculate that the river will be runnable at 1.6 feet and may be on the high side of runnable at that level.

*Normal Wet Period:* No available statistics on seasons. Since this section is medium-sized, it should normally be runnable approximately December through May.

# Allegheny River Watershed

137

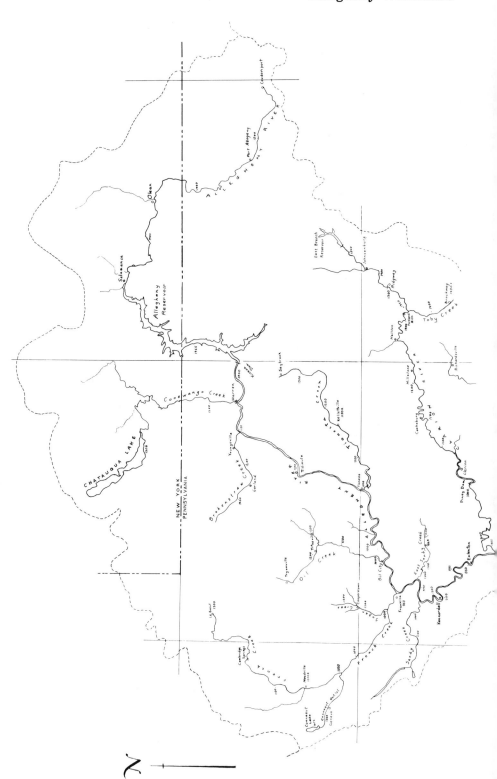

# Allegheny River

## A. Coudersport to Salamanca                        78 miles

| Class | Grad | Size (Area/Volume) | Scene/Poll. | Level |
|-------|------|--------------------|-------------|-------|
| A | 3/11 | Medium (248/464) | A-B/A-B | 3.0-?? |
| | | Port Allegany | | Port Allegany |
| | | Medium (550/936) Eldred | | |
| | | Large (1,608/2,777) Salamanca | | |

*Topographic Maps:* Coudersport, Austin, Roulette, Port Allegany, Bullis Mills, Eldred, Portville (NY), Olean (NY), Knapp Creek (NY), Limestone (NY), Salamanca (NY)

*County Maps:* Potter, McKean, Cattaraugus (NY)

*Description:* At Coudersport, the river is about 15 feet wide, and access is limited by sheer concrete channel walls. The trip from Coudersport to Olean (56 miles) is a scenic run through rural flat country. There are good camping sites all along this stretch. The backwater of the dam fluctuates, but it will usually start a little below Salamanca. Coudersport to Port Allegany is a good trout stream. [Checked 1988]

*Shuttle:* State numbered highways run all along the river; use a road map.

*Gauges:* Port Allegany. This gauge should read above 3.0 feet. This corresponds to a flow of 300 cfs. The Eldred gauge also on this section, should read above 4.6 feet.

*Normal Wet Period:* The Allegheny is normally canoeable downstream of Port Allegany until the end of May, and downstream of Olean until the middle of June.

# B. Salamanca to Kinzua Dam                  33 miles

| Class | Grad | Size (Area/Volume) | Scene/Poll | Level |
|-------|------|--------------------|-----------|-------|
| A | lake | Large (1,608/2,777) Salamanca | A-B/A-B | 4.0-?? Salamanca |
| | | Large (2,180/3,770) Kinzua | | |

*Topographic Maps:* Salamanca (NY), Little Valley (NY), Red House (NY), Steamburg (NY), Cornplanter Run, Cornplanter Bridge, Clarendon

*County Maps:* Cattaraugus (NY), McKean, Warren

*Other Maps:* A map of the reservoir showing camping facilities, access points, etc. is available free from the Corps of Engineers, District Engineer, Pittsburgh District, Federal Building, 1000 Liberty Avenue, Pittsburgh, Pennsylvania 15222.

*Description:* The Allegheny Reservoir, about 30 to 35 miles long, offers pleasant flatwater canoeing with a number of developed campsites for use by boaters. [Checked 1988]

*Shuttle:* State numbered highways run all along the river; use a road map or get a National Forest map from Allegheny National Forest Headquarters, Warren, Pennsylvania 16365.

*Gauges:* Salamanca. This gauge should read above 4.0 feet. This corresponds to a flow of 1,639 cfs. This is for the upper reaches of this section. The lower reaches are in the lake and therefore no gauge is necessary.

*Normal Wet Period:* The Allegheny Reservoir is canoeable all year round.

# C. Kinzua Dam to West Monterey                    120 miles

*Class  Grad*    *Size (Area / Volume)*    *Scene / Poll  Level*
  B      3/3     Large (3,660/6,442)       A-B/A-B   1.7-4.9
                 West Hickory                        Franklin
                 Large (5,982/10,550) Franklin
                 Large (7,671/13,090) Parker

*Topographic Maps:* Clarendon, Warren, Youngsville, Cobham, Tidioute, West Hickory, Tionesta, President, Oil City, Franklin, Kennerdell, Eau Claire, Emlenton, Parker

*County Maps:* Warren, Forest, Venango, Butler, Clarion, Armstrong

*Other Maps:* A brochure called *Allegheny River Access Sites* covering this section of the river is available from the Western Pennsylvania Conservancy, 316 Fourth Avenue, Pittsburgh, Pennsylvania 15222. Access points are also shown on the *Pennsylvania Fishing and Boating Map* published by the Pennsylvania Fish Commission and Pennsylvania Department of Transportation.

*Description:* The size of the Allegheny and the constant release of water from the dam make the river canoeable all year round. Scenery on this entire stretch of the Allegheny is generally pleasant and rural with mostly small towns and many clusters of vacation cottages. The stretch from Oil City to Franklin is somewhat less attractive than the rest because of the nearness of the highway and the refinery at Reno. The Western Pennsylvania Conservancy has a more detailed description of a trip from Franklin to Kennerdell. [Reported 1988]

*Camping:* Camping is possible on many of the islands of the upper Allegheny, at the Forest Service Buckaloons Campground, and at some commercial campgrounds. Island camping is primitive and campers should be prepared to bury human wastes so that late summer users of the islands do not find offensive conditions. Campgrounds offer flush toilets and some have showers.

*Liveries:* Several liveries along the upper Allegheny offer canoe rental and shuttles for paddlers without equipment.

Their location as of 1988 has been shown in the list below. They may also be willing to accommodate the launch/take-out of a private trip, or to arrange a shuttle for you.

*Difficulties:*  The only real rapid on the Allegheny is the 0.2 mile stretch (Class II) between the two highway bridges in Oil City.  The river drops several feet here, causing very fast water.  When the river is high, this fast water forms large standing waves that could swamp a heavily loaded canoe; in low water, the channel narrows to the left and runs through a partially submerged rock garden of boulders at a fast clip.  Inexperienced canoeists and those with heavily loaded boats should stop and scout (along the left bank). Lining is easiest along the right bank.

*Shuttle:* Numerous public access points have been established for the use of boaters and fishermen; The following established access points are available.

| Location | Owner / Operator | River mile |
|---|---|---|
| Kinzua Dam | Corps of Engr | 197 Left |
| Allegheny Outfitters | Commercial | 189 Right |
| (814) 723-1203 | | |
| Clifford Betts Park | Warren Boro | 187 Right |
| Crescent Park | Warren Boro | 188 Right |
| Starbrick | Pa Fish Comm | 185 Right |
| Buckaloons | All. Nat. Forest | 181 Right |
| (814) 968-3232 | | |
| Cloverleaf Camp | Commercial | 174 Left |
| (814) 484-3353 | | |
| Conklin Run | Pa Game Comm | 174 Right (1) |
| Indian Waters Livery | Commercial | 172 Left |
| (814) 484-3252 | | |
| Perry Magee Run | Pa Game Comm | 171 Right |
| Bonnie Brae | Pa Fish Comm | 169 Left |
| Tidioute | Tidioute Boro | 167 Right |
| West Hickory | Pa Fish Comm | 158 Left |
| Eagle Rock Campground | Livery | 153 Left |
| (814) 755-4444 | | |
| Indian Valley Campground | Livery | 153 Right |
| (814) 755-3578 | | |
| Tionesta | Pa Fish Comm | 153 Left |
| Tionesta Island | Private | 152 Left (2) |
| President | Semi-public | 145 Left (3) |
| President Campground | Commercial | 144 Left |
| (814) 679-2935 | | |
| Oil City | Pa Fish Comm | 130 Left (4) |
| Hallstown Marine | Commercial | (5) |
| (814) 432-3449 | | |
| Franklin | Pa Fish Comm | 123 Right (6) |
| Fisherman's Cove | Pa Fish Comm | 114 Right |
| Kennerdell | Private | 108 Left |
| Emlenton (5th St) | Emlenton Boro | 90 Left |
| Emlenton (6th St) | Emlenton Boro | 90 Left |
| Parker Bridge | Redevelop. Auth | 83 Right |
| Parker | Parker Boro | 83 Right |
| West Monterey | Semi-public | 79 Left (3) |

(1) (2) (3) (4) (5) (6) see notes on next page

(1) Undeveloped, no markings, minimum parking.

(2) Turn at highland street in Tionesta, ramp on right on island.

(3) The access points at President and West Monterey are "semi-public", and boaters should exercise special courtesy toward the residents when parking cars, changing clothes, etc. The ramp at President is right at the door of the church; don't disturb the services.

(4) There is a paved bike trail between Oil City and Franklin (1990). Plans are to extend it further downstream.

(5) Hallstown Marine is not directly on the Allegheny, but is upstream on French Creek.

(6) Park on side street downstream of State Route 322 bridge.

*Gauges:* Franklin. This gauge should read between 1.7 and 4.9 feet. This corresponds to a flow of 510 cfs to 8,300 cfs. The Kinzua gauge at the head of this section should read between 7.5 and 8.5 feet. This corresponds to a flow of 600 cfs to 2,350 cfs.

*Normal Wet Period:* Since this section of the river is dam controlled and two of the purposes of the Kinzua Dam is low flow augmentation and flood control this section is virtually never too low; however, it is periodically too high. The Franklin gauge is above 1.7 feet 99% of the time and above 4.9 feet 38% of the time.

# D. West Monterey to Pittsburgh                    79 miles

| Class | Grad | Size (Area / Volume) | Scene / Poll | Level |
|-------|------|---------------------|--------------|-------|
| A | Pool | Huge (8,389/13,290) | B-D/B-C | |
| | | Rimer | | Natrona |
| | | Huge (8,973/15,490) Kittanning | | |
| | | Huge (11,410/19,670) Natrona | | |

*Topographic Maps:* Parker, Rimersburg, East Brady, Templeton, Mosgrove, Kittanning, Leechburg, Freeport, New Kensington East, New Kensington West, Braddock, Pittsburgh East, Pittsburgh West

*County Maps:* Armstrong, Allegheny

*Other Maps:* A set of detailed navigation charts is available for $6.00 from the District Engineer, Pittsburgh District Corps of Engineers, Federal Building, 1000 Liberty Ave., Pittsburgh, Pennsylvania 15222. A brochure coving this stretch of the river is also available from the Western Pennsylvania Conservancy, 316 Fourth Avenue, Pittsburgh, Pennsylvania 15222.

*Description:* This section of the Allegheny, although closer to Pittsburgh, is generally less attractive for canoeing than the upper reaches; both the scenery and the water quality deteriorate as you approach the city, and the lack of any helpful current means that progress will be slower, especially with head winds. The Allegheny is held back in flat pools by eight dams with locks, to allow the passage of commercial barge traffic. Scenery is mostly B down to Freeport; below that the Allegheny is mostly an industrial river. The Western Pennsylvania Conservancy has a more detailed description of a trip starting and ending at the Deer Creek Access and circling Twelve Mile and Fourteen Mile Islands. See address above. In the Oakmont area and around Herrs Island you can sometimes see rowers in their narrow boats with the long oars. [Reported 1989]

*Difficulties:* Be sure you know where the dams are; they are fatally dangerous from either the upstream or downstream side, and it's easy to miss noticing them from upstream. To pass through a lock, approach it close to shore and keep clear of large boats to give them room to maneuver. Have a 50-foot line available in each boat and follow the lockmaster's instructions. See more detailed instructions for lock passage under the write-up for the Ohio River.

Barges are moving faster than they look, sometimes almost silently. Keep clear of large boats. They need lots of room to maneuver. Stay clear not only of the physical barge itself, but also of the very turbulent wake created by the push-boat. These boats not only make wake out the back, but some also have additional propellers pointed sideways, so that the wake may come straight out the side.

Power boaters are also a hazard in this section.

*Shuttle:* The charts mentioned above, as well as the topographic maps, show the navigable parts of the rivers labeled with the mileage from the Point at Pittsburgh. Access points and dams on this section of the Allegheny are listed on the next page with their mile numbers.

*Gauge:* Kittanning, Natrona, Acmetonia

*Normal Wet Period:* This section of the river is used commercially by barges, and is dam controlled. The Corps of Engineers operates its dams on the principal of low flow augmentation and flood control, this section is never too low to canoe. There are times when it is too high.

| Location,Owner/Maintainer | | River mile |
|---|---|---|
| West Monterey | | 79.0 Left |
| Limit of Navigation (9-foot depth) | | 71.9 |
| East Brady | Pa Fish Comm | 69.5 Right |
| mouth of Red Bank Creek, Pa Fish Comm | | 64.0 Left (1) |
| Lock and Dam # 9 | | 62.2 Left |
| Rimer | | 60.1 Left |
| mouth of Mahoning Creek, Private | | 55.4 Left |
| Templeton | Pa Fish Comm | 54.5 Left |
| Lock and Dam # 8 | | 52.6 Left |
| Mosgrove (mouth of Pine Creek), private | | 50.8 Left |
| mouth of Cowanshannock, Pa Fish Comm | | 48.5 Left |
| Lock and Dam # 7 | | 45.7 Right |
| Kittanning ramp | Kittanning Muni | 44.8 Left |
| Applewood, Pa Fish Comm | | 43.9 Right |
| Manorville,Manorville Twp | | 43.0 Left |
| Rosston (mouth of Crooked Creek) | | |
| | Pa Fish Comm | 40.1 Left |
| Lock and Dam # 6 | | 36.3 Right |
| Clinton, abandoned ferry road | | 34.4 Left and Right |
| Lock and Dam # 5 | | 30.4 Right |
| Freeport ramp | Freeport Boro | 29.1 Right |
| Lock and Dam # 4 | | 24.2 Right |
| Tarentum | Tarentum Boro | 21.8 Left |
| Tarentum ramp | Pa Fish Comm | 21.7 Left |
| Springdale east ramp | | 17.5 Right |
| Springdale west ramp | Pa Fish Comm | 16.4 Right |
| Lock and Dam # 3 | | 14.5 Left |
| Harmarville ramp | Pa Fish Comm | 13.2 Right |
| Oakmont ramp | Oakmont Boro | 12.0 Left |
| Lock and Dam # 2 | | 6.6 Left |
| Tenth Street Wharf | | 0.2 Left (3) |
| Clemente Park | City of Pittsburgh | 0.1 Right |
| Point Park | State Park | 0.0 Left (2,3) |

(1) Access not recommended. See write up on the Red Bank Creek

(2) Has five to ten foot vertical walls

(3) No automobile access near the water edge within the state park.

# Pine Creek
# (Allegheny County)

## A. North Park Lake to Allison Park          6.6 miles

| Class | Grad | Size (Area/Volume) | Scene/Poll | Level |
|-------|------|--------------------|------------|-------|
| C-I | 7/26 | Tiny (45/75) estimate | C/B-C | |

*Topographic Maps:* Glenshaw

*County Maps:* Allegheny

*Description:* If it were not for the trash in the creek bed, the occasional water treatment plant and the Wildwood Mine, this would be a pretty run. Except for the last mile or two, it is reasonably remote, often running at the base of a high cliff. It is flowing water with riffles and small ledges. [Checked 1981]

*Difficulties:* In 1981 there was a 3-foot dam at Wildwood Mine/Country Club. If there is enough water, the spillway is runnable in a kayak, but it is too narrow for an open canoe.

*Shuttle:* Wildwood Road parallels Pine Creek below the spillway from North Park Lake. Choose your put-in. The easy take-out is across from the ballfield on Duncan Avenue in Allison Park.

*Gauges:* None.

*Normal Wet Period:* No available statistics on seasons. Since this section is tiny, it should normally be runnable only after a heavy rain or during spring snowmelt.

# B. Allison Park to Etna                       6.5 miles

*Class  Grad     Size (Area / Volume)      Scene / Poll   Level*
I-II    5/16      Small (67/112)            D/C
                  Etna

*Topographic Maps:* Glenshaw

*County Maps:* Allegheny

*Description:*  This is a fine stream for a study of the construction and maintenance of retaining walls. [Checked 1981]

*Difficulties:*  The run is basically Class I but it also has five Class II double ledges, all of which deserve respect, especially from beginners.  The first two are between Burchfield Road (near Kitchen Fair) and the lumber yard. They are not hard for paddlers with Class II experience, but beginners should exercise caution.  The third is at the Glenshaw Glass plant just downstream from the State Route 8 bridge.  This is a man-made dam or weir with a drop of 3 to 4 feet.  Scout from the left bank.  Much more intimidating is the recent blasted cutoff channel across the road from the Shaler (K-mart) Plaza in Etna.  This is a very steep and jagged drop of about 10 feet.  It is visible from the highway and should be scouted from the Burger King parking lot.  Note the four foot culvert diverting some of the main flow through the levee at the same spot.  There are also a few fallen trees.

*Shuttle:*  Put in at the ball field in Allison Park, access off Duncan Avenue.  Follow State Route 8 south to a take-out at the parking lot behind Pantone Auto Parts store and warehouse.

*Gauges:*  None.

*Normal Wet Period:*  No available statistics on seasons. Since this section is tiny, it should normally be runnable only after a heavy rain or during spring snowmelt.

# Deer Creek

## State Route 910 to Little Deer Creek            8.0 miles

| Class | Grad | Size (Area/Volume) | Scene/Poll | Level |
|-------|------|--------------------|------------|-------|
| I | 9/26 | Tiny (51/85) | C/B-C | |
| | | Harmarville | | Streamside |

*Topographic Maps:* New Kensington West, Glenshaw

*County Maps:* Allegheny

*Description:* A run which could be pretty if it were not so close to town. It is an interesting run, if you can ignore the civilization. The creek winds from level plain, against tall cliffs, through a golf course and camp, into the industrial suburbs of Harmarville. [Reported 1975]

*Difficulties:* Watch for fallen trees. There are also civilized hazards such as dead washing machines and old tires. Toward Harmarville it becomes more industrialized.

*Shuttle:* Put in at the strip mine north of Dorseyville. Use State Route 910 and Rich Hill Road. Take out at the mouth of Little Deer Creek on Rich Hill Road.

*Gauges:* Lower, enlarged section of piers of the bridge from State Route 910 to the tank farm should be covered by water. The bridge is near Indianola.

*Normal Wet Period:* No available statistics on seasons. Since this section is tiny, it should normally be runnable only after a heavy rain or during spring snowmelt.

# Buffalo Creek
# (Armstrong County)

## A. Worthington to West Winfield                 8.5 miles

| Class | Grad | Size (Area/Volume) | Scene/Poll | Level |
|-------|------|--------------------|------------|-------|
| I-II  | 12/22 | Small (90/150) estimate | A-B/A-B | 1.6-2.6 Freeport |

*Topographic Maps:* Worthington

*County Maps:* Armstrong, Butler

*Description:* This is a pretty stream not far from Pittsburgh, making it somewhat of an oddity. This upper section can be run only in higher-than-average spring runoff. It requires more skill than the lower section. [Checked 1990]

*Difficulties:* In 1989 a low dam was built just above the first bridge, which is about 2 miles below Worthington and just upstream of Shadyside Village. This dam is just downstream of the mural-decorated sportman's club. Carry around the dam. Below here there are three Class II drops. The first is 0.2 miles below the church camp. The second is just above the new (1986) concrete bridge about 3 miles further downstream. The third is 0.5 miles further downstream, where the river abruptly squeezes into a narrow channel on river right. There are often trees down in the river, especially near the church camp.

*Shuttle:* Use Wilson Road; leaving the river at Shadyside village (Buffalo Creek), climb out of the valley on the west side (river right). Go south 2 miles, cross the Blaine Bridge, go another mile. Turn right/west, go 1.5 miles to reach West Winfield; turning left/east takes you to Slate Lick, from where the further-down access points can be reached. To eliminate a couple of miles of flatwater put in at Shadyside Village downstream of the mural-decorated sportsman's club, and just below the dam . Alternately, you can stretch the trip by about 3 miles by taking out at Boggsville Bridge on US Route 228. The Boggsville take-out is on the left side about 100 feet downstream of the bridge.

*Gauges:* Freeport. This gauge should read between 1.6 and 2.6 feet. This corresponds to a flow of 105 cfs to 505 cfs. This Corps of Engineer gauge is not currently available on a daily basis, but the Corps has said that it is scheduled to be updated the summer of 1989 and daily readings should be available.

*Normal Wet Period:* This section is normally runnable from early January through mid May, and does not have a season when it is too high. The Freeport gauge is above 1.6 feet 45% of the time and above 2.6 feet 8% of the time.

## B. West Winfield to Freeport               11.0 miles

| Class | Grad | Size (Area / Volume) | Scene / Poll | Level |
|-------|------|----------------------|--------------|-------|
| I | 10/10 | Small(137/194) | B/B | 1.7-2.8 |
|   |       | Freeport |  | Freeport |

*Topographic Maps:* Worthington, Freeport

*County Maps:* Butler, Armstrong

*Description:* This section is neither as pretty nor as difficult as the upper section. On the lower 6 miles of this section, most of the land on both sides is posted. You will not be permitted to leave your boat. [Checked 1989]

*Difficulties:* After you pass a one-lane bridge about 0.75 miles below Boggsville, there are some old bridge piers on which driftwood may pile up, partially blocking passage for canoes.

*Shuttle:* To get to the take-out from West Winfield, proceed to State Route 28 at Slate Lick. Go south and exit at State Route 356. Turn left/east toward Freeport. At the bottom of the hill, turn left rather than cross the bridge. Bear right onto Mill Road and take out at an old flour mill a few hundred yards downstream from the brick kilns on the left bank. Or, you can paddle out into the Allegheny and go upstream to the municipal launching ramp. You can shorten the trip by putting in at Boggsville, on river left below the bridge. There are bridges at the intermediate villages of Boggsville and Iron Bridge, but you may be hassled by the local residents who appear to have been abused by boaters and fishermen in the past.

*Gauges:* Freeport. This gauge should read between 1.7 and 2.8 feet. This corresponds to a flow of 129 cfs to 624 cfs. This Corps of Engineer gauge is not currently available on a daily basis, but the Corps has said that it is scheduled to be updated the summer of 1989 and daily readings should be available.

*Normal Wet Period:* This section is normally runnable from early January through mid May, and does not have a season when it is too high. The Freeport gauge is above 1.7 feet 40% of the time and above 2.8 feet 6% of the time.

# Kiskiminetas River

## A. Saltsburg to Salina                    6.7 miles

| Class | Grad | Size (Area/Volume) | Scene/Poll | Level |
|-------|------|--------------------|-----------|-------|
| B | 6/6 | Large (1,723/2,872) Avonmore | B/B | 3.5-8.0 Vandergrift |

*Topographic Maps:* Saltsburg, Avonmore

*County Maps:* Indiana, Armstrong, Westmoreland

*Description:* This is a pretty stretch of river running between wooded hills. Pollution from mine acid has been reduced, but is still a factor. [Reported 1988]

*Difficulties:* None

*Shuttle:* In Saltsburg, put in where State Route 981 crosses Loyalhanna Creek a few yards from where it joins the Conemaugh to form the Kiskiminetas. Alternatively, put in on the Kiskiminetas on river right just upstream from the new bridge. Take out at Salina on river right just upstream of town. Intermediate access is available at the Avonmore Bridge, upstream on river right. A good one-day trip can be taken by adding the 6.9 miles of the Conemaugh River. Put in just below the flood control dam and take out at Salina. At Salina, take out on the right, somewhat upstream of town.

*Gauges:* Vandergrift. This gauge should read between 3.5 and 8.0 feet. This corresponds to a flow of 700 cfs to 6,700 cfs. The Tunnelton gauge on nearby Conemaugh River will probably read between 3.0 and 6.7 feet.

*Normal Wet Period:* This section is normally runnable from early November through mid August, and it does not have a too high season. The Vandergrift gauge is above 3.5 feet 77% of the time and above 8.0 feet 11% of the time.

# B. Salina to Freeport                    21.0 miles

| Class | Grad | Size (Area / Volume) | Scene / Poll | Level |
|-------|------|----------------------|--------------|-------|
| B | 3/3 | Large (1,825/3,106) | C/B | 3.0-6.7 |
|   |     | Vandergrift |   | Tunnelton |

*Topographic Maps:* Avonmore, Vandergrift, Leechburg, Freeport

*County Maps:* Armstrong, Westmoreland

*Description:* Coal mines dot the east bank from Salina to Apollo, where the scenery becomes industrial. Problems with sewage pollution have been controlled, but mine acid is still noticeable, though much reduced from earlier years. The last 2 miles are in the backwater of the Allegheny. To reach the take-out in Freeport, paddle across the Allegheny, then 1 mile downstream. [Checked 1987]

*Difficulties:* Watch out for power boat traffic on the Allegheny. Just above the mouth, on the Allegheny River is Lock and Dam #5. Stay well clear of the backwash.

*Shuttle:* At Salina, put in on the right just upstream of town. From Salina, head northwest on State Route 819 to Oklahoma (opposite Apollo), then west about 1 mile on State Route 4034. Turn north on State Route 356 for about 10 miles and cross the Allegheny into Freeport. The municipal ramp is 0.5 miles upstream from the bridge. Intermediate access is available at Apollo on river right, just downstream of the State Route 66 bridge, behind the senior citizens' highrise. There is also access at Leechburg on river right downstream of the highway bridge, near the shopping center.

*Gauges:* Vandergrift. We do not have enough information to report runnable levels on this section. A reading of 5.8 feet on this gauge corresponds to the mean flow of 3,106 cfs. Since this is a large size river, we speculate that the river is runnable most of the year; at 5.8 feet it may be too high. The Tunnelton gauge on nearby Conemaugh River will probably read between 3.0 and 6.7 feet.

*Normal Wet Period:* No available statistics on seasons. Since this section is large, it should normally be runnable all year, but it may be too high from February to April.

# Loyalhanna Creek

## A. Rector to Ligonier                    4.9 miles

| Class | Grad | Size (Area / Volume) | Scene / Poll | Level |
|-------|------|----------------------|--------------|-------|
| II | 8/20 | Small (70/117) estimate | B/A | 4.5-5.3 Kingston |

*Topographic Maps:* Ligonier

*County Maps:* Westmoreland

*Description:* The first 2 miles are very narrow with downed trees. This section has excellent scenery through Rolling Rock Farms. The lower 3 miles are lined with cottages. [Reported 1980]

*Difficulties:* Downed trees.

*Shuttle:* Put in at the State Route 381 bridge near Rector. Shuttle on State Route 381 and US Route 30. Take out by the State Route 711 bridge at Ligonier.

*Gauges:* Kingston. This gauge should read between 4.5 and 5.3 feet. This corresponds to a flow of 1,040 cfs to 1,770 cfs.

*Normal Wet Period:* This section does not have a normally runnable season nor a normally too high season. The Kingston gauge is above 4.5 feet 5% of the time and above 5.3 feet 2% of the time.

# B. Ligonier to Kingston Dam                    6.9 miles

| Class | Grad | Size (Area/Volume) | Scene/Poll | Level |
|-------|------|--------------------|------------|-------|
| II | 18/50 | Small (120/200) | C/A | 3.2-5.3 |
| | | Kingston | | Kingston |

*Topographic Maps:* Ligonier, Stahlstown, Derry

*County Maps:* Westmoreland

*Description:* This is an excellent spring and autumn whitewater stream. The difficulty of this run does not vary too much with water level changes. At low levels, there is much maneuvering. At higher levels, there is less maneuvering, but faster water and larger standing waves. The stream roughly parallels US Route 30. It passes through Story Book Forest, Idlewild Park, and along many summer homes. At Kingston Dam the shores are industrialized. [Checked 1990]

*Difficulties:* There are two high ledges that should be scouted and a low-water bridge which must be portaged. The low water bridge at high levels of water acts like a dam with a recirculating hydraulic.

*Shuttle:* For the whitewater stretch, put in between Story Book Forest and Ligonier where the stream comes within 20 yards of US Route 30 (about 0.5 miles west of Ligonier). By putting in at Darlington (below Story Book Forest) a mile of slow water can be eliminated. Take out above Kingston Dam. Alternate put-ins are available at any of the several cross-roads above Story Book Forest.

*Gauges:* Kingston. This gauge should read between 3.2 and 5.3 feet. This corresponds to a flow of 315 cfs to 1,770 cfs. The dam where State Route 217 crosses US Route 30 can also be used as a local gauge. At low levels all of the water flows on the river right side of the dam and it is too low. At a minimum level the center and river left side of the dam will have just a small amount of water flowing over.

*Normal Wet Period:* This section is normally runnable from late December through late May and does not have a normally too high season. The Kingston gauge is above 3.2 feet 28% of the time and above 5.3 feet 2% of the time.

# C. Kingston Dam to Latrobe                          4.6 miles

| Class | Grad | Size (Area/Volume) | Scene/Poll | Level |
|-------|------|--------------------|------------|-------|
| I-II  | 9/15 | Small (172/303)    | B/A        | 3.4-5.0 |
|       |      | Kingston           |            | Kingston |

*Topographic Maps:* Derry, Latrobe

*County Maps:* Westmoreland

*Description:* Below the dam the stream runs between the east and west lanes of US Route 30 for about 0.5 miles before it leaves the main road. The stream is wide and winds through a series of lazy S turns. The bottom is generally rocky except for the slab rock that creates a river-wide 6-inch ledge about 0.5 miles past the first bridge. Used in conjunction with the pool above the dam and the last rapid above the pool, this section could be a good afternoon run for a solo open canoe school or a poling school. [Checked 1989]

*Difficulties:* Dam just above the put-in can be portaged. At high water levels, there are no eddies and two river-wide ledges produce hazardous hydraulics. Ledge under the railroad bridge at Legion-Keener Park should be run center or right.

*Shuttle:* Put in on the westbound side of US Route 30 below the dam at Kingston. Go west on US Route 30 to State Route 982 North. Cross the bridge. This is the second bridge crossing the stream and is a good alternate. The take-out is in Legion-Keener Park on Spring Street. Follow signs in downtown Latrobe to the stadium.

*Gauges:* Kingston. This gauge should read between 3.4 and 5.0 feet. This corresponds to a flow of 380 cfs to 1,470 cfs. The dam where State Route 217 crosses US Route 30 can also be used as a local gauge. At low levels all of the water flows on the river right side of the dam and it is too low. At a minimum level the center and river left side of the dam will have just a small amount of water flowing over.

*Normal Wet Period:* This section is normally runnable from late December through late May and does not have a normally too high season. The Kingston gauge is above 3.4 feet 23% of the time and above 5.0 feet 3% of the time.

# D. Latrobe to New Alexandria                          12 miles

*Class   Grad    Size (Area / Volume)    Scene / Poll   Level*
B-I      3/8     Medium (265/439)        C/D
                 New Alexandria                        Kingston

*Topographic Maps:* Latrobe, Saltsburg

*County Maps:* Westmoreland

*Description:* This section below Latrobe is entirely within the boundary limits of the Loyalhanna Reservoir flood control project, and as such is subject to water backed up from the lake below New Alexandria. However, except for extreme flooding, water rarely backs up beyond the last bridge above New Alexandria. The stream is essentially flat and contained by flood control levees until the third bridge (below the brewery). Below here the stream flows among wooded hills marred only by a few homes and one reclaimed strip mine. Below the piers of an old bridge (fourth bridge) there is a boulder section of no special difficulty but good playing for beginners. Plan your take-out according to reservoir level and beware of mud banks in New Alexandria. [Reported 1988]

*Difficulties:* New Alexandria mud banks. This mud is thick and not very solid. You will sink into it and will have to pull your feet out with each step.

*Shuttle:* Put in at Latrobe's Legion-Keener Park on Spring Street or at the Rolling Rock brewery or the third bridge. Shuttle on State Route 981 and take out at the site of the old bridge upstream of the present US Route 22 bridge. There is now a boat launching ramp on river left. One could continue downstream to the bridge 2 miles upstream of New Alexandria.

*Gauges:* Kingston. We do not have enough information to report runnable levels on this section. Readings comparable to the section above would be a good guess.

*Normal Wet Period:* No available statistics on seasons. Since this section is medium-sized, it should normally be runnable approximately December through May.

# E. Loyalhanna Dam to Saltsburg                     4.0 miles

| Class | Grad  | Size (Area / Volume)              | Scene / Poll | Level      |
|-------|-------|-----------------------------------|--------------|------------|
| B-I   | 10/15 | Medium (292/481)<br>Loyalhanna Dam | B/B          | Loyalhanna |

*Topographic Maps:* Saltsburg

*County Maps:* Westmoreland

*Description:* This section depends on water release from Loyalhanna Dam. The run starts in a minor wooded canyon and joins the Conemaugh among farm fields. [Reported 1980]

*Difficulties:* None.

*Shuttle:* Put in at bridge on access road to Loyalhanna Dam from State Route 981. Take out in Saltsburg across from the mouth of the Loyalhanna.

*Gauges:* Loyalhanna Dam Outflow. We do not have enough information to report runnable levels on this section. A reading of 2.1 feet on this gauge corresponds to the mean flow of 481 cfs. Since this is a medium-sized river, we speculate that the river will be runnable at 2.1 feet and may be on the high side of runnable at that level.

*Normal Wet Period:* Dam controlled.

# Crabtree Creek

## Crabtree                                          4.0 miles
## to New Alexandria (Loyalhanna Creek)

| Class | Grad | Size (Area / Volume) | Scene / Poll | Level |
|-------|------|----------------------|--------------|-------|
| II    | 9/25 | Tiny (19/32)         | B/B          |       |
|       |      | Shieldsburg          |              |       |

*Topographic Maps:* Latrobe, Saltsburg

*County Maps:* Westmoreland

*Description:* This is a tiny stream piercing a minor canyon to join Loyalhanna Creek. The gradient and character is fast and uniform for the 2.0 mile run from the put-in to Loyalhanna Creek. The last 2.0 miles are on Loyalhanna Creek, which is normally in near-flood when Crabtree Creek is runnable. [Reported 1980]

*Difficulties:* Trees, low bridge at mid-run, and mud banks at the take-out in New Alexandria.

*Shuttle:* Put in on a side road about 1 mile from US Route 119 in Crabtree (Turn off US Route 119 at Carbone's Restaurant). Shuttle on US Route 119 to US Route 22 at New Alexandria. Take out at the site of the old bridge upstream of the present US Route 22 bridge.

*Gauges:* None. The Kingston gauge downstream on Loyalhanna Creek will probably be above 4.5 feet.

*Normal Wet Period:* No available statistics on seasons. Since this section is tiny, it should normally be runnable only after a heavy rain or during spring snowmelt.

# Fourmile Run

## State Route 130 to Darlington 10.0 miles

| Class | Grad | Size (Area/Volume) | Scene/Poll | Level |
|-------|------|--------------------|------------|-------|
| 1.8mileIII-IV | 28/80 | Tiny (39/65) | B/A | |
| 8.2mileI-II | | Darlington | | |

*Topographic Maps:* Stahlstown, Derry

*County Maps:* Westmoreland

*Description:* This heavily used trout stream is receiving increased pressure from permanent and summer home sites. Roughly the first third of the trip, above Bethel Church Road (State Route 2033), is a delightful mountain stream, cutting steeply through a wooded gorge with mixed softwood and hemlock cover. At low water levels this portion of the trip is a technical Class III, with almost continuous maneuvering to avoid shoals and get positioned for the runnable chutes in the small ledges; one significantly steeper section is mentioned below. At higher water levels this upper section becomes continuous Class IV with complex cross currents.

Below Bethel Church Road, it's a pleasant valley stream, passing behind summer homes and over low ledges that dam up small pools for the summer homes; much of the run is in a valley formed as the stream cut through the ridge. About a mile below Bethel Church Road the stream braids through an island complex in many small channels, providing ample opportunity for trees to partly or completely block the channel and requiring short carries or Class II maneuvering by paddlers. Several tributaries enter near Jefferson School Road (State Route 2008), and the creek continues from there relatively unobstructed for the last 6.2 miles into Darlington. [Checked 1989]

*Difficulties:* Trees could block the creek almost anywhere in the upper half. Several cables (fences and remains of foot bridges) cross the creek near water level. The steepest section is next to the foundations of a former mill about a 0.2 miles upstream from the concrete bridge on Hoods Mill Road. (This bridge is 0.9 miles south (upstream) of the

intersection of Hoods Mill Road and Bethel Church Road.)
The gradient starts picking up as you approach the mill
race, culminating in a 4- to 5-foot sloping ledge beside the
ruins of the mill and a pair of smaller drops below. The mill
race is visible from both the creek and the road; it's easy to
scout on the shuttle since the road runs within 30 to 50 feet of
the river here.

*Shuttle:* Put in where Fourmile Run crosses under State
Route 130, west of Stahlstown. The shuttle route roughly
follows the stream on Hoods Mill Road (no state number),
Bethel Church Road (State Route 2033), Fourmile Run Road
(State Route 2037), and Darlington-Rector Road (State Route
2043). Take out at Idlewild Bridge near Darlington; this
bridge crosses Loyalhanna Creek about 100 yards below (and
well within sight of) the mouth of Fourmile Run. The
shuttle route runs close to the stream, and intermediate
access can be had at a number of bridges on or within sight
of the shuttle route or at a few places where the shuttle road
runs alongside the stream.

*Gauge:* There is no gauge on this creek. The Kingston
gauge downstream on Loyalhanna Creek will probably be
between 4.5 and 6.0 feet. Drive upstream from the take-out
and observe the level at bridges and along the roadside.
Minimum level for the upper third is reached when the
small rapids above and below the concrete bridge on Hoods
Mill Road (the bridge near the former mill site) are
runnable without scraping. A lake on Fourmile Run about
2 miles above the put-in may significantly affect flow on the
upper third, so Kingston may not be a reliable indicator.

*Normal Wet Period:* No available statistics on seasons.
Since this section is tiny, it should normally be runnable
only after a heavy rain or during spring snowmelt.

# Mill Creek
# (Westmoreland County)

## Waterford to Ligonier                                    5.0 miles

| Class | Grad | Size (Area / Volume) | Scene / Poll | Level |
|-------|------|----------------------|--------------|-------|
| II | 30/55 | Tiny (33/55) Ligonier | C/A | |

*Topographic Maps:* Wilpen, Ligonier, Stahlstown

*County Maps:* Westmoreland

*Description:* This is a small, meandering tree-lined stream draining the area just north of Ligonier. It flows in pastures and periodically makes a radical change in course which causes tree problems. From Waterford to Oak Grove the stream width permits trees to bridge the stream. The best of the run begins at State Route 711 below Oak Grove and continues to the mouth of the stream. [Reported 1990]

*Difficulties:* Major tree blockages possible near Oak Grove (behind the Buick garage) and on the outskirts of Ligonier.

*Shuttle:* Put in on State Route 271 at the downstream edge of Waterford. Shuttle State Route 271 to State Route 711 then US Route 30. Take out along US Route 30 near the Ligonier sewage treatment plant.

*Gauges:* None. The Kingston gauge downstream on Loyal-hanna Creek will probably read between 4.5 and 6.0 feet. There is also a staff gauge on US Route 30 on the downstream right pier. A reading of zero is plenty for the last half, minus 0.25 is okay.

*Normal Wet Period:* No available statistics on seasons. Since this section is tiny, it should normally be runnable only after a heavy rain or during spring snowmelt.

# Conemaugh River

## A. Johnstown to New Florence                12.9 miles

| Class | Grad | Size (Area / Volume) | Scene / Poll | Level |
|-------|------|----------------------|--------------|-------|
| I I | 7/11 | Medium (715/1,281) | A/B-C | 3.0-?? |
| | | Seward | | Seward |

*Topographic Maps:* Johnstown, Vintondale, New Florence

*County Maps:* Cambria, Indiana, Westmoreland

*Description:* This is a polluted river with pretty wooded hills. The river emerges from Johnstown's concrete flood channel into the glory of the Conemaugh gorge through Laurel Mountain. The presence of highways and railroads on both sides is easily ignored, but a major power line does detract from the beauty. [Reported 1982]

*Difficulties:* The river presents no difficulty through the gorge, but immediately at the end there is a Class II rapid past a mine dump on the right shore. Below this point the river returns to Class I. About 1.25 miles below Seward there is a power plant with a dam. Carry on the left. Note this is not the power plant in New Florence that is obvious from the road.

*Shuttle:* The put-in is an inclined ramp on Stony Creek near the junction with the Little Conemaugh. It is a short paddle to the main river. From the put-in take State Route 56 northwest to US Route 22. Go west to Clyde, turn right 100 feet beyond the Clyde volunteer fire department building, continue 3 miles to State Route 2008. Turn left for 100 yards then right on State Route 2009. Go a short distance (200 yards) across the railroad tracks to the concrete bridge crossing the river.

*Gauges:* Seward. This gauge should read above 3.0 feet. This corresponds to a flow of 1,080 cfs.

*Normal Wet Period:* This section is normally runnable from late February through late May. The Seward gauge is above 3.0 feet 35% of the time.

# B. New Florence to Torrance

13.0 miles

| Class | Grad | Size (Area/Volume) | Scene/Poll | Level |
|-------|------|--------------------|-----------|-------|
| I-III | 10/13 | Medium (715/1,281) | A-B/B | 2.4-4.0 |
| | | Seward | | Seward |

*Topographic Maps:* New Florence, Rachelwood, Wilpen, Bolivar

*County Maps:* Indiana, Westmoreland

*Description:* This section has wide open riffles and long quiet pools. The rapids are fairly continuous from Bolivar to Torrance. The remains of an old barge canal can be seen along the left shore as you cut through Chestnut Ridge. [Checked 1988]

*Difficulties:* There is one Class III rapid at the mouth of Richards Run, just above Bolivar. The rapid is at the end of a long sweeping 180 degree bend to the left. There is a mine portal on the right 200 yards above the rapid.

*Shuttle:* The put-in is on State Route 2009 in New Florence. To get to the take-out, follow State Route 217 south from State Route 27. Follow signs to Torrance State Hospital. Past the hospital, take the left to the river. Take out at the point where a pipeline bridge crosses the river. This is a Class III road in wet weather. An alternate take-out is on the other side of river about one mile further downstream in the town of Strangford. Follow US Route 22/119 from Blairsville and exit at the US Route 119 exit. Turn right and then right again along old US Route 22. In about 0.5 miles turn left onto Strangford Road. Park by a railroad culvert. To take out you will have to tow your boat through the large culvert and then carry about 150 feet to the road.

*Gauges:* Seward. This gauge should read between 2.4 and 4.0 feet. This corresponds to a flow of 365 cfs to 2,760 cfs.

*Normal Wet Period:* This section is normally runnable from mid November through early July and does not have a season when it is too high. The Seward gauge is above 2.4 feet 77% of the time and above 4.0 feet 10% of the time.

## C. Torrance to Conemaugh Dam                17.0 miles

| Class | Grad | Size (Area/Volume) | Scene/Poll | Level |
|-------|------|--------------------|------------|-------|
| A | flat | Medium (890/1,483) estimate | D/C | |

*Topographic Maps:* Bolivar, Blairsville

*County Maps:* Indiana, Westmoreland

*Description:* The backwaters of the flood control dam above Tunnelton are not good canoeing as the level is normally held low and considerable silt is exposed, leaving no access to the water. Mine acid pollution is quite noticeable on the lower Conemaugh and Kiskiminetas. [Reported 1989]

# D. Conemaugh Dam to Saltsburg          6.9 miles

| Class | Grad | Size (Area/Volume) | Scene/Poll | Level |
|-------|------|--------------------|-----------|-------|
| C | 6/6 | Large (1,358/2,882) Tunnelton | B/B | 3.0-6.7 Tunnelton |

*Topographic Maps:* Blairsville, Saltsburg

*County Maps:* Indiana, Westmoreland

*Description:*   This stream has wooded banks with a few farms. It is a wide stream as creeks in Western Pennsylvania go and offers pleasant canoeing. During the first mile you can hear the whine of a mine fan. Just upstream of the first bridge is a very visible junkyard.   [Reported 1990]

*Difficulties:* None.

*Shuttle:* The Corps of Engineers maintains a nice picnic area with restrooms at the dam. In 1990 they wanted you to check in at the office before putting in. After exiting from the office parking lot, turn left and drive past the maintenance building.   Continue downhill to the put-in under the old stone arch bridge just below the dam.   The park gate is locked in the evenings so park in a spot that will be unlocked when you return.   After leaving the park, go straight.  Turn right onto State Route 3003 and then turn left onto State Route 3002. Continue on State Route 3002 until it joins Point Street in Saltsburg.  Follow Point Street to the river.  The take-out is the short road which is designed for fire equipment access.  Do not park near the pipe.  This is just upstream of the bridge across the Kiskiminetas on river right.  A longer trip may be had by adding the 6.7 miles described under the Kiskiminetas River.

*Gauges:* Tunnelton.   This gauge should read between 3.0 and 6.7 feet. This corresponds to a flow of 720 cfs to 7,850 cfs.

*Normal Wet Period:* This section is normally runnable from mid November through late June and does not have a season when it is too high.

# Blacklick Creek

## A. Wehrum to Heshbon                        12.0 miles

| Class | Grad | Size (Area / Volume) | Scene / Poll | Level |
|-------|------|----------------------|--------------|-------|
| I-II  | 18/20 | Small (150/250) estimate | C-D/C | ??-4.1 Josephine |

*Topographic Maps:* Vintondale, New Florence

*County Maps:* Cambria, Indiana

*Description:* This trip has two rapids within sight of Heshbon. Otherwise it is flat flowing water. Both rapids are normally Class II. Scout from the take-out during shuttle. It is possible to carry and/or line from the beginning of the rapids to the take-out. [Checked 1988]

*Difficulties:* None.

*Shuttle:* Put in along State Route 2013 about 2.5 miles north of US Route 22. To get to the take-out, go south on State Route 2013. Turn west onto US Route 22. Go about 8 miles then turn north onto State Route 259. Go about 2.7 miles to the river crossing.

*Gauges:* Josephine. This gauge should read below 4.1 feet. This corresponds to a flow of 388 cfs.

*Normal Wet Period:* The Josephine gauge is above 4.1 feet 31% of the time.

# B. Heshbon to Josephine                                6.2 miles

*Class*  *Grad*    *Size (Area / Volume)*      *Scene / Poll*  *Level*

III-IV  26/66    Medium (195/370)         C-D/C    3.8-4.6
                 Josephine (above Two Lick)              Josephine

*Topographic Maps:* New Florence, Bolivar

*County Maps:* Indiana

*Description:* This river has been devastated by the 1977 flood and subsequent restoration of the railroad. Rapids now are smooth swept ledges with waves and holes, boulder piles and shallow-outs of flood-swept rocks, or small rock gardens. Many of the large boulders have been pushed out of the stream bed for the railroad. The widening of the stream bed by the flood is apparent, but at the mid-point of the trip there is a calm stretch away from the railroad that went unscathed, leaving a trace of the Blacklick of old. The run starts intensely and gradually eases. Mid-run has two steep isolated drops. The last mile is Class I. [Checked 1988]

*Difficulties:* There is a steep boulder drop immediately below Aulds Run, 0.6 miles below the put-in. Within a mile below the coal tipple there is a difficult shallow rocky area, marked by a large boulder at its approach. The run is directly into the late afternoon sun, which adds to the difficulty of running these intricate rapids.

*Shuttle:* Put in where State Route 259 crosses the river about 2.7 miles north of US Route 22. To get to the take-out, go south on State Route 259. Turn west onto US Route 22. Turn right onto US Route 119 towards Black Lick. Go about 3.0 miles to the river crossing.

*Gauges:* Josephine. This gauge should read between 3.8 and 4.6 feet. This corresponds to a flow of 225 cfs to 794 cfs.

*Normal Wet Period:* The Josephine gauge is above 3.8 feet 40% of the time and above 4.6 feet 10% of the time.

## C.  Josephine to Conemaugh Lake            11.0 miles

| *Class* | *Grad* | *Size (Area / Volume)* | *Scene / Poll* | *Level* |
|---|---|---|---|---|
| B | 5/15 | Medium (390/671) | C-D/C | |
| | | Blacklick (below Two Lick) | | Josephine |

*Topographic Maps:* Bolivar, Blairsville

*County Maps:* Indiana, Westmoreland

*Description:* A few rapids occur early around Josephine. Below this is the flood limit of Conemaugh Lake, but it is normally free flowing to State Route 217. [Checked 1986]

*Shuttle:* Put in where State Route 119 crosses the river about 3.0 miles north of US Route 22.  To get to the take-out go south on US Route 119.  Turn west onto US Route 22.  Go about 3 miles and turn west onto State Route 217.  Go north 100 yards and turn left onto State Route 3009.  Go 3 miles and turn left/west onto State Route 3007.  Go 2 miles and turn left onto State Route 3002.  Go 0.5 miles and turn left/south on State Route 3003. Continue through Tunnelton to the dam. Take out at the mouth of Blacklick Creek, using the old railroad grade on the left. There is an alternative take-out at State Route 217.

*Gauges:* Josephine. We do not have enough information to report runnable levels on this section.

*Normal Wet Period:*   No available statistics on seasons. Since this section is medium-sized, it should normally be runnable approximately December through May.

# Two Lick Creek

## A. Wandin                                    5.4 miles
## to Clymer (State Route 403 Bridge)

| Class | Grad | Size (Area/Volume) | Scene/Poll | Level |
|-------|------|--------------------|------------|-------|
| I | 15/20 | Small (70/117) estimate | A-B/B-C | |

*Topographic Maps:* Commodore, Clymer

*County Maps:* Indiana

*Description:* The South Branch is a stocked trout stream, but acid mine drainage from Wandin to Clymer changes it from trout to an acid stream. The scenery is lovely, with hemlock and rhododendron. There are enough chutes, riffles, and rocks to make the trip interesting. A highway bridge at Diamondville and two railroad bridges within the next 0.5 mile may have log jams. The next bridge is State Route 286 after a long rapid. The State Route 403 take-out bridge is about a 0.5 miles downstream. [Reported 1988]

*Difficulties:* Fallen trees are the worst problem. State Route 403 bridge has low clearance for boaters, perhaps none in high water.

*Shuttle:* To reach the put-in from Clymer, take State Route 403 east for about 3 miles from the light in Clymer. Turn left onto State Route 1012 following the signs to Diamondville. Follow this road through Diamondville. After you cross a deep railroad cut, turn right, remaining on State Route 1012. Wandin is another mile. Put in at a small bridge near a railroad underpass on a polluted feeder stream. It will be a short run to the main stem. The take-out is at the State Route 403 bridge in Clymer.

*Gauges:* Visually check upstream at the State Route 286 bridge. This is a rocky section, so if it looks good the rest of the stream will be runnable.

*Normal Wet Period:* No available statistics on seasons. Since this section is small, it should normally be runnable approximately January through April.

# B. Clymer (State Route 403 Bridge)          4.5 miles
# to Two Lick Reservoir(2.5 miles stream, 2.0 miles
lake)

| Class | Grad | Size (Area/Volume) | Scene/Poll | Level |
|-------|------|--------------------|-----------|-------|
| C | 12/14 | Small (80/133) estimate | B-C/B-C | |

*Topographic Maps:* Clymer, Brush Valley

*County Maps:* Indiana

*Description:* This stream quickly merges with Dixon Run, which is usually black from the upstream mines. Clymer has a new sewage treatment plant since the big flood of 1977 and the sewage smell should be reduced as you paddle through the town. After a mile the stream breaks away from State Route 286 and flows through a deeper valley toward the reservoir. You will encounter a small bridge before getting into the backwater of the dam. Then there are about 2 miles of flatwater before you reach the Allen Bridge take-out. There is another 3 miles from the Allen Bridge to the dam. [Checked 1989]

*Difficulties:* State Route 403 bridge has low clearance for boaters. In high water you may not be able to make it under the bridge.

*Shuttle:* Put in on the downstream side of the State Route 403 bridge at the ballfield in Clymer. To find the take-out from Clymer take State Route 286 west toward Indiana, turn left at Exxon station at the bottom of the hill onto State Route 1005, go straight at the next two crossroads, and head down to the lake and bridge. Paddle under the bridge and to the left shore near a picnic area for take-out. Alternate take-out is on the right side, 2.5 miles down the lake at the Old US Route 422 bridge (East Pike or Philadelphia Street East Extension from Indiana).

*Gauges:* None

*Normal Wet Period:* No available statistics on seasons. Since this section is small, it should normally be runnable approximately January through April.

## C. Indiana Waterworks to Homer     7.0 miles
## City (State Route 56 Bridge)

| Class | Grad | Size (Area/Volume) | Scene/Poll | Level |
|-------|------|--------------------|------------|-------|
| I-II | 13/17 | Small (100/167) estimate | A/B-C | 3-12 inches Flood gates open |

*Topographic Maps:* Brush Valley, Indiana

*County Maps:* Indiana

*Description:* This section has a remoteness about it due to the forest and abundance of rhododendron. It is 100 percent dam controlled from the Two Lick Reservoir, owned by the downstream power plant. Normally, under minimum flow conditions, the stream is runnable with a lot of route picking through shallows. Solo runs are better for boats and paddlers. To convert this stream into a Class I-II, the dam must open a flood gate 3 to 6 inches. If the dam gates are open, the current will be swift and have several long rapids prior to the first bridge. There are usually some nice waves just below this bridge. The stream alternates between slow moving and Class I rapids from the State Route 954 bridge to where you see US Route 119. [Reported 1989]

*Difficulties:* The locals have made 2 or 3 rock dams across the stream. If the flow is minimal you may have to get out and carry over. Just below where the stream parallels US Route 119, there is a Class II S-turn. At high flows the current pushes you into the trees on the outside of the bends and has Class II waves at the bottom. Next there are four bridges. Just above the fourth one is an island with a hydraulic on river right. Easiest run is left of center and down the left side of the island.

*Shuttle:* To reach the put-in, take State Route 954 south from Indiana for about 2 miles to the first big dip. Turn left just short of the Two Lick bridge. Go about 0.4 miles and bear right at the "Y", following the valley. Continue until the road looks like it stops at the Indiana Water Works. It is about a 100-yard carry to the stream. To reach the take-out, retrace your steps to State Route 954. Turn right/north back towards Indiana. Go a short distance and turn left/south on US Route 119. Continue into Homer City and there turn right/west onto State Route 56. Take out on river left just past the new State Route 56 bridge.  Parking has been permitted in the FMC parking area.

*Gauges:*  Since the flow is 100 percent controlled it is best to call the Two Lick Reservoir, (412) 357-1234, and inquire about the amount of water being released.  For good runs the gate must be open at least 3 inches.  An ideal level is 6 inches. An opening of 18 inches puts Homer City's low areas on flood alert.  The normal operation is:  When the lake rises to a maximum height, the operators release water until it reaches a minimum level and then close the gates.  The dam operators might be able to guess when they will be releasing after a rainfall.  In this section most of the river water volume is controlled by the powerplant dam.  They tend to regulate flow based on electricity demand; therefore, the actual flow could vary greatly from the 7AM reported level.   The Graceton gauge further downstream will probably read above 2.5.

*Normal Wet Period:*  Dam controlled.


## D.  Homer City (State Route 56 Bridge)          7.0 miles
## to Blacklick Bridge

| Class | Grad | Size (Area/Volume) | Scene/Poll | Level |
|-------|------|--------------------|------------|-------|
| C-II  | 7/8  | Small (171/284) | B-C/B-C | 2.5-?? |
|       |      | Graceton |  | Graceton |

*Topographic Maps:*  Indiana, Bolivar

*County Maps:*  Indiana

*Description:*  The stream is noticeably larger after picking up a major feeder stream, Yellow Creek.  In low water there is usually a sewage smell at the start of the trip.  The paddle route is easy with several small islands.  This gauge is read and reported daily.   In general the stream seems quite remote and the scenery varies from pasture fields to woods, to swamp, to small cliffs, to rhododendron thickets at water's edge.  There is a DANGER sign on a railroad bridge warning about the powerplant catch dam ahead.  Portage is on the left.  This 4-foot dam does create the classic deathtrap especially in high water.  There is always debris caught in the hydraulic.   The stream has several large gooseneck turns, and both head toward the power plant, giving you a brief deja vu view. Look for ducks along the slow sections. Two Lick flows into the Blacklick Creek about a mile above the take-out. At the junction, the Two Lick appears to flow under the two bridges, but this is actually upstream on the Blacklick. Just to the right and several hundred yards downstream is the Class II rapid. The stream breaks wide and is fast. The best plan is to run it on the left. In higher water you can run the center, then cut left. [Checked 1989]

*Difficulties:* The powerplant dam with its hydraulic. A good portage trail is on the left side near the dam. Follow the signs. When putting in downstream of the dam, be sure to avoid the dam's hydraulic.

*Shuttle:* Put in where State Route 56 crosses the river about 0.7 miles west of US Route 119. To get to the take-out follow US Route 119 south from Homer City to the traffic signal light in Blacklick, turn right toward the stream. The bridge is only 0.25 miles away. Several good parking areas are on the far side of the bridge.

*Gauges:* Graceton. This gauge should read above 2.5 feet. This corresponds to a flow of 144 cfs. In this section most of the river water volume is controlled by the powerplant dam. The flow is regulated based on electrical demand. This can cause the daytime flow to vary greatly from the 7AM reported level.

*Normal Wet Period:* The Graceton gauge is above 2.5 feet 47% of the time.

# Yellow Creek
# (Indiana County)

## A. Yellow Creek State Park Dam Outlet        3.0 miles
## to Ferrier Run Road

| Class | Grad | Size (Area/Volume) | Scene/Poll | Level |
|-------|------|--------------------|-----------|-------|
| I-II | 24/29 | Tiny (40/67) | A/A | |
| | | estimate | | |

*Topographic Maps:* Brush Valley

*County Maps:* Indiana

*Description:* The problem with paddling this section is that
you are not allowed to land a boat on the spillway or
breastwork of the State Park dam. This results in either a
0.5-mile carry to the put-in or a 1.25-mile paddle on the lake
and 0.25-mile carry. If you paddle the lake, take out to the
right of the outlet tower on the inclined road to the top of the
dam. Then carry across the breastwork and down to where
the outlet and spillway meet.

This is a trout stream and is lined with beautiful
overhanging hemlocks and rhododendron thickets. The
first 1.5 miles is easy paddling with riffles and chutes and
lots of room to pick a route. The second half is a lot faster,
starting with a roaring chute after a long quiet section.
Other difficulties are tight turns with fast current and fallen
trees. This proves to be an exciting run when the water is
up. The take-out is on the right side at the old Ferrier Run
Road bridge abutment (no bridge). Within the last 100 yards
or so, there is another exciting chute-ledge which has a big
wave you must crash through. [Checked 1987]

*Difficulties:* Respectable Class I-II stream with downed
trees blocking or partially blocking the paddling route.

*Shuttle:* To put in below the lake, take US Route 422 bypass
east from Indiana; take Chestnut Ridge exit, right about 100
yards, sharp right back toward bypass, left about 400 yards
and down over the hill to the gate at the parking lot. Carry
equipment past the gate and follow the road to the right

towards the dam, cross the breastwork and continue down to the junction of the spillway and dam outlet where you can put in. For the lake put-in, follow US Route 422 to State Route 259 (just past Pikes Peak Nursery). Turn right, away from the marked routes, and follow the blacktop lane to the North Shore Boat Launch on Yellow Creek Lake. To find the take-out point, follow State Route 954 south past the US Route 422 ramp and turn left on a blacktop lane which parallels US Route 422 Bypass. At the next dip, in about 1.1 miles, turn right on Ferrier Run Road. This dirt roads ends at the stream.

*Gauges:* None.

*Normal Wet Period:* No available statistics on seasons. Since this section is tiny, it should normally be runnable only after a heavy rain or during spring snowmelt.

## B. Ferrier Run Road to State Route 954 Bridge 2.5 miles

| Class | Grad | Size (Area/Volume) | Scene/Poll | Level |
|-------|------|--------------------|-----------|------|
| I-II | 32/46 | Tiny (55/92) estimate | A/A-B | 2.3-?? Homer City |

*Topographic Maps:* Brush Valley, Indiana

*County Maps:* Indiana

*Description:* It's well worth the extra effort to carry up stream 100 yards to catch the chute/ledge in this section. There is no warm-up on this stretch because the rapids and rocks start right away. In lower water you have to watch for rocks, and in higher water you get a lot of choppy waves. The hardest rapid is just above the backwater of the Waterworks Dam. This rapid, which was man-made by bulldozers creating a barrier 3 to 4 feet high, is runnable through a narrow chute on the extreme right. It is best to eddy out on the right side and walk down to see if there are any logs or strainers. The rapids on this lower section are more technical because of the many rocks. [Checked 1987]

*Difficulties:* Scout the 3-foot man-made drop above the Waterworks Dam. Portage the dam on the right side, land

100 feet upstream from the breastwork. The dam is about 15 feet high. It has a nasty hydraulic at the bottom. Launch downstream beyond the strong backwater created by the dam.

*Shuttle:* To find the put-in follow the instructions for the take-out on Section A, above. To get to the take-out follow State Route 954 south into the Yellow Creek valley. Take out on the left side of the stream, upstream of the bridge.

*Gauges:* Homer City. This gauge should read above 2.3 feet. This corresponds to a flow of 85 cfs. There is a gauge 100 yards upstream of the Waterworks Dam on stream left, but the gauge is not reported. If it reads 3.0 feet, the stream will be a rocky run. Between 3.5 and 4.5 feet is a very exciting level. Above that, the gauge is washed out and the stream is quite fast, with bigger standing waves. To get to the gauge, take a stripmine road which runs up the left side of the stream and a side road to the Waterworks Dam, and hike up to the gauge. The easiest way to check the water level is to look upstream at the State Route 954 rapid. If it looks obviously low, do not go. If the water is so high it is frightening, do not go.

*Normal Wet Period:* No available statistics on seasons. Since this section is tiny, it should normally be runnable only after a heavy rain or during spring snowmelt.

## C. State Route 954 Bridge                          3.5 miles
   to State Route 56 Bridge

| Class | Grad | Size (Area/Volume) | Scene/Poll | Level |
|-------|------|--------------------|-----------|-------|
| I-II | 23/80 | Tiny (57/107) | A-C/A-C | 2.3-?? |
|       |       | Homer City |  | Homer City |

*Topographic Maps:* Indiana

*County Maps:* Indiana

*Description:* Launch upstream of the bridge on the left side. Within sight of the bridge the stream divides into three channels. The best chute is the first branch to the right; the other two run through narrow brushy routes. However, the best chute is quite swift and flows toward the bank with some overhanging trees. Run it tight on the inside of the turns. After a mile or so you paddle out of the woods into the barrens of a mining area. Here the water changes from trout stream quality to a vile yellow brew of acid mine drainage. In several sections the stream becomes quite wide, if you run it too low, you will have to walk your boat a little. After passing an old coal tipple the stream approaches the US Route 119 bridge, where there is a lot of concrete rubble which is very tough on boats. The left span under the bridge ends in a 3-foot vertical drop; the right side is runnable, but narrow (this is the best side to walk the boat if water is low). Next is a small iron bridge and then the Main Street bridge in Homer City where there is a big rock in the center of stream. This is a good gauge (see below). After a swift S-turn rapid, Yellow Creek flows into Two Lick Creek. The State Route 56 bridge is just downstream of the junction. Take out on the left side downstream of the bridge. [Checked 1987]

*Difficulties:* Watch out for the first rapid where the stream narrows and splits into three. You may want to stop on the left side and scout the hidden end of the chute. The US Route 119 bridge is dangerous on the left side due to a 3-foot vertical drop and a lot of sharp concrete rubble. Run under the right span of the bridge; it is narrow, but has no vertical drops.

*Shuttle:* The put-in is on the bridge where State Route 954 crosses the creek. Turn south to get to State Route 56. Follow State Route 56 west through Homer City to the bridge. The FMC company has a large parking area at the take-out and has allowed boaters to use their property in the past.

*Gauges:* Homer City. This gauge should read above 2.3 feet. This corresponds to a flow of 85 cfs. A large rock in the center of the stream just upstream of the Main Street bridge in Homer City is a good indicator. If you see more than a foot of the rock it will be a tough trip with scraping and boat walking. If you just see the rock and can pull into the eddy behind it, the level is about just right. If higher than that, the stream washes out many interesting rapids making the course straightforward with bigger waves.

*Normal Wet Period:* No available statistics on seasons. Since this section is tiny, it should normally be runnable only after a heavy rain or during spring snowmelt.

# Blacklick Creek,
# South Branch

## Nanty Glo to Vintondale                              7.1 miles

| Class | Grad | Size (Area/Volume) | Scene/Poll | Level |
|-------|------|--------------------|------------|-------|
| II-III | 42/105 | Tiny (47/78) | B/B | |
| | | Vintondale | | |

*Topographic Maps:* Nanty Glo, Vintondale

*County Maps:* Cambria

*Description:* Small stream paddlers may want to extend the trip 5 miles by putting in at the State Route 271 bridge above Nanty Glo. The first mile from State Route 271 is continuous Class II and then the stream flattens to fast flowing to Nanty Glo. This section is very scenic as it passes through game lands. It also passes by some spoil piles, but overall the scenery gets a B rating. Below Nanty Glo the stream contains many Class II and Class III rapids. The most notable section begins below the State Route 3047 bridge following a loop in the stream. [Reported 1987]

*Difficulties:* Several drops in the section below Nanty Glo will require scouting.

*Shuttle:* Put in either at Nanty Glo or at the State Route 271 bridge above Nanty Glo depending on your desire for small stream paddling. To get to the take-out go west on State Route 271. About 2.5 miles from the railroad crossing in Nanty Glo turn left onto State Route 3047 which parallels the stream for the entire length. The take-out is at a streamside park near the junction of the North Branch below Vintondale.

*Gauges:* Josephine. This gauge further downstream on the Blacklick Creek will probably read below 5.5 feet.

*Normal Wet Period:* No available statistics on seasons. Since this section is tiny, it should normally be runnable only after a heavy rain or during spring snowmelt.

# Blacklick Creek, North Branch

## Two miles below State Route 271 to Vintondale

10.0 miles

| Class | Grad | Size (Area/Volume) | Scene/Poll | Level |
|-------|------|--------------------|------------|-------|
| II-III | 36/50 | Small (69/115) Vintondale | B/C | |

*Topographic Maps:* Colver, Strongstown, Vintondale

*County Maps:* Cambria

*Description:* The stream is a Class II meandering plateau stream for the first 4 miles. Numerous small reservoirs in the watershed cause the first few miles of stream bed to dry up during low flow periods and become overgrown with brush. There are some islands with tree hazards. The stream leaves the plateau in several miles of Class III past US Route 422 to Red Mill. The last mile or so is wide and shallow with numerous islands. About 2 miles of tiny Elk Run from State Route 271 to the North Branch at US Route 422 can be run as an alternate to the North Branch above US Route 422. It is shallow and predictable until it abruptly leaves the railroad. There is a 3-foot ledge and steep, narrow rocky rapids of hard Class III difficulty. [Reported 1981]

*Difficulties:* The passages between the islands are choked with trees. You will have to do some canoe dragging to run this trip.

*Shuttle:* Follow State Route 271 south out of Nicktown for about 2.5 miles to an intersection where State Route 271 bears hard left shortly after crossing the creek. Proceed straight ahead onto the unnumbered intersecting road. Put in about 2 miles further, where this road crosses the creek. To get to the take-out go south on State Route 271 through Twin Rocks. Take the first right (State Route 3047) south of Twin Rocks to Vintondale which is about 2.5 miles. Go through Vintondale crossing the South Branch and continue on another 0.25 miles which brings you to the North Branch crossing. Take out near the iron furnace.

*Gauges:* None.

*Normal Wet Period:* No available statistics on seasons. Since this section is small, it should normally be runnable approximately January through April.

# Tubmill Creek

## State Route 711 to Bolivar                      5.6 miles

| Class | Grad | Size (Area/Volume) | Scene/Poll | Level |
|-------|------|--------------------|------------|-------|
| I-II | 20/40 | Tiny (54/90) | B/B | |
| | | Bolivar | | |

*Topographic Maps:* Rachelwood, Wilpen, Bolivar

*County Maps:* Westmoreland

*Description:* Before putting in, scout the upper 3 miles from the Laurel Valley High School to the junction with Hendricks Creek. This section is tiny and brush choked. Hendricks Creek from the vicinity of Camp Kaufmann may be more suitable, although still tiny. Below the junction the stream is wide, calm, and in a pastoral setting until the outskirts of Bolivar. The last 2 miles contain the steepest gradient with a long rapid of uniform waves and small holes at high water. [Reported 1981]

*Difficulties:* Trees above the junction with Hendricks Creek. The gradient changes suddenly in Bolivar.

*Shuttle:* Put in where State Route 711 crosses the stream. To reach the take-out, go about 0.5 miles southwest on State Route 711. Turn right/northwest onto State Route 1006. Go about 5 miles to a "T" intersection with State Route 259 in Bolivar. Turn right/north. Take out on a Bolivar side street, walk up the railroad, or paddle upstream on the Conemaugh.

*Gauges:* None.

*Normal Wet Period:* No available statistics on seasons. Since this section is tiny, it should normally be runnable only after a heavy rain or during spring snowmelt.

# Little Conemaugh River

## A. Lilly to Portage                                    5.6 miles

| Class | Grad | Size (Area / Volume) | Scene / Poll | Level |
|---|---|---|---|---|
| III-IV | 53/100 | Small (60/100) estimate | C-D/C | |

*Topographic Maps:* Cresson, Ebensburg

*County Maps:* Cambria

*Description:* This stream is tiny, especially at the start. Small streams joining in Lilly make this run possible.

*Difficulties:* About 1 mile downstream of Lilly in Cassandra between 3 railroad bridges, the gradient picks up to 100 feet per mile, but the small size keeps the excitement down. [Reported 1981]

*Shuttle:* State Route 53 follows the run at various distances. Take out at the State Route 53 bridge near Portage.

*Gauges:* None.

*Normal Wet Period:* No available statistics on seasons. Since this section is small, it should normally be runnable approximately January through April.

## B. Portage to South Fork                               10.4 miles

| Class | Grad | Size (Area / Volume) | Scene / Poll | Level |
|---|---|---|---|---|
| I | 12/20 | Small (100/167) estimate | C/C | |

*Topographic Maps:* Ebensburg, Beaverdale, Geistown, Nanty Glo

*County Maps:* Cambria

*Description:* This is a gentle meandering stream in a valley with wide valley floor. [Reported 1981]

*Difficulties:* None.

*Shuttle:* State Route 53 parallels the run.

*Gauges:* None.

*Normal Wet Period:* No available statistics on seasons. Since this section is small, it should normally be runnable approximately January through April.

## C. South Fork to Johnstown                    10.2 miles

| Class | Grad | Size (Area / Volume) | Scene / Poll | Level |
|-------|------|----------------------|--------------|-------|
| II-III | 23/30 | Medium (183/328) East Conemaugh | B/B-C | East Conemaugh |

*Topographic Maps:* Geistown, Nanty Glo, Johnstown

*County Maps:* Cambria

*Description:* This run follows the route of the 1889 Johnstown Flood when the South Fork Dam broke. About a mile below the put-in is a beautiful 1 mile loop of Class III difficulty ending at a massive, double arch railroad bridge. The next 2 miles to Mineral Point is Class II, continuing 2 more miles to the loop cut. Bethlehem Steel of Johnstown has diverted the stream across the top of a 1 mile loop to create a slag dump. The falls created here should be carried on the left through the railroad cut. The next 4 miles is Class III with rapids created by slag. [Reported 1981]

*Difficulties:* Small dam 0.5 miles below the put-in. Carry on the left. Loop Cut Falls is a 20-foot falls which should be carried on the left. It is 2 miles below Mineral Point where the river makes a left turn into a deep rock cut. Because the cut was created by dynamiting, the rock within the cut has very sharp edges. A spill going through the rapid would result in lots of nasty slashes. The last mile is in a concrete channel and ends at a small dam/weir at the mouth. This is a uniform river-wide drop with concrete walls on either side. Look at it during the shuttle and consider the alternate take-out.

*Shuttle:* To reach the take-out from South Fork, take State Route 53 west to downtown Johnstown. Take out at the junction with Stony Creek. Note that this take-out involves dealing with a miserable small dam and its concrete walls near the mouth. A better take-out is located about 2.6 miles further upstream at a concrete emergency access ramp. Head north on State Route 271 from Johnstown. At the third crossing of the stream, the ramp is on river right, upstream of the bridge. Do not block the ramp, as it is emergency access for fire vehicles.

*Gauges:* East Conemaugh. We do not have enough information to report runnable levels on this section. Seward gauge on Conemaugh River will probably read between 2.7 and 4.0 feet.

*Normal Wet Period:* No available statistics on seasons. Since this section is medium-sized, it should normally be runnable approximately December through May.

# Little Conemaugh River, South Fork

## Beaverdale to South Fork                        7.3 miles

| Class | Grad | Size (Area/Volume) | Scene/Poll | Level |
|-------|------|--------------------|-----------|-------|
| III   | 58/100 | Small (64/107)<br>South Fork | C/C | |

*Topographic Maps:* Beaverdale, Geistown

*County Maps:* Cambria

*Description:* The South Fork has been run from Lloydell, where size and gradient are extreme; however, even the most adventurous canoeists will prefer to start at Beaverdale for 2 small, steep miles to Sidman. Below Sidman the stream enters the limits of the old South Fork Dam of Johnstown Flood fame. The pace through here is enjoyable. Below US Route 219 is a minor canyon with small ledges and playing waves. [Reported 1981]

*Difficulties:* Trees above Sidman. Boat-swamping waves below US Route 219.

*Shuttle:* State Route 869 parallels the stream.

*Gauges:* None. Check level at put-in, South Fork Dam site, and take-out.

*Normal Wet Period:* No available statistics on seasons. Since this section is small, it should normally be runnable approximately January through April.

# Stony Creek

## A. Shanksville to Kantner (US Route 30)      7.0 miles

| Class | Grad | Size (Area / Volume) | Scene / Poll | Level |
|-------|------|----------------------|--------------|-------|
| I V   | 61/80 | Small (85/142) | A / A | 0.1-?? |
|       |       | estimate |  | Streamside |

*Topographic Maps:* Stoystown

*County Maps:* Somerset

*Description:* This river section has a wide variety to offer. It starts easy, plunges furiously, and then levels off with medium-difficulty rapids. [Reported 1981]

*Difficulties:* The river is Class III for about a mile below the put-in. About 0.4 miles below the covered bridge with a railroad retaining wall on the left, and 100 feet beyond a sharp bend to the right, there is a brush dam blocking most of the left side of the river. It is sometimes possible to paddle around on the right in low water, but it is dangerous to do so in high water. At least one person is known to have been swept into the dam and nearly killed. **Round all right-hand bends with caution. Scout the brush dam before running.** This brush dam has been there for many years. Because of the character of the riverbed, it will probably always be there. After this, the river goes wild for the next mile or two. The rapids become Class IV, very tight with much maneuvering necessary. Past this difficult section, the river becomes Class II-III to the end, except for a complex sloping ledge 0.5 miles above Mostollar.

*Shuttle:* To find the put-in take State Route 1007 from Kantner to Shanksville, turn off onto an obscure tree-lined lane 0.25 miles south of State Route 1019 that seems to enter a farmer's field, and put in at the covered bridge. Take out at the bridge in Kantner or upstream at the Mostollar Bridge, 1.5 miles west of Lambertsville.

*Gauges:* A canoeists gauge on bridge abutment at US Route 30 across Stony Creek. There should be at least 0 feet showing on the gauge for a low, but acceptable, run. One foot would probably be a very good run. A reading of above

3.0 feet would probably be dangerous. This painted gauge probably runs 3 to 4 feet when Hollsopple reads 5 to 6 feet.

*Normal Wet Period:* No available statistics on seasons. Since this section is small, it should normally be runnable approximately January through April.

# B. Kantner (US Route 30) to Hollsopple    12.0 miles

| Class | Grad | Size (Area/Volume) | Scene/Poll | Level |
|-------|------|--------------------|-----------|-------|
| I/II | 19/30 | Medium (244/407) Hollsopple | C-D/C | 3.0-5.0 Hollsopple |

*Topographic Maps:* Stoystown, Hooversville

*County Maps:* Somerset

*Description:* This little-paddled section offers possibilities to novices. Stream is open with little difficulty except for one Class II rapid under the highway bridge at Landstreet. The last 1.5 miles is Class B. [Reported 1981]

*Shuttle:* Use State Route 403.

*Gauges:* Hollsopple. This gauge should read between 3.0 and 5.0 feet.

*Normal Wet Period:* No available statistics on seasons. Since this section is medium-sized, it should normally be runnable approximately December through May.

# C. Hollsopple to Kring    8.5 miles

| Class | Grad | Size (Area/Volume) | Scene/Poll | Level |
|-------|------|--------------------|-----------|-------|
| I V | 34/66 | Medium (375/625) estimate | A-B/B-C | 3.4-3.9 Ferndale |

*Topographic Maps:* Hooversville, Johnstown

*County Maps:* Somerset, Cambria

*Description:* At a level of 3 feet on the Hollsopple gauge, this creek is an honest Class IV. Several of the rapids are like the best part of Entrance Rapids on the Youghiogheny, with water boiling around and over large rocks, and curlers set at rapidly changing angles to the main stream. There are many hydraulics in which one could play, and some in which one definitely would not want to play. The banks are generally scenic, and there is some access to the creek on foot. At lower water levels the river is easier, but it is generally more suited to rafts and covered boats than to open equipment. [Reported 1987]

*Difficulties:* About a mile downstream from Hollsopple, the river begins to get cluttered, signifying the approach to the first real rapid. One must move to the left side of the river, go over a slight drop and down a chute bordered by long curler waves. You are, in effect, entering the open part of a "V" and heading for the point where two big curlers meet. At this point, the currents get interesting and you may need your roll. You may infer that this is a closed-boat run. The 0.75 miles between the mouth of Shade Creek and the railroad bridge is marked with sloping ledges and hydraulics. The next mile below the railroad bridge has mixed ledges and boulder drops in plunge-pool fashion as the river makes two large right bends. At a point where the river turns sharply back to the left, there is a small island. Here the railroad rejoins the river. There is a major drop at the base of the island. If in doubt, run the right side of the island, tight to island. This is the left side of the right channel, or better yet, scout the rapid. About a mile from this is Border Dam, which is unrunnable. Carry on the left. A few hundred yards below the dam is the Pipeline Hydraulic. It should be scouted and probably carried on the right. In high water (over 5 feet at Hollsopple), it is Class VI (risk of life). Above 3 feet it is just tough. About 0.5 miles downstream, a line of waves on the right leads into a dangerous hydraulic. It is easily avoided to the left.

*Shuttle:* Put in at the State Route 403 bridge. To get to the take-out, go north on State Route 403. Go about 6 miles and turn right onto State Route 4041. Go about 1 mile to the creek in Kring.

*Gauges:* Ferndale. This gauge should read between 3.4 and 3.9 feet. This corresponds to a flow of 495 cfs to 840 cfs. The Hollsopple gauge is painted on the center pier of the State Route 403 bridge and must be read at the site. For open canoes 1.5 feet on the Hollsopple gauge is minimum and

2.2 feet is maximum. At 3.25 feet on the Hollsopple gauge, the Stony is very fast and wild (Class IV-V). If the Stony is too high, try Shade Creek from Dark Shade Creek to Seanor. If the Stony is too low, try Blacklick Creek from Heshbon to Josephine.

*Normal Wet Period:* The Ferndale gauge is above 3.4 feet 35% of the time and above 3.9 feet 25% of the time.

## D. Kring to Johnstown                  7.0 miles

| Class | Grad | Size (Area/Volume) | Scene/Poll | Level |
|-------|------|--------------------|------------|-------|
| B-I | 11/20 | Medium (451/771) | D/C | |
| | | Ferndale | | Ferndale |

*Topographic Maps:* Johnstown

*County Maps:* Somerset, Cambria

*Description:* The first 1.5 miles is Class I. Below Ferndale is Johnstown with its concrete-lined channels. The attraction here is the city, with bridges and buildings above the concrete river. [Reported 1982]

*Difficulties:* Pipe crossing creates hole on left, 0.5 miles below Kring.

*Shuttle:* State Route 403 between Ferndale and downtown Johnstown.

*Gauges:* Ferndale. We do not have enough information to report runnable levels on this section. A reading of 3.8 on the Ferndale gauge corresponds to the mean flow of 771 cfs. Since this is a medium-sized river, we speculate that the river will be runnable at 3.8 and may be on the high side of runnable at that level.

*Normal Wet Period:* No available statistics on seasons. Since this section is medium-sized, it should normally be runnable approximately December through May.

# Bens Creek

## North Fork of Bens Creek                    3.0 miles
## to Stony Creek

| Class | Grad | Size (Area/Volume) | Scene/Poll | Level |
|-------|------|--------------------|-----------|-------|
| II | 35/55 | Tiny (49/82) | B/B | |
| | | Bens Creek | | |

*Topographic Maps:* Johnstown

*County Maps:* Somerset

*Description:* This is a straightforward small stream with lots to offer the novice paddler. The Shaffer Covered Bridge, which dates back to the 19th century, is the one-third mark of the run. The stream has continuous stretches of Class II rapids. [Reported 1982]

*Difficulties:* Downed trees.

*Shuttle:* The put-in is next to the Stardust Hotel at an old gas station. This is located several miles north of Thomas Mills on State Route 985, heading towards Johnstown. The take-out is at the Ideal Park Bridge near the town of Bens Creek on State Route 985.

*Gauges:* Ferndale. This gauge on nearby Stony Creek will probably read above 4.0 feet.

*Normal Wet Period:* No available statistics on seasons. Since this section is tiny, it should normally be runnable only after a heavy rain or during spring snowmelt.

# Paint Creek

## Windber to Stony Creek                                    2.7 miles

| Class | Grad | Size (Area/Volume) | Scene/Poll | Level |
|-------|------|--------------------|------------|-------|
| V+ | 130/200 | Tiny (37/62) | C/C | |
| | | Paint Creek | | |

*Topographic Maps:* Windber, Hooversville

*County Maps:* Somerset, Cambria

*Description:* Scout the entire run. Then decide whether to run it. The lower mile has two waterfalls 6 to 10 feet in height. The last half mile down to the Stony drops 100 feet. Although the pollution rating is C, you will be so busy with the stream that you will not notice it on the water. [Checked 1988]

*Difficulties:* Every boat length. After one slide there is an undercut rock on the right.

*Shuttle:* Put in below the State Route 601 bridge and below the falls in Windber. From the put-in, take State Route 601 across State Route 56 toward Paint Boro. Take the first right turn with a sign in Paint (State Route 4022) to the junction with Stony Creek.

*Gauges:* Ferndale. We do not have enough information to report runnable levels on this section. This gauge on nearby Stony Creek will probably give a good estimate of runnability.

*Normal Wet Period:* No available statistics on seasons. Since this section is tiny, it should normally be runnable only after a heavy rain or during spring snowmelt.

# Shade Creek

## Dark Shade Creek to Stony Creek                    9.8 miles

| Class | Grad | Size (Area/Volume) | Scene/Poll | Level |
|-------|------|--------------------|------------|-------|
| III   | 56/75 | Small (97/162) | A/A | 12-9 bricks |
|       |       | Seanor |  | Hillsboro Bridge |

*Topographic Maps:* Windber, Hooversville

*County Maps:* Somerset

*Description:* From the put-in on the Clear Shade Creek, run about 100 yards down to the junction with the Dark Shade. The river widens considerably when the two streams join to form the Shade Creek. From the junction of the Clear and Dark Shades to Hillsboro, rapids are formed by sediment and rock buildup from the 1977 flood. [Checked 1987]

*Difficulties:* About 2 miles into the run there is a 4-foot ledge. Run it on the right where there is a chute. The left drops straight off. About 2/3 of the way to Hillsboro, a significant strainer (tree pile) occupies about 200 yards of river and an island. The right-hand channel is a dead end. You will have to carry out if you commit to it. If you recognize the strainer, go left. At Hillsboro the character of the stream changes to steep drops separated by swift moving water. About 0.75 miles below the Hillsboro Bridge the stream makes a sharp right bend with a sheer 100-foot canyon wall on the left. It is here that the stream deposited an 8-foot pile of stones and rocks that forms a natural dam. There is a sluiceway on the left that leads smack into a rock if you do not make the necessary right turn at the bottom of the drop. A sweet Class III+. Major flooding in 1977 and the subsequent rebuilding, dredging, channelizing and blasting have substantially altered the character of parts of this stream.

*Shuttle:* The put-in is on the Clear Shade at State Route 160. To get to the take-out, go north on State Route 160. Turn left/north onto State Route 56. Turn left/west onto State Route 601. Take out at Seanor 0.5 miles above junction with Stony Creek. This trip can be broken into two smaller segments by accessing Hillsboro. This would cut the trip roughly in half.

*Gauges:* Hillsboro center bridge pier. This gauge should read between 12 to 9 bricks showing. Ferndale. This gauge further downstream on Stony Creek will probably read between 3.6 and 4.6. A quick check on the level is possible by looking at the river from the bridge in Seanor. If this looks runnable, the entire section should have adequate water, as this is about the shallowest point on the run. Note that the Shade rises and falls faster than the Stony.

If the Shade is too low, and if you are an experienced canoeist with a decked boat, try the nearby Stony Creek or the Blacklick Creek. These are more difficult streams.

*Normal Wet Period:* No available statistics on seasons. Since this section is small, it should normally be runnable approximately January through April.

# Clear Shade Creek

## Ashtola Road to Shade Creek                    5.5 miles

| Class | Grad  | Size (Area/Volume) | Scene/Poll | Level |
|-------|-------|--------------------|------------|-------|
| I V   | 45/90 | Tiny (31/52)       | A/A        |       |
|       |       | Reitz              |            |       |

*Topographic Maps:* Ogletown, Windber

*County Maps:* Somerset

*Description:* The first 3 miles is a Class II plateau stream to the Windber Reservoir. The last 2 miles plunge through a small canyon at a fast pace. The 1977 flood rearranged these last 2 miles allowing the possibility of periodic changes over the next few years. The canyon starts as large boulders with small pools, then becomes uniform fast gradient among small boulders. [Reported 1981]

*Difficulties:* Fallen trees within 0.5 miles below dam.

*Shuttle:* From take-out follow State Route 160 north approximately 2 miles to Ashtola Road (State Route 1033). Turn right for about a 4 mile drive to Ashtola. In Ashtola make a sharp turn to the right and go about 4 miles to the stream.

*Gauges:* None. Ferndale gauge on nearby Stony Creek will probably give a good estimate of runnability.

*Normal Wet Period:* No available statistics on seasons. Since this section is tiny, it should normally be runnable only after a heavy rain or during spring snowmelt.

# Dark Shade Creek

## Cairnbrook to Clear Shade Creek               1.9 miles

| Class | Grad | Size (Area/Volume) | Scene/Poll | Level |
|-------|------|--------------------|------------|-------|
| IV-V | 60/160 | Tiny (36/60) | A/B | |
| | | Reitz | | |

*Topographic Maps:* Windber

*County Maps:* Somerset

*Description:* This is a very tight stream with very rapid drops. The last half mile drops 80 feet. It is almost comparable to the Upper Youghiogheny in difficulty. It is only runnable with much water in the Shade. Run with covered boats only. [Checked 1982]

*Difficulties:* Everything below the slag dump on river right.

*Shuttle:* Use State Route 160.

*Gauges:* Ferndale. This gauge further downstream on Stony Creek will probably read above 3.6.

*Normal Wet Period:* No available statistics on seasons. Since this section is tiny, it should normally be runnable only after a heavy rain or during spring snowmelt.

# Quemahoning Creek

## Boswell to Reservoir                                    3.4 miles

| Class | Grad | Size (Area/Volume) | Scene/Poll | Level |
|-------|------|--------------------|-----------|-------|
| III   | 50/65 | Small (98/163)    | A/B       |       |

Jerome Junction (below reservoir)

*Topographic Maps:* Boswell, Hooversville

*County Maps:* Somerset

*Description:* Two miles of flatwater can be added by putting in at US Route 30. The gradient begins immediately below Boswell. The first drops are among car-sized boulders. The middle mile is steepest with uniform rocky gradient. The closing rapids within sight of US Route 219 are small ledges. [Reported 1982]

*Difficulties:* Possible downed trees.

*Shuttle:* Start at the crossroads of US Route 30 and US Route 219. Take US Route 219 north for about 1 mile. A left turn will take you 1.5 miles to the put-in at Boswell, while a right turn will take you 1.5 miles to the take-out at the reservoir.

*Gauges:* None. Check the level at the put-in and from the US Route 219 bridge.

*Normal Wet Period:* No available statistics on seasons. Since this section is small, it should normally be runnable approximately January through April.

# Crooked Creek
# (Indiana County)

## A. US Route 119
## to Creekside (State Route 110)

6.5 miles

| Class | Grad | Size (Area / Volume) | Scene / Poll | Level |
|-------|------|---------------------|--------------|-------|
| I | 8/8 | Tiny (50/83) | A-B/B | |
| | | Route 119 | | Idaho |

*Topographic Maps:* Clymer, Ernest

*County Maps:* Indiana

*Description:* You must catch this section when the water is high, but not overflowing. The high clay banks are lined with trees or brush and many of the turns are tight. Watch for downed trees. Trees vary from hemlocks and rhododendron to large sycamores. Quite a pleasant trip. You usually see or surprise a deer or two and some ducks. The fastest chute is just upstream of the Chambersville Bridge; a fun change from the mostly slow water. [Checked 1988]

*Difficulties:* Downed trees blocking or partially blocking your path. If you extended the trip upstream, a major tree fall blocks the stream completely about 1 mile above US Route 119.

*Shuttle:* Take US Route 119 north from Indiana until the stream crosses the road, about 9 miles. There is a parking area on the left side just before the bridge, with a short carry down through some tall pine trees. To get to the take-out from here, continue past the bridge 100 yards, turn left onto State Route 110 to Creekside. This route follows the stream. The trip can be extended 2 miles upstream by putting in at the Kintersburg covered bridge.

*Gauges:* Idaho. We do not have enough information to report runnable levels on this section.

*Normal Wet Period:* No available statistics on seasons. Since this section is tiny, it should normally be runnable only after a heavy rain or during spring snowmelt.

## B. Creekside to Shelocta                    8.1 miles

| Class | Grad | Size (Area/Volume) | Scene/Poll | Level |
|---|---|---|---|---|
| I | 5/5 | Small (90/150) estimate | A-B/B | 2.7-5.0 Idaho |

*Topographic Maps:* Ernest, Elderton

*County Maps:* Indiana

*Description:* The stream lies in a narrow, winding channel with high wooded banks. The whole stretch is Class I water with fast current. [Checked 1989]

*Difficulties:* Downed trees. There are two ledges, less than 1 foot high about 0.5 miles and 0.75 miles from the start.

*Shuttle:* Put in at the State Route 110 bridge in Creekside. To reach the take-out, go southwest on State Route 954. Go about 1.3 miles and continue on State Route 4002 when State Route 954 turns left. Turn south onto State Route 4001. Go a short distance and turn right on US Route 422. Go 1.5 miles and turn left onto State Route 156. This road immediately crosses the creek in Shelocta.

*Gauges:* Idaho. This gauge should read between 2.7 and 5.0 feet. This corresponds to a flow of 85 cfs to 1450 cfs.

*Normal Wet Period:* This section is normally runnable from early January through mid May. The Idaho gauge is above 2.7 feet 59% of the time and above 5.0 feet 3% of the time.

## C. Shelocta to Girty                    10.5 miles

| Class | Grad | Size (Area/Volume) | Scene/Poll | Level |
|---|---|---|---|---|
| I | 4/6 | Small (175/295) Idaho | B/B | 3.0-4.5 Idaho |

*Topographic Maps:* Elderton, McIntyre, Whitesburg

*County Maps:* Indiana, Armstrong

*Description:* There are some nice riffles between the bridges in Shelocta that require some rock dodging. Below the State

Route 156 bridge the stream was rerouted along the new US Route 422 and is wider and shallower than the normal streambed. After about 3 miles of winding, Plum Creek sneaks in from the right. Now the stream heads toward the Keystone power plant and their catch dam with about a 7-foot vertical drop. Portage on the left through dense growth of young trees and rocks or on the right using streamside roadbed. The backwater of the dam gives plenty of time to determine how close you want to paddle before you portage. If the water is high, take out well upstream so you do not get washed over. If the water is just flowing over the center section it is safe to paddle up to and land on the edge on the left side. Below the dam 0.5 miles is the Idaho gauge (on right), and less than 0.25 miles later is another low dam. The outlet causes a very strong back current toward the dam. It is probably best to land and portage this dam on the left although a right side portage is possible with extreme caution for the back current. The stream seems to widen out from this point which makes you work and pick your way through the shallows, riffles, and chutes if the stream is on the low side. There are some very large boulders in the stream just above the State Route 210 bridge. [Checked 1988]

*Difficulties:* At the powerplant dam portage on either side. At the smaller dam about 0.75 miles downstream portage either side. The small one has a much stronger back current, so launch well down stream of the grip of the back current. Note: If the water is breaking across the entire length of powerplant dam (very high volume) beware of the increased hydraulic action on the dam.

*Shuttle:* From Shelocta, proceed west 6.5 miles along State Route 156. Turn right/north on State Route 2027. Go 1 mile to Girty. Intermediate access is available at South Bend. To get there, at the State Route 156 bridge, take the side road along the right/north bank of the creek.

*Gauges:* Idaho. This gauge should read between 3.0 and 4.7 feet. This corresponds to a flow of 170 cfs to 1080 cfs.

*Normal Wet Period:* This section is normally runnable from early January through mid May. The Idaho gauge is above 3.0 feet 40% of the time and above 4.5 feet 5% of the time.

# D. Girty to Cochrans Mills                    7.2 miles

| Class | Grad | Size (Area/Volume) | Scene/Poll | Level |
|-------|------|--------------------|-----------|-------|
| I-II | 9/11 | Medium (200/333) estimate | B/B | 2.7-4.0 Idaho |

*Topographic Maps:* Whitesburg

*County Maps:* Armstrong

*Description:* Numerous small ledges and rock gardens. The creek runs close to overhanging cliffs and once past the gas pumping station is fairly scenic. An often-run alternative trip is to put in at South Bend at the western bridge of State Route 156, run 3.2 miles to Girty, continue 4.2 miles to Mateer Bridge. [Checked 1990]

*Difficulties:* None, except the mud banks at the take-out.

*Shuttle:* To reach the take-out, go north across the Girty Bridge, turn left/west onto State Route 2026. Go 2.0 miles to the fork. Bear right at the fork and follow this road to the Cochrans Mills bridge. For the Mateer bridge, bear left at the fork. To extend the trip upstream about 3 miles, the road to South Bend from Girty runs along the right/north bank of the river.

*Gauges:* Idaho. This gauge should read between 2.7 and 4.0 feet. This corresponds to a flow of 85 cfs to 770 cfs. If you can get over the shallows at the bridge in Girty, the rest of the stream is runnable.

*Normal Wet Period:* This section is normally runnable from late December through late May. The Idaho gauge is above 2.7 feet 59% of the time and above 4.0 feet 8% of the time.

# E. Cochrans Mills to Crooked Creek Dam    8.0 miles

| Class | Grad | Size (Area/Volume) | Scene/Poll | Level |
|-------|------|--------------------|-----------|-------|
| A | Lake | Medium (278/423) Crooked Creek Dam | B/B | |

*Topographic Maps:* Whitesburg, Leechburg

*County Maps:* Armstrong

*Description:* Depending on the water level in Crooked Creek Lake, the reservoir backwater sometimes reaches all the way to Girty. If the lake level is low (860 ft), this section is a slow flowing stream; if the lake is up (880 ft), then this stretch becomes flat.

The backwaters of Crooked Creek Dam provide good still-water canoeing, boating, waterskiing and swimming. To get away from the power boats paddle upstream from the boat launch area. One can paddle several miles even in late summer when the water is low. The banks are attractive and there is a good swimming spot just before the current begins to get strong. [Checked 1989]

*Difficulties:* In the reservoir itself there are numerous power boats towing water skiers at high speed.

*Shuttle:* Several access points are available in the park. Obtain a Crooked Creek Reservoir map at the park office.

*Gauges:* Call Crooked Creek Park for the reservoir level.

*Normal Wet Period:* Lakes are canoeable all year except when frozen.

## F.  Crooked Creek Dam                    7.0 miles
## to Rosston (Allegheny River)

| Class | Grad | Size (Area/Volume) | Scene/Poll | Level |
|-------|------|--------------------|-----------|-------|
| B | 5/5 | Medium (292/487)<br>Crooked Creek Dam | B/B | |

*Topographic Maps:*  Leechburg

*County Maps:*  Armstrong

*Description:*  This flat stream flows through farm land between mud banks. [Checked 1985]

*Difficulties:*  None.

*Shuttle:*  Put in below the dam on river left, at the outflow picnic area. Drive west 0.9 miles on State Route 2019. Turn north on State Route 66 to Ford City, south along State Route 128 to the bridge on the Allegheny River. Instead of crossing the bridge turn left and follow the river bank 1 mile to Rosston. Alternately you can extend the trip by taking out downstream on the Allegheny.

*Gauges:*  Crooked Creek Outflow. Call the Corps of Engineers at Crooked Creek Recreational Area to determine the amount of water being released.

*Normal Wet Period:*  This section is entirely dam controlled.

# Cowanshannock Creek

## A. Greendale to State Route 28/66     8.0 miles

| Class | Grad | Size (Area/Volume) | Scene/Poll | Level |
|-------|------|--------------------|------------|-------|
| II | 18/26 | Tiny (40/67) estimate | A-B/A | 6-?? blocks SR 85 bridge |

*Topographic Maps:* Rural Valley, Mosgrove

*County Maps:* Armstrong

*Description:* This is a beautiful small volume Class II stream. Rapids are short and frequent and take a bit of maneuvering. There are low water bridges, fords, small ledges and fallen trees. It takes some care to get through without banging and scraping, but nothing is hairy except the tree problem. Scenery is outstanding, from farms to steep walled areas. From State Route 85 bridge to the take-out is Class C-I. [Checked 1988]

*Difficulties:* Some fallen trees must be carried around or over.

*Shuttle:* Pick a spot along State Route 85.

*Gauges:* None. There is a streamside gauge using the stone block retaining wall on right bank near Sunnyside, where State Route 85 crosses. 4.5 to 5.5 blocks showing should be okay.

*Normal Wet Period:* No available statistics on seasons. Since this section is tiny, it should normally be runnable only after a heavy rain or during spring snowmelt.

# B. State Route 28/66                        3.6 miles
# to Allegheny River

| Class | Grad | Size (Area/Volume) | Scene/Poll | Level |
|-------|------|--------------------|-----------|---------|
| I V | 36/80 | Small (63/105) mouth of stream | B/A | |

*Topographic Maps:* Mosgrove, Kittanning

*County Maps:* Armstrong

*Description:* This is a beautiful creek flowing through a deep gorge. It is very tight and continuous -- you need to do lots of maneuvering. There is a trail along river right offering a look at the stream. [Checked 1987]

*Difficulties:* Lots of potential for pinning and strainers. At high water levels, some very large holes are present. There are several drops of 2 to 4 feet. The first of these, just around a right-hand bend, should be scouted. In addition, watch out for logs or railroad ties sticking up out of the holes. The trip is short, but plan to do lots of scouting.

*Shuttle:* Via Kittanning, from the put-in at State Route 28/66, to the road along the east bank of the Allegheny. Take-out is at the Pennsylvania Fish Commission boat launch area.

*Gauges:* None

*Normal Wet Period:* No available statistics on seasons. Since this section is small, it should normally be runnable approximately January through April.

# Pine Creek
# (Armstrong County)

## A. Echo to Pine Furnace                                      7.0 miles

| Class | Grad | Size (Area/Volume) | Scene/Poll | Level |
|-------|------|--------------------|------------|-------|
| I-II | 20/30 | Tiny (20/33) estimate | A-B/B | |

*Topographic Maps:* Rural Valley, Mosgrove

*County Maps:* Armstrong

*Description:* Echo to Oscar is flowing water with many trees down. From Oscar to Pine Furnace the volume picks up and the creek runs mostly along the base of a cliff and through stands of hemlock. [Reported 1974]

*Difficulties:* There is a steady drop of 30 feet per mile for 2 miles of the section between Oscar and Pine Furnace. At high water levels this section is continuous standing waves with obstacles to turn around.

*Shuttle:* Do it with the topographic maps, but be warned that in 1974 the road from State Route 28/66 to Pine Furnace was much worse than the map suggests. To reach the take-out from Echo, go west on State Route 1028. This road will take you through Oscar. Go about 6 miles and turn right on an unnumbered road to Pine Furnace.

*Gauges:* None.

*Normal Wet Period:* No available statistics on seasons. Since this section is tiny, it should normally be runnable only after a heavy rain or during spring snowmelt.

# B. Pine Furnace to State Route 28/66            1.5 miles

*Class  Grad*    *Size (Area / Volume)*    *Scene / Poll  Level*
26/28          Tiny (30/50)                   B/B

*Topographic Maps:* Mosgrove

*County Maps:* Armstrong

*Description:* Not run at this time

# C. State Route 28/66                             3.0 miles
# to Allegheny River

*Class  Grad*    *Size (Area / Volume)*    *Scene / Poll  Level*
II-III 39/100        Tiny(38/63)                 B/B
                     Mosgrove

*Topographic Maps:* Mosgrove

*County Maps:* Armstrong

*Description:* This small stream starts and ends with flat but fast moving water. Most of the river consists of long continuous Class II and III rapids. The river meanders with high current from shore to shore in a narrow, wooded valley. The only eddies are small and along the shore or behind bends in the river. The rapids are mostly submerged rocks with holes and rows of standing waves, with a few exposed rocks or ledges. [Reported 1987]

*Difficulties:* About 100 yards above the fourth bridge, a single sloping ledge (4 to 5 feet high) crosses the entire river and forms a major hydraulic across the current. This may be runnable, but is significantly more difficult than anything else on this section. Scout and/or carry on the right.

*Shuttle:* Head north from the put-in on State Route 28/66. Turn left/west at the first road onto State Route 1034. It will cross the river twice on the way to the Allegheny River at Mosgrove.

*Gauge:* Two streamside gauges were observed during this run. The first bridge on the shuttle from State Route 28/66 had six cut stone blocks exposed. The water level was also bank full under the State Route 28/66 put-in bridge.

*Normal Wet Period:* No available statistics on seasons. Since this section is tiny, it should normally be runnable only after a heavy rain or during spring snowmelt.

# Mahoning Creek

## A. Big Run (Upper Bridge)                    10.9 miles
## to Punxsutawney (State Route 436 Bridge)

| Class | Grad | Size (Area/Volume) | Scene/Poll | Level |
|-------|------|--------------------|-----------|-------|
| C | 7/11 | Small (158/277) Punxsutawney | B-C/B | Punxsutawney |

*Topographic Maps:* McGees Mills, Punxsutawney

*County Maps:* Jefferson

*Description:*

*Difficulties:* The remains of an old dam, most of which is silted in, provides a 4-foot drop. Paddle down the right side and carry the canoe over the concrete. The dam is about a mile below the Cloe Bridge (9th bridge, if you count bridges). There is another very old dam or pipeline across the stream which sets up a diagonal small ledge about 0.5 miles further down next to the rail yards. [Reported 1982]

*Shuttle:* To get to the put-in, follow US Route 119 north from Punxsutawney. Continue through Big Run, turn right at the small bridge near the main road, then immediately right on the levee road. To get to the take-out, follow US Route 119 south into Punxsutawney, then take State Route 36 north through town. On the west end of town, turn left above the Skat gas station and turn right to pass under the high State Route 436 bridge. Take out where the street passes near the stream.

*Gauges:* Punxsutawney. We do not have enough information to report runnable levels on this section. A reading of 2.2 on the Punxsutawney gauge corresponds to the mean flow of 277 cfs. Since this is a small river, we speculate that the runnable level will be at least 2.2 and perhaps more.

*Normal Wet Period:* No available statistics on seasons. Since this section is small, it should normally be runnable approximately January through April.

# B. Punxsutawney (State Route 436 Bridge) to Lower Valier Bridge                    9.5 miles

| Class | Grad | Size (Area/Volume) | Scene/Poll | Level |
|-------|------|--------------------|-----------|-------|
| B | 3/3 | Small (158/269) | B/A-B | |
| | | Punxsutawney | | Punxsutawney |

*Topographic Maps:* Punxsutawney, Valier

*County Maps:* Jefferson

*Description:* A very slow and winding section. Six ox-bow loops wander back and forth. [Reported 1982]

*Difficulties:* None.

*Shuttle:* From the junction of State Route 36 and State Route 436 in Punxsutawney, take State Route 436 south to US Route 119 and turn right/south. Go about 1.0 miles then turn right on State Route 210 (Trade City Road). Follow this 1.5 miles and turn right toward Valier. Go straight through the village, then turn left. The lower bridge is another 0.5 miles.

*Gauges:* Punxsutawney. We do not have enough information to report runnable levels on this section. A reading of 2.2 on the Punxsutawney gauge corresponds to the mean flow of 277 cfs. Since this is a small river, we speculate that the runnable level will be at least 2.2 and perhaps more.

*Normal Wet Period:* No available statistics on seasons. Since this section is small, it should normally be runnable approximately January through April.

## C. Valier to State Route 839 Access Area    17.1 miles
## (Milton Loop Boat Launch)

| Class | Grad | Size (Area/Volume) | Scene/Poll | Level |
|-------|------|--------------------|------------|-------|
| C | 7/9 | Medium (200/333) estimate | B/B | |

*Topographic Maps:* Valier, Dayton

*County Maps:* Jefferson, Indiana, Armstrong

*Description:* The scenery from Valier to the dam is quite pretty. The Mahoning Dam sometimes backs water up to the mouth of the Little Mahoning Creek which is about 2 miles above the Mahoning Lake State Route 839 take-out. At summer lake levels, however, you will have less than a mile of flatwater paddling. [Checked 1982]

*Difficulties:* There is only one major riffle between Valier and the Little Mahoning, which should pose no problem.

*Shuttle:* The best car shuttle route for this section of the stream runs along the north side of the stream using State Routes 4028 and 4026. The best take-out is the Milton Loop launch ramp for Mahoning Lake, about a quarter mile below the State Route 839 bridge. One can choose to shorten the trip by 2 miles of potential flatwater by taking out at Little Mahoning Creek near the State Route 4026 bridge.

*Gauges:* McCormick. This gauge on nearby Little Mahoning Creek will probably read between 1.9 and 2.6.

*Normal Wet Period:* No available statistics on seasons. Since this section is medium-sized, it should normally be runnable approximately December through May.

# D. State Route 839 (Milton Loop Launch)   6.0 miles
to Mahoning Dam

*Class  Grad    Size (Area/Volume)    Scene/Poll  Level*
  A    Lake    Medium (321/561)
                Dayton

*Topographic Maps:* Dayton, Distant

*County Maps:* Armstrong

*Description:* This is flatwater above the Corps of Engineers
Flood Control Dam. The lake is slightly over 5 miles long in
a narrow valley. The first 2 miles retain the appearance of a
river. The last three widen out. If the lake is down
10-20 feet, then the moving water will extend to within
3 miles of the dam. The lake has a ten horsepower limit on
motorboats. [Reported 1989]

*Difficulties:* None.

*Shuttle:* Put in at the Milton Loop Boat Launch on the north
side of the lake abut 0.25 miles downstream of where State
Route 839 crosses the lake. Take out on the right side of the
lake by the dam above the log boom. There is a 0.25 miles
trail up to the road. From here it is another 0.5 miles to the
put-in for the next section. An alternate put-in for this
section is to take State Route 4026 upstream on the river
right for about 3 miles to the junction with the Little
Mahoning Creek.

*Gauges:* None.

*Normal Wet Period:* Lakes are canoeable all year except
when frozen.

# E. Mahoning Dam to Putneyville 6.5 miles

| Class | Grad | Size (Area/Volume) | Scene/Poll | Level |
|---|---|---|---|---|
| I-II | 12/13 | Medium (344/601) | A-B/A | 2.8-3.9 |
| | | Mahoning Dam | Mahoning Dam | Outflow |

*Topographic Maps:* Distant

*County Maps:* Armstrong

*Description:* Downstream of Mahoning Dam the stream cuts through and snakes around some 300 to 400 foot slopes. There are several short, swift and powerful chutes on this section with standing waves. However, most of it is easy paddling. [Checked 1990]

*Difficulties:* Three or four places between Eddyville and Putneyville, the river narrows to less than half its usual width, the current picks up speed, and rocks, ledges, or standing waves require attention.

*Shuttle:* McCrea Furnace is a tough one without a map. McCrea Furnace is about 0.5 miles below the Corps of Engineers dam, and about 2.0 miles north of the village of Belknap.

To reach the put-in from State Route 28/66, turn east at Baum onto State Route 1018 and follow the brown signs for Mahoning Lake. This will take you on State Route 1018, past the turn off to Belknap (State Route 1025). About 0.25 miles past the Belknap road, turn left onto an unnumbered road. Go about a mile to a "T" intersection. Turn left, go another mile to a "Y" and bear left. Then go another mile to a second "Y" with the left going uphill (this will be the shuttle road) and the right arm continuing level. Go right and put in along the river or at the bridge. Respect private property.

To reach the put-in from Putneyville go south on State Route 1025 until State Route 1008 comes in from the left. Bear right and continue on State Route 1025 for about 0.1 miles. Here go straight on a dirt road rather than turning right to follow the paved State Route 1025. Continue straight on this dirt road until it tees, at which point turn left and continue to the river.

To get to the take-out, start back up the hill on the other branch of the "Y". Take the first right turn (northwest). After 0.4 miles, cross State Route 1010, and continue on for 0.7 miles. Turn right/north on State Route 1025. Follow this for 4 miles to Putneyville. This section can be lengthened by putting in where State Route 28/66 crosses the creek.

*Gauges:* Mahoning Dam Outflow. This gauge should read between 2.8 and 3.9 feet. This corresponds to a flow of 345 cfs to 1050 cfs.

*Normal Wet Period:* Completely controlled by Mahoning Dam. This section is normally runnable from early December through late May and there is not a normally too high season. The Mahoning Dam Outflow gauge is above 2.8 feet 45% of the time and above 3.9 feet 15% of the time.

# F. Putneyville to Allegheny River                16.5 miles

| Class | Grad | Size (Area/Volume) | Scene/Poll | Level |
|-------|------|--------------------|-----------|-------|
| I | 7/13 | Medium (425/708) | A-B/A | 3.0-?? |
|   |   | mouth of stream | Mahoning dam outflow | |

*Topographic Maps:* Distant, Templeton

*County Maps:* Armstrong

*Description:*  The first mile below Putneyville is a rock garden that requires at least a gauge reading of 3.0 to avoid scraping.  The remainder is flat and flowing.  The scenery of gentle bends and steep hillsides is interrupted 3 miles from the Allegheny by a coal mine and coke oven operations. Cottages and homes dot the last 2 miles.  Otherwise the stream valley is empty. [Checked 1989]

*Difficulties:*  None.

*Shuttle:*  The put-in is where State Route 1025 crosses the creek in Putneyville.  To get to the take-out, go north about 2 miles and cross US Route 28/66 at Distant.  Turn west onto State Route 1004.   Go 5.5 miles to Widnoon and turn left/south on State Route 1003.  Go 3 miles to the take-out. This section can be shortened by putting in where State Route 28/66 crosses the creek.

*Gauges:*  Mahoning Dam Outflow.  This gauge should read above 3.0 feet. This corresponds to a flow of 480 cfs.

*Normal Wet Period:*  Completely controlled by Mahoning Dam.   This section is normally runnable from early January through late May.  The Mahoning Dam Outflow gauge is above 3.0 feet 35% of the time.

# Little Mahoning Creek

## A. Nashville to Rochester Mills                     6.0 miles

| Class | Grad | Size (Area/Volume) | Scene/Poll | Level |
|-------|------|--------------------|------------|-------|
| II | 25/40 | Tiny (20/33) | A/A | |
| | | estimate | | McCormick |

*Topographic Maps:* Rochester Mills

*County Maps:* Indiana

*Description:* This is a trout stream all the way to the backwaters of Mahoning Dam. This section is the fastest if you catch it with enough water, when it is narrow and swift. There are so many tight turns that you can lose sight of the boat in front of you. The high banks are wooded with rhododendron and hemlocks. [Reported 1982]

*Difficulties:* About 2 miles above Rochester Mills the stream splits, the right branch usually carrying the higher volume. After several hundred yards the right branch of the stream has a blind turn to the left where the current slows. Downed trees may have to be portaged, especially on the upper part.

*Shuttle:* The new high-level bridge connects Rochester Mills, south of the stream, with State Route 236 on the north. To get to the put-in go east on State Route 236 a few hundred yards, then turn right and go down to the water at the site of the old bridge. To reach the take-out drive across the bridge and turn left/east away from town. Go 4 miles to the bridge at Nashville (one-house town). There is also access at the halfway point of the trip, at the mouth of the North Branch of the Little Mahoning.

*Gauges:* McCormick. We do not have enough information to report runnable levels on this section. Look at the creek from the new bridge at Rochester Mills for the best indicator. McCormick is reported daily to the Mahoning Dam. Call (814) 257-8811.

*Normal Wet Period:* No available statistics on seasons. Since this section is tiny, it should normally be runnable only after a heavy rain or during spring snowmelt.

## B. Rochester Mills                          4.0 miles
## to upstream of US Route 119

| Class | Grad | Size (Area/Volume) | Scene/Poll | Level |
|-------|------|--------------------|-----------|-------|
| C-I | 14/22 | Small (60/100) | A-B/A | |
| | | estimate | | McCormick |

*Topographic Maps:* Rochester Mills, Marion Center

*County Maps:* Indiana

*Description:* The first of four dams is close to the put-in. The next three dams are in a series about 2 to 3 miles into the run. Ducks have been seen on the pools caused by these dams. [Reported 1981]

*Difficulties:* The four low dams always have logs stuck in the drops or at the walls. All should be portaged.

*Shuttle:* Put in at the old bridge along State Route 236. Take-out is also along State Route 236 about 0.25 miles short of US Route 119 where the road runs close to the stream. The US Route 119 bridge is posted no trespassing.

*Gauges:* McCormick. We do not have enough information to report runnable levels on this section. Look at the creek from the new bridge at Rochester Mills for the best indicator. McCormick is reported daily to the Mahoning Dam. Call (814) 257-8811.

*Normal Wet Period:* No available statistics on seasons. Since this section is tiny, it should normally be runnable only after a heavy rain or during spring snowmelt.

## C. Upstream of US Route 119      5.0 miles
## to State Route 210

| Class | Grad | Size (Area/Volume) | Scene/Poll | Level |
|-------|------|--------------------|-----------|-------|
| C | 6/6 | Small (70/117) estimate | A-B/A | 3.0-?? McCormick |

*Topographic Maps:* Marion Center

*County Maps:* Indiana

*Description:* The stream winds back and forth in the valley and is bordered by many willow trees. You may get a glimpse of beavers, muskrats, kingfishers, or ducks anywhere along this stream. [Reported 1981]

*Difficulties:* None.

*Shuttle:* Put-in about 0.25 miles upstream of US Route 119 bridge along State Route 236. The US Route 119 bridge is posted due to abuse by fishermen. Head downstream on State Route 236 and cross US Route 119 and drive down the valley. The road parallels the stream at the Mottarns Mill bridge. Cross State Route 210 to a dirt road at the pig farm. Take out at a convenient point along this road. As the stream bends away from the road there is a church camp. You can drive into this area to check on the take-out.

*Gauges:* McCormick. This gauge should read above 3.0 feet. This corresponds to a flow of 180 cfs.

*Normal Wet Period:* The McCormick gauge is above 3.0 feet 28% of the time.

222 Allegheny Watershed

# D. State Route 210 to McCormick    4.0 miles

| Class | Grad | Size (Area/Volume) | Scene/Poll | Level |
|---|---|---|---|---|
| B | 4/4 | Small (80/133) estimate | A-B/A | 3.0-?? McCormick |

*Topographic Maps:* Marion Center

*County Maps:* Indiana

*Description:* This is the most peaceful and quiet section of the entire stream with the exception of the Mahoning Lake. [Reported prior to 1975]

*Difficulties:* There is a man-made rock pile dam next to a camp near the bottom end. If there is no break in the dam you should land and carry your boat over the rocks.

*Shuttle:* Take State Route 210 south toward Plumville, to just a mile past Georgeville. Take a right next to a cemetery. The sign should read McCormick or Smicksburg. Cross the Mahoning at the bottom of the hill and turn on the old road about 400 yards on the right. This road runs back to the stream.

*Gauges:* McCormick. This gauge should read above 3.0 feet. This corresponds to a flow of 180 cfs.

*Normal Wet Period:* The McCormick gauge is above 3.0 feet 28% of the time.

# E. McCormick    5.0 miles
## to State Route 954 (Smicksburg)

| Class | Grad | Size (Area/Volume) | Scene/Poll | Level |
|---|---|---|---|---|
| C-I | 6/6 | Small (87/153) McCormick | A-B/A | 3.0-?? McCormick |

*Topographic Maps:* Marion Center, Plumville

*County Maps:* Indiana

*Description:* Almost the entire section is in the flood plain of Mahoning Dam which is 18 to 20 miles downstream.

However, it is not as bad as it sounds.  There are many
riffles and chutes which make the trip interesting, plus an
abundance of waterfowl and wildlife.  [Reported prior to
1975]

*Difficulties:* None.

*Shuttle:* If you follow the road along the stream you will see
a thriving Amish community in the Smicksburg area.  Take
out at the State Route 954 bridge.

*Gauges:* McCormick.  This gauge should read above
3.0 feet.  This corresponds to a flow of 180 cfs.

*Normal Wet Period:* The McCormick gauge is above 3.0 feet
28% of the time.

# F.  State Route 954 (Smicksburg)        5.0 miles
## to the 'Forks' Junction with Mahoning

| Class | Grad | Size (Area/Volume) | Scene/Poll | Level |
|-------|------|--------------------|-----------|-------|
| C | 5/5 | Small (113/188) | A-B/A | 3.0-?? |
|   |     | mouth of stream |       | McCormick |

*Topographic Maps:* Plumville, Dayton

*County Maps:* Indiana

*Description:* The scenery changes from flat land to scenic
steep cliffs on some of the bends.  There are enough rocks,
riffles, and chutes to make the trip interesting.  If the dam
has recently backed water up over the area, the banks may
be a real mess of mud.  [Reported prior 1975]

*Difficulties:* None.

*Shuttle:* From the bridge take State Route 954 south
0.25 miles (through the village) and turn right, then right
again after 100 yards.  This will take you over the stream on
a high bridge.  Follow this road about 4 miles to the bridge at
the river junction.  To extend the trip another 6.5 miles,
continue to a boat launch on the Dayton side of Mahoning
Lake.  See the Distant topographic map.  Take-out is at the
junction of the Little Mahoning with the main Mahoning at

a small bridge. If this looks too messy, paddle up the main Mahoning to a better location.

*Gauges:* McCormick. This gauge should read above 3.0 feet. This corresponds to a flow of 180 cfs.

*Normal Wet Period:* The McCormick gauge is above 3.0 feet 28% of the time.

# Red Bank Creek

## A. Brookville to Summerville                    10.5 miles

| Class | Grad | Size (Area/Volume) | Scene/Poll | Level |
|-------|------|---------------------|------------|-------|
| C-I | 6/10 | Medium (220/367) | B/B | |
| | | Brookville | | Brookville |

*Topographic Maps:* Brookville, Corsica, Summerville

*County Maps:* Jefferson

*Description:* The first half of this run flows in a shallow valley and is paralleled only by the railroad. Occasional strip mine scars can be seen. At mid-run, State Route 28 joins the stream which now flows against low hills with a broad flat valley. [Reported 1987]

*Difficulties:* None on Red Bank. Paddlers should not attempt to put in on the North Fork above Brookville for access to Red Bank. There is a dangerous drop on the North Fork under the US Route 322 bridge. See warning and description for that stream.

*Shuttle:* Put in near the junction of Sandy Lick Creek and North Fork behind the White-Brook, Inc. building in Brookville. This is river left, upstream of the Pickering Street bridge (concrete bridge above State Route 36 steel bridge). Take State Route 28 south to Summerville. In Summerville take a left/east turn on any road towards the river. Pick a spot along the river road that will not antagonize the locals.

*Gauges:* Brookville. This gauge was recalibrated in 1989. Please report new data. The St. Charles gauge further downstream will probably read above 3.8 feet.

*Normal Wet Period:* St. Charles above 3.8 feet 40 percent of the year.

# B. Summerville to New Bethlehem           16.5 miles

| Class | Grad | Size (Area/Volume) | Scene/Poll | Level |
|-------|------|--------------------|------------|-------|
| C-I   | 6/11 | Medium (350/583)   | B/B        | 3.8-5.5 |
|       |      | estimate           |            | St. Charles |

*Topographic Maps:* Summerville, New Bethlehem

*County Maps:* Jefferson, Clarion, Armstrong

*Description:* The first 5 miles has sweeping bends in a wide valley. Just below the run's only railroad bridge, the creek enters a shallow canyon about 300 feet deep that continues for the middle 5 miles of the run. Little Sandy Creek enters the Red Bank while in this canyon. The canyon ends at State Route 536 at Mayport and State Route 28 rejoins the stream. The final 5 miles is again in a wide valley with a series of towns ending with New Bethlehem. The last mile is on the backwater of the dam in New Bethlehem. [Reported 1987]

*Difficulties:* None. Take out on river right above the dam in New Bethlehem. Stay well clear of chute on river right at the dam.

*Shuttle:* State Route 28 connects New Bethlehem to Summerville. At Summerville take a right-hand turn on any road to the river. Alternate put-ins are available at Heathville for a 12 mile trip, and Mayport for a 5.5 mile trip.

*Gauges:* St. Charles. This gauge should read between 3.8 and 5.5 feet. This corresponds to a flow of 575 cfs to 1,710 cfs.

*Normal Wet Period:* This section is normally runnable from early December through late May and does not have a season where it is too high. The St. Charles gauge is above 3.8 feet 40% of the time and above 5.5 feet 15% of the time.

# C. New Bethlehem                                        27.8 miles
## to Rimer on the Allegheny River

| Class | Grad | Size (Area/Volume) | Scene/Poll | Level |
|-------|------|--------------------|------------|-------|
| I | 9/29 | Medium (528/873) | A/B | 3.6-6.9 |
| | | St. Charles | | St. Charles |

*Topographic Maps:* New Bethlehem, Distant, Templeton, Sligo, East Brady

*County Maps:* Clarion, Armstrong

*Description:* This is a major tributary of the Allegheny that is freeflowing, unlike many of its neighbors to the north and south. This section enters a canyon that reaches 500 feet deep in places and maintains a serpentine course against high hills with a mixture of hardwood and evergreens. Shortly below New Bethlehem there is a 3 mile loop that comes within 500 feet of closing on itself. The loop is visible from above on the shuttle road near Distant. The 11.7 mile section between Climax and Lawsonham has 15 feet per mile average gradient. The current is reasonably swift but the rocks are small. [Checked 1989]

*Difficulties:* As you approach St. Charles there is a riffle, an 800 foot long section of Class II whitewater. It can be carried, or there may be an easy route along the right-hand shore. If you chose the section of this trip that includes the Allegheny River be aware of the lock and dam about 2 miles downstream from the mouth. See the description of the Ohio River for locking through a lock and dam. One wants to approach it along the left-hand shore and remain clear of any barge traffic.

*Shuttle:* Put in on stream right, just below a small 5-foot dam at the bridge where State Route 28/66 crosses the creek in New Bethlehem. To find the take-out, take State Route 28/66 south, leave 28/66 by going straight in Distant, turn right a quarter of a mile past Kellersburg, take right fork 1.6 miles past Widnoon (at Tidal). At Lawsonham, take out immediately below the bridge on the right. Ask the McCennas if you can use this grassy spot; they are very friendly. Follow this road 3 miles to mouth of the Red Bank and the Allegheny River. This take-out is about 50 yards downstream from the mouth. It is terribly steep and across the railroad tracks from the cars. A better take-out is at Lock and Dam No. 9 on the Allegheny River 2 miles downstream from the mouth of the Red Bank. Continue straight at Tidal to Rimer and follow access road 2 miles upstream to the lock. This section has a number of intermediate access points. Two of the more commonly run trips are New Bethlehem to St. Charles, and Climax to Lawsonham.

| | |
|---|---|
| New Bethlehem to Climax | 6.1 miles |
| Climax to St. Charles | 2.6 miles |
| St. Charles to Lawsonham | 9.1 miles |
| Lawsonham to Allegheny River | 6.0 miles |
| Allegheny River to Lock and Dam | 2.0 miles |
| Lock and Dam to Rimer | 2.0 miles |

*Gauges:* St. Charles. This gauge should read between 3.6 and 6.9 feet. This corresponds to a flow of 475 cfs to 3,120 cfs.

*Normal Wet Period:* This section is normally runnable from late November through late May and does not have a season where it is too high. The St. Charles gauge is above 3.6 feet 45% of the time and above 6.9 feet 5% of the time.

# Little Sandy Creek
# (Jefferson County)

## Worthville to Mayport         8.0 miles
## (Red Bank Creek)

| Class | Grad | Size (Area/Volume) | Scene/Pol | Level |
|-------|------|--------------------|-----------|-------|
| I | 15/30 | Small (73/122) | A-B/A | |
| | | mouth | | |

*Topographic Maps:* Summerville, New Bethlehem

*County Maps:* Jefferson, Armstrong, Clarion

*Description:* From Worthville to the State Route 3003 bridge below Langeville this is a pastoral stream running through farms and near roads. The steep mud banks are slippery but not high, and you should expect numerous fallen trees. A sandstone outcropping just downstream from the mouth of Ferguson Run offers the opportunity to hunt fossils while you eat lunch. At State Route 3003, the creek enters a 300 foot deep gorge, lined with rhododendron, laurel, hemlock and wild roses. If you catch the creek with water in late June, you will find the fragrance delightful and the display stunning. In the gorge, the gradient picks up to a steady 25 feet per mile, which appears as continuous riffles rather than distinct rapids. The trip ends with 1.5 miles on the Red Bank Creek, which will be flowing at a pretty good rate whenever the Little Sandy is up. [Reported 1989]

*Difficulties:* Expect fallen trees partially or completely blocking the river.

*Shuttle:* To reach Worthville from State Route 28, turn sharp right on State Route 536 about 5 miles northeast of the New Bethlehem bridge. Cross the Red Bank Creek at Mayport. This will be the take-out. Turn left after crossing the bridge in Mayport continuing on State Route 536. About 2.5 miles after the northeast edge of North Freedom, turn left on an unnumbered road just after crossing Nolf Run. Follow this road for 1.5 miles and turn left when it joins State Route 3003 just before crossing the Little Sandy. Follow State Route 3003 through Langeville, bearing right where

3003 forks left. After a mile this road becomes State Route 3031, which takes you to Worthville. The put-in is the State Route 3014 bridge over the Little Sandy immediately after turning right on a side road. To reach the take-out, retrace your steps. There is intermediate access at the State Route 3003 bridge.

*Gauge:* St. Charles. This gauge on nearby Red Bank Creek will probably read above 6.3 feet.

*Normal Wet Period:* No available statistics on seasons. Since this section is small, it should normally be runnable approximately January through April.

# Red Bank Creek, North Fork

**Richardsville**      10.0 miles
**to Dr. Walter W. Dick Park in Brookville**

| Class | Grad | Size (Area/Volume) | Scene/Poll | Level |
|-------|------|--------------------|------------|-------|
| I | 13/17 | Small (98/163) | A/A | |
| | | mouth of stream | | Brookville |

*Topographic Maps:* Munderf, Hazen, Brookville, Sigel

*County Maps:* Jefferson

*Description:* This gem of a stream is clean and pristine throughout the run. The size is sufficient and the difficulty low enough so that paddlers can relax and soak up the beauty of the seven-mile valley. The first 2 miles below Richardsville has a wide valley floor with meandering stream. Then in a sharp loop, the stream turns south and enters a shallow canyon that provides a beautiful valley. Most of the valley below this point is part of one estate, and paddlers should respect the property owner's rights. A seemingly out-of-place grass bank on river right about 3 miles below the bridge marks the site of the owner's home. The spectacular home and setting blends well with the valley. Another mile reveals the high bridge of I-80 at the take-out. Recommended take-out is at the recreational area on river right at the dam. [Reported 1990]

*Difficulties:* None for the recommended take-out. Paddlers attempting to proceed downstream for the additional mile into Brookville or to the mouth of the North Fork must be aware of the sudden drop under the US Route 322 bridge. This drop is a killer! The approach has a flood levee on stream right with a sign reading "DANGER - SUDDEN DROP - KEEP OUT". Paddlers should take out immediately when seeing the sign as there is very little opportunity to take out above the bridge.

*Shuttle:* State Route 4005 (formerly State Route 968) from US Route 322 near the "sudden drop" bridge. This road crosses the put-in north of Richardsville. Access to the park is Water Plant Road in Brookville from US Route 322. An alternate put-in is about 4 miles below Richardsville on State Route 4006 due west out of Richardsville. This put-in drops paddlers into the heart of the valley.

For small-stream aficionados this stream can be run as high as the Munderf-Warsaw road with several tree problems above Richardsville.

*Gauges:* Brookville. This gauge was recalibrated in 1989. Please report new data. The St. Charles gauge further downstream will probably read between 4.5 and 8.0 feet.

*Normal Wet Period:* No available statistics on seasons. Since this section is small, it should normally be runnable approximately January through April.

# Sandy Lick Creek

## Reynoldsville to Brookville                    20.0 miles

| Class | Grad | Size (Area / Volume) | Scene / Poll | Level |
|-------|------|----------------------|--------------|-------|
| I-II | 8/19 | Small (114/190) | B/B | |
| | | Reynoldsville | | Brookville |

*Topographic Maps:* Reynoldsville, Coolspring, Brookville

*County Maps:* Jefferson

*Description:* This is a pleasant wooded stream along a railroad. The upper half has occasional light rapids which become more frequent on the lower half of the trip. This is very pleasant canoeing with fast current for easy paddling. As you approach Port Barnett there are many chains of curious, tiny, man-made islands in mid-stream. [Reported prior 1975, State Game Lands to Port Barnett checked 1988]

*Difficulties:* A long rock garden (Class II) about a mile above the Fuller Run Road bridge needs quick rock dodging.

*Shuttle:* Put in at the US Route 322 bridge in Reynoldsville. The banks are steep and slippery. Follow US Route 322 west to where you cross the stream in Brookville. There are several intermediate points for put-ins and take-outs. One is in the middle of the State Game Lands Number 249, where a side road crosses the stream about 2 miles south of US Route 322. Another put-in is where State Route 2025 crosses about 2 miles south of US Route 322. An alternate take-out is about 2 miles upstream of Brookville in Port Barnett. It is located about 100 yards south of US Route 322 on State Route 2023 by a tall free-standing chimney.

*Gauges:* Brookville. This gauge was recalibrated in 1989. Please report new data. Check the rapids at Brookville for runnability. This is one of the shallower spots on the run. The St. Charles gauge on the nearby Red Bank will probably read between 4.3 and 6.0 feet.

*Normal Wet Period:* No available statistics on seasons. Since this section is small, it should normally be runnable approximately January through April.

# Mill Creek
# (Jefferson County)

## Allen Mills to Port Barnett                    9.0 miles

| Class | Grad  | Size (Area / Volume) | Scene / Poll | Level |
|-------|-------|----------------------|--------------|-------|
| II    | 35/52 | Tiny (53/88)         | A/B          |       |
|       |       | mouth of stream      |              | Brookville |

*Topographic Maps:* Hazen, Brookville

*County Maps:* Jefferson

*Description:* This stream offers 4 miles of delightful Class II in a pretty valley. The whitewater is small rocky drops and occasional small ledges. The scenery is mature hemlock and pines on river left and deciduous brushy forest on the right. A railroad is in the valley, but mostly hidden from the water. Access is very limited, requiring a 2-mile run through alder and downed trees to enjoy the remainder of the Creek below Horm Run. The stream changes character below Interstate-80. The gradient eases, the run becomes Class I, a few homes appear. There is a boulder dam that can be run. [Reported 1989]

*Difficulties:* Trees and alder dominate the first 2 miles. Possible downed trees throughout the run. The boulder dam at a big home is run right of center. An alternate put-in 1 mile upstream at Allens Mills bridge is not recommended due to a beaver dam just downstream The swamp above the beaver dam and the remaining stream are almost totally choked with alder. (A brush-cutting trip would do wonders.)

*Shuttle:* To reach the put-in, go northeast from Interstate 80 about 5 miles on State Route 830 to the bridge. Return west on State Route 830, cross Interstate 80 to US Route 322. Turn right/west on US Route 322 and go about 5 miles to the old tall chimney at Port Barnett. Parking is across Mill Creek upstream of the bridge. Warning: State Route 830 has been rerouted. Some old maps show the connection from Interstate 80 to Allen Mills as State Route 310.

*Gauges:* Brookville. This gauge was recalibrated in 1989. Please report new data. The St. Charles gauge on nearby Red Bank Creek will probably read above 7.0 feet.

*Normal Wet Period:* No available statistics on seasons. Since this section is tiny, it should normally be runnable only after a heavy rain or during spring snowmelt.

# Clarion River

## A. Johnsonburg to Ridgway                                    8.5 miles

| Class | Grad | Size (Area / Volume) | Scene / Poll | Level |
|-------|------|----------------------|--------------|-------|
| C-I | 8/11 | Medium (204/385) Johnsonburg Medium (303/591) Ridgway | B/B | 2.2-?? Johnsonburg |

*Topographic Maps:* Ridgway

*County Maps:* Elk

*Description:* This stream differs radically from the downstream Clarion sections. The valley above Ridgway is wide and relatively flat with considerable industrial development. The valley is the corridor for US Route 219 and Conrail. The river is wide enough to be free from tree hazards and meanders slightly in its course to Ridgway. [Reported 1987]

*Difficulties:* There are two dams on the run. The first is a rock and timber structure near a power substation on the edge of Ridgway. This can be run, over the broken-down sections, but should be scouted. The second is a 6-foot industrial dam near the take-out. Portage on the right. Note there are two additional dams in Johnsonburg, but the specified put-in is below both of these dams.

*Shuttle:* US Route 219. Put in at the ball field, below the paper mill in Johnsonburg, along US Route 219. Take out at Love's Canoe on State Route 948 in Ridgway.

*Gauges:* Johnsonburg. This gauge should read above 2.2 feet. This corresponds to a flow of 330 cfs. The Ridgway gauge will probably read above 4.0 feet.

*Normal Wet Period:* The Johnsonburg gauge is above 2.2 feet 32% of the time.

# B. Ridgway to Cooksburg                    44 miles

| Class | Grad | Size (Area/Volume) | Scene/Poll | Level |
|-------|------|--------------------|-----------|-------|
| C-I | 6/10 | Medium (303/591) | A/B | 3.0-?? |
| | | Ridgway | | Ridgway |
| | | Medium (807/1,462) Cooksburg | | |

*Topographic Maps:* Ridgway, Portland Mills, Carman, Hallton, Munderf, Sigel, Cooksburg

*County Maps:* Elk, Jefferson, Forest

*Other Maps:* The Western Pennsylvania Conservancy publishes a detailed map showing bridges, towns, and access sites.

*Description:* The sections between Ridgway and Mill Creek and between Piney (Deer Creek) and Parker are popular with cruising canoeists due to the scenery, wildlife, fishing and camping. Cleanup efforts are reducing the pollution from strip mine drainage and a paper mill above Ridgway. There are many possible camping spots along the river, including nice spots at Portland Mills (mile 9) across from Bear Creek and just above the Y rapid (mile 16). Another good camping spot (capacity of about 40) is on river right at a bend 1.0 mile downstream of Heath Station (mile 26). Clear Creek State Park also has camping. [Checked 1989]

*Difficulties:* None

*Shuttle:* Pun it at Love's Canoe on State Route 949. Shuttle via State Route 949. There are many possibilities for put-in and take-out spots between Ridgway and Cooksburg. Rental canoes and shuttles are available from several outfitters at or near Cooksburg. This trip can be split into two parts. Ridgway to Belltown bridge (off State Route 949) is 27 miles and the remaining section to Cooksburg of 16 miles.

*Gauges:* Ridgway. This gauge should read above 3.0 feet. This corresponds to a flow of 270 cfs. The Cooksburg gauge at the downstream end of the trip will probably read between 2.8 and 5.0 feet.

*Normal Wet Period:* The Ridgway gauge is above 3.0 feet 60% of the time.

# C. Cooksburg to Mill Creek                    11.8 miles

| Class | Grad | Size (Area/Volume) | Scene/Poll | Level |
|-------|------|--------------------|-----------|-------|
| C-I | 6/20 | Medium (807/1,462) | A/B | 2.3-?? |
| | | Cooksburg | | Cooksburg |

*Topographic Maps:* Cooksburg, Lucinda, Strattanville, Clarion

*County Maps:* Forest, Jefferson, Clarion

*Other Maps:* The Western Pennsylvania Conservancy publishes a detailed map showing bridges, towns, and access sites.

*Description:* This section is remote below Gravel Lick. There are no roads or railroads along almost 10 miles of river before coming to Mill Creek. It consists of long pools, with riffles interspersed. The last 2 miles is the backwater of Piney Dam. In the backwaters there are numerous motorboats and sometimes the water level drops to where the banks become unattractive. [Checked 1989]

*Difficulties:* Motorboats with waterskiers above Piney Dam.

*Shuttle:* The put-in is located just off State Route 36 by the parking lot of the Cook Forest State Park Office. To get to the take-out drive south from Cooksburg on State Route 36 for about 1.9 miles to where the main highway turns east and a dirt road goes west. Turn west onto the dirt road and go through the woods for 4.0 miles. Turn right/west onto State Route 1003, travel another 0.5 miles to Fisher. In Fisher go straight onto State Route 1001. Drive 5.0 miles to the edge of Strattanville, turn right/north, go 2.0 miles to the Mill Creek access ramp.

*Gauges:* Cooksburg. This gauge should read above 2.3 feet. This corresponds to a flow of 350 cfs.

*Normal Wet Period:* The Cooksburg gauge is above 2.3 feet 80% of the time.

# D. Mill Creek to Callensburg                    21.0 miles

| Class | Grad | Size (Area / Volume) | Scene / Poll | Level |
|-------|------|----------------------|--------------|-------|
| C-I   | 6/10 | Medium (951/1,787)   | B/B          |       |
|       |      | Piney Dam            |              | Piney Dam |

*Topographic Maps:* Strattanville, Clarion, Knox

*County Maps:* Clarion

*Other Maps:* The Western Pennsylvania Conservancy
publishes a detailed map with towns and access sites.

*Description:* First 11.5 miles are the backwater of Piney Dam operated by Pennsylvania Electric Co. There is heavy motorboat traffic in this area. Pool level rises about 1.5 feet when water is being held, and drops the same amount in the afternoon while power is being generated. Portage the dam on the left at the gravel road leading to the parking lot. One can use the phone there to determine the water release schedule. From the dam down there are some Class I rapids and numerous riffles. [Checked 1989]

*Difficulties:* If you outrun the released water, you will find yourself in a rock garden with minimal water.

*Shuttle:* From the Mill Creek access ramp drive south 2.0 miles to Strattanville. Turn right/west onto US Route 322, go into Clarion. Take US Route 68 South for 11.0 miles to Sligo, turn right/west onto State Route 58. Go 4.0 miles to the Callensburg bridge. To avoid 11 miles of flatwater, put in at the Pennelec Recreation Area. To reach this area at the base of the dam, go south on State Route 68 from Interstate 80. About 0.8 miles from the Interstate turn right/west onto State Route 3016 (Brush Road). Continue for about 2 miles and turn right/north onto State Route 2007. The recreation area is about 1 mile from the turn.

*Gauges:* Piney Dam. We do not have enough information to report runnable levels on this section. Call the Piney Dam substation (814) 226-8630.

*Normal Wet Period:* Water releases from Piney Dam can make it runnable at any time during the year.

# E. Callensburg to Parker                                17.0 miles

| Class | Grad | Size (Area/Volume) | Scene/Poll | Level |
|-------|------|--------------------|-----------|-------|
| B | 6/6 | Large (1,246/2,252) | A-B/B | |
| | | St. Petersburg | | Piney Dam |

*Topographic Maps:* Knox, Emlenton, Parker

*County Maps:* Clarion

*Other Maps:* The Western Pennsylvania Conservancy publishes a detailed map showing bridges, towns, and access sites.

*Description:* The trip from Callensburg to Parker is pleasant when the water conditions are right. The car shuttle is only 8 miles for a 17-mile trip on the water. The scenic values are not comparable to those above Piney Dam. The dam and power-generating facilities are operated by the Pennsylvania Electric Company. Because of the nature of these operations, the flow below the dam can change suddenly. Before canoeing, call the Piney Dam substation (814) 226-8630 in Clarion to determine the amount and timing of water to be released. The crest moves about 2 miles/hour. [Checked 1989]

*Difficulties:* None.

*Shuttle:* Use State Route 368.

*Gauges:* Piney Dam. We do not have enough information to report runnable levels on this section. Call the Piney Dam substation (814) 226-8630.

*Normal Wet Period:* Dam controlled, but usually dry after early August.

# Toby Creek
# (Clarion County)

## A. State Route 1013                                    7.0 miles
## to State Game Lands #72

| Class | Grad | Size (Area/Volume) | Scene/Poll | Level |
|-------|------|--------------------|------------|-------|
| I | 23/47 | Tiny (25/42) estimate | A/B | |

*Topographic Maps:* Lucinda, Strattanville

*County Maps:* Clarion

*Description:* Putting in on this tiny stream is like stepping back to the days of virgin timber in the state. The valley is dominated by mature hemlock with occasional pockets of deciduous trees and a few meadows. The forest floor is mostly open. There is no alder, although a few tree carries are required. Acid runoff is evident in lower parts of the run. [Reported 1989]

*Difficulties:* Trees, especially at islands. A low-water bridge. A runnable 2-foot dam with mildly sloping concrete face.

*Shuttle:* The put-in is reached by taking State Route 1005 north from Clarion to the second left turn past the Helens Furnace historical marker. This is State Route 1013. The take-out is the second bridge above Clarion lake. This is the lower bridge in State Game Lands Number 72. From the put-in retrace your path towards Clarion. Turn right/west 1.25 miles before the bridge across Clarion Lake. Note this turn on the way to the put-in so you will recognize it on the shuttle.

*Gauges:* Cooksburg. This gauge on nearby Clarion River will probably read above 7.0 feet.

*Normal Wet Period:* No available statistics on seasons. Since this section is tiny, it should normally be runnable only after a heavy rain or during spring snowmelt.

# B. State Game Lands #72 to Clarion Lake   2.1 miles

| Class | Grad | Size (Area/Volume) | Scene/Poll | Level |
|-------|------|---------------------|------------|-------|
| III | 29/60 | Tiny (35/58) | A/A | |
| | | mouth of stream | | |

*Topographic Maps:* Strattanville, Fryburg, Clarion

*County Maps:* Clarion

*Description:* Surprise! This is a whitewater gem. Rapids range from short steep boulder drops to shallow ledges with many small holes. A couple of sizeable holes can be found. Much of the stream flows on bedrock. There are many opportunities to play. Acid drainage is evident from the rock color but the valley is otherwise beautiful. [Reported 1989]

*Difficulties:* Major problems to Class I paddlers who miss the take-out for the upper section.

*Shuttle:* The put-in is reached by going north from Clarion on State Route 1005. Go 1.25 miles past the bridge over Clarion Lake and turn left/west. Recommended take-out is the Clarion side of the bridge across Clarion Lake on State Route 1005. An alternate take-out at the beginning of the lake is found by taking the first road away from the lake. Access to the stream is poor at the alternate take-out.

*Gauges:* Cooksburg. This gauge on nearby Clarion River will probably read above 6.5 feet.

*Normal Wet Period:* No available statistics on seasons. Since this section is tiny, it should normally be runnable only after a heavy rain or during spring snowmelt.

# Mill Creek (Clarion County)

**2nd Bridge below State Route 949**                    10.5 miles
**to Clarion Lake**

| Class | Grad | Size (Area/Volume) | Scene/Poll | Level |
|-------|------|--------------------|-----------|-------|
| II | 23/52 | Tiny (59/98) | A/A | |
| | | mouth of stream | | |

*Topographic Maps:* Corsica, Strattanville

*County Maps:* Jefferson, Clarion

*Description:* This stream is a gem for whitewater paddlers looking for wilderness setting and Class II difficulty. The otherwise perfect setting is marred slightly by a recent pipeline and silty water coming from the upstream watershed. Scenery is dominated by hemlock and mature forests in a beautiful canyon. The area of this run is mostly within State Game Lands and therefore controlled. The run breaks roughly into thirds. The first third is small volume, uniform gradient with small rocks, easy maneuvering. The next third is Class I continuing past the Strattanville-Fisher road (State Route 1001). The final third is a Class II plunge to the lake over bedrock ledges with waves and small holes. The whitewater ends within a few hundred yards of the take-out. The price for enjoying the upper Class II stretch is 1.5 miles of tiny stream with alder and trees. [Reported 1989]

*Difficulties:* Trees and alder through the first 1.5 miles. Possible downed trees throughout.

*Shuttle:* The put-in is reached by taking State Route 949 north from US Route 322 in Corsica to a bridge. Follow Township road on south bank downstream 1 mile to a hilltop, turn right, continue a 0.5 miles to a crossroads, turn right again, follow this road 0.75 miles to the put-in. Take-out is the Mill Creek Pennelec access area on Clarion Lake. Turn north off US Route 322 in Strattanville and follow signs to the Pennelec Recreation Area. An alternate put-in for a 3-mile whitewater run into the lake is State Route 1001 between Strattanville and Fisher.

*Gauges:* Cooksburg. This gauge on nearby Clarion River will probably read above 6.5 feet.

*Normal Wet Period:* No available statistics on seasons. Since this section is tiny, it should normally be runnable only after a heavy rain or during spring snowmelt.

# Millstone Creek, West Branch

## Forest Service Road 130 to Clarion River    12.2 miles

Class  Grad    Size (Area / Volume)      Scene / Poll  Level
I-II   34/47        Tiny (24/40)              A / A
                junction with East Branch

*Topographic Maps:* Marienville East, Marienville West, Sigel

*County Maps:* Forest, Elk

*Description:* The run from Forest Service Road 130 to the Marienville-Loleta road is tiny and in mixed woods and meadow. Swamp conditions with alder and tree jams are common. Beaver dams can be found. Below the Marienville-Loleta bridge the stream maintains a near-uniform character and gradient in an isolated canyon among mixed hardwoods and hemlock forests. Canoe camping is possible in a small stream whitewater setting. This one is a gem. [Reported 1989]

*Difficulties:* Lots of trees and brush above the Marienville-Loleta road. A few trees at islands below.

*Shuttle:* To get to the put-in, locate the intersection of State Route 66 and State Route 2005 in Marienville. North of this intersection you will find Forest Service Road 130, which heads due east from State Route 66. Follow it for 2 miles to the stream. To get to the take out, return to Marienville. Take State Route 2005 south to the Loleta Recreation Area. Turn right on the road which runs along the East Branch, and continue to the take out at the junction with the Clarion.

*Gauges:* Ridgway. This gauge on nearby Clarion River will probably read between 8.5 and 9.5 feet. Check conditions along Marienville-Loleta road before running.

*Normal Wet Period:* No available statistics on seasons. Since this section is tiny, it should normally be runnable only after a heavy rain or during spring snowmelt.

# Millstone Creek, East Branch

## A. Gurgling Run                                          5.7 miles
## to Loleta Recreation Area

*Class*  *Grad*   *Size (Area/Volume)*    *Scene/Poll*  *Level*
III+    42/112       Tiny (26/43)             A/A
                  junction with West Branch

*Topographic Maps:* Marienville East

*County Maps:* Elk

*Description:* Observed from Forest Service Road 131, the East Branch appears too small to run and only Class I. However, from the put-in to Lick Run there are three sections away from the road with steep rocky drops mixed with easier, fast flowing stream. The steepest section is around Muddy Fork. The few cabins near Muddy Fork are unobtrusive. [Reported 1989]

*Difficulties:* Fallen trees are always possible. The size from Gurgling Run to unnamed run downstream is small enough so that spinning around may not be possible. Drops below Muddy Fork may require scouting. A gas pipeline near the cabins must be portaged. Loleta Recreation Area has two dams, fifty yards apart. During the recreation season both must be portaged if continuing downstream. Out of season the upper drop of one foot can be run and take out on the swimming beach to carry the lower dam.

*Shuttle:* From the put-in on Forest Service Road 228 at Gurgling Run continue along the stream following this route and then Forest Service Road 131 to the Loleta Recreation Area on State Route 2005. Alternatively chose a put-in or take-out any place convenient along Forest Service Road 131.

*Gauges:* Ridgway. This gauge on nearby Clarion River will probably read above 8.0 feet. Check conditions along Forest Service Road 131 before running.

*Normal Wet Period:* No available statistics on seasons. Since this section is tiny, it should normally be runnable only after a heavy rain or during spring snowmelt.

## B. Loleta Recreation Area                                   4.0 miles
## to Clarion River

| Class | Grad | Size (Area/Volume) | Scene/Poll | Level |
|-------|------|--------------------|-----------|-------|
| II-III | 35/52 | Tiny (54/90) | A/A | |
| | | mouth of stream | | |

*Topographic Maps:* Marienville East, Sigel

*County Maps:* Elk

*Description:* This is one of several delightful alternatives in the Clarion Basin during high water conditions. The pace is continuous Class II with a couple of rocky drops to add to the excitement. The Forest Service Road maintains its distance, leaving an isolated valley. Only a pipeline right-of-way mars the scenery. [Reported 1989]

*Difficulties:* Fallen trees are possible.

*Shuttle:* Forest Service Road road from Loleta Recreation Area, along the river to the mouth at the junction with the Clarion River.

*Gauges:* Ridgway. This gauge on nearby Clarion River will probably read above 6.0 feet. Check conditions along Forest Service Road 131 before running.

*Normal Wet Period:* No available statistics on seasons. Since this section is tiny, it should normally be runnable only after a heavy rain or during spring snowmelt.

# Spring Creek

## Duhring to Hallton                              10.5 miles

| Class | Grad | Size (Area/Volume) | Scene/Poll | Level |
|-------|------|--------------------|------------|-------|
| I | 15/25 | Small (88/147) mouth of stream | A/A | |

*Topographic Maps:* Russell City, Lynch, Hallton

*County Maps:* Forest, Elk

*Description:* Duhring to Forest Service Road 130 bridge is remote with beaver dams and other wildlife in mixed woodlands. The pace is very relaxed through here. Some homes are visible from the water. Below Forest Service Road 130 the pace quickens with steady wave action. The five-mile run from Forest Service Road 130 to the mouth is an alternative with easy shuttle in the valley. A good alternative to high-water Clarion runs. [Reported 1989]

*Difficulties:* Trees around islands, beaver dam.

*Shuttle:* Put in where Forest Service Road 124 crosses the creek north of Duhring. To reach the take-out, turn left/south on Forest Service Road 131 just west of the put-in, then turn left/east on Forest Service Road 130 in Lamona-ville, and follow 130 to towards Hallton. In the summer of 1989, the demise of a bridge over Big Run made it no longer possible to travel by Forest Service Road 130 to Hallton. This shortened this run by about 1 mile. This stream was run two days after the bridge was washed out, so the bridge may be repaired by now. If you choose to run both the East Branch and Spring Creek, shuttle by way of Forest Service Road 136 over Owl's Nest and through Sackett and Four Corners.

*Gauges:* Wilcox. This gauge on nearby West Branch of Clarion River will probably read above 2.5 feet.

*Normal Wet Period:* No available statistics on seasons. Since this section is small, it should normally be runnable approximately January through April.

# Spring Creek, East Branch

## Pigs Ear to Duhring                                  5.5 miles

| Class | Grad | Size (Area / Volume) | Scene / Poll | Level |
|-------|------|----------------------|--------------|-------|
| II | 11/30 | Tiny (24/40) mouth of stream | A / A | |

*Topographic Maps:* Russell City, Lynch

*County Maps:* Elk, Forest

*Description:* This section is a remote headwaters stream in the depths of the National Forest. Unfortunately, it is also in a producing oil and gas field. Numerous wells and pipes are found in the valley but do not detract from the beauty. Whitewater is minor rocky rapids and sharp corners. [Reported 1989]

*Difficulties:* Trees, pipe crossing on cables.

*Shuttle:* To get to the put-in, use State Route 66, turn south on a Forest Service road a 0.2 miles east of State Route 948 junction. This Forest Service Road road is marked to Hi-La Fish Hatchery at Pigs Ear. To get to the take-out, return to State Route 66 and turn west to Forest Service Road 131. Turn towards the river at Duhring.

*Gauges:* Ridgway. This gauge on nearby Clarion River will probably read above 7.0 feet. Check conditions at put-in. Spring Creek at the take-out has additional water from the West Branch, and will not give an adequate indication of conditions.

*Normal Wet Period:* No available statistics on seasons. Since this section is tiny, it should normally be runnable only after a heavy rain or during spring snowmelt.

# Bear Creek (Elk County)

## Forest Service Road 339                    9.0 miles
## to Junction with Clarion at Arroyo

| Class | Grad | Size (Area/Volume) | Scene/Poll | Level |
|-------|------|--------------------|------------|-------|
| I | 20/26 | Tiny (41/68) | A/A | |
| | | mouth of stream | | |

*Topographic Maps:* Portland Mills

*County Maps:* Elk

*Description:* This is a gem. The scenery is excellent with occasional signs of campsites along Forest Service roads that follow parts of the run and a few homes along stream sections not controlled by the National Forest. The action is steady, tree problems are few. Rhododendron and hemlock dominate the lower 2 miles. [Reported 1989]

*Difficulties:* Four cabled and posted fish refuge areas are located on the run. Each is about 50 yards long. Three are easily carried. Fallen trees are a possibility. One welded-pipe foot bridge has collapsed near water level. Two Class II rapids occur within the first 0.5 miles below the Hallton-Ridgway bridge. Both can be navigated safely on the left.

*Shuttle:* Put in at the Bear Creek Picnic Area, about 2 miles east of Owls Nest. Shuttle on Forest Service Road 339 to Owl's Nest, and then Forest Service Road 339 to Arroyo bridge. A 3.3 mile shorter run can be had by taking out in Portland Mills.

*Gauges:* Ridgway. This gauge on nearby Clarion River will probably read above 7.0 feet. Check riffles at Hallton-Ridgway bridge or conditions at put-in.

*Normal Wet Period:* No available statistics on seasons. Since this section is tiny, it should normally be runnable only after a heavy rain or during spring snowmelt.

# Little Toby Creek
# (Elk County)

## Brockway to Clarion River                    11.0 miles

| Class | Grad | Size (Area/Volume) | Scene/Poll | Level |
|-------|------|--------------------|-----------|-------|
| I | 10/14 | Small (91/152) | A-B/A-B | |
| | | Brockway | | |

*Topographic Maps:* Carman

*County Maps:* Jefferson, Elk

*Description:* This scenic stream runs through mixed hardwood forests north into the Clarion River near Portland Mills. For the most part it runs as a Class I stream through a steep, wooded valley about 500 feet deep. It starts out in Brockway as a flat stream with levees, which soon turn into open woods. The stream bed is sand and gravel, but boulders in the creek form Class I rapids. Much of the surrounding land is State Game Lands. [Checked 1989]

*Difficulties:* This creek needs a lot of water to be enjoyable.

*Shuttle:* Put in near the US Route 219 bridge in Brockway. With permission, the emergency rescue station makes a good put-in. To reach the take-out, go north on US Route 219 one or two blocks to reach State Route 28. Turn left/west at the light. Go 4 blocks to the Post Office and turn right/north on Clay Point Road. At the "T" with State Route 1010, turn right. Follow 1010 until it ends in Blowtown and turn right on State Route 4005. Continue on State Route 4005 which becomes State Route 949 in Green Briar. Follow 949 to the river just past Portland Mills.

*Gauges:* Wilcox. This gauge on nearby West Branch of the Clarion River will probably read above 2.0 feet. There is a gauge on the State Route 28 bridge in Brockway which was under construction in 1989.

*Normal Wet Period:* No available statistics on seasons. Since this section is small, it should normally be runnable approximately January through April.

# Mill Creek (Elk County)

## A. State Route 948 to Ridgway Reservoir    9.0 miles

| Class | Grad | Size (Area/Volume) | Scene/Poll | Level |
|-------|------|--------------------|-----------|-------|
| III | 25/28 | Tiny (25/42) | A/A | |
| | | Ridgway Reservoir | | |

*Topographic Maps:* James City, Portland Mills

*County Maps:* Elk

*Description:* Also known as Big Mill Creek, this is the upper of the two Mill Creeks that run into the Clarion. This small tributary of the Clarion drains a near-wilderness area in the southeastern part of the Allegheny National Forest. Portions of the stream are fenced off for fish propagation by the Pennsylvania Fish commission requiring skillful cable ducking or short portages. Note: the signs say it is illegal to be within the fenced off area. We (the editors) have be told by the Fish Commission that this was not the intent and that they would investigate rewording of the signs. The size picks up near the reservoir. You will probably want to combine this run with the next section. [Reported 1987]

*Difficulties:* There is no difficulty at the reservoir dam. Carry over the middle of the dam and put in on the downstream left. It is a tiny stream this high up and fallen trees are a certainty.

*Shuttle:* A put-in on State Route 948 is possible. The take-out is on the left side, 0.3 miles below the dam. A dirt road (Forest Service 143) along the upper 6 miles gives general access for alternatives. To get to the take-out, go south on State Route 948 to Ridgway. Turn right on State Route 3002. Go about 2 miles to the river crossing.

*Gauges:* Wilcox. This gauge on nearby West Branch of the Clarion River will probably read above 4.3 feet.

*Normal Wet Period:* No available statistics on seasons. Since this section is tiny, it should normally be runnable only after a heavy rain or during spring snowmelt.

# B. Ridgway Reservoir                    2.2 miles
# to Clarion River

| Class | Grad | Size (Area/Volume) | Scene/Poll | Level |
|-------|------|--------------------|-----------|-------|
| III | 32/33 | Tiny (32/53) | A/A | |
| | | mouth of stream | | |

*Topographic Maps:* Portland Mills

*County Maps:* Elk

*Description:* This small tributary of the Clarion drains the southeastern area of Allegheny National Forest. The gradient picks up below the dam to make the last 2 miles a pleasant whitewater run. [Reported 1987]

*Difficulties:* Possibility of fallen trees because of its small size.

*Shuttle:* To reach the reservoir, take West Main Street out of Ridgway, which becomes State Route 3002 when State Route 948 turns right. Near hilltop at edge of town, State Route 3002 has a sharp left turn followed in 100 yards by a sharp right with side road to the right between. This road leads to reservoir. To get to the take out, return to Ridgway. Take State Route 949 west. Go about 3 miles to the area across from the mouth of Mill Creek. Take out on left bank of Clarion across from mouth of Big Mill Creek and carry up bank to State Route 949.

Alternate put-ins are Sandy Beach Recreation Area on State Route 3002 for a 1.6 mile run, or at the bridge on Forest Service Road 135 (Bingham Road) off State Route 4001 for a 4.3 mile run beginning above the reservoir. Alternate take-outs are any place along the Clarion above Portland Mills.

*Gauges:* Wilcox. This gauge on nearby West Branch of the Clarion River will probably read above 4.3 feet.

*Normal Wet Period:* No available statistics on seasons. Since this section is tiny, it should normally be runnable only after a heavy rain or during spring snowmelt.

# Elk Creek

## Daguscahonda to Ridgway                              6.4 miles

| Class | Grad | Size (Area/Volume) | Scene/Poll | Level |
|-------|------|--------------------|-----------|-------|
| I-III | 15/25 | Small (64/107) | B-C/B | |
| | | mouth of stream | | |

*Topographic Maps:* Ridgway

*County Maps:* Elk

*Description:* This small tributary of the Clarion east of Ridgway offers a surprise series of ledges for whitewater paddlers in an otherwise Class I-II run. Below the US Route 219 truck bypass the stream enters an industrial and urban valley with channelization. [Reported 1987]

*Difficulties:* Above the State Route 120 bridge there is a strong possibility of downed trees. At the US Route 219 truck bypass, the stream is channelized with a bridge pier in the channel. Large boulders were placed in 200 yards of the channel beginning at the bridge to reduce water velocity and offer Class II difficulty at low levels with unknown conditions at high flows. Paddlers should scout from the shuttle. A series of ledges occurs behind the industrial buildings below the bypass giving this run its Class III rating. Channelization in Ridgway offers no difficulties.

*Shuttle:* State Route 120. Put in at Daguscahonda Run or on side road bridge about 0.5 miles downstream. Take out at the junction with the Clarion at Love's Canoe on State Route 948 in Ridgway. Above Daguscahonda the stream is large enough to paddle but major tree falls make it impractical.

*Gauges:* Wilcox. This gauge on nearby West Branch of the Clarion River will probably read above 4.3 feet.

*Normal Wet Period:* No available statistics on seasons. Since this section is tiny, it should normally be runnable only after a heavy rain or during spring snowmelt.

# Clarion River, West Branch

## Rocky Run to Johnsonburg                        9.9 miles

| Class | Grad | Size (Area/Volume) | Scene/Poll | Level |
|-------|------|--------------------|------------|-------|
| I | 13/18 | Small (63/126) | B/B | 2.0-3.0 |
|   |       | Wilcox |     | Wilcox |

*Topographic Maps:* Wilcox, Ridgway

*County Maps:* Elk

*Description:* This stream flows through a wide valley on the eastern edge of Allegheny National Forest. The 3 miles above Wilcox is small enough for downed trees to be troublesome. Below Wilcox, the stream is open with sufficient size to minimize obstructions and meanders slightly in its due southward course. US Route 219 and a Conrail railroad track follow the stream and often dominate the scenery. [Reported 1987]

*Difficulties:* Paddlers may want to look at the first US Route 219 underpass on the north edge of Johnsonburg. The sheet piling and appearance of this curved water channel are imposing from the water but offer no difficulty to the informed paddler.

*Shuttle:* The put-in is on Horner Road about 3 miles above Wilcox. Take US Route 219 to get to the take-out at ball field between US Route 219 and river just below the paper mill in Johnsonburg. For a 3 mile shorter trip put on at the mouth of Wilson Run in Wilcox.

*Gauges:* Wilcox. This gauge should read between 2.0 and 3.0 feet. This corresponds to a flow of 125 cfs to 415 cfs. The Ridgway gauge further downstream will probably read above 4.5 feet.

*Normal Wet Period:* The Wilcox gauge is above 2.0 feet 30% of the time and above 3.0 feet 4% of the time.

# Clarion River, East Branch

**Glen Hazel to Johnsonburg**                            6.2 miles

| Class | Grad | Size (Area / Volume) | Scene / Poll | Level |
|-------|------|---------------------|--------------|-------|
| I | 11/15 | Small (73/138) | A/B | 2.0-?? |
| | | East Branch Clarion River Dam | | |
| | | Small (80/133) Glen Hazel | | East Br Dam |

*Topographic Maps:* Glen Hazel, Wilcox, Ridgway

*County Maps:* Elk

*Description:* This little tributary of the Clarion is controlled by the East Branch Dam and flows through Bendigo State Park. For most of the run, the stream is small and winding in the relatively wide and flat valley. [Reported 1987]

*Difficulties:* There are some weirs which can be run if the water is sufficient. The first dam is about 0.5 miles downstream from the Glen Hazel road bridge. The second is in Bendigo State Park and is a 3-4 foot recreational dam; carry either side. At the upper edge of Johnsonburg there is a 6 foot dam; carry on right. Just below US Route 219 in Johnsonburg, there is a 3 foot industrial dam; scout and carry is recommended. This dam is walled in on both sides, so you will need to carry around the buildings and across US Route 219. Portage on the right. Weirs built in CCC days should be checked before running.

*Shuttle:* Put in at Glen Hazel road bridge or drive dirt road upstream right towards dam. To get to the take-out, go southwest on State Route 1004. Take out at the ball field between US Route 219 and the river below paper mill in Johnsonburg. A take-out at the first bridge as you approach Johnsonburg avoids the last two dams and reduces the trip by 1 mile.

*Gauges:* East Branch Dam. This gauge should read above 2.0 feet. This corresponds to a flow of 70 cfs. The Ridgway gauge further downstream will probably read above 4.5 feet.

*Normal Wet Period:* The East Branch Dam gauge is above 2.0 feet 60% of the time.

# Sandy Creek

## A. Goddard State Park to Raymilton          9.0 miles

| Class | Grad | Size (Area / Volume) | Scene / Poll | Level |
|-------|------|----------------------|--------------|-------|
| C | 8/13 | Small (100/167) estimate | A-B/A-B | |

*Topographic Maps:* Sandy Lake, Polk

*County Maps:* Mercer, Venango

*Description:* This is a very nice run from below the dam in Goddard State Park, past the village of Sandy Lake, until one gets into the swamps. They start about 1.5 miles below the town and the terrain is still beautiful except there are numerous trees, fences, and logs. This is a good wildlife river, with very heavy cover. [Reported prior to 1975]

*Difficulties:* After entering the swamps below the town of Sandy Lake there are lots of downed trees. These are not as dangerous as the usual downed tree situation, since in the swamp the water does not flow very fast. One should still be very careful to avoid a pinning.

*Shuttle:* Put in below the dam in Goddard State Park. To get to the take-out, go east on US Route 62. Turn right/south onto State Route 3015. Continue on to the river crossing in Raymilton.

*Gauges:* Rouseville. This gauge on nearby Oil Creek will probably read above 4.0 feet.

*Normal Wet Period:* No available statistics on seasons. Since this section is small, it should normally be runnable approximately January through April.

# B. Raymilton to Pecan                          8.5 miles

| Class | Grad | Size (Area/Volume) | Scene/Poll Level |
|-------|------|--------------------|------------------|
| I-II  | 14/14 | Small (161/268) mouth of stream | A-B/B 8-5.5 blocks SR 965 bridge |

*Topographic Maps:* Polk

*County Maps:* Venango

*Description:* Several picnic spots are close to good chutes to play in. Wildlife is often sighted. The stream becomes polluted from Polk to the Allegheny. The short stretches through Raymilton and Polk are the only sights of civilization in otherwise very rugged country. [Checked 1987]

*Difficulties:* Many trees are down above Polk. There is a rumor of a dam of unspecified characteristics somewhere above the State Route 965 bridge.

*Shuttle:* To reach the take-out, go south from Raymilton on State Route 3015 for about 1 mile. Turn left/north on State Route 965. At the junction with US Route 62, turn right/east on State Route 62. In Polk turn right/east onto State Route 3024. At the junction with State Route 8 turn right/south. Shortly after the turn, State Route 8 will fork with old Route 8 on the right and by-pass Route 8 going left. You will want the right hand fork for old Route 8, not the divided highway. Continue on old State Route 8, now State Route 3013 for about 1.5 miles to Pecan and the take-out. Just just before the road crosses the creek high up, go down to creek level on a dirt road named Poverty Valley Road. Running the last 3 miles to the Allegheny river adds about 7 miles to the shuttle from Pecan through Five Points to the Fisherman's Cove access ramp on the Allegheny river. Pecan is not on some maps, but is called Mays Mill instead.

*Gauges:* Bridge abutment on State Route 965. More than 8 blocks showing indicates it is too low to run. Real fun with between 8 to 5.5 blocks showing. The Rouseville gauge on nearby Oil Creek will probably read above 3.0 feet.

*Normal Wet Period:* No available statistics on seasons. Since this section is small, it should normally be runnable approximately January through April.

# South Sandy Creek

## State Game Lands #39 to Pecan  8.5 miles

| Class | Grad | Size (Area/Volume) | Scene/Poll | Level |
|-------|------|--------------------|------------|-------|
| I-II | 23/28 | Tiny (31/52) | A/A | |
| | | mouth of stream | | |

*Topographic Maps:* Polk

*County Maps:* Venango

*Description:* This is an extremely beautiful run through a hemlock valley with an understory of moss, ferns, and skunk cabbage. The gradient, though high for a Class I-II stream, is steady. The creek runs over many small gravel bars and rock gardens. It is only about 25 feet wide at the put-in but widens on the way down. The only sign of civilization is an old iron furnace ruins. [Checked 1990]

*Difficulties:* About 3 to 4 miles within the run there are several Class II ledges.

*Shuttle:* To get to the put-in, go north from Pearl on State Route 3013 (old State Route 8) for 0.1 miles, and turn west on a dirt road (Slatertown Road). Follow this road for about 2.2 miles to the river following the signs to State Game Lands #39. To get to the take-out at Pecan (Mays Mill), return to old State Route 8 (State Route 3013) and turn right/north. Just after the road crosses the creek high up, go down to creek level on a dirt road on the right named Poverty Valley Road. This take-out will have you paddling 2.5 miles on the Sandy Creek.

*Gauges:* Rouseville. This gauge on nearby Oil Creek will probably read between 4.5 and 6.5 feet. Eyeball it at the put-in. There will be more water soon after the put-in so do not shy away if it looks minimal.

*Normal Wet Period:* No available statistics on seasons. Since this section is tiny, it should normally be runnable only after a heavy rain or during spring snowmelt.

# East Sandy Creek

## Van to Allegheny River                              10.5 miles

| Class | Grad | Size (Area/Volume) | Scene/Poll | Level |
|-------|------|--------------------|-----------|-------|
| II | 21/25 | Small (54/90) | A/A | IV-?? |
|  |  | Van |  | Van |
|  |  | Small (103/172) mouth of stream |  |  |

*Topographic Maps:* Cranberry, Kennerdell

*County Maps:* Venango

*Description:* The entire run is in a narrow forested valley. The creek is shallow and narrow but fast when the water is up. Its starts as continuous Class I. The 2 to 3 miles above State Route 257 has six Class II rapids and the mile or two below has long stretches of Class II. [Checked 1990]

*Difficulties:* There may be downed trees, especially on the upper section. In high water, maneuvering gets tricky.

*Shuttle:* Put in where US Route 322 crosses the creek in Van. Go west on US Route 322 for about 7.5 miles, turn south on Astral road which is about 0.5 miles west of Victory Heights. Go 2.6 miles to the mouth of the creek, ignoring the "Dead End" sign. The last mile is rough and will require vehicles with moderate clearance. For a 7-mile trip, take out at Deep Valley Park (State Route 257). Go west on US Route 322 for about 5 miles. Turn south at Egypt Corners (1 mile west of Cranberry), and go 2.5 miles to the creek.

*Gauges:* Southwest corner of center pier on Van bridge. The gauge consists of marks about 4 inches apart with the fifth labeled "V" and the tenth labeled "X". A reading of III (i.e. two lines below the "V") was too low at Van but adequate below the State Route 257 bridge. Alternately look at the stream from the State Route 257 bridge. This is the shallowest part of the run. The Rouseville gauge on nearby Oil Creek will probably read above 3.5 feet.

*Normal Wet Period:* No available statistics on seasons. Since this section is small, it should normally be runnable approximately January through April.

# French Creek

## A. State Route 474 (Pa - NY border)          15.3 miles
## to Union City Dam

| Class | Grad | Size (Area/Volume) | Scene/Poll | Level |
|-------|------|--------------------|-----------|-------|
| I | 10/20 | Small (92/153) | A/A | |
| | | Wattsburg | | Wattsburg |

*Topographic Maps:* Wattsburg, Union City, Waterford

*County Maps:* Erie

*Description:* Above Wattsburg the creek is narrow and fast flowing with a few good rapids. Strainers can be expected on the curves. Below Wattsburg the creek widens and flattens out, with occasional strainers. This section ends at the dam for the Union City Reservoir. This is a unique member of the Corps of Engineers' Pittsburgh District flood control projects, a dry-bed reservoir. According to the Corps' description, "The dam functions as an uncontrolled detention structure that automatically stores and releases water during periods of peak flow. A 520-foot-long concrete conduit, 4.5 feet wide by 8 feet high, runs through the base of the dam to allow for uncontrolled discharge of waters. The conduit permits normal flows of French Creek to pass through unimpeded. When the amount of water entering the reservoir, however, exceeds the dam's capacity to discharge it through the drainage conduit a temporary lake is formed. If the flow of waters into the lake fills the reservoir to capacity the excess waters are then discharged into a side-channel spillway constructed through the right abutment of the dam. At maximum flood pool Union City Reservoir will extend 7.4 miles up French Creek. As the water inflow decreases, the stored water gradually drains out, and once again the reservoir bed becomes dry. The lake forming process usually occurs during late winter and early spring as a result of melting snow and spring rains. The resulting lake usually lasts only for two or three months." The conduit through the dam and the side-channel spillway are restricted areas which may be marked with floats. Plan to take out on the left-hand shore and walk up the service road to your car. [Reported 1988]

*Difficulties:* Strainers. Observe the pool level at the float line at the take-out. If the area is mud flats, plan to take out at the Hatch Hollow Road bridge just above this area. The mud in the pool bottom is very soft. It is extremely dangerous to broach against the floats in a moving current that close to the breastworks.

*Shuttle:* The put-in is where State Route 474 crosses the creek near the state line. To get to the take-out, go south on State Route 474 to Wattsburg, then south on State Route 8 to Union City. Turn right/west onto State Route 97 for about 2.5 miles. Turn right on Hare Road leading to the Union City Dam. If recent decreases in the reservoir level have left mud flats in the area near the dam, then go north from the intersection of Hare and Haugh Roads (near overlook area parking lot) for about 2 miles. Turn right at the "T" on Juva Road, go another 1.5 miles and turn right on Hatch Hollow Road. Continue about .25 miles to the bridge.

*Gauges:* Wattsburg. We do not have enough information to report runnable levels on this section. If the riffle upstream of the State Route 474 bridge is passable then the entire section is runnable.

*Normal Wet Period:* No available statistics on seasons. Since this section is small, it should normally be runnable approximately January through April.

# B. Union City Dam                    27.0 miles
# to Cambridge Springs

*Class  Grad    Size (Area/Volume)     Scene/Poll  Level*
  B     4/10    Medium (222/439)        A/A      2.3-5.0
                Union City  Dam                  Union City

*Topographic Maps:* Waterford, Millers Station, Cambridge
    Springs

*County Maps:* Erie, Crawford

*Description:* The stream is straightforward until below the
two railroad bridges about 6 miles below US Route 6. Below
here the creek has many sharp turns and fallen trees
requiring lots of climbing around and over. The course
becomes serpentine in a swamp-like setting until Cambridge Springs. A place of abundant wildlife. [Checked
1988]

*Difficulties:* Strainers and logs just beneath the muddy
water.

*Shuttle:* The put-in is 2.5 miles west of Union City on State
Route 97. Continue west on State Route 97 to US Route 6/19.
Turn south to Cambridge Springs. In Cambridge Springs
turn west on Poplar Street about 250 yards from bridge,
continue to the end and turn left at the fairgrounds.

*Gauges:* Union City Outlet. This gauge should read
between 2.3 and 5.0 feet. This corresponds to a flow of 55 cfs
to 1310 cfs. This gauge is about 1 mile below the dam. If the
shallows under the State Route 97 road bridge look passable,
then the section is runnable.

*Normal Wet Period:* The Union City Outlet gauge is above
2.3 feet 75% of the time and above 5.0 feet 7% of the time.

# C. Cambridge Springs to Seagertown          15.0 miles

*Class  Grad    Size (Area/Volume)      Scene/Poll  Level*
  I     2/4     Medium (597/1,064)         B/B      2.0-??
                    Venango            Meadville (see note)
            Medium (629/1,056) Seagertown

*Topographic Maps:* Cambridge Springs, Blooming Valley, Meadville

*County Maps:* Crawford

*Description:* Parts of the small towns of Cambridge Springs and Seagertown can be seen from French Creek. The stream winds through farming country and is bordered by some summer homes. However, much of the stream passes through uninhabited forest. Camping sites are plentiful and nice, especially on the east bank. Unfortunately, the highway sounds from US Route 6/19 can be heard much of the time. Heron and kingfisher are often seen. [Checked 1989]

*Difficulties:* At Seagertown, just below the concrete bridge for State Route 198 and above the Pennsylvania Fish Commission access point, is a 3-foot low-water bridge which should be portaged.

*Shuttle:* To find the put-in turn west onto Poplar Street about 250 yards from the bridge, continue to the end and turn left at the fairgrounds. Follow US Route 6/19 south to the Pennsylvania Fish Commission access area about 0.25 miles south of Seagertown.

*Gauges:* Meadville on French Creek. This gauge should read above 2.0 feet. Note there is also a nearby Meadville gauge on Cussewago Creek. Be sure to get the correct one. There is an outside gauge on the bridge at the intersection of US Route 6/19 and State Route 198 in Seagertown. A level of 4.5 feet was adequate.

*Normal Wet Period:* No available statistics on seasons. Since this section is medium-sized, it should normally be runnable approximately December through May.

# D. Seagertown to Meadville          20.0 miles
## to Cochranton

*Class  Grad     Size (Area/Volume)     Scene/Poll  Level*
  B     4/6     Medium (629/1,056)            2.0-??
                 Seagertown      Meadville (see note)

*Topographic Maps:* Meadville, Geneva, Cochranton

*County Maps:* Crawford

*Description:* Between Seagertown and Meadville the stream crosses US Route 6/19 twice, but otherwise remains separated from the highway by mixed farmland, marshland, and woods. Occasional stretches of cottages follow the stream. Several island complexes offer choices, but no significant difficulty in the major channel. Meadville is an industrial city viewed from the stream, but passed quickly. Below Meadville, French Creek is a wide well-defined channel. Railroad and highway maintain their distance and long sections down to Conneaut Outlet can be found without cottages. The last 3 miles to Cochranton have several stretches of cabins. [Checked 1989]

*Difficulties:* None.

*Shuttle:* About 0.25 miles south of Seagertown on US Route 6/19 is a Pennsylvania Fish Commission put-in. Go south on US Route 6/19 to Meadville and take US Route 322 to Cochranton. Turn right/southwest onto State Route 173 to the take-out about a mile further where the road crosses the creek.

*Gauges:* Meadville on French Creek. This gauge should read above 2.0 feet. Note there is also a nearby Meadville gauge on Cussewago Creek. Be sure and get the correct one. We do not have enough information to report runnable levels on this section. There is an outside gauge on the bridge at the intersection of US Route 6/19 and State Route 198 in Seagertown. A level of 4.5 feet was adequate.

*Normal Wet Period:* No available statistics on seasons. Since this section is medium-sized, it should normally be runnable approximately December through May.

# E. Cochranton to Utica                                   8.8 miles

| Class | Grad | Size (Area/Volume) | Scene/Poll | Level |
|-------|------|-------------------|------------|-------|
| C | 3/3 | Medium (998/1,722) | B-C/B | 1.6-5.5 |
|   |   | Carlton |   | Utica |
|   |   | Medium (1,028/1,756) Utica |   |   |

*Topographic Maps:*  Cochranton, New Lebanon, Utica

*County Maps:*  Crawford, Mercer, Venango

*Description:*  This is mostly flat fast moving water with a few shallows around small islands.  There are cottages along the shore. [Checked 1989]

*Difficulties:*  The first island below Cochranton often has a strainer in the right-hand channel.  Spots to land and camp or picnic are scarce.  Most of the shoreline is privately owned.  Avoid the first island below Carlton, but it is possible to camp on the others.  Take care at the take-out at Utica, as the shoreline is privately owned.  Ask permission beforehand and do not leave a mess.

*Shuttle:*  Put in under the State Route 173 bridge about 1 mile west of Cochranton.  Take State Route 173 northeast about a mile.  Turn right/south onto US Route 322.  Turn right onto State Route 3017.  Go 3 miles to the French Creek bridge. Intermediate access is available at Carlton, but because of landowner problems you should not use the upstream side of the bridge, nor leave parked cars at this point.

*Gauges:*  Utica.  This gauge should read between 1.6 and 5.5 feet.  This corresponds to a flow of 179 cfs to 3850 cfs.

*Normal Wet Period:*  The Utica gauge is above 1.6 feet 85% of the time and above 5.5 feet 12% of the time.

# F.  Utica to Franklin                                    7.0 miles

| Class | Grad | Size (Area/Volume) | Scene/Poll | Level |
|-------|------|--------------------|-----------|---------|
| C-I | 6/6 | Medium (1,028/1,837) | B-C/B | 1.6-5.5 |
|     |     | Utica                |       | Utica |

*Topographic Maps:*  Utica, Franklin

*County Maps:*  Venango

*Description:*  This one of the largest tributaries of the Allegheny.  It offers good current with riffles, walleye fishing, occasional minor rapids on corners, and a few eddies with playing opportunities.  [Checked 1989]

*Difficulties:*  At the mouth of Sugar Creek, a long island keeps most of Sugar Creek on the left and most of French Creek on the right.  At the lower end of the island, French Creek bends left.  Stay in the center to avoid boulders on the right.  At high water, this confluence creates 2 to 4-foot standing waves.  Spots to land and camp or picnic are scarce.  Most of the shoreline is privately owned.  Take care at the put-in in Utica, as the shoreline is privately owned.  Ask permission beforehand and do not leave a mess.

*Shuttle:*  Put in at the State Route 3017 bridge in Utica.  To get to the take-out, go north on State Route 3017.  Turn right/south onto US Route 322.  Go through Franklin.  Go 0.3 miles past the oil refinery, and park on the extra-wide berm 0.1 miles before Foster Corner.  Alternatively, one can take-out at the Pennsylvania Fish Commission launching ramp on the west bank of the Allegheny River just below the US Route 322 bridge.  This take-out is 3.2 miles below the Foster Corner take-out, making the trip from Utica 10.2 miles long.  Hallstown Marine (814) 432-3449 is located on French Creek about 200 yards below the mouth of Sugar Creek.  They will be happy to answer questions about water level.  They also rent canoes and will arrange private shuttles for various streams in the area.

*Gauges:*  Utica.  This gauge should read between 1.6 and 5.5 feet.  This corresponds to a flow of 179 cfs to 3,850 cfs.

*Normal Wet Period:*  The Utica gauge is above 1.6 feet 85% of the time and above 5.5 feet 12% of the time.

# Sugar Creek

## Cooperstown to French Creek                    7.5 miles

| Class | Grad | Size (Area/Volume) | Scene/Poll | Level |
|-------|------|--------------------|-----------|-------|
| I-II | 16/27 | Small (166/267) | B/A | |
| | | Sugar Creek | | Sugar Creek |

*Topographic Maps:* Dempseytown, Utica, Franklin

*County Maps:* Venango

*Description:* This stream flows mostly between high mud banks through forest. This is an interesting and beautiful ride for the novice at levels up to 1.0 foot above the low mark. Beyond this, have plenty of experience or you will surely get it fast. [Checked 1989]

*Difficulties:* Trees down in bends are the greatest hazard. After passing the mouth of Lake Creek, look for a picnic area on the left bank to warn of a bad "S" bend which is tricky in high water. If you continue into French Creek at low water, go right of the island at the confluence. The left channel is likely to be low.

*Shuttle:* Put in along State Route 427 in the town of Cooperstown. To get to the take-out, go south on State Route 427. Turn left/east onto US Route 322. Go about 3 miles and take a sharp U turn to the right onto State Route 4010. This road is between US Route 322 and French Creek for about 0.5 miles. The take-out is on Sugar Creek between the road bridge and the railroad bridge. Parking will be a problem since there is not much room. An alternate put-in which extends the trip for about 3 miles is at Fedderman's bridge on State Route 4009 using a portion of the East Branch Sugar Creek. Hallstown Marine (814) 432-3449 is located on French Creek about 200 yards below the mouth of Sugar Creek. They will be happy to answer questions about water level. They also rent canoes and will arrange private shuttles for various streams in the area.

*Gauges:* Sugar Creek. We do not have enough information to report runnable levels on this section. The Rouseville gauge on nearby Oil Creek will probably read between 3.7

and 5.0 feet. If too high consider the East Branch of Sugar Creek. A streamside gauge is the road bridge at the take-out. A minimum of 2 blocks showing is necessary. If French Creek is high, the backwater from French Creek can give you a misleading high reading.

*Normal Wet Period:* No available statistics on seasons. Since this section is small, it should normally be runnable approximately January through April.

# Sugar Creek, East Branch

## Wallaceville to Cooperstown                    7.0 miles

| Class | Grad | Size (Area/Volume) | Scene/Pol | Level |
|-------|------|--------------------|-----------|-------|
| I-II | 12/20 | Tiny (49/82) | B/A | |
| | | mouth of stream | | |

*Topographic Maps:*  Dempseytown, Franklin

*County Maps:*  Venango

*Description:*  When everything else in northern Venango County is too high, try the East Branch of Sugar Creek. This stream starts as an intimate brook running through tight Class I and II riffles in a hemlock forest. It picks up tributaries as it runs past farms and camps and finally enters Cooperstown as an open Class I small stream. Just before the State Route 4009 bridge the creek passes through an area of extensive tornado damage. Although  the creek is now clear, the banks are populated by eerie skeletons of broken but still-standing trees. Where the stream has cut away the banks on curves, you can see evidence of glaciation: Layers of fine-grained lake sand on top of coarse stream gravel. [Reported 1989]

*Difficulties:*  Fallen trees partially or completely blocking the stream above State Route 4009.

*Shuttle:*  To reach the put-in, go south from Wallaceville on State Route 428. You will first cross Little Sugar Creek and then 50 yards later Prather Creek. Put in on either of these; they join shortly and a mile later enter the East Branch. To reach the take-out, go back north on State Route 428 to Wallaceville, turn left/west on State Route 4022. At the junction with State Route 427, turn left/south and proceed to Cooperstown and the take-out on the main stem of Sugar Creek.

*Gauge:*  Rouseville. This gauge on nearby Oil Creek will probably read above 4.5 feet.

*Normal Wet Period:*  No available statistics on seasons. Since this section is tiny, it should normally be runnable only after a heavy rain or during spring snowmelt.

# Conneaut Outlet Marsh

## A. Geneva Dike Area                                    5.5 miles

*Class   Grad     Size (Area/Volume)      Scene/Poll  Level*
 A     Marsh      Small(75/125)             A/A
                 mouth of stream

*Topographic Maps:*  Conneaut Lake, Geneva

*County Maps:*  Crawford

*Description:* The following is extracted from a write-up available from Western Pennsylvania Conservancy. See Appendix D to get their address and to request the complete write-up with much more detail. The outlet of Conneaut Lake runs southeast through swamp and marsh lands which are now State Game Lands and a Bird Sanctuary. The view from the put-in at Geneva Dike is a sea of water and low vegetation, but paddlers heading northwest along the outlet will discover that this open marsh undergoes a gradual transformation into wooded swamp as they approach Conneaut Lake. From the put-in you will be able to paddle "upstream" for about 2.5 miles to the turn around at Mud Pike bridge. You could have put in here at the lake and paddled to the Geneva access area.

About 0.75 miles southeast from the dike you will encounter a Game Propagation Area which is posted off limits to all access and activities. This area is about 0.5 miles across before it connects to the next section of the marsh. The dike itself is about a two foot drop, with a runnable drop at either end. [Checked 1990]

*Difficulties:* There will be some beaver dams to lift and slide the canoe over. The last 0.5 miles to the lake and the turn-around point is a sluggish woodland creek with downed trees that will be require a little effort to get the canoe across. Since there is minimal current this presents no danger. During the duck and geese hunting seasons of October through December there are a lot of hunters in the area. It is best to paddle only on Sundays (no hunting allowed) during those months.

*Shuttle:* Take Interstate 79 to Exit 35. After exiting turn west on State Route 285 toward Geneva. Cross US Route 19 and go about 2.6 miles to Geneva. Make a right at the second intersection in Geneva, immediately before the sign listing mileages to Conneaut Lake and Linesville. Follow this road past several dozen houses, over the railroad tracks, and into the marsh on a dike. Cross a small bridge and park on the wide gravel road. This section could also be a trip by putting in on Conneaut Lake at the Pennsylvania Fish Commission access area. To get to the take-out, go east on State Route 285 to Geneva. Turn right/north and follow the instructions above.

*Gauge:* None for the marsh trip. If you put in at the lake, there is a staff gauge on the lake face of the Route 6 bridge. It's sufficient to judge the riffle under the bridge; if you have enough to clear this you'll be fine.

*Normal Wet Period:* Usually runnable.

## B. Interstate 79 Area                              3.7 miles

| Class | Grad | Size (Area / Volume) | Scene / Poll | Level |
|-------|------|----------------------|--------------|-------|
| A | Marsh | Small (90/150) estimate | A / A | |

*Topographic Maps:* Geneva

*County Maps:* Crawford

*Description:* See above. This section covers from the eastern end of the bird sanctuary to the dam at State Route 2003, with Interstate 79 crossing in the middle. The state has "mowed" several paths through the swamp grasses. These paths are 15-20 feet wide, but they are not the only way to go. Explore some of the natural side passageways and open areas. From the put-in under Interstate 79 either paddle "upstream" about 1.7 miles to the bird sanctuary or "downstream" about 2.0 miles to the dam with many side trips possible. The marsh is about 0.5 miles wide. [Checked 1988]

*Difficulties:* If the water level is high then you may not be able to pass under the US Route 19 bridge. In this case it is not hard to carry over. If you run down to French Creek instead of taking out where you put in then plan to carry over the 4-foot dam/causeway at State Route 2003. Note also the remarks about hunting season in the previous section.

*Shuttle:*   Put in and take out at an access area under Interstate 79 on the north side of the marsh. To reach this area, exit Interstate 79 at Exit 35 which is State Route 285. Head east on State Route 285 for about a mile. In Custard turn left/north on State Route 2003. Cross the dam that forms the marsh and take the first left onto a dirt road. Follow this to another left that obviously takes you under the interstate.

*Gauge:*   None. This is a marsh.

*Normal Wet Period:*   Usually runnable.

## C. Interstate 79 area to French Creek          6.0 miles

| Class | Grad | Size (Area/Volume) | Scene/Pol | Level |
|-------|------|--------------------|-----------|-------|
| B | 1/1 | Small (101/168) mouth of stream | B/A | |

*Topographic Maps:*   Geneva, Cochranton

*County Maps:*   Crawford

*Description:*   This trip is the subject of a detailed write-up available from the Western Pennsylvania Conservancy. Scenic and ecological values are outstanding due to the Conservancy's protection efforts. The trip offers a 2-mile section of marsh (open wetland), swamp (wooded wetland), and lazy farmland/woodland stream. [Reported 1988]

*Difficulties:*   Downed trees can be numerous in the swamp. They are not dangerous, because there is no current, but they all have to be gotten over or around. The bridge at State Route 2003, 2 miles below Interstate 79, has a dam that should be carried.

*Shuttle:*   To get to the put-in see the previous section. To get to the take-out, come back to State Route 285 and continue east for another 3.5 miles. As the highway bends to the right, take a small road forking to the left, going downhill to the bank of French Creek. Make a sharp left turn, and go north about 0.5 miles to the Pennsylvania Fish Commission Access Area, just above the mouth of Conneaut Outlet.

*Gauge:* None.

*Normal Wet Period:* No available statistics on seasons. Since this section is small, it should normally be runnable approximately January through April.

# Cussewago Creek

## Crossingville to Meadville                            28.5 miles

| Class | Grad | Size (Area/Volume) | Scene/Pol | Level |
|-------|------|--------------------|-----------|-------|
| C | 2/2 | Small (90/130) | AB/A | |
| | | Meadville | Meadville (see note) | |

*Topographic Maps:* Edinboro South, Meadville

*County Maps:* Crawford

*Description:* Water is initially fairly clear. In spite of high mud banks, the scenery is usually good, mostly woodsy, with very little trash and lots of wildlife. Only a few riffles -- mostly in Meadville and at the remains of an old mill weir about the middle of the trip. The rest of the run is flat. [Reported 1988]

*Difficulties:* Scores of fallen trees to carry. Only the last 5 miles are relatively unimpeded. There is a 2-foot weir in Meadville, between the 1st and 2nd bridges; run the washout on the left.

*Shuttle:* Put in on State Route 98 southwest of Crossingville. Take out at the mouth in Meadville.

*Gauge:* Meadville on Cussewago Creek. Note there is also a nearby Meadville gauge on French Creek. Be sure and get the correct one. There is a staff gauge on the left abutment of (probably) the second road bridge from the start. A level of 2.1 was okay in riffles, plenty everywhere else. The Union City Outflow gauge on nearby French Creek will probably read above 4.6 feet.

*Normal Wet Period:* No available statistics on seasons. Since this section is small, it should normally be runnable approximately January through April.

# Oil Creek

## A. Centerville to Titusville                    12.0 miles

| Class | Grad | Size (Area/Volume) | Scene/Poll | Level |
|-------|------|--------------------|-----------|-------|
| I | 7/10 | Medium (250/417) estimate | B/A | 3.0-5.0 Rouseville |

*Topographic Maps:* Centerville, Titusville North

*County Maps:* Crawford

*Description:* This is a pretty section of river, but it needs a lot of water to be pleasant canoeing rather than hiking. It should be run only in higher-than-average spring water levels. Camping is possible along this section by permission only. [Reported prior to 1975]

*Difficulties:* Fallen trees add difficulty to the first 3 miles.

*Shuttle:* Use State Route 8 for the shuttle.

*Gauges:* Rouseville. This gauge should read between 3.0 and 5.0 feet. This corresponds to a flow of 550 cfs to 2,250 cfs.

*Normal Wet Period:* The Rouseville gauge is above 3.0 feet 28% of the time and is above 5.0 feet 4% of the time.

## B. Titusville to Rouseville                    12.0 miles

| Class | Grad | Size (Area/Volume) | Scene/Poll | Level |
|-------|------|--------------------|-----------|-------|
| I | 10/12 | Medium (300/538) Rouseville | B/A-B | 2.5-5.0 Rouseville |

*Topographic Maps:* Titusville South, Oil City

*County Maps:* Venango

*Description:* This section runs through Oil Creek State Park. The last 3 miles are "civilized" with some houses. No overnight camping is permitted along this section. The creek flows over a gravel bed down a wooded valley. The region is rich in the history of the early days of the American oil industry. Below State Route 8 to the mouth of Oil Creek at Oil City, pollution becomes a problem due to refineries along the shore. [Checked 1989]

*Difficulties:* Near Drake Well the deepest channel is on the right. In medium or low water some difficulty may be experienced about 3 miles below Drake Well Park at the remains of an old logging dam. There is a drop of about 1.5 feet. Run through the center. About a mile above the State Route 8 bridge and below the former town of Petroleum Junction and present State Park headquarters, there is an ice breaker structure. It resembles a dam, but it lets water pass through. Its purpose is to break up river ice so it does not jam and cause floods in Oil City. This structure is not runnable. The main spillway on the left side may look tempting at high water, but there are a couple of ice-breaking piers inside the wave that would break boats as handily as ice. A portage trail runs on the left side of this structure. Note however, that the trail starts no more than 50 yards above the dam, and the cutout in the bank accommodates only a couple of boats at once. If the water is high and you have several boats, be sure they space themselves far enough apart to allow early arrivals to get out before late arrivals try to enter the eddy. Alternatively you can take out on the right about 0.2 miles above the structure.

*Shuttle:* Put in at Drake Well Park at the head of the bike trail or at the State Route 27 bridge west of Titusville. Take out at Rynd Farm Bridge (State Route 8) or at the picnic area about 0.5 miles upstream. An alternative take-out with convenient parking is the bike trail access park, just north of Petroleum Junction. Dropping a bike here, or renting one, would provide a one-motor-vehicle shuttle.

*Gauges:* Rouseville. This gauge should read between 2.5 and 5.0 feet. This corresponds to a flow of 300 cfs to 2,250 cfs.

*Normal Wet Period:* The Rouseville gauge is above 2.5 feet 45% of the time and is above 5.0 feet 4% of the time.

# Pithole Creek

## Pithole to Oleopolis                                    6.5 miles

| Class | Grad | Size (Area/Volume) | Scene/Poll | Level |
|-------|------|--------------------|------------|-------|
| III | 44/70 | Tiny(42/70) mouth of stream | A-B/A | |

*Topographic Maps:* Pleasantville, President

*County Maps:* Venango

*Description:* This small stream drains an area that once boasted a major oil community that is now a ghost town. A mostly wilderness hemlock valley is all that remains with a stream that paddlers are slowly discovering. The run is roughly split by a stone bridge on a secondary road east of Plumer. The run starting at Pithole offers a very small, meandering headwater stream with gradient increasing towards the stone bridge. Active oil and gas wells can be found along the otherwise deserted valley. About a mile below the stone bridge, a blind left turn leads to a 2-3 foot ledge. This is the first in a series of half a dozen that punctuate the next 1.5 miles of almost continuous Class III rock-dodging. At medium levels all offer straight passage, but this is not always obvious, so it is worth scouting them. The stream gradually flattens out again for the junction with the Allegheny, offering good whitewater to within sight of the mouth. [Checked 1989]

*Difficulties:* Potential for tree problems. First mile below the stone bridge is very continuous. Several narrow drops have potential for pins.

*Shuttle:* To reach the Pithole put-in, turn east off State Route 227 on State Route 1006 toward the Pithole historical site. About 1.5 miles later in quick secession the road bends right, a dirt road enters from the left, you cross west Pithole Creek, the road bends left and another dirt road enters on the right. Turn right on this second dirt road, it crosses Pithole Creek in about 0.2 miles. If you get to the historical site, you have gone too far. Take out in Oleopolis on State Route 1005 (the Oleopolis road) accessed from State Route 227. The State Route 1004 (the stone bridge east of Plumer) offers an alternative put-in. The bridge is reached by turning east off State Route 227 about 1 mile north of the Oleopolis road. Pithole can be run from the second bridge above Pithole, adding 3 miles, but size, trees, and several above-water pipe crossings make this section undesirable.

*Gauges:* Rouseville. This gauge on nearby Oil Creek will probably read between 4.0 and 5.0 feet. Check levels at the stone bridge on State Route 1004 for enough water.

*Normal Wet Period:* No available statistics on seasons. Since this section is tiny, it should normally be runnable only after a heavy rain or during spring snowmelt.

# Tionesta Creek

## A. Sheffield to Lynch                                      9.0 miles

| Class | Grad | Size (Area/Volume) | Scene/Poll | Level |
|-------|------|--------------------|-----------|-------|
| I     | 7/8  | Medium (233/426)   | A/A       | 2.8-?? |
|       |      | Lynch              |           | Lynch  |

*Topographic Maps:* Sheffield, Lynch

*County Maps:* Warren, Forest

*Description:* This is an excellent open canoe stream if you can catch it up. The size is adequate to minimize problems with trees. The valley setting is very nice with highway and cottages mostly unobtrusive. This section is narrower and more winding than the section downstream. There is no access at the junction of the headwater branches and the 2 mile paddle from Sheffield on the West Branch is more enjoyable than the 0.5 mile trip from State Route 666 on the South Branch. [Reported 1988]

*Difficulties:* Possible trees.

*Shuttle:* The Sheffield put-in is on a side road near the junction of State Route 666 and State Route 948. Take out at the Lynch Gauge. An optional take-out is at the State Route 666 bridge in the valley for a 5.5 mile trip from Sheffield.

*Gauges:* Lynch. This gauge should read above 2.8 feet. This corresponds to a flow of 890 cfs. Check conditions at State Route 666 bridge in valley.

*Normal Wet Period:* The Lynch gauge is above 2.8 feet 12% of the time.

# B. Lynch to Kellettville                    15.0 miles

| Class | Grad | Size (Area/Volume) | Scene/Poll | Level |
|-------|------|--------------------|-----------|----|
| C-I | 5/8 | Medium (233/426) | A/A | 2.1-?? |
|   |   | Lynch |   | Sheffield |
|   |   | Medium (307/594) Mayburg |   |   |

*Topographic Maps:* Lynch, Mayburg, Kellettville

*County Maps:* Forest

*Description:* This is an excellent open canoe run. The Tionesta shares a National Forest valley with State Route 666 throughout this run. The road, small villages and cabin groupings along its length are not visually obtrusive and road noise is minor. Occasional Class I rapids add to the interest. This is an excellent camping river with plenty of campsite possibilities. Fishing is reported as excellent with a healthy population of fresh water mussels. Property ownership is an unknown. Approaching Kellettville, paddlers will notice remnants of mid-1980's tornadoes that devastated forested areas in this region. This damage was very intense around Kellettville. Minister Creek State Park is about half between Lynch and Kellettville. It provides a convenient camp ground for those driving to the stream the night before a trip. [Checked 1988]

*Difficulties:* None.

*Shuttle:* State Route 666 follows alongside the stream for the entire length. One could choose from any number of put-in or take-out spots.

*Gauges:* Sheffield. This gauge should read above 2.1 feet.

*Normal Wet Period:* No available statistics on seasons. Since this section is medium-sized, it should normally be runnable approximately December through May.

# C. Kellettville to Nebraska Bridge 11.4 miles

| Class | Grad | Size (Area / Volume) | Scene / Poll | Level |
|-------|------|----------------------|--------------|-------|
| C-I | 7/7 | Medium (469/824)<br>Nebraska | A-B/A | 2.1-??<br>Sheffield |

*Topographic Maps:* Kellettville, Tylersburg, Tionesta

*County Maps:* Forest

*Description:* This continues the excellent canoe camping, fishing, and general paddling stream from the upper reaches of the watershed. State Route 666 disappears from the valley at the put-in and the remaining secondary road is frequently unnoticed. Camping opportunities are many. The tornado damage in the first mile below Kellettville is impressive. Below here the stream enters the flood pool from Tionesta lake, but normal pool elevation leaves all but the last mile or so as free flowing stream. About 0.25 miles above the bridge on the right is a high overlook covered with pine trees. Turn right up a small stream just among the pines. Swimming is pleasant below the overlook. [Checked 1987]

*Difficulties:* None

*Shuttle:* From the put-in in Kellettville go 2.5 miles northwest on State Route 666 to Whig Hill, turn left onto State Route 4004. Go 7.5 miles to Kiser Corners. Turn left onto State Route 3004, go 2.5 miles to Nebraska Bridge.

*Gauges:* Sheffield. This gauge should read above 2.1 feet.

*Normal Wet Period:* No available statistics on seasons. Since this section is medium-sized, it should normally be runnable approximately December through May.

## D. Tionesta Reservoir                 5.5 miles
## below Nebraska Bridge

*Class  Grad    Size (Area / Volume)     Scene / Poll  Level*
  A     Lake    Medium (469/824)
                Nebraska
        Medium (479/891) Tionesta Creek Dam

*Topographic Maps:* Tionesta

*County Maps:* Forest

*Description:* Tionesta Reservoir offers enjoyable paddling in a relatively short, serpentine, shaded lake. About 1.5 miles below Nebraska Bridge the lake turns left with a grassy slope on the left shore. Below here the reservoir opens up. Tionesta Dam is earth filled with the outlet provided by a tower on the right-hand shore away from the dam. One can paddle to the crest of the dam for a direct portage route if continuing downstream. From the base of the dam to the Allegheny River is an additional 1.0 mile. A pleasant canoe-camping trip may be had by putting in at the boat launching area of Tionesta Reservoir and paddling up Tionesta Creek a few miles to Nebraska Bridge. Beyond this bridge about 0.25 miles on the right is a high overlook covered with pine trees. Turn right up a small stream just among the pines. Swimming is pleasant below the overlook. [Reported 1988]

*Difficulties:* If you paddle to the junction with the Allegheny beware of the low head dam in the Allegheny River below the mouth of Tionesta Creek on the left side of the island.

*Shuttle:* To get to the put-in/take-out, head west out of Tionesta on State Route 4004. After about 4 miles turn right/south on State Route 3004. Nebraska Bridge is about 2.5 miles after this turn. If you want to haul over the dam and continue downstream, retrace your shuttle to Tionesta, and turn left/south on State Route 36. Go 0.3 miles until it crosses the creek, or make your selection from the Allegheny River descriptions.

*Gauges:* Tionesta Dam Outflow. This gauge would be meaningful for the mile of stream below the dam.

*Normal Wet Period:* None.

# Salmon Creek

## A. Forest Service Road 128                6.8 miles
## to Forest Service Road 145

| Class | Grad | Size (Area / Volume) | Scene / Poll | Level |
|-------|------|----------------------|--------------|-------|
| III   | 43/89 | Tiny (40/67) estimate | A / A | |

*Topographic Maps:* Lynch, Mayburg, Marienville West

*County Maps:* Forest

*Description:* Don't let the steep gradient fool you, this is not a screamer! It's like a swamp trip confined to a very narrow channel with plenty of small rocky drops above Forest Service Road 216. The scenery includes mature hardwoods, hemlocks, brushy shores, meadows, and micro-canyons. At Forest Service Road 128 the stream is very small. An alternate put-in at Forest Service Road 216 eliminates 2.8 miles of the smallest and steepest parts and most of the trees. Above Forest Service Road 216 the run is totally within the National Forest. Below, it plays with the boundary and some development is evident. [Reported 1989]

*Difficulties:* Alder bushes; trees in short, steep rocky drops.

*Shuttle:* The put-in is reached by taking Forest Service Road 128 from the center of Marienville. The take-out is reached from Marienville by taking State Route 66 southwest and following State Route 3004 toward Muzette. Forest Service Road 145 leaves this road to the right about 1.5 miles from State Route 66.

*Gauges:* Cooksburg. This gauge on nearby Clarion River will probably read above 8.0 feet. Note this gauge is not very close to this stream, so it should be used as a guideline only. Plenty of rain is needed in the area in order to run this headwater stream. Check the put-in for enough water.

*Normal Wet Period:* No available statistics on seasons. Since this section is tiny, it should normally be runnable only after a heavy rain or during spring snowmelt.

# B. Forest Service Road 145 to Kellettville     7.1 miles

| Class | Grad | Size (Area/Volume) | Scene/Poll | Level |
|-------|------|--------------------|-----------|-------|
| I I | 25/42 | Tiny (55/92) | A/A | |
| | | mouth of stream | | |

*Topographic Maps:* Marienville West, Mayburg, Kellettville

*County Maps:* Forest

*Description:* The stream is within the National Forest throughout the run and enjoys a mixture of mature forests, occasional meadows, beaver dams and a small canyon. It is very small at the put-in and trees and brush can be problems early on. Below Little Salmon Creek the size is adequate to eliminate all but obstructions from major tree falls. This run has a whitewater section that is out of place in this part of the state. The first hint is "Shark Rock", aptly named and requiring paddlers to journey past the jaws to continue downstream. This starts a series of rocky, Class II rapids intermixed with long sections of easy water. A more difficult rapid appears with no obvious outlet. This requires a 50-yard carry on either shore, or Class IV skillful eddy-hopping to a short left side lift over. The final drop here is unrunnable as the small size flows through and under large boulders choked with trees. The difficulty dissolves below here with occasional small rapids. Forest Service Road 145 is never far away through the most difficult parts. [Reported 1989]

*Difficulties:* Trees and some brush above Little Salmon Creek. One unrunnable rapid.

*Shuttle:* Forest Service Road 145 parallels the run. Forest Service Road 127 completes the shuttle for the last mile into Kellettville. Take-out at the Corps of Engineers campground with 150 yard carry from stream to the campground, or along the river road on right side of the island in Tionesta about 1.5 miles below the mouth of Salmon Creek, or on Forest Service Road 145 about 1 mile above the mouth of Salmon Creek where Forest Service Road 145 is very close to the stream (best take-out).

*Gauges:* Cooksburg. This gauge on nearby Clarion River will probably read above 8.0 feet. Note this gauge is not very close to this stream, so it should be used as a guideline only. Plenty of rain is needed in the area in order to run this headwater stream. Check the put-in for acceptable conditions.

*Normal Wet Period:* No available statistics on seasons. Since this section is tiny, it should normally be runnable only after a heavy rain or during spring snowmelt.

# Tionesta Creek, West Branch

## Weldbank to Sheffield                                    6.0 miles

| Class | Grad | Size (Area/Volume) | Scene/Poll | Level |
|-------|------|--------------------|-----------|-------|
| C-I | 7/9 | Small (128/248) | B/B | |
| | | Sheffield | | |

*Topographic Maps:* Clarendon, Sheffield

*County Maps:* Warren

*Description:* This stream emerges from a highlands plateau to become an excellent open canoe creek beginning at Sheffield. Above Sheffield the transition from swamp to definitive channel is slow. See description of Tionesta Creek for the section below Sheffield. The stream has been run as far upstream as Forest Service Road 154 near Clarendon, but the first 2.5 miles is nearly a hopeless swamp. The swamp outlet near Weldbank is the limit of reasonable navigation with paddlers still paying a heavy price of downed trees as the stream gathers size. The stream is very small and well hidden, giving a remote appearance from the water. [Reported 1987]

*Difficulties:* Trees. Above Weldbank, trees, and more trees.

*Shuttle:* The put-in is about 3 miles north of Sheffield along US Route 6. Put in at Weldbank where the river turns away from the road. Head back/south on US Route 6 to Sheffield and take State Route 666 south out of Sheffield. Chose your distance.

*Gauges:* Lynch. This gauge further downstream on the main stem will probably read above 3.0 feet.

*Normal Wet Period:* No available statistics on seasons. Since this section is small, it should normally be runnable approximately January through April.

# Tionesta Creek, South Branch

## Brookston to Barnes                                    5.3 miles

| Class | Grad | Size (Area/Volume) | Scene/Poll | Level |
|-------|------|--------------------|------------|-------|
| I-II  | 14/22 | Small (85/156)    | C/B        |       |
|       |      | Barnes             |            |       |

*Topographic Maps:* Russell City, Ludlow, Sheffield

*County Maps:* Forest, Warren

*Description:* This high-elevation stream in Allegheny National Forest flows in a shallow valley shared with State Route 948 and several villages that minimize the wilderness experience. [Reported 1987]

*Difficulties:* Many trees above State Route 948. Generally open below State Route 948.

*Shuttle:* State Route 948. Put in on Beam Farm Road (Brookston) and take out at State Route 666 bridge near Barnes. This trip can be extended to Lynch on the main branch; see the write-up for Sheffield to Lynch.

*Gauges:* Lynch. This gauge further downstream on the main stem will probably read above 3.0 feet. At State Route 948 bridge, 10 blocks showing without cap on downstream left is adequate.

*Normal Wet Period:* No available statistics on seasons. Since this section is small, it should normally be runnable approximately January through April.

# Brokenstraw Creek

## Garland to Youngsville                              12.0 miles

| Class | Grad | Size (Area/Volume) | Scene/Poll | Level |
|-------|------|--------------------|------------|-------|
| C-I   | 8/14 | Medium (321/587)   | A/A        |       |
|       |      | Youngsville        |            | Youngsville |

*Topographic Maps:* Pittsfield, Youngsville

*County Maps:* Warren

*Description:* The creek meanders through a broad flood plain and runs by several small towns. It has sharp turns and at several points there are narrow channels along islands with fast water. [Reported prior to 1975]

*Difficulties:* There is a pipeline across the creek in Youngsville just upstream from the old US Route 6 bridge. Brokenstraw is runnable as far upstream at the State Route 426 bridge below Columbus. But from here to Spring Creek and Garland, watch out for low hanging cables across the river.

*Shuttle:* Roads run along the entire north bank of the river. Use US Route 6 and State Route 27. An alternate take-out is 2 miles further at the mouth of the Brokenstraw near Buckaloons.

*Gauges:* Youngsville. We do not have enough information to report runnable levels on this section. A reading of 3.0 on the Youngsville gauge corresponds to the mean flow of 587 cfs. Since this is a medium-sized river, we speculate that the river will be runnable at 3.0 and may be on the high side of runnable at that level.

*Normal Wet Period:* No available statistics on seasons. Since this section is medium-sized, it should normally be runnable approximately December through May.

# Kinzua Creek

## Westline to Forest Service Road 150       5.5 miles
## (Meade Run)

| Class | Grad | Size (Area/Volume) | Scene/Poll | Level |
|-------|------|--------------------|-----------|-------|
| I | 18/29 | Small (46/78) | A/A | 3.0-?? |
| | | Guffey | | Guffey |

*Topographic Maps:* Westline

*County Maps:* McKean

*Description:* The creek runs through mixed hardwood and hemlock forest. The bed of coarse gravel and cobbles periodically forms shoals that produce small riffles. Several short stretches of the shore line are fenced off for fish propagation be the Pennsylvania Fish Commission. They have said (1989) that it is okay to canoe through these areas. The Forest Service roads on either side are lightly traveled and unobtrusive. [Reported 1989]

*Difficulties:* None.

*Shuttle:* Westline can be reached from US Route 219 by turning west on State Route 3000 at Tallyho. Put in at the bridge in Westline. Forest Service roads parallel the creek on both sides. To shuttle on the south side (river left), go back along State Route 3000 for about 150 feet and turn right onto Forest Service Road 321. Follow this road to Forest Service Road 150. Turn right and proceed 150 to 200 feet to the take-out bridge.

*Gauge:* Guffey. This gauge should read above 3.0 feet. This corresponds to a flow of 137 cfs.

*Normal Wet Period:* The Guffey gauge is above 3.0 feet 15% of the time.

# Allegheny Portage Creek

## Wrights to Port Allegany                    5.5 miles

| Class | Grad | Size (Area/Volume) | Scene/Pol | Level |
|-------|------|--------------------|-----------|-------|
| I-II  | 16/20 | Small (61/102) mouth | B/A |  |

*Topographic Maps:*  Keating Summit, Norwich, Port
  Allegany

*County Maps:*  McKean

*Description:*  A very small clear brook winding like crazy
through bottomland woods in a narrow pastoral valley.
Only a few tree problems but many sharp woody bends -- this
is alder country!  The last mile is drab and trashy.
[Reported 1977]

*Difficulties:*  A few trees down.

*Shuttle:*  State Route 155 runs along the creek.  Put in at a
bridge on a side road in Wrights.  To reach the take-out go
north on State Route 155.  As you enter Port Allegany turn
left/west and go 0.3 miles to where the road crosses the
Allegheny river.  This will be about 0.2 miles downstream of
the junction of this stream with the Allegheny.  You can add
a mile to the trip be continuing to where US Route 6 crosses
the Allegheny River.

*Gauge:*  Port Allegany.  This gauge is about 1.4 miles
downstream from the mouth on the Allegheny River.  We do
not have enough information to report runnable levels on
this section.

*Normal Wet Period:*  No available statistics on seasons.
Since this section is small, it should normally be runnable
approximately January through April.

# Monongahela River Watershed

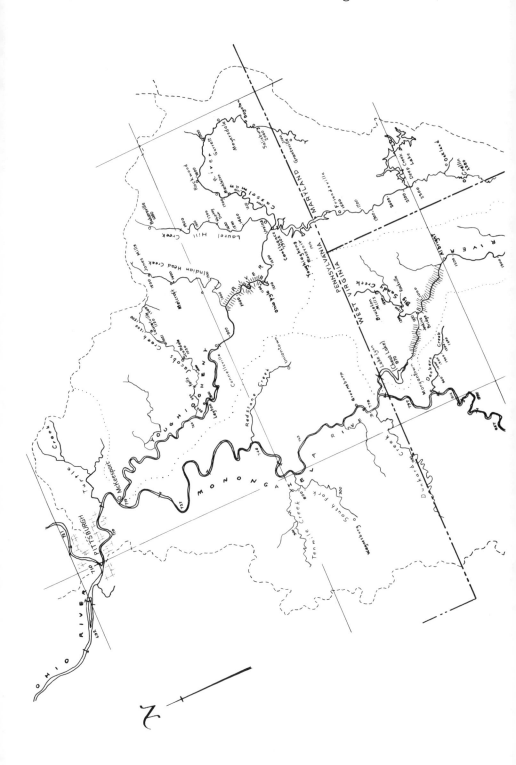

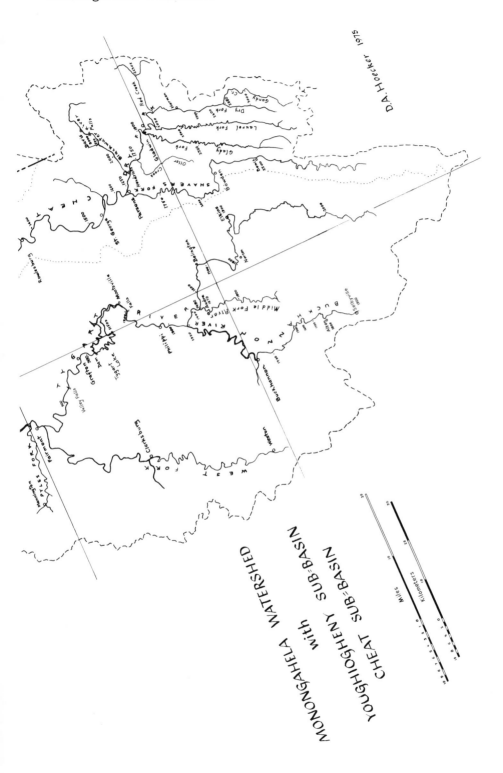

MONONGAHELA WATERSHED
with SUB-BASIN
YOUGHIOGHENY SUB-BASIN
CHEAT SUB-BASIN

D.A. Hoecker 1975

# Monongahela River

## Fairmont, West Virginia to Pittsburgh          128 miles

| Class | Grad | Size (Area/Volume) | Scene/Poll | Level |
|-------|------|--------------------|-----------|-------|
| A | Pool | Large (2,720/4,494) | D/C | |

Pt Marion
Large (4,407/8,090) Greensboro
Large (5,213/8,973) Charleroi
Huge (7,337/12,500) Braddock

*Topographic Maps:* Fairmont West (WVa), Fairmont East (WVa), Rivesville (WVa), Morgantown South (WVa), Morgantown North (WVa), Masontown, Carmichaels, Mather, California, Fayette City, Donora, Monongahela, Glassport, McKeesport, Braddock, Pittsburgh East, Pittsburgh West

*County Maps:* Marion (WVa), Monongalia (WVa), Greene, Fayette, Washington, Westmoreland, Allegheny

*Other Maps:* A set of detailed navigation charts is available for $6.00 from the District Engineer, Pittsburgh District Corps of Engineers, Federal Building, 1000 Liberty Ave., Pittsburgh, Pennsylvania, 15222.

*Description:* This is a wide flat river with little visible current. The wind direction and speed is often a bigger factor than the current. The stream is controlled by dams with navigation locks. There is a lot of motorboat and barge traffic. This traffic is faster but often less maneuverable than canoe traffic, and it creates considerable wake turbulence. This is a river in transition from a former high-pollution condition to a much lower level of pollution. Fish are evident until about 20 miles upstream of Pittsburgh. The water starts blue-green at Fairmont, giving way to murkiness as you approach the industry in Pittsburgh. Pollution is obvious, but not offensive until you get past Lock and Dam No. 3 which is within 20 miles of Pittsburgh. It is an area of abandoned ferry crossings, and coal mine operations with many bridges. Towns are built right up to the water's edge. A trip on this river is for people who like their canoeing with conveniences (restaurants, stores, ice cream stands, etc.). [Reported 1989]

*Difficulties:* Be sure you know where the dams are; they are fatally dangerous from either the upstream or downstream side, and it's easy to miss noticing them from upstream. Plan to be on the lock side of the river well above the lock and dam. To pass through a lock, approach it close to shore and keep clear of large boats to give them room to maneuver. Have a 50-foot line available in each boat and follow the lockmaster's instructions. See more detailed instruction on lock passage, under the write-up for the Ohio River.

Keep clear of large boats and barge tows. Barges are moving faster than they look, sometimes almost silently. They need lots of room to maneuver. Stay clear not only of the physical barge itself, but also of the very turbulent wake created by the push-boat. These boats not only make wake out the back, but some also have additional propellers pointed sideways, so that the wake may come straight out the side. Not only are barges hard to maneuver, they are slow to turn and stop. This means that by the time a barge captain sees a canoe, it is too late to avoid it. In addition the barges themselves block the captain's line of sight far in front of the boat.

This section of the river contains power boaters as well. Most of them will stay well clear of you, but others may want to create some waves for you to deal with.

*Shuttle:* Numerous public access points have been established for the use of boaters and fishermen; they are shown on the *Pennsylvania Fishing and Boating Map* published by the Pennsylvania Fish Commission and Pennsylvania Department of Transportation, the *Allegheny River Access Sites* published by the Western Pennsylvania Conservancy, and the *Navigation Charts for the Monongahela River* published by the Corps of Engineers. The table on the following page lists these access points and the river mile distance from the Pittsburgh Point.

*Gauge:* Call the weather service recording. If they say "not safe for recreational boating" it is probably too high.

*Normal Wet Period:* All year, see comment under gauge.

The following established access points are available.

| Location | river mile |
|---|---|
| Fairmont | 127.3 Right |
| Pricketts Creek | 120.7 Right |
| Opekiska Lock and Dam | 115.4 Right |
| Hildebrand Lock and Dam | 108.0 Left |
| Uffington | 104.5 Right |
| Morgantown Lock and Dam | 102.0 Left |
| Morgantown | 101.1 Right |
| Star City | 97.8 Right |
| Pt. Marion Lock and Dam | 90.8 Left |
| Pt. Marion | 90.3 Right |
| Lock and Dam # 7 | 85.0 Left |
| Greensboro | 84.5 Left |
| Greys Landing Lock and Dam under construction | |
| | 82.0 Right |
| Rice's Landing | 68.5 Left |
| Ten Mile Creek | 65.6 Left |
| Fredericktown | 63.8 Right |
| Maxwell Lock and Dam | 61.2 Right |
| West Brownsville | 56.0 Left |
| California | 51.8 Left |
| Roscoe | 48.5 Left |
| Speers | 43.4 Left |
| Charleroi | 42.3 Left |
| Lock and Dam #4 | 41.5 Right |
| North Charleroi | 41.1 Left |
| Webster | 36.4 Right |
| Forward Township | 34.1 Right |
| Monongahela (Pa Fish Comm) | 33.2 Left |
| Monongahela Borough | 31.9 Left |
| New Eagle | 30.1 Left |
| Lock and Dam #3 | 23.8 Right |
| Elizabeth Riverfront Park | 23.1 Right |
| Coal Valley | 18.5 Left |
| McKeesport (Left bank of Youghiogheny) | |
| | 15.5 Right |
| Lock and Dam #2 | 11.2 Right |
| Braddock | 10.7 Right |
| Pittsburgh (Birmingham Bridge) | 2.2 Left |
| Station Square | 0.1 Right |
| Point State Park | 0.0 Left |

# Turtle Creek

## A. West Export to Abers Creek                    4.1 miles
## (Pennsylvania Turnpike)

| Class | Grad | Size (Area/Volume) | Scene/Poll | Level |
|-------|------|--------------------|-----------|-------|
| I | 22/40 | Tiny(45/75) estimate | C/C | |

*Topographic Maps:* Murrysville

*County Maps:* Westmoreland

*Description:* This close-to-Pittsburgh stream demonstrates that many acres of trees can still be found close to town. The section above the restaurant with the footbridge runs behind warehouses, restaurants, and light industry. The mile below the foot bridge takes lots of maneuvering around chunks of rock apparently stirred up by industrial construction. From there to the Turnpike it is flowing with some riffles. This one is a good poling stream. [Checked 1987]

*Difficulties:* None. Some sections might go to Class II with standing waves when the rest of the creek is deep enough to get a good paddle stroke.

*Shuttle:* Via old William Penn Highway, US Route 22 and Abers Creek Road.

*Gauges:* None. On US Route 22 in Murrysville there is a restaurant with a footbridge to the parking lot. It used to be a Hardees and is now (1989) Busy Day Gourmet. Stand on the footbridge looking downstream. Look at the corrugated drainpipe (1.5 foot diameter) near water level in the retaining wall on river right. Its lower lip should be a few inches under water for poling, more for paddling.

*Normal Wet Period:* No available statistics on seasons. Since this section is tiny, it should normally be runnable only after a heavy rain or during spring snowmelt.

# B. Abers Creek to Trafford                    5.0 miles

| Class | Grad | Size (Area/Volume) | Scene/Poll | Level |
|-------|------|--------------------|-----------|-------|
| I | 6/22 | Tiny (56/76) Trafford | B-C/C | |

*Topographic Maps:* Murrysville, Braddock

*County Maps:* Westmoreland

*Description:* [Reported 1987]

*Difficulties:* Trees have fallen about 0.25 miles below Saunders Station Bridge. Be sure to get out at the Forbes Road bridge above the old Westinghouse plant in Trafford. Below the plant, at the State Route 130/993 bridge, is a dangerous dam, about 6 feet high, both unrunnable and unportageable. The plant area is reputed to contain PCB and the concrete stream banks are fenced off very effectively to prevent all access. These fences form a cul-de-sac from which retreat would be exceedingly difficult. Do *not* continue beyond the Forbes Road bridge.

*Shuttle:* Via Abers Creek Road to Saunders Station Road to Haymaker Road, to Forbes Road.

*Gauges:* None.

*Normal Wet Period:* No available statistics on seasons. Since this section is tiny, it should normally be runnable only after a heavy rain or during spring snowmelt.

# C. Trafford to Monongahela River            7.5 miles

| Class | Grad | Size (Area/Volume) | Scene/Poll | Level |
|-------|------|--------------------|-----------|-------|
| I | 7/9 | Small (148/247) mouth of creek | D/B | |

*Topographic Maps:* Braddock

*County Maps:* Westmoreland, Allegheny

*Description:* Below Trafford, Turtle Creek runs through an urban stream channel. Shortly below State Route 48 is

Pitcairn. The stream bed runs on smooth bedrock for 100 yards with surfing waves and small holes. Below Pitcairn begins a flood channel that extends through Wilmerding, Turtle Creek, and East Pittsburgh. The scenery consists of concrete stream walls for 3 miles and buildings beyond. Local fishermen catch catfish and bass in this channel. Westinghouse Bridge brings an end to the concrete; scout the flood control dam here before the run to be sure you can get through. Below here the right bank is dominated by the Edgar Thompson works of USX, and the mouth of Turtle Creek is marked by 19 railroad tracks. [Reported 1987]

*Difficulties:* Do not attempt to combine this section with the previous section, which terminates shortly above an unrunnable dam. See description above. There is some Class II water around Pitcairn. Before running, scout the flood control dam under the Westinghouse Bridge. This dam has a huge gate that normally is 20 feet above the water and is lowered into Turtle Creek when the Monongahela is in flood. This prevents high water on the Monongahela from backing up Turtle Creek while huge pumps carry Turtle Creek's normal flow past the dam.

*Shuttle:* The put-in is not easy to find. Fencing along Turtle Creek in Trafford effectively blocks direct access from Trafford. From First Street there is a foot trail on river left along the Conrail mainline. This is not advised. The recommended put-in adds 0.5 to 1.0 miles by putting in on Brush Creek. Go down First street to the dead end. Take Stewart Street which is the underpass under the railroad nearby. Follow Stewart out of town and pick your access as it follows the creek. Best access is 0.2 miles past an athletic field where the road parallels the stream. Take out at Corps of Engineers Lock and Dam #2 on river right on the Monongahela River just downstream of the mouth of Turtle Creek.

*Gauges:* None.

*Normal Wet Period:* No available statistics on seasons. Since this section is small, it should normally be runnable approximately January through April.

# Brush Creek

## Manor to Trafford                                         11.8 miles

| Class | Grad | Size (Area / Volume) | Scene / Poll | Level |
|-------|------|----------------------|--------------|-------|
| I | 15/20 | Tiny (58/97) | C/B | |
| | | mouth of creek | | |

*Topographic Maps:* Irwin, McKeesport, Braddock

*County Maps:* Westmoreland, Allegheny

*Description:* Brush Creek is surprisingly pleasant; it flows through or past numerous communities and shares a valley with State Route 993 and a Conrail mainline. These are evident, but lush vegetation keeps the towns, highway, and railroad at bay. The unavoidable railroad bridges are old stone structures that add a class touch to the run. There are also two loops where the run escapes local civilization. [Reported 1987]

*Difficulties:*

*Shuttle:* Put in at the mouth of Bushy Run near Manor or behind Manor Borough Maintenance Building on Brush Creek Road. Take out is at recommended put-in for Turtle Creek in Trafford, or just continue the additional 6 miles to the Monongahela. Alternate put-ins are at State Route 993 bridge, 7 miles upstream of Trafford, or the recreational area downstream of the Turnpike bridge and 10 miles above Trafford.

*Gauges:* None.

*Normal Wet Period:* No available statistics on seasons. Since this section is tiny, it should normally be runnable only after a heavy rain or during spring snowmelt.

# Youghiogheny River

## A. Swallow Falls State Park    5.7 mile
## to Sang Run "The Top Yough"

| Class | Grad | Size (Area/Volume) | Scene/Poll | Level |
|-------|------|--------------------|------------|-------|
| V-VI | 42/130 | Medium (200/333) estimate | A/A | 0.8-2.7 Sang Run |

*Topographic Maps:* Sang Run (Md)

*County Maps:* Garrett (Md)

*Description:* The Top Yough (this section) and the Upper Yough (the next section) are undoubtedly two of the most difficult runs reviewed in this guide. Together they comprise one of the premier whitewater challenges in the East. If you are adequately prepared and in good company this will be a superb experience; but if you or your paddle mates are not expert boaters, expect a catastrophe. The gradient is steep, the current swift, and the stream is strewn with boulders and holes. There is no evidence of civilization except at the put-in and take-out.

Put in at Swallow Falls State Park below Lower Swallow Falls. In the middle of the first Class V rapid Muddy Creek pours into the Yough from river left. Catch an eddy and glance upstream at the splendid falls, before continuing your descent.

Most of the rapids can be scouted from eddies. At lower levels (1.8-2.0) the river is highly technical, and there are numerous pinning possibilities. At higher levels (2.5-2.8) large holes and explosion waves abound. Above 3 feet the eddies become upstream rapids, and the whole river is Class VI.

Only those who have mastered the Tygart Gorge and Cheat Canyon should consider this. Because of the continuity and difficulty of the rapids, rescue is difficult. A solid roll is an absolute necessity. The remnant of a trail runs along river right, otherwise the mountain sides are choked with dense undergrowth of rhododendron and hemlock. [Checked 1990]

*Difficulties:* About 1.5 miles into the run lurks the Suck Hole, a Class V which nearly everyone elects to carry. There is no distinguishing feature for this rapid so it is best to be with someone who knows the river, or be prepared to do a lot of scouting. At first glance Suck Hole seems just to be another Class V series of drops punctuated by mid-stream boulders. But look carefully at the "inviting" eddy on river right just after the first drop. Notice the water sliding out backwards into a tremendous undercut stuffed with logs, debris and other assorted goodies.

*Shuttle:* Put in at Swallow Falls State Park. Take out near the power station at Hoyes Run, but please do so quickly and without fanfare. Due to strict Maryland Department of Natural Resources Wild and Scenic River Regulations some local property owners are hostile to paddlers. Under no circumstances should shuttle vehicles be left on private property. You might want to add about 3 miles of flatwater to the trip and paddle down to the Sang Run bridge (the Upper Yough put-in).

*Gauges:* Sang Run. This gauge should read below 2.7 feet. This corresponds to a flow of 262 cfs. Use this gauge with caution! The levels cited are for natural flow only. The water from the Deep Creek power station dumps in below this section but above the gauge. If there is a dam release when you check the gauge you will need to subtract 4 to 5 inches from the reading. For instance, in the summer during a mid-morning dam release the Sang Run gauge may read 2.2 but this section will not be runnable. The "Upper" would be the appropriate run. There are seldom dam releases on weekends.

Note that the character of this river changes dramatically with every two-inch increment on the gauge, and during a heavy rain the levels can change very quickly. The Top Yough can be run in early spring and after heavy summer rains. If a dam release raises the level too high for a run on the Upper, the Top Yough or nearby Bear Creek should be exciting alternatives.

*Normal Wet Period:* Runnable only after a rain.

# B. Sang Run to Friendsville, Md.     9.3 miles
# "The Upper Yough"

| Class | Grad | Size (Area/Volume) | Scene/Poll | Level |
|-------|------|--------------------|-----------|-------|
| V-VI | 56/100 | Medium (295/646) | A/A | 1.8-2.8 |
| | | Friendsville | | Sang Run |

*Topographic Maps:* Sang Run (Md), Friendsville (Md)

*County Maps:* Garrett (Md)

*Description:* This section, often called the Upper Yough, is one of the ultimate white-water runs in the East. After 3 miles of flatwater, the river drops continuously through a beautiful gorge, although the paddler may not notice anything except water and rocks on the first few trips. For 6 miles there are no pools, only eddies in which to rest and regroup. The river is characterized by rapids that drop away so steeply that the paddler cannot see through to the bottom of any of the major rapids. The beginning and ending of the major rapids are arbitrarily designated rocks in the river and are separated by only slightly smaller rapids. The river should be attempted only by very experienced closed boaters with excellent boat control and a 99-percent-plus roll on lesser rivers. Swimmers face a probability of injury and loss of equipment. An overgrown logging railroad follows the river along the left above National Falls and along the right below. The first several trips should be done only in the company of other paddlers who already know the river. The rapids are so continuous and so concealed by the drops and boulders that scouting is not possible if the paddler expects to finish before dark. The first-time paddler should be prepared for a long and exhausting, but exhilarating day.

A number of rafting companies offer trips on this section. This is some of the most intense and difficult rafting in the United States. Rafters should be aware that some of the private rafting trips that have been attempted have not been completed. Other private trips have lost their equipment and some have required outside rescue. [Checked 1990]

*Difficulties:* The 14 major rapids (all individually Class IV+ or V) are as follows  Gap Falls, Bastard Falls, Charlie's Choice, Triple Drop, National Falls, Tommy's Hole, Zinger,

Hinzerling, Meat Cleaver, Powerful Popper, Lost and
Found, Cheeseburger Falls, Wright's Hole, and Double
Pencil Sharpener. Memorizing the names in order helps
considerably in maintaining your perspective on the river.
Without the names as milestones, the river can seem an
endless series of disappearing rapids. All of the major
rapids include blind entries with steep and technical
maneuvering. Most of the rapids are long and include
numerous pinning and broaching possibilities.

The best chance for a safe and enjoyable trip on the Upper
for a first time paddler is with a group of experienced
paddlers who know the intricacies of this river. Before
considering this section a paddler should feel comfortable
with rivers such as the Tygart Gorge and the lower Big
Sandy.

*Shuttle:* From Friendsville follow Bishoff Road to a sharp
right turn onto Hoyes-Sang Run Road and follow it to the
put-in. The residents of Sang Run (the put-in) have a
history of great concern over their property rights and have
posted all obvious river access points with no trespassing
notices. A rafting company has acquired access property at
the put-in and allows private boaters to put in there. Stop in
Friendsville and check for directions to the legal put-in.
Shuttle vehicles should not be left at the Sang Run as there
is no legal or secure parking available. Check in
Friendsville for hiring a shuttle driver (or bring your own) to
return the vehicle to Friendsville.

*Gauges:* Sang Run. This gauge should read below 2.8 feet.
This corresponds to a flow of 318 cfs. Use this gauge with
caution! The levels are for natural flow only. The Sang Run
bridge gauge can be viewed only from the put-in bridge. It
includes the outflow from Deep Creek Lake used to generate
peaking power for the Pennsylvania Electric Company.
During the week power plant operation adds considerable
water to the river. For gauge information call Pennsylvania
Electric Company, Hoyes Generating Station (301) 334-3165.
"Two turbines" is the best level for decked boats. It takes the
water two hours after release to reach Sang Run, another
hour to reach Gap Falls, and 7 more to reach Friendsville.
The Corps of Engineers Friendsville gauge can be used for
this stream to a certain extent. A reading of 2.9 feet on this
gauge (natural water) is minimal for decked boats. Be very
cautious if the gauge reads over 4 feet.

At Sang Run, there is a gauge on the bridge; 1.5 feet is minimum, but that is a good first time level. A level of 2.5 feet is as high as most experts will run. Remember, this is a Class V-VI river. Approach with great caution.

*Normal Wet Period:* Weekdays. This river is generally runnable only Monday through Friday when the natural flow is augmented by power generation releases out of Deep Creek Lake. On weekends, the peaking power plant does not operate, but in the spring or after heavy rains, the river is runnable in natural water. In fact, at this time, the peaking release can be dangerous, converting a difficult but manageable trip into a nightmare.

## C. Friendsville to Confluence          5.0 miles

| Class | Grad | Size (Area/Volume) | Scene/Poll | Level |
|-------|------|--------------------|-----------|-------|
| A | Lake | Medium (295/637) | A/A | |
|   |      | Friendsville |  | |
|   |      | Medium (436/878) | Youghiogheny Dam | |

*Topographic Maps:* Friendsville, Ohiopyle, Confluence

*County Maps:* Garrett (Md), Somerset, Fayette

*Other Maps:* A map of the reservoir showing camping facilities, access points, etc. is available free from the Corps of Engineers, District Engineer, Pittsburgh District, Federal Building, 1000 Liberty Avenue, Pittsburgh, Pennsylvania 15222.

*Description:* This is a Corps of Engineers recreation lake. [Checked 1988]

*Difficulties:* Power boats.

*Shuttle:* Several access points are available on the lake. Obtain the map from the office at the foot of the dam, or from above.

*Gauges:* Not applicable.

*Normal Wet Period:* This is a lake so it is always canoeable unless it is iced over.

## D. Confluence to Ohiopyle          11.0 miles
## "The Middle Yough"

*Class  Grad    Size (Area/Volume)    Scene/Poll  Level*
I-II    9/20    Medium (436/856)      A-B/A       1.8-3.5
                Youghiogheny Dam                  Confluence
        Large (1,029/2,005) Confluence

*Topographic Maps:* Confluence, Ohiopyle

*County Maps:* Somerset, Fayette

*Description:* The 11-mile stretch between Confluence and
Ohiopyle is a favorite run, especially for instructing
whitewater students and in the late summer when nothing
else is runnable. The river cuts through Laurel Ridge with
wooded mountainsides along the river. An abandoned
railroad along the left bank has been converted into a bicycle
path. This stretch begins easy and gets more difficult as
Ohiopyle is approached. Below the Ramcat Hollow put-in
are 2 miles of Class I-II rapids. In this section there are
four significant rapids. The next 3 miles is a long flat
shallow section called the "Doldrums". At lower water
levels you will have to be really sharp to get through without
dragging. After the river makes a major left bend the pools
shorten and the rapids begin to intensify with the best rapids
occurring in the last mile to Ohiopyle. [Checked 1990]

*Difficulties:* Near Confluence in 1989 the Corps of Engineers
had constructed two 3-foot rock dams across the river to
aerate the water from the power plant. These were removed
in the spring of 1990. It is not known if they will try
something else. At Ohiopyle, a take-out has been built by the
state, on river left above the island which is 0.25 miles above
the highway bridge. An alternative take-out is on either
bank immediately below the highway bridge. Do not attempt
to run beyond this point as there is a 20-foot waterfall just
downstream. At higher water levels you should use the
State Park take-out. If you use State Park take-out you will
miss the "Zee" rapid on river right.

*Shuttle:* The normal put-in is at Confluence above the road
bridge and below the Corps of Engineers campground on the
river left. One can eliminate about 2.0 miles of flatwater by
putting in downstream along the left side of the river at the

Ramcat Hollow State Park put-in. To get to the take-out, continue up Ramcat Hollow road to State Route 2012, Turn right towards Ohiopyle. At the tee in Ohiopyle turn right. There is an official take-out on river left about 400 yards upstream of the bridge. To use the take-out below the highway bridge, park on river right along the railroad tracks and haul your boats up to the cars. A bicycle trail from the Ramcat Hollow put-in, along river left to the take-out offers an option of a easy 9 mile bike ride for the shuttle.

*Gauges:* Confluence. This gauge should read between 1.8 and 3.5 feet. This corresponds to a flow of 550 cfs to 2,100 cfs. The Ohiopyle gauge at the end of the section will probably read between 1.3 and 3.5 feet.

The following graph shows the correlation between the 7:00 AM readings for the Confluence and Ohiopyle gauges during the 1988 canoeing season. Values are in feet. For example, readings just below 3.5 at Confluence correspond to readings just above 3.5 at Ohiopyle.

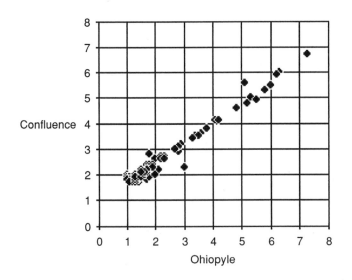

*Normal Wet Period:* Due to the dam at Confluence and the cooperation of the Corps of Engineers there is usually enough water for a good run, but it is normally too high from early January to mid May. The Confluence gauge is above 1.8 feet 92% of the time and above 3.5 feet 28% of the time.

*Hostel:* AYH accommodations are available at the Ohiopyle Youth Hostel in Ferncliff Park at Ohiopyle. For reservations call (412) 329-4476 or write to Ohiopyle Youth Hostel, PO Box 99, Ohiopyle, Pennsylvania, 15470.

## E. Ohiopyle to Bruner Run                    10.1 miles
## "The Lower Yough"

| Class | Grad | Size (Area/Volume) | Scene/Poll | Level |
|-------|------|--------------------|------------|-------|
| III-IV | 17/45 | Large (1,200/2,000) estimate | A/A | 1.9-3.5 Confluence |

*Topographic Maps:* Ohiopyle, Mill Run, Ft. Necessity

*County Maps:* Fayette

*Description:* The stretch from Ohiopyle Falls to Bruner Run is a favorite trip for rafters and advanced canoeists in closed boats. In addition to the exciting rapids and beautiful scenery there are frequent opportunities for swimming in the fairly clean but chilly water. Unless there are people in the party who have run this section before, a considerable amount of scouting is required. Because the Corps of Engineers maintains the water level throughout the summer, it is not unusual to find boaters from Ohio, Indiana, Illinois, and Washington, DC as well as hordes of local boaters. [Checked 1990]

*Difficulties:* Besides the normal problems of a Class III-IV river, this stretch of river is populated by a high density of inexperienced rafters. After the first rapid one can stand on shore and watch a continuous stream of rafts with very few breaks in traffic. As this is a Class III-IV river it is pushing the limits of an open boat. It is being run successfully in open boats, but the water level and skill of the paddler is critical. Many open boats have been destroyed on this section.

The current quota system allows 88 rafters on the river every 15 minutes and during the summer this quota is filled from 7:00 AM to 3:00 PM. Because of the filled quotas advanced reservations for rafters are generally required. Weekend time slots are being reserved for several months ahead of time. There is also a quota for boaters; however, during the summer of 1988 the boater's quota did not fill except for some prime times on weekends. Reserve with Ohiopyle State Park, Ohiopyle, Pennsylvania 15470.

Entrance Rapids is a series of ledges and hydraulics twisting several hundred yards. Cucumber Drop, immediately following, channels to the far right, with a final chute left of center and a large hole in the center. The next significant rapid is the Railroad Bridge Rapid. After a drop over a ledge, turn sharply left to miss "Charlie's Washing Machine". The river then opens up into flowing shallows for a couple of miles. The Dimple is a large rock near the left shore with water flowing directly into it. There is a narrow channel to the right of the Dimple at the top of a long left-curving rapid with the "Swimmer's Rapids" hydraulic at the bottom. The standing waves here are favorites of closed boaters for surfing. Swimmers hydraulic is a good one to play in, as it seldom, if ever, will hold a boat. Double Hydraulic follows a long rock garden. It can be sneaked on the right. Immediately after is the Gate (also known as River's End, World's End, the Pipestem).

*Shuttle:* Put in below the falls at Ohiopyle at the State Park put-in. There is a quota system on this river, see above. The take-out requires a 1.5 mile bus trip up a steep hill from the river to the parking area, for which you must buy a ticket at the put-in. The shuttle leaves Ohiopyle to the south, takes the right-hand fork in Ohiopyle towards the Campground, and follows the signs to Bruner Run. When parking be sure to get off the road, as there are many boaters cars and commercial trip busses along this narrow road.

*Gauge:* Confluence. This gauge should read between 1.9 and 3.5 feet. This corresponds to a flow of 610 cfs to 2,100 cfs. The Ohiopyle gauge at the start of the section will probably read between 1.4 and 3.5 feet. For decked boats 3.5 feet on the Confluence gauge is okay and it has been run at 4.0 to 4.5 by experienced paddlers. At the 5.0 foot level the commercial rafting tours stop operating. If Confluence is too high, try the Casselman from Markleton to Fort Hill for a fun run. Check also to see if the Laurel Hill is runnable.

The graph in the previous section shows the correlation between the 7:00 AM readings for the Confluence and Ohiopyle gauges during the 1988 canoeing season.

*Normal Wet Period:* The dam at Confluence and the cooperation of the Corps of Engineers usually provide enough water for a good run, but it is normally too high from early January to mid May. The Confluence gauge is above 1.9 feet 85% of the time and above 3.5 feet 28% of the time.

# F. Bruner Run to South Connellsville    9.0 miles

| Class | Grad | Size (Area/Volume) | Scene/Poll | Level |
|-------|------|-----|-----|-----|
| II-III | 10/17 | Large (1,300/2,167) estimate | A-B/A | 2.4-?? Confluence |

*Topographic Maps:* Mill Run, South Connellsville

*County Maps:* Fayette

*Description:* This trip starts tough and gets easy. The rapids start right at the put-in with no chance for a warm-up. They end well above the mouth of Indian Creek. The gorge has beautiful scenery with Class C-I whitewater consisting of shallow riffles. [Checked 1989]

*Difficulties:* The first few rapids are Class III, but there are easy routes. The dam at South Connellsville can not be run. Lower boats over the right side and continue to the US Route 119 take-out or take out above the dam at an alternate take-out.

*Shuttle:* When the Bruner Run take-out shuttle is running (see section above) private cars cannot drive to the Bruner Run river access (the put-in for this section). Check with the rangers in Ohiopyle or the shuttle vehicle drivers for the ride down the hill. The shuttle for this section is horrendously long. Use State Road maps for the trip from Bruner Run to South Connellsville. There is city-supplied access under the US Route 119 bridge in South Connellsville. An alternate take-out that avoids the dam and cuts off 2.5 miles of flatwater is just upstream of South Connellsville at a foot bridge. Go north on State Route 711 through South Connellsville. Turn right on Pittsburgh Street; go a couple miles until the road dead ends. Turn right and curve down to the river on a dirt road. Park in an industrial parking lot. Carry boats up hill and across railroad tracks to get to cars. Do not block access to the gate. It is possible to continue to the put-in of the next section, but you must carry around dams at a filtration plant and a power plant.

*Gauges:* Confluence. This gauge should read above 2.4 feet. This corresponds to a flow of 960 cfs. If the water level is too high, one can try Fort Hill to Harnedsville, or Rockwood to Markleton on the Casselman.

*Normal Wet Period:* This section is normally runnable from mid November through late September. The Confluence gauge is above 2.4 feet 62% of the time.

## G. South Connellsville to Dawson          5.7 miles

| Class | Grad | Size (Area/Volume) | Scene/Poll | Level |
|-------|------|--------------------|------------|-------|
| C-I | 5/6 | Large (1,350/2,580) | A/B | 2.1-4.5 |
|  |  | Connellsville |  | Connellsville |

*Topographic Maps:* South Connellsville, Connellsville, Dawson

*County Maps:* Fayette

*Description:* After leaving Connellsville, sparse population and wooded banks make this a pleasant trip. At mid-trip the remains of the Schenley Distillery on river right offers a reminder of the valley's history. [Reported 1989]

*Difficulties:* None.

*Shuttle:* Put in at Connellsville under the US Route 119 bridge on the upstream left side of the river. Follow State Route 201 west and then State Route 819 north to Dawson. At Dawson the take-out is on the river right some 200 yards upstream from the bridge. The road is chained where it leads into the firemen's carnival area. The take-out is on the other side of the chain. Park on the main road and do not block access to the area. A take-out just 50 feet upstream of the bridge, should not be used because of local landowner problems. It is possible to run from the take-out of the previous section, but you must carry around dams at a filtration plant and a power plant.

*Gauges:* Connellsville. This gauge should read between 2.1 and 4.5 feet. This corresponds to a flow of 630 cfs to 4,300 cfs. The shallowest place on the entire trip extends across the river just below the bridge at Dawson. If this can be canoed, the water level is adequate.

*Normal Wet Period:* Dam controlled. The Connellsville gauge is above 2.1 feet 81% of the time and above 4.5 feet 15% of the time.

# H. Dawson to Whitsett                    9.7 miles

| Class | Grad | Size (Area / Volume) | Scene / Poll | Level |
|-------|------|----------------------|--------------|-------|
| C-I | 6/8 | Large (1,400/2,333) estimate | B-C/B | 2.1-4.5 Connellsville |

*Topographic Maps:* Dawson, Fayette City

*County Maps:* Fayette

*Description:* This section of the Youghiogheny River is characterized by shallow riffles and calm pools. In higher water, the riffles develop into regular standing wave patterns. The last mile is flatwater, but just upstream of Layton there are many nice flat rocks for sunning and swimming. [Checked 1989]

*Shuttle:* The put-in is described as the take-out for the section above. A commonly used take-out at Layton will cut about 2.3 miles from the trip. Park either at the canoe livery for $3.00 per car for access/parking (1989) or there is a dirt road which starts between the main road and the railroad tracks and then curves in under the main road to get to the river. The Whitsett take-out is about 2 miles downstream from Layton, or about 1 mile northwest of Perryopolis on the river left where the paved but unnumbered road follows the stream bank for over 0.5 miles, offering river level access.

*Gauges:* Connellsville. This gauge should read between 2.1 and 4.5 feet. This corresponds to a flow of 630 cfs to 4,300 cfs. The shallowest place on the entire trip extends across the river just below the bridge at Dawson. If this can be canoed, the water level is adequate.

*Normal Wet Period:* Dam controlled. The Connellsville gauge is above 2.1 feet 81% of the time and above 4.5 feet 15% of the time.

# I. Whitsett to McKeesport                    28.8 miles
## "The Bottom Yough"

| Class | Grad | Size (Area/Volume) | Scene/Poll | Level |
|-------|------|--------------------|-----------|-------|
| C | 1/1 | Large (1,700/3,043) | C/B | |
| | | Sutersville | | Sutersville |

*Topographic Maps:* Fayette City, Dawson, Smithton, McKeesport

*County Maps:* Fayette, Westmoreland

*Description:* Aside from the villages of West Newton, Sutersville, and Blythedale there is little development visible from river level for the 25 miles to the Boston Bridge. Even here industrial sites are mostly screened by trees and brush. The Western Pennsylvania Conservancy has a detailed write-up of the Sutersville to Boston section. See appendix D for the address. [Checked 1982]

*Difficulties:* This section of the Youghiogheny can be canoed all year. However, caution should be exercised in early spring and after heavy rains as the current may be swift, and floating debris can be dangerous.

*Shuttle:* See Section H above for the description of the put-in at Whitsett. There are several take-outs and put-ins in the area of West Newton. The West Newton Sportsmen's Association has a public launching area at the downstream end of town. From West Newton to Sutersville the road runs next to the river. A good put-in at Sutersville is behind the Recreation Park. At Sutersville, the road crosses the river and continues downstream, skirting the villages of Blythedale, Industry, and Buena Vista. From Buena Vista, take the Greenock road for 2.5 miles, then bear left on Renzie road and go about a mile into Boston. The Pennsylvania Fish Commission has built a paved access ramp at Boston. It is on the left bank, just below the bridge. Another one has been built near the McKeesport sewer plant, on the left bank at the mouth of the Youghiogheny.

This section can be broken into sections in several different ways.

| | |
|---|---|
| Whitsett to Smithton | 4.0 miles |
| Smithton to West Newton | 6.5 miles |
| West Newton to Sutersville | 3.0 miles |
| Sutersville to Boston | 11.5 miles |
| Boston to McKeesport | 3.8 miles |

*Gauges:* Sutersville. We do not have enough information to report runnable levels on this section. A reading of 4.8 on the Sutersville gauge corresponds to the mean flow of 3034 cfs. Since this is a large size river, we speculate that the river is runnable most of the year; at 4.8 it may be too high. The Connellsville gauge upstream will probably read between 2.0 and 4.5 feet.

*Normal Wet Period:* Dam controlled.

# Sewickley Creek

## Yukon to Youghiogheny River                12.0 miles

| Class | Grad | Size (Area/Volume) | Scene/Poll | Level |
|-------|------|--------------------|-----------|-------|
| III | 13/33 | Small (165/275) mouth of creek | C/C | |

*Topographic Maps:* Smithton, Donora, McKeesport

*County Maps:* Allegheny, Westmoreland

*Description:* The water is very polluted with both mine acid and human pollution. Garbage and debris decorate the banks, bridge piers and downed trees. The first 3 miles are generally flat and flowing Class I. The river then drops over several small ledges and enters a deep gorge. In the gorge there are more ledges and hydraulics with chutes and rocks of Class III difficulty, some of them undercut. The chutes over some of the ledges can be identified by the piles of suds. [Reported 1980]

*Difficulties:* The vertical shore line of the gorge allows very few eddies, and makes for difficult scouting. About 1 mile downstream from the Mill Grove bridge three rusting steel cables drop off the right bank and slant diagonally into the main current.

*Shuttle:* Go south from Yukon then east on Interstate 70. Take the exit to West Newton, cross the Youghiogheny and proceed north along the river to the mouth of Sewickley Creek.

*Gauges:* None.

*Normal Wet Period:* No available statistics on seasons. Since this section is small, it should normally be runnable approximately January through April.

# Jacobs Creek

## A. Acme to Laurelville                                4.5 miles

| Class | Grad | Size (Area / Volume) | Scene / Poll | Level |
|-------|------|----------------------|--------------|-------|
| I V | 125/164 | Tiny (30/50) | A-B/A | zero-.5 |
| | 3 mile@140 | estimate | | streamside |
| | | | | 34"-24" |
| | | | | Freemans Falls |

*Topographic Maps:* Mammoth

*County Maps:* Westmoreland

*Description:* Jacobs Creek rises in the farmland on the crest of Chestnut Ridge and blasts 500-plus feet down to the valley floor in a little over 4 miles. You have probably seen the creek; it shares its tiny valley with the Pennsylvania Turnpike just west of Donegal. The Turnpike is not intrusive; you are too busy with the stream to think about it.

The drop is spread out fairly evenly, so the creek is almost continuous Class III water studded with concentrated descents of 4 to 6 feet or more, sometimes in the form of ledges with chutes, sometimes as cascades, and sometimes simply as steeper places. Some of these are complex enough to be rated Class IV, but the creek also earns a Class IV rating for being continuous whitewater without any pools and with very few eddies. With more water, it would probably become Class V.

From the canoeist's eye level, the stream often disappears from sight--downward. It drops away so fast that you can not see the bottom of a descent until you are halfway through it. And this happens too often to scout. The most amazing thing about this little creek is that it is runnable at all. Few other runnable rivers have a sustained gradient even approaching the 140 ft/mile, and they are all described as Class V or VI for only the most expert canoeists. Jacobs Creek is nothing to take lightly, but if the fallen trees were cleared out it would be delight for the intermediate closed boat paddler. [Checked 1985]

*Difficulties:* Surprisingly few, considering the gradient. Fallen trees are the biggest problem. With low water, one can pull out and carry around, but higher water could make this a real problem. The river falls away from the paddler so fast that the best course is sometimes hard to spot, but the creek is so small that there are not many choices. There is usually an eddy at the end of each big descent, but there are no pools.

There is a waterfall, Freeman Falls (unrunnable), and a dam (runnable) just before the creek crosses under the Turnpike from north to south (this is the put-in). There is a dam (unrunnable) where you first encounter houses at the foot of the ridge. The pool for the dam has silted up and is non-existent. Take out as soon as you reach the houses.

*Shuttle:* From Donegal, west on State Route 31. For the put-in, turn right at Acme, cross the Turnpike, find the creek in about 0.25 mile. Ask the owners for permission to put in below the waterfall. For the take-out, follow State Route 31 to the Laurelville bridge.

*Gauges:* Minimum level is 34 inches below the crest of the dam at Freeman falls, or 0.9 feet at the Mennonite Church Camp. Appreciably more water could drastically change the character of the run. We estimate that 1.0 foot would make the run Class V. The creek rises after a day of rain. Check along the Turnpike east of New Stanton to decide whether you want to run it.

*Normal Wet Period:* No available statistics on seasons. Since this section is tiny, it should normally be runnable only after a heavy rain or during spring snowmelt.

# B. Laurelville to Scottdale                    10.0 miles

*Class  Grad     Size (Area / Volume)      Scene / Poll  Level*
  I      12/76      Small (60/100)           A-B/A-B
                    estimate

*Topographic Maps:* Mammoth, Mt Pleasant, Connellsville

*County Maps:* Westmoreland, Fayette

*Description:* Jacobs Creek has a mile or so of Class I-II whitewater below State Route 31 before entering two braided sections followed by what are different forms of wetlands (swamps and marshes) stretching most of the way to US Route 119. There are good passages among the islands in the braiding sections. Next comes the silted remains of an old lake that is now revegetated as a grassy wetland. The dam is breached with only a small riffle at the dam site. After a drop under an old bridge, the creek enters the short pool of the present Bridgeport dam (3 feet high). The rest of the distance to US Route 119 is a marsh with some trees and one low bridge obstruction. Below US Route 119 the stream reenters a conventional channel and heads for Scottdale among homes and varied industry. [Reported 1985]

*Difficulties:* The first mile below State Route 31 has Class I-II rapids. Plan to carry around the Bridgeport dam.

*Shuttle:* Take State Route 31 into Mount Pleasant and State Route 819 to Scottdale. Continue through Scottdale on State Route 819 to the bridge about 0.25 miles past the cemetery.

*Gauges:* None available.

*Normal Wet Period:* No available statistics on seasons. Since this section is small, it should normally be runnable approximately January through April.

# C. Scottdale to Chaintown                        5.0 miles

| Class | Grad | Size (Area / Volume) | Scene / Poll | Level |
|-------|------|----------------------|--------------|-------|
| B | 4/4 | Small (80/133) estimate | C/B | |

*Topographic Maps:* Connellsville, Dawson

*County Maps:* Westmoreland, Fayette

*Description:* This is a lazy moving section through mixed farm and woodlands. Occasional homes dot the hillsides.

*Difficulties:* none

*Shuttle:* To get to the take-out, go west on State Route 819. Go 2.0 miles and bear right onto State Route 1006. Twist and turn for 2.2 miles and then turn right/north onto State Route 1041. Drive about 1.0 miles to the Chaintown Bridge.

*Gauge:* None available.

*Normal Wet Period:* No available statistics on seasons. Since this section is small, it should normally be runnable approximately January through April.

# D. Chaintown to town of Jacobs Creek   7.1 miles  at Youghiogheny River

| Class | Grad | Size (Area / Volume) | Scene / Poll | Level |
|-------|------|----------------------|--------------|-------|
| II-III | 32/41 | Small (95/158) Jacobs Creek | B/B | 4.7-6.9 Connellsville |

*Topographic Maps:* Dawson

*County Maps:* Westmoreland, Fayette

*Description:* The stream starts out trashy but cleans up after the first 2 or 3 miles. The creek is flat and flowing for the first couple of miles. Shortly after the second railroad bridge it picks up real rapids and an unrunnable waterfall (see difficulties). After the waterfall it is Class II-III rapids separated by short pools. The rapids are open, with maneuvering and waves but nothing long or terrifying.

The waterfall would be beautiful if it had not been defaced by painted graffiti (this area has been known as Blue Hole to generations of high schoolers). You may find the ruins of a mill where you put in below the waterfall and the ruins of an iron furnace (Alliance Furnace) about 2 miles above the town of Jacobs Creek. The iron furnace is on the left shortly after a strip mine on the right descends to river level. If you walk up the hill from the furnace you may find coal works and ruins of a road and building. The historical marker for this furnace is along the shuttle route. If you are into ruins, stop on the way home to see the coke ovens visible from the road between Jacobs Creek and Smithton. [Checked 1988]

*Difficulties:* Waterfall on a blind left-hand bend after the second railroad bridge. After passing this bridge always have an eddy in sight that you are 100 percent sure of making. As soon as rapids start, more than just riffles, get out on the left side and scout. The portage is on the left. If the water is low enough, you can carry on top of the berm of the former mill race. In higher water you will have to haul the boats up 50 feet up the hill to a jeep trail around the falls.

*Shuttle:* Take State Route 3073 north out of Chaintown for 3.5 miles. Turn left onto State Route 981, then left again onto State Route 3035, left onto State Route 3033 and a final left onto State Route 3029 to the river. Follow a dirt road on river right upstream for about 100 yards to the take-out at the old bridge abutment.

*Gauges:* On the old bridge abutment on river right about 100 yards above the road bridge in the town of Jacobs Creek, ignoring the concrete slab on top, seven blocks should give a good run. There is a staff gauge bolted to a tree on river right about 0.2 miles upstream from the take-out, just upstream of a small island. This gauge should read above 2.2 feet. The Connellsville gauge on nearby Youghiogheny River will probably read between 4.7 and 6.9 feet.

*Normal Wet Period:* No available statistics on seasons. Since this section is small, it should normally be runnable approximately January through April.

# Dunbar Creek

## Above Dunbar to Connellsville                         6.4 miles

*Class  Grad      Size (Area / Volume)      Scene / Poll  Level*
III-IV  59/112        Tiny (26/43)                B/A
                         Dunbar
             Tiny (38/63) Connellsville

*Topographic Maps:* South Connellsville, Connellsville

*County Maps:* Fayette

*Description:* Dunbar Creek drains a tiny watershed on Chestnut Ridge in the vicinity of Jumonville. The beginning of the trip has braided channels, many downed trees, and the remains of several old dams. The largest old dam is about a mile below the put-in and at the bottom of the worst of the islands and split channels; it has trees in the washout channel and should be carried. The next mile is comparable to the lower Savage River with even gradient, plenty of speed and small waves, and a few one-shot play spots. The gradient picks up for the next 2 miles into Dunbar. The steepest section is near Furnace Hill where the road is away from the stream. Here the run enters a small man-made canyon of slag and other industrial waste. Most of the run can be scouted from the boat, but one 4-foot drop next to a truck-size slag boulder deserves special attention. Shortly below this a debris pile chokes most of the stream. Below Dunbar the gradient diminishes and the stream becomes Class I-II with some tree hazards. [Reported 1989]

*Difficulties:* Old dam about a mile below the put-in should be carried. A couple of Class IV drops should be scouted and perhaps carried. Dunbar is noteworthy because the stream flows under the local tavern and hotel. Two channels are open to the paddler, but they should be scouted from shore during the shuttle. Downed trees can present problems at any point.

*Shuttle:* To reach the put-in from Connellsville, head south for the State Game Lands by way of US Route 119. Turn left onto State Route 1053 (the road between Dunbar and

Ohiopyle State Park). Pass through Dunbar continuing along side the stream for about 2 miles. Pick your put-in. One suggestion is where the stream leaves the main road. Return to Connellsville and take out under the US Route 119 bridge. On the river you will paddle about a mile on the Youghiogheny, and through town to reach this bridge.

*Gauges:* Streamside. There is a concrete ledge just upstream of the first highway bridge above Dunbar. Optimal level when it is 3/4 covered.

*Normal Wet Period:* No available statistics on seasons. Since this section is tiny, it should normally be runnable only after a heavy rain or during spring snowmelt.

# Indian Creek

## A. Jones Mills
## to Indianhead Lake on State Route 381

16.0 miles

| Class | Grad | Size (Area/Volume) | Scene/Poll | Level |
|---|---|---|---|---|
| I-II | 13/20 | Tiny (33/55) | A/A | |
| | | Melcroft | | White Bridge |

*Topographic Maps:* Seven Springs, Donegal, Mill Run

*County Maps:* Westmoreland, Fayette

*Description:* From Jones Mills to Melcroft the creek is fast-flowing and narrow. There may be downed trees. There is a Class I rapid just below Champion, and a ledge or low runnable dam just above Melcroft. From Melcroft to State Route 653, the creek is slightly bigger. It flows over gravel bars, mostly straight shots, not many eddies. Not far above State Route 653 the Class I-II rapids begin. Between State Route 653 and the lake at State Route 381, the river is an honest Class II. This is a nice trip. It is pretty except for a shantytown on the left bank just above State Route 653. [Checked 1981]

*Difficulties:* There is a series of rock dams in conjunction with the summer homes about halfway down the run.

*Shuttle:* The river runs roughly along State Route 381, so you can pick a trip according to your tastes.

*Gauges:* White Bridge. We do not have enough information to report runnable levels on this section. Under the State Route 653 bridge is the shallowest part, so if you can get through there, the level is adequate. The Ursina gauge on nearby Laurel Hill Creek will probably read above 2.0 feet.

*Normal Wet Period:* No available statistics on seasons. Since this section is tiny, it should normally be runnable only after a heavy rain or during spring snowmelt.

# B. Indianhead Lake                                4.9 miles
## to Youghiogheny River at Camp Carmel

| Class | Grad | Size (Area/Volume) | Scene/Poll | Level |
|---|---|---|---|---|
| V-VI | 57/80 | small (125/208)<br>mouth of creek | A/A | White Bridge |

*Topographic Maps:* Mill Run, South Connellsville

*County Maps:* Fayette

*Description:* The character of the river swiftly changes from a valley stream to a let's-get-down-off-the-mountain stream. The gradient is very steep and the rapids are big and technical. [Checked 1981]

*Difficulties:* One rapid just beyond a hanging bridge has a dangerous undercut rock (Class VI) and should be scouted carefully. Most people choose not to run it. There are several other dangerous rapids. Scout carefully.

*Shuttle:* Put in on the reservoir near State Route 381, paddle across along the left bank. Carry around the dam at the end of the reservoir. Give the dam wide clearance as it is extremely dangerous. The creek runs into the Youghiogheny River about 3 miles upstream of South Connellsville. South Connellsville is the closest good take-out. Alternately, take out at Camp Carmel on the left side of the Youghiogheny.

*Gauges:* White Bridge. We do not have enough information to report runnable levels on this section. There is also a painted gauge where State Route 653 crosses the creek (slightly off the direct route to the creek, but well worth checking). Two inches on this painted gauge would probably be a good low level. Three feet is too high. The Ursina gauge on nearby Laurel Hill Creek will probably read above 2.0 feet.

*Normal Wet Period:* No available statistics on seasons. Since this section is tiny, it should normally be runnable only after a heavy rain or during spring snowmelt.

# Meadow Run

## A. State Route 381 to State Route 2011        5.0 miles

| Class | Grad | Size (Area/Volume) | Scene/Poll | Level |
|-------|------|--------------------|------------|-------|
| II-III | 53/90 | Tiny (30/50) estimate | A/A | |

*Topographic Maps:* Fort Necessity, Ohiopyle

*County Maps:* Fayette

*Description:* This is a extremely beautiful run. Occasional well-maintained summer homes dot the shore, but for the most part the banks are covered in mountain laurel. The creek runs through the back of Nemacolin Woodlands, past wrought-iron gates at the mouth of Beaver Creek, and along the lawn of a small church. The third small iron bridge marks the take-out at the Park office on State Route 2011. [Reported 1984]

*Difficulties:* Downed trees block the stream in several places. One of these is right around a bend from the put-in; it may be simpler to put in below it. Two low dams should be scouted. The first is intact; the second is broken out on the left side and may be passable there.

*Shuttle:* Follow US Route 40 to Farmington and turn left/north on State Route 381 toward Ohiopyle. The put-in is about a mile from the corner at the bridge crossing the small creek by the logging company on the left. To reach the take-out, follow State Route 381 north to State Route 2011 and turn right toward the park office, where the road crosses Meadow Run.

*Gauge:* Ursina. This gauge on nearby Laurel Hill Creek will probably read above 2.1 feet. Check the put-in; more tributaries join soon. A drain pipe on the bridge should not be more than a foot above the water. If Meadow Run is up, Indian Creek is probably up, too.

*Normal Wet Period:* No available statistics on seasons. Since this section is tiny, it should normally be runnable only after a heavy rain or during spring snowmelt.

# B. State Route 2011                    3.0 miles
## to Youghiogheny River

*Class  Grad      Size (Area / Volume)      Scene / Poll   Level*
IV-V   88/135       Tiny (41/68)              A / A
                    mouth of stream

*Topographic Maps:* Ohiopyle

*County Maps:* Fayette

*Description:* As it passes the trail to the rafting customers'
gathering point, this delightful stream changes character
and makes a run for the Youghiogheny. [Reported 1984]

*Difficulties:* Shortly after the rafting gathering point the
gradient increases to about 110 feet per mile as you reach the
Cascade. It's runnable, but many choose to carry; the best
carry is on the left, but the best spot for a safety rope (for
those who choose to run) is on the right. Two more spots
require special attention. The first is a 4-5 foot drop to the
left of a large undercut rock at the bottom of a zig-zag. The
second is the top of the slide, where you must get out in time
to avoid running it (the last eddy looks possible but may not
be). Most people who have run the slide purposefully have
needed stitches at the take-out, so carry around.

*Shuttle:* To reach the put-in, follow State Route 381 to State
Route 2011 and turn toward the park office, where the road
crosses Meadow Run. Meadow Run enters the Youghiogheny River at Entrance Rapid. If you don't feel like
working your way back upstream to the Yough put-in,
paddle the rest of the Loop on the Yough. This section can
be combined with the previous section.

*Gauge:* Ursina. This gauge on nearby Laurel Hill Creek
will probably read above 2.1 feet. If Meadow Run is up,
Indian Creek is probably up, too.

*Normal Wet Period:* No available statistics on seasons.
Since this section is tiny, it should normally be runnable
only after a heavy rain or during spring snowmelt.

# Casselman River

## A. US 40 Grantsville, Md. to Salisbury, Pa.   6.7 miles

| Class | Grad | Size (Area/Volume) | Scene/Poll | Level |
|-------|------|--------------------|------------|-------|
| I | 15/23 | Small (63/119) | B/A | |
| | | Grantsville | | Grantsville |

*Topographic Maps:* Grantsville, Avilton, Meyersdale

*County Maps:* Garrett, Somerset

*Description:* This is an easy stretch with Class I riffles running through a beautiful hemlock woods. If you can paddle the first riffle below the put-in, you will be okay for the entire run. [Checked 1981]

*Difficulties:* Several barbed wire fences cross the creek. There is also a very low dam.

*Shuttle:* East on US Route 40 then north on US Route 219 to Salisbury.

*Gauges:* Grantsville. We do not have enough information to report runnable levels on this section. The Markleton gauge further downstream will probably read above 2.8 feet.

*Normal Wet Period:* This section is normally runnable from early March through mid April.

## B. Salisbury to Garrett                    15.0 miles

| Class | Grad | Size (Area/Volume) | Scene/Poll | Level |
|-------|------|--------------------|------------|-------|
| I | 6/7 | Small (125/208) estimate | B/A | Grantsville |

*Topographic Maps:* Meyersdale

*County Maps:* Somerset

*Description:* This stream flows through farm country with occasional towns and some strip-mined areas. [Checked 1981]

*Difficulties:* None.

*Shuttle:* Along US Route 219. This section could be split into two trips at the halfway point of Meyersdale.

*Gauges:* Grantsville. We do not have enough information to report runnable levels on this section. The Markleton gauge further downstream will probably read above 2.7 feet.

*Normal Wet Period:* This section is normally runnable from late December through late May.

# C. Garrett to Rockwood                           7.5 miles

| Class | Grad | Size (Area / Volume) | Scene / Poll | Level |
|-------|------|----------------------|--------------|-------|
| I-II | 15/20 | Medium (250/417) | A/A | 2.2-3.6 |
| | | estimate | | Markleton |

*Topographic Maps:* Meyersdale, Murdock, Rockwood

*County Maps:* Somerset

*Description:* Once you leave Garrett, the only sign of civilization is the railroad track that runs alongside the creek. The first half of the trip has almost continuous rapids of Class I and easy Class II. After 3 miles or so the gradient tapers off and flowing water carries you into Rockwood. [Checked 1990]

*Difficulties:* Canoeists with no whitewater experience should take along someone with experience. Paddlers comfortable on the Middle Yough should have no trouble. Beware of poison ivy at the Rockwood access point.

*Shuttle:* State Route 653 runs between Garrett and Rockwood. Access is available near the bridge of the main cross route in each town; downstream on river left seems to work.

*Gauge:* Markleton. This gauge should read between 2.2 and 3.6 feet. This corresponds to a flow of 390 cfs to 1,770 cfs.

*Normal Wet Period:* This section is normally runnable from early December through late May and it has no season when it is too high. The Markleton gauge is above 2.2 feet 43% of the time and above 3.6 feet 7% of the time.

# D. Rockwood to Markleton 7.0 miles

| Class | Grad | Size (Area/Volume) | Scene/Poll | Level |
|-------|------|--------------------|------------|-------|
| II-III | 20/38 | Medium (325/542) Markleton | A/A | 2.1-3.5 Markleton |

*Topographic Maps:* Rockwood, Markleton

*County Maps:* Somerset

*Description:* At Rockwood the Casselman picks up from an easy Class I-II stream to good intermediate whitewater. This is the easiest of the intermediate sections, with Fort Hill to Harnedsville somewhat more difficult and Markleton to Fort Hill requiring solid Class III skills. The river begins to take on the Casselman character here, with boulders forming eddies and occasionally blocking easy view of the channel and hydraulics good enough to stop and play. As the river passes Casselman, the three quarters point, the pace picks up as the rapids become somewhat steeper and more continuous. [Checked 1990]

*Difficulties:* Nothing you wouldn't expect from a Class II-III river. But don't antagonize the landowner on river right at Markleton.

*Shuttle:* Rockwood is easy to find on State Route 653. In Rockwood turn east on State Route 2016 towards the river. Put in downstream left of the bridge. To get to Markleton, you can return to State Route 653, then go south on State Route 281 through Kingwood. About a mile after Kingwood, turn left on State Route 3011, which goes to the river. A shorter but slightly trickier route is available on the other (east) side of the river. From Rockwood go about a 0.25 miles east on State Route 2016. Turn right on State Route 3011, and continue to Markleton. Whichever way you get to Markleton, avoid the area around the bridge on river right. You can take out along the dirt road about a 0.3 miles upstream on river right, or you can pay the homeowner at the bridge on river left ($2.00 per car in 1990) to let you use his yard and to watch your car.

*Gauge:* Markleton. This gauge should read between 2.1 and 3.5 feet. This corresponds to a flow of 340 cfs to 1,630 cfs.

*Normal Wet Period:* This section is normally runnable from early December through early June and it has no season when it is too high. The Markleton gauge is above 2.1 feet 48% of the time and above 3.5 feet 8% of the time.

# E. Markleton to Fort Hill                    6.0 miles

| Class | Grad | Size (Area / Volume) | Scene / Poll | Level |
|-------|------|----------------------|--------------|-------|
| III | 29/36 | Medium (382/661) Markleton | A / A | 2.0-3.5 Markleton |

*Topographic Maps:* Markleton, Confluence

*County Maps:* Somerset

*Description:* This, the most difficult section of the Casselman, is a classic Class III drop-and-pool river. The rapids range in length from 50 yards to a third of a mile with continuous maneuvering at low to moderate water levels. They are, however, separated by good pools. Some require one or two specific moves to be in the one right place; others are long rock gardens with many routes. Intermediates should plan for a full (long) day the first time to allow for scouting and playing. The world's finest lunch rock, the lunch rock that defines the standard for all lunch rocks, is about a third of the way down, just above the railroad bridge. It has ledges and benches of natural rock, a good spot to play, good boat access, and plenty of room to sun. [Checked 1990]

*Difficulties:* The second rapid after Markleton comes up quickly as the river squeezes right and then bends left. It should be scouted at least the first time. There is a large nasty rock with accompanying hole on the right side. It can be totally avoided by running far left. About 3 miles into the run and just into a bend, the river appears to be dammed up by boulders. This is a complex drop and could be tricky to the inexperienced. Stay to the far left if in doubt, but remember that it will still be a double drop. In very high water a sneak route exists on the far right. At any level, the more entertaining descent is through the center and this requires a sharp right-hand turn. The Railroad Rapid (you can not see the railroad bridge until you are into the rapid) is a long turn to the left. The sneak route is on the inside of the curve, on the left. As you approach the second railroad bridge, avoid the extreme left as there are some keeper-sized hydraulics there in very high water. In low water it is a sharp, dry drop. There are several other rapids that require scouting as the course is not obvious from the top. Toward the end of the trip there is a large boulder garden. At high levels, most of the rapids have fast-flowing pools alongside the main rapid. Only the boulder garden is unavoidable.

The rock structure of this section of the river is such that it grabs and bends canoe poles.

*Shuttle:* Both Markleton and Fort Hill are on side roads off State Route 281. Look for signs at the intersections with State Route 281. Markleton is on State Route 3011, Fort Hill is on State Route 3001. At Markleton, avoid the area around the bridge on river right. You can take out along the dirt road about a 0.2 miles upstream on river right, or you can pay the homeowner at the bridge on river left ($2.00 per car in 1988) to let you use his yard and to watch your car.

*Gauges:* Markleton. This gauge should read between 2.0 and 3.5 feet. This corresponds to a flow of 290 cfs to 1,630 cfs. The bridge at Fort Hill should show between 10 and 3 bricks.

The following graph shows the correlation between the 7:00 AM reading for the Markleton gauge with the level later in the day at the Ft. Hill bridge during the 1988 canoeing season. Values for Markleton are in feet; values for Ft. Hill are in "bricks" -- the number of bricks showing above water level on the bridge pier on river right. For example, readings of 2.6 at Markleton corresponded to readings of 6 and 7 bricks at Ft. Hill. There is more variation in this correlation than in correlations between Corps of Engineers gauges because the readings are taken at different times of the day and the count of bricks is accurate to only about half a brick.

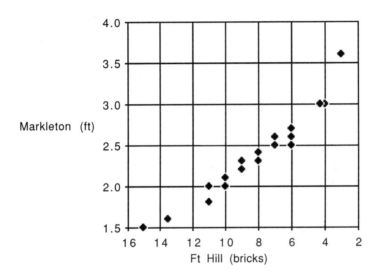

If this section is too high, try nearby Laurel Hill Creek.

*Normal Wet Period:* This section is normally runnable from early December through early June and it has no season when it is too high. The Markleton gauge is above 2.0 feet 52% of the time and above 3.5 feet 8% of the time.

# F. Fort Hill to Harnedsville                     5.7 miles

| Class | Grad | Size (Area/Volume) | Scene/Poll | Level |
|-------|------|--------------------|-----------|-------|
| II-III | 24/33 | Medium (425/708) estimate | A/B | 2.0-4.0 Markleton |

*Topographic Maps:* Confluence

*County Maps:* Somerset

*Description:* This section is mostly fast-flowing water, with some ledges and fairly open rapids. The scenery is good, giving way to more settled farm land. Most of the rapids occur at wide places in the river and many are straightforward, open descents. A few more are like larger rock gardens, but not requiring too much maneuvering, There are only two or three potential trouble spots. [Checked 1989]

*Difficulties:* No really difficult spots below Fort Hill unless you choose to make it so. About midway there is a nice rapid that turns sharply to the right as a beautiful waterfall enters the stream from the left. The river is divided by a large boulder at this point. An easy, but wavy, run to the right, an interesting fandango on the left!

*Shuttle:* From Fort Hill go west to State Route 281, then south to Ursina. Cross and follow the signs to Harnedsville which will turn you left, back across the Laurel Hill Creek. At Harnedsville the take-out is on the right side of the river with parking on the left.

*Gauges:* Markleton. This gauge should read between 2.0 and 4.0 feet. This corresponds to a flow of 290 cfs to 2,330 cfs. The bridge at Fort Hill should show no more than 10 bricks. If the Fort Hill to Harnedsville section is too high, try the Laurel Hill Creek.

*Normal Wet Period:* This section is normally runnable from early December through early June and it has no season when it is too high. The Markleton gauge is above 2.0 feet 52% of the time and above 4.0 feet 5% of the time.

# G. Harnedsville to Confluence                3.5 miles

| Class | Grad | Size (Area/Volume) | Scene/Poll | Level |
|-------|------|--------------------|-----------|-------|
| I | 7/10 | Medium (590/983) Markleton | A-B/B | 2.0-4.0 Markleton |

*Topographic Maps:*  Confluence

*County Maps:*  Somerset

*Description:*  This is a pretty section of river except for the last 0.6 miles, which is flood controlled by a levee. [Reported 1989]

*Difficulties:*  There is an easy ledge a short distance below Harnedsville. The rest of the river is just fast flowing water.

*Shuttle:*  To get to the take-out go west on State Route 523 and park in Confluence about 30 yards south of the bridge over the Laurel Hill Creek. Upon entering Laurel Hill Creek at the end of the Casselman, paddle a short distance up Laurel Hill Creek to the take-out.

*Gauges:*  Markleton. This gauge should read between 2.0 and 4.0 feet. This corresponds to a flow of 290 cfs to 2,330 cfs.

*Normal Wet Period:*  This section is normally runnable from early December through early June and it has no season when it is too high. The Markleton gauge is above 2.0 feet 52% of the time and above 4.0 feet 5% of the time.

# Laurel Hill Creek

## A. Laurel Hill State Park                    8.2 miles
## to Whipkey Dam

| Class | Grad | Size (Area/Volume) | Scene/Poll | Level |
|-------|------|--------------------|-----------|-------|
| III | 31/50 | Small (60/100) estimate | A/A | 2.1-?? Ursina |

*Topographic Maps:* Rockwood, Kingwood

*County Maps:* Somerset

*Description:* This trip begins easy and ends easy, but in the center section there are some large ledges. The scenery is beautiful, especially as the trip starts in the state park. There are cottages along the shores as you approach Whipkey Dam. This dam backs up water for about 1 mile, almost to State Route 653. [Checked 1990]

*Difficulties:* The first ledge in this section is really a 4-foot waterfall. It comes up suddenly around a left turn. There are also two fairly tight rapids that could be tricky in high water. Carry Whipkey Dam on the river right by taking out at the upstream end of the retaining wall, or on the embedded stairways in the wall. If you use the stairway, be careful to avoid the overflow spillway if it has flowing water.

*Shuttle:* Put in at Trent where State Route 3029 crosses the creek. From Trent, go east 2.5 miles to Posys Corner Trailer Park. Turn right and follow State Route 281 south about 4 miles to 0.25 miles north of Kingwood. Turn right/west on the road to Scullton. Bear right at the fork 0.1 miles from State Route 281 and go 1.5 miles to Whipkey Dam. Take out after carrying Whipkey Dam, or put in and paddle the 50 yards to the bridge and then take out. An alternate put-in which avoids a mile of flat, flowing water is in the State Park. An alternate take-out which avoids the backwater of Whipkey Dam is at State Route 653.

*Gauges:* Ursina. This gauge should read above 2.1 feet. This corresponds to a flow of 620 cfs.

*Normal Wet Period:* This section does not have a season when it is normally runnable nor when it is too high. The Ursina gauge is above 2.1 feet 12% of the time.

## B. Whipkey Dam to Ursina            8.0 miles

| Class | Grad | Size (Area/Volume) | Scene/Poll | Level |
|-------|------|--------------------|------------|-------|
| III | 40/70 | Small (121/266) Ursina | A/A | 1.9-3.1 Ursina |

*Topographic Maps:* Kingwood, Confluence

*County Maps:* Somerset

*Description:* This section is a favorite trip for intermediate whitewater canoeists. A gentle start builds to four long challenging rapids in the middle section, which has large gradient and very few pools. The island after the first big rapids makes a good lunch spot, as does a large rock outcropping about 0.5 miles below this island. Allow time to enjoy the scenery. The last section braids into several channels winding around small islands. The easiest route is through the main largest channel. [Checked 1990]

*Difficulties:* Appropriate to a typical Class III stream. Every thing hard is around a left-hand bend. Downed trees block some of the braided channels near the end of the run.

*Shuttle:* From Whipkey Dam, go south and turn right/south onto State Route 281. About 1 mile further, take the right fork. Several take-outs are available. The favorite is the fishing access area about 3 miles upstream from Ursina. Another is near the covered bridge about 1 mile further downstream.

*Gauges:* Ursina. This gauge should read between 1.9 and 3.1 feet. This corresponds to a flow of 430 cfs to 1,620 cfs. At 1.7 this is more like a hike; at 3.5 its holes will hold a canoe. It is still a delightful closed boat run up to 4.5.

*Normal Wet Period:* This section is normally runnable from early March through mid April and it has no season when it is normally too high. The Ursina gauge is above 1.9 feet 20% of the time and above 3.1 feet 1% of the time.

# Whites Creek

## Unamis to Harnedsville                                    7.0 miles

| Class | Grad | Size (Area/Volume) | Scene/Poll | Level |
|-------|------|--------------------|------------|-------|
| III   | 80/100 | Tiny (36/60) | A/A | |
|       |      | mouth of creek     |            |       |

*Topographic Maps:* Accident (Md), Confluence

*County Maps:* Somerset

*Description:* This very small trout stream is continuous Class II, with a number of Class III drops thrown in. A good indication of the nature of this run can be had by gawking from the State Route 523 bridge. [Reported 1988]

*Difficulties:* As is often the norm with streams of this size there are many trees down and bends that obstruct one's view. After passing under a power line crossing there is a 3-foot dam which is preceded by a 75-foot pool. There is an easy carry on the right. A low-water bridge, 1 mile below Listonberg, is no problem in low water.

*Shuttle:* To get to the put-in, start at Listonburg and head east on State Route 2004. Then immediately turn right onto State Route 3004. About 1.5 miles after a stream crossing, put in at the State Route 3004/80 marker where the stream nears the roadway. This will avoid a braided area just downstream of the next bridge about a tenth of a mile further. The take-out is along State Route 653, south of Harnedsville, were the creek joins the Casselman river.

*Gauges:* Markleton. This gauge on nearby Casselman River will probably read above 5.0 feet. Look at the stream from the State Route 523 bridge.

*Normal Wet Period:* No available statistics on seasons. Since this section is tiny, it should normally be runnable only after a heavy rain or during spring snowmelt.

# Coxes Creek

## Somerset to Rockwood                                    10.5 miles

| Class | Grad | Size (Area / Volume) | Scene / Poll | Level |
|-------|------|----------------------|--------------|-------|
| III   | 29/55 | Tiny (55/92)<br>mouth of stream | B/B | |

*Topographic Maps:* Somerset, Murdock, Rockwood

*County Maps:* Somerset

*Description:* This Casselman tributary flowing out of Somerset offers a surprise to those who have car scouted the Class II lower 5 miles from Milford. The Somerset flatwater gives way to a steep wilderness run of about 3 miles. The stream is small throughout. A mile below Roberts the West Branch joins, size increases and the gradient tames down. [Reported about 1985]

*Difficulties:* Trees are possible on the small headwater section.

*Shuttle:* Put in at State Route 281 in Somerset or along any side street in Somerset. Follow State Route 3015 along the creek to the take-out in Rockwood where State Route 653 crosses, or continue the additional 0.4 miles onto the Casselman and the State Route 2016 bridge.

*Gauge:* None.

*Normal Wet Period:* No available statistics on seasons. Since this section is tiny, it should normally be runnable only after a heavy rain or during spring snowmelt.

# Bear Creek
# (Garrett County, Md)

## US Route 219 Bridge to Friendsville        6.7 miles

| Class | Grad | Size (Area/Volume) | Scene/Poll | Level |
|-------|------|--------------------|------------|-------|
| III-IV | 75/120 | | A-B/A | |

*Topographic Maps:* Friendsville (Md), Accident (Md)

*County Maps:* Garrett (Md)

*Description:* This tiny trout stream, never more than 25 feet wide, becomes an interesting alternative to the Upper Youghiogheny when rain or snowmelt has been heavy. The first 4 miles are continuous Class I-II rapids as the stream meanders through scenic rhododendron and hemlock forest. There are occasional unobtrusive houses and camps. The last 4 miles, where all the gradient is, can easily be scouted from the shuttle road. There are at least five Class IV rapids, separated only by swift-moving Class II-III whitewater. Eddies are tiny and difficult to catch, as well as being few and far between. There are lots of opportunities to pin a boat in the shallow swift current; however, the small volume of the stream and the proximity of the road make this an attractive late winter run. [Reported 1982]

*Difficulties:* As with all small streams, downed trees are an ever present danger. No strainers were present in the final, more difficult, 3 miles as of 1982, but one should scout this carefully. All Class IV rapids but one can be seen from the road. The exception, perhaps the most technical drop, is hidden behind a log house. Take time to look on the shuttle. Only expert closed boaters should attempt the last 3 miles of this stream.

*Shuttle:* Put in under the bridge where the stream crosses under US Route 219. Take out about 0.25 miles above Friendsville, in a small grassy field. The stream has been channelized in Friendsville, and it would be difficult to terminate the trip in the swift continuous current, which is devoid of eddies.

*Gauges:*  If the Youghiogheny from Sang Run to Friendsville is too high, drive through Friendsville to the bridge over Bear Creek on the Addison-Friendsville Road. If this looks okay, follow the stream via US Route 219 and scout from the car. If the shallow section under the US Route 219 bridge is runnable, then give it a try.

*Normal Wet Period:*  No available statistics on seasons. Since this section is tiny, it should normally be runnable only after a heavy rain or during spring snowmelt.

# Bear Creek, South Branch

## Accident, Maryland to Bear Creek          5.9 miles

| Class | Grad | Size (Area/Volume) | Scene/Poll | Level |
|-------|------|--------------------|------------|-------|
| III-IV | 107/154 | | A/A | |

*Topographic Maps:* McHenry (Md), Sang Run (Md),
   Accident (Md), Friendsville (Md)

*County Maps:* Garrett (Md)

*Description:* The first half to two-thirds of this run consists
of a rather steady gradient with rapids of about Class III
difficulty, much of the creek being a little wider than the
length of a boat. Then it gets steeper with bigger rocks
studding the streambed and one drop after another. This
stream is sometimes called Little Bear Creek, but it should
not be confused with the Little Bear Creek, which flows into
Bear Creek east of US Route 219, 2 miles northeast of
Accident.

*Difficulties:* The major difficulty throughout was created by
logs and trees, sometimes completely across the stream,
sometimes only across part of it, sometimes above water
level, sometimes at water level, sometimes a little below
water level. [Reported 1985]

*Shuttle:* To get to the put-in, follow Bear Creek Road out of
Friendsville to Accident Road, which intersects from the
right; follow Accident Road to Accident. At the intersection
with US Route 219, turn right on US Route 219 past the
Meadow Motel. Drive south about 2 miles. In a depression
at the tight bend in the road, there are two turn-offs to the
right about 100 yards apart. They are opposite ends of the
same short road paralleling US Route 219, and the put-in is
along this road. To get to the take-out, return along
Accident Road. A few hundred yards from the intersection
with Bear Creek Road, a bridge crosses the South Branch of
Bear about 25 yards from its junction with the Bear Creek
main stem. This is about a mile east of Friendsville.

*Gauges:* If it's too scrapy to float a boat at the put-in, don't even think about running it.   The Friendsville gauge on nearby Youghiogheny River will probably read between 4.3 and 5.0 feet.

*Normal Wet Period:* No available statistics on seasons. Since this section is tiny, it should normally be runnable only after a heavy rain or during spring snowmelt.

# Peters Creek

## Snowden to USX Clairton Works                    7.0 miles

*Class   Grad    Size (Area / Volume)    Scene / Poll   Level*
  I      14/20      Tiny (51/85)              C/B
                     estimate

*Topographic Maps:* Glassport

*County Maps:* Allegheny

*Description:* This small poling stream is often very shallow. Although close to the city, it is isolated in its valley with only a couple of houses along its banks. In most places the stream is very pretty, in a couple of places it is very trashy. The last mile passes alongside the slag dump and material storage yard for the Clairton Works. This stream is short and close to Pittsburgh so it makes a good run in the winter, or very early in the spring. [Checked 1990]

*Difficulties:* Shallow water, and the tunnel under the Clairton Works downstream from the take-out. The tunnel has a sign indicating that hot water is discharged into the tunnel and steam sometimes pours out of the tunnel. The tunnel is long, with several turns, and you can not see from one end of the tunnel to the other.

*Shuttle:* The put-in is near Snowden where the Piney Fork joins Peters Creek. The take-out is along side State Route 837 upstream of the tunnel. An alternate put-in is further upstream at Finleyville. From there to Snowden the gradient is steeper, so you will need more water.

*Gauges:* None. If you can make the shallows in the first 0.25 mile, then the rest should be okay.

*Normal Wet Period:* No available statistics on seasons. Since this section is tiny, it should normally be runnable only after a heavy rain or during spring snowmelt.

# Redstone Creek

## Smock to Albany                                    8.5 miles

| Class | Grad | Size (Area/Volume) | Scene/Poll | Level |
|-------|------|--------------------|-----------|-------|
| II | 15/20 | Small (74/101) | C/C | 0.8-?? |
| | | Waltersburg | | Waltersburg |
| | | Small (109/182) mouth of creek | | |

*Topographic Maps:* New Salem, Fayette City, California

*County Maps:* Fayette

*Description:* The creek is aptly named; it flows through several old mining towns, and past many mine outflows. The mine acid drainage gives the creek its reddish color and bottom. The old towns give it a sewage smell. There are however remote stretches between the towns that are pretty. Below Linn to the take-out at Albany the river becomes a flat Class I stream. [Reported 1988]

*Difficulties:* About 50 yards below a cast iron bridge the creek flows straight into a sheer hillside and turns left at a 90 degree angle. A rock sits in the middle of all this and can be difficult to spot. The standing and reactionary waves will give you a good gyration. At the bridge in Grindstone there is a strainer that blocks over 80 percent of the river. It is passable if you are very careful, or it may be portaged around on the island. Make a short side trip on the shuttle to check it out from the bridge. Below Grindstone is a two foot ledge.

*Shuttle:* To get to the put-in head west from Smock and take the right-hand fork of the Y at the WWII memorial. Follow this road about 0.7 miles to the intersection with the put-in bridge and the Smock Gun Club road.

*Gauges:* Waltersburg. This gauge should read above 0.8 feet. This corresponds to a flow of 69 cfs.

*Normal Wet Period:* The Waltersburg gauge is above 0.8 feet 40% of the time.

# Dunlap Creek

## Allison to Brownsville                                    6.2 miles

| Class | Grad  | Size (Area/Volume) | Scene/Poll | Level   |
|-------|-------|--------------------|------------|---------|
| II    | 26/40 | Tiny (33/43)       | BC/C       |         |
|       |       | Allison            |            | Allison |
|       |       | Tiny (42/70) mouth of stream |   |         |

*Topographic Maps:* New Salem, Carmichaels, California

*County Maps:* Fayette

*Description:* This small stream flows northwestward into the Monongahela River. Like several nearby streams (Dunkard Creek, Georges Creek, Redstone Creek, Ten Mile Creek, and Whiteley Creek), it resembles a mountain stream as it cuts down through the bedrock of the Appalachian Plateau, seeking the level of the Monongahela River. The creek is characterized by many ledges, which vary from sloping to level, jagged to smooth, and alone or in series. At low water, most of the holes below the ledges were surfable to some extent with no keepers. At higher levels some of the ledges and holes will probably wash out and others may reach Class III. There is a lot of trash along the hillsides, banks, and creek bottom; the stream flows through some ghastly abandoned strip mines above Brownsville; and the water smells of sewage. However the creek is remote, supports wildlife, and features historical features including an abandoned railroad tunnel and old mine buildings. It will never be famous for its scenic beauty or its death-defying rapids, but it is nevertheless worth running. The film "Maria's Lovers" was filmed in the area of Brownsville near the take-out. [Reported 1989]

*Difficulties:* Strainers are common, especially in the slower water above Brownsville. Some of the ledges appear just around blind curves.

*Shuttle:* To find the put-in, take State Route 166 south from US Route 40 just east of Brownsville. Follow 166 for 2 to 3 miles to the first creek crossing, which is Dunlap Creek (check water level here). After crossing the creek, take the first left and follow the road to a bridge over Dunlap Creek.

To get to the take-out, follow State Route 166 north to US Route 40; turn west to Brownsville. Just before the high level bridge over the Monongahela River turn right. Turn left at a stop sign and follow this street under the bridge, down the hill into downtown Brownsville; turn left at the third light and follow that street until you reach the creek. There is a lot of crime in this area.

*Gauges:* Allison. We do not have enough information to report runnable levels on this section. Visually judge navigability from the State Route 166 bridge.

*Normal Wet Period:* No available statistics on seasons. Since this section is tiny, it should normally be runnable only after a heavy rain or during spring snowmelt.

# Ten Mile Creek

## A. Ten Mile to Marianna                              6.3 miles

| Class | Grad | Size (Area/Volume) | Scene/Poll | Level |
|---|---|---|---|---|
| I | 7/7 | Small (100/167) | B/A | 2.2-?? |
| | | Marianna | | Marianna |

*Topographic Maps:* Amity, Ellsworth

*County Maps:* Washington

*Description:* This stream is moving flatwater with occasional riffles, small ledges, and a covered bridge. The scenery is very nice except in the town of Marianna. [Checked 1972]

*Difficulties:* In the town of Marianna, there is a 3-foot dam for a water filtration plant. It can be recognized by the round intake house on the left end of the dam. At reasonable water levels, the dam can be portaged on the right behind the abutment. At higher levels, water may be flowing in this path, forcing a more difficult portage on the left. State Route 2020 runs along side the creek at this point. Stop and scout the dam during the shuttle.

*Shuttle:* Put in at the first bridge west of the town of Ten Mile. Follow State Route 2020 through Marianna. This road enters a "T" intersection with the bridge across Ten Mile Creek on the left. Take out downstream of this bridge.

*Gauges:* Marianna. This gauge should read above 2.2 feet. This corresponds to a flow of 335 cfs.

*Normal Wet Period:* No available statistics on seasons. Since this section is small, it should normally be runnable approximately January through April.

# B. Marianna to Clarksville 9.0 miles

| Class | Grad | Size (Area/Volume) | Scene/Poll | Level |
|-------|------|--------------------|-----------|-------|
| I-II | 11/23 | Small (150/250) | B/A | 2.0-?? |
| | | Marianna | | Marianna |
| | | Medium (338/563) mouth of stream | | |

*Topographic Maps:* Ellsworth, Mather

*County Maps:* Washington, Greene

*Description:* The stream starts slowly, flowing between channelized but grassy banks through Marianna. It soon enters woods and farmlands. After 3 miles or so it passes under Davis Bridge, a Burr truss covered bridge built in 1889, but now closed and in poor repair. Here the pace picks up, with several series of easy Class II rapids alternating with pools. There is usually a 200-foot wooded cliff on one side and farmlands, houses or woods on the other. The bottom is often smooth bedrock, and fish are plentiful. [Reported 1989]

*Difficulties:* A 3-foot dam at Deemston should be portaged. The dam is about 200 feet upstream from a steel truss bridge, the first bridge after the covered bridge. At low water, concrete will be showing above water at the right of the dam and in the center. If this is clearly showing, you can land on it and lift over. Otherwise get out upstream from the dam and carry around on either side. The topographic maps show another dam about 1.5 miles downstream from Deemston. It is actually a washed-out, low-water bridge. Numerous reinforcing bars stick up from the remains, but it can be run with caution and good boat control.

*Shuttle:* Put in at the bridge just downstream from Marianna. Follow signs to Clarksville via State Route 2049 and State Route 1013. In Clarksville, turn left on State Route 1011, cross the creek, (the road becomes State Route 2039 at this point), cross under the railroad track, and take out just below the footbridge and the waste water treatment plant. An alternative take-out is available 1.5 miles of flatwater further downstream at the county park and boat ramp.

*Gauges:* Marianna. This gauge should read above 2.0 feet. This corresponds to a flow of 275 cfs. The State Route 1011/2039 bridge has several rows of tiles near the water line. No more than 5 should be showing for a good run.

*Normal Wet Period:* No available statistics on seasons. Since this section is small, it should normally be runnable approximately January through April.

## C. Clarksville to East Bethlehem          2.5 miles
## junction with Monongahela

| Class | Grad | Size (Area/Volume) | Scene/Poll | Level |
|-------|------|--------------------|------------|-------|
| A | Pool | Medium (388/647) mouth of stream | D/B | |

*Topographic Maps:* Mather, Carmichaels

*County Maps:* Washington, Greene

*Description:* Not run at this time, but appears to be flat.

*Difficulties:* Several marinas for docking power boats between Clarksville and the Monongahela.

# Ten Mile Creek, South Fork

## A. Waynesburg to Jefferson    7.0 miles

| Class | Grad | Size (Area/Volume) | Scene/Poll | Level |
|-------|------|--------------------|-----------|-------|
| C-I | 7/8 | Small (180/201) Jefferson | B/A-B | 2.0-?? Jefferson |

*Topographic Maps:* Waynesburg, Mather

*County Maps:* Greene

*Description:* Although the drainage area is mainly rolling farmlands, the creek runs largely in a wooded valley, often with a 200-foot cliff on one side or the other. Gently flowing pools alternate with easy riffles. It is remote enough that the wildlife is abundant, and the water supports fish, primarily bass. [Checked 1990]

*Difficulties:* None if the indicated take-out is used. If you take out on the east side of Jefferson see difficulties in the next section.

*Shuttle:* State Route 188 follows the stream from Waynesburg to Jefferson, crossing it several times. The put-in is at the second crossing east of Interstate 79, at a pumping station due north of Green County Airport. The take-out is at the third and last crossing of State Route 188 east of Interstate 79, just west of Jefferson. Shuttle directly along State Route 188.

*Gauges:* Jefferson. This gauge should read above 2.0 feet. This corresponds to a flow of 160 cfs.

*Normal Wet Period:* This section is normally runnable from late December through late April. The Jefferson gauge is above 2.0 feet 30% of the time.

# B. Jefferson to Clarksville                               9.0 miles

| Class | Grad | Size (Area / Volume) | Scene / Poll | Level |
|-------|------|---------------------|--------------|-------|
| I-II | 10/17 | Small (108/201) | B-C/A-B | 2.0-?? |
| | | Jefferson | | Jefferson |
| | | Small (199/332) mouth of stream | | |

*Topographic Maps:* Mather

*County Maps:* Greene, Washington

*Description:* At first, easy riffles alternate with pools, but note the low-water bridge mentioned in difficulties. After a couple of miles the pace begins to pick up, and the last mile into Clarksville is almost continuous Class I to easy Class II. These rapids are fairly wide-open but with some maneuvering necessary. About .25 miles after joining the main fork, there is a long Class II "staircase".

The construction of several waste water treatment plants has substantially improved the water quality, and fish and birds are now plentiful. The wooded hillsides support a superb assortment of wild flowers, including some of the lushest carpets of trillium we have ever seen. Unfortunately, *Trillium grandiflorum* alternates with *Frigidarium discardum,* Every place a road runs along the creek, home appliances cascade down the hillside. Aside from the trash heaps and the half-mile-long mine dump about a mile below the put-in, it is a pleasant, pretty run. [Checked 1990]

*Difficulties:* About a 0.3 miles below the put-in (State Route 188 bridge near Jefferson) is a low water bridge. Sloping concrete abutments descend to a river-level roadway that will have water running over it whenever the creek is runnable. Most of the water passes through square culverts under both end abutments. Stay clear of these. Scout the bridge during the shuttle. At some levels the upstream curb on the roadway will be almost at water level and one can land in the middle and lift over the drop on the downstream side. At higher levels it might be possible to paddle between the left abutment and the shore where the bank has eroded away for 10 feet or so.

*Shuttle:* Put in where State Route 188 crosses the creek near Jefferson. This is the easternmost place where State Route 188 crosses the creek. Go through either Mather (west from bridge, then right) or Jefferson (east from bridge, left in town) to join State Route 1011 east of Mather. Go north (up the hill) on State Route 1011; Take the right fork at the top of the hill to follow State Route 1011 to the take-out. Note that the designation changes to State Route 2039 as it crosses the Main Fork of Ten Mile Creek in Clarksville. Take out as for the Main Fork, just below the footbridge and before the banks turn to concrete.

*Gauges:* Jefferson. This gauge should read above 2.0 feet. This corresponds to a flow of 160 cfs. On the left abutment of the State Route 1011/2039 bridge in Clarksville, 13 bricks showing yields a low but quite runnable level. In addition, the shuttle runs along the creek for a mile south of Clarksville. If this section looks good, you are probably okay.

*Normal Wet Period:* This section is normally runnable from late December through late April. The Jefferson gauge is above 2.0 feet 30% of the time.

# Whiteley Creek

## State Route 2011 to State Route 88                2.5 miles

| Class | Grad | Size (Area / Volume) | Scene / Poll | Level |
|-------|------|----------------------|--------------|-------|
| III   | 18/25 | Tiny (54/90) | B/B | |
|       |       | mouth of creek | | |

*Topographic Maps:* Garards Fort, Masontown

*County Maps:* Greene

*Description:* Only about 2.5 miles of this river was paddled. Road scouting suggests it may be possible to start further upstream, and a trip could be extended about 2 miles downstream if one could find access through or around the coal processing plant, or were willing to take-out across the Monongahela River at Mt. Sterling. The river contains a half-mile gorge with 20 foot vertical walls on both banks. This is caused by the river cutting through the resistant layer of bedrock that forms the bluffs along the Monongahela River. After the gorge the river is pooled for about 0.6 miles to the take-out. The scenery is attractive throughout the run. [Reported 1988]

*Difficulties:* There is a runnable 2-foot ledge about 100 yards downstream of a railroad bridge. The 0.7 mile gorge contains numerous smaller ledges and a boulder field. A lot of maneuvering is required to follow the stream's sinuous path. There are few eddies.

*Shuttle:* To get to the put-in, head west out of Mapletown on State Route 2016. In 0.5 miles you will cross a horseshoe bend of the stream; take the right-hand turn between the two crossings. Immediately take the left-hand fork and follow the stream to a put-in that you like. The take-out is back through Mapletown to State Route 88 and then north to where the stream crosses the road near the filtration plant.

*Gauges:* None available.

*Normal Wet Period:* No available statistics on seasons. Since this section is tiny, it should normally be runnable only after a heavy rain or during spring snowmelt.

# Georges Creek

## US Route 119 to New Geneva                8.0 miles

| Class | Grad | Size (Area/Volume) | Scene/Poll | Level |
|-------|------|--------------------|------------|-------|
| II | 18/20 | Tiny (16/18) | /C | |
| | | Smithfield | | Smithfield |
| | | Small (65/108) mouth of creek | | |

*Topographic Maps:* Smithfield, Masontown

*County Maps:* Fayette

*Description:* Georges Creek is a fun run. There are lots of Class I rapids with no long pools between them. The drop of 20 feet per mile is continuous throughout and the water just keeps on moving along. Although the creek passes through some remote areas, there are also stretches with trash along the bank. [Reported 1988]

*Difficulties:* As always on small streams, the potential for trees down and strainers is present.

*Shuttle:* The put-in is where the creek crosses US Route 119 about 1.5 miles south of Smithfield. Continue south on US Route 119. If you have the maps, take a right at Locust Hill, go about a 0.3 miles to Tomcat Hollow Road and turn right/north. The third crossing of the stream is the take-out. Without the maps, pass through Locust Hill and continue on US Route 119 to State Route 166. Turn north on State Route 166 towards New Geneva. Just after coming down off the Monongahela bluff and immediately after crossing the creek, turn right onto Tomcat Hollow road. This road crosses the creek at the take-out about 0.5 miles from State Route 166.

*Gauges:* Smithfield. We do not have enough information to report runnable levels on this section.

*Normal Wet Period:* No available statistics on seasons. Since this section is tiny, it should normally be runnable only after a heavy rain or during spring snowmelt.

# Dunkard Creek

## State Route 2019 to Monongahela River          8.0 miles

| Class | Grad | Size (Area / Volume) | Scene / Poll | Level |
|-------|------|----------------------|--------------|-------|
| I | 6/7 | Medium (229/276) | C/ | |
| | | Shannopin | | Shannopin |
| | | Medium (235/429) mouth of creek | | |

*Topographic Maps:* Morgantown North, Masontown

*County Maps:* Greene

*Description:* Many active underground coal mines and facilities border the creek. The railroad is owned by a coal company. Below Bobtown a collapsed railroad bridge in the creek has one end on the pier and the other in the creek. It is eerie and foreboding to paddle under. [Reported 1988]

*Difficulties:* Some small ledges that demand caution, but are not really dangerous.

*Shuttle:* The put-in is at the bottom of the hill about 1 mile from Bobtown. Head northwest out of Bobtown on State Route 2008 and follow the road as it turns southwest on State Route 2019. The take-out is located where State Route 88 crosses the creek mouth at the Monongahela River. Alternatively, head west on a dirt road on the north side of the creek for about 0.5 mile to avoid paddling the pool formed by the backwater of the Monongahela. An alternative put-in that adds more miles of flatwater can be found by continuing on as the road follows the creek. The stream has been run from about 3 miles above the designated put-in.

*Gauges:* Shannopin. We do not have enough information to report runnable levels on this section. A reading of 2.8 feet on the Shannopin gauge corresponds to the mean flow of 276 cfs. Since this is a medium-sized river, we speculate that the river will be runnable at 2.8 feet and may be on the high side of runnable at that level.

*Normal Wet Period:* No available statistics on seasons. Since this section is tiny, it should normally be runnable only after a heavy rain or during spring snowmelt.

# Cheat River

## A. Parsons to Rowlesburg                          36 miles

| Class | Grad | Size (Area/Volume) | Scene/Poll | Level |
|-------|------|--------------------|-----------|-------|
| C-I   | 7/8  | Medium (718/1,697) | A-B/A-B   | 2.9-5.0 |
|       |      | Parsons            |           | Parsons |

*Topographic Maps:* Parsons (WVa), St. George (WVa), Rowlesburg (WVa)

*County Maps:* Tucker (WVa), Preston (WVa)

*Description:* This scenic run is ideal for canoe camping. There are several islands to camp on. There are many wide flat areas. Rowlesburg to the cement plant downstream is flat. [Checked 1988]

*Difficulties:* None

*Shuttle:* Trip length possibilities are wide open as West Virginia Route 72 follows the stream closely. Put-in and take-out spots are numerous and as variable as the canoeist's interest. This section can be broken into several good one-day trips.

*Gauges:* Parsons. This gauge should read between 2.9 and 5.0 feet. This corresponds to a flow of 440 cfs to 2,600 cfs. The Albright Bridge gauge further downstream will probably read between 3.0 and 4.5 feet.

*Normal Wet Period:* No available statistics on seasons. Since this section is medium-sized, it should normally be runnable approximately December through May.

# B. Rowlesburg to Lick Run                 5.2 miles
# "The Narrows"

| Class | Grad | Size (Area/Volume) | Scene/Poll | Level |
|-------|------|--------------------|-----------|-------|
| III | 19/23 | Large (972/2,284) | A-B/A-B | |
| | | Rowlesburg | | Rowlesburg |

*Topographic Maps:* Rowlesburg (WVa), Kingwood (WVa)

*County Maps:* Preston (WVa)

*Description:* "The Narrows" has a great feeling of isolation in its large wooded valley. Hidden behind the trees on the left shore is WVa State Route 72, while the railroad is hidden on the right. At lower level the Class III rapids are open and obvious with little maneuvering required, but a fairly strong push hides in the powerful currents. At higher levels large standing waves and deep holes offer a lot more excitement. At Rowlesburg the river is wide and generally shallow. The best part, "the Narrows", is the 5 miles, beginning at the cement plant 2 miles below Rowlesburg, and ending at Lick Run on river left upstream from the railroad bridge. Above Lick Run the river is alive with aquatic life and known for fishing. The orange covered rocks at Lick Run is from mine acid and this kills the fish below here. [Checked 1988]

*Difficulties:* The biggest rapid, psychologically and actually, is called "Calamity Rock". It can be scouted from the road. This rock is preceded by a long rock garden. Stay right as you proceed through the rock garden and can begin to see the drop at Calamity. The runnable chute is on the right of the rock; it is narrow. In low water (0.5 foot or below at the Albright Bridge gauge), this is a tricky S-turn with little power. In higher water the chute is straight through into a boiling hydraulic with very strong side eddies. For scouting, there is a good pool on the right above Calamity Rock, most of the way through the rock garden. At 2 feet (on the Albright Bridge gauge) Calamity Rock juts up out of the water; at 4 feet it is covered by water and has a strong hydraulic just below it. Avoid the rock; it might be a calamity. The next two rapids "Winds" and "Rocking Horse" both have high standing waves down the center with occasional holes tucked in between.

*Shuttle:* West Virginia Route 72 follows this section closely, so many shuttle possibilities are available. There are numerous wide shoulders for parking.

*Gauges:* Rowlesburg. We do not have enough information to report runnable levels on this section. A reading of 3.9 on the Rowlesburg gauge corresponds to the mean flow of 2,284 cfs. Since this is a medium-sized river, we speculate that the river will be runnable at 3.9 and may be on the high side of runnable at that level. The Albright Bridge gauge further downstream will probably read between 0.5 and 4.0 feet. This section is runnable at zero on the Albright Bridge gauge, although it involves technical maneuvering. At 4 feet, there are huge standing waves and river-wide rollers to contend with. It is suitable for open canoes with experienced whitewater paddlers up to 3.0 feet. Experienced closed boats and rafts have run it up to 8 feet. Note the Albright Bridge gauge is painted on the highway bridge in Albright and should not be confused with the Albright power station gauge, which is reported by phone.

The following graph shows the correlation between the 7:00 AM readings for the Parsons and Albright Bridge gauges during the 1988 canoeing season. Values are in feet. For example, readings of 2.0 feet at the Albright power station corresponded to readings of 1.7 to 2.8 feet at Parsons. Note that Parsons is about 50 miles upstream from the Albright power station, so water level changes in the headwaters are reflected in the Parsons reading before they reach Albright. For example, the day Parsons was 7.1 and Albright Power Station 3.1, the river at both stations was rising; the following day Parsons had dropped to 6.6 and Albright Power Station had risen to 5.0; and the day after that Parsons was down to 4.9 and the Albright Power Station to 3.9. In other words, the crest at Parsons was about a day before the crest at Albright.

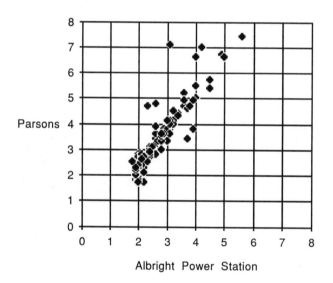

Albright  Power  Station

*Normal Wet Period:*   No available statistics on seasons. Since this section is medium-sized, it should normally be runnable approximately December through May.

# C. Lick Run to Albright Bridge      6.3 miles

| Class | Grad | Size (Area/Volume) | Scene/Poll | Level |
|-------|------|--------------------|--------------------|-------|
| I | 8/8 | Large (1,000/1,667) estimate | /C | 0.5-4.0 Albright Bridge |

*Topographic Maps:* Kingwood (WVa)

*County Maps:* Preston (WVa)

*Description:* Not reported at this time. This section is mostly visible from the accompanying roads and is generally flat. [Checked 1988]

*Difficulties:* Beware of the dam at the power plant in Albright. It is a low head dam with the proverbial dangerous hydraulic.

*Gauges:* Albright Bridge. This gauge should read between 0.5 and 4.0 feet.

*Normal Wet Period:* No available statistics on seasons. Since this section is medium-sized, it should normally be runnable approximately December through May.

# D. Albright to Jenkins Bridge      11.4 miles
# "The Canyon"

| Class | Grad | Size (Area/Volume) | Scene/Poll | Level |
|-------|------|--------------------|--------------------|-------|
| IV-V | 25/43 | Large (1,300/2,167) estimate | A/B minus | 0.5-5.0 Albright Bridge |

*Topographic Maps:* Kingwood (WVa), Valley Point (WVa)

*County Maps:* Preston (WVa)

*Description:* This is a steep-walled canyon with beautiful scenery and fantastic rock formations worn away by the river. It is deep enough and inaccessible enough to be protected from the ravages of civilization. At least, one can not see much intrusion from the bottom of the canyon. The Canyon proper begins 0.75 miles below Albright. This section is for rafts and experienced closed boaters only. At low water (0.0 foot at Albright) there is not enough water for an open canoe to drop over the ledges and at slightly higher levels there are countless opportunities for pinning an open boat. The first rapid is known as Decision Rapid. If you have trouble here, get out while you still can. The end is many miles away. There are the vague remains of an old logging road high on the right bank, for walking out.

The more maneuverable C-1's and K-1's can run comfortably at levels down to 0.9 feet at Albright. At 2.5 feet on the Albright Bridge gauge, commercial trips switch to high water operation. At this level, there are large hydraulics to catch and tumble a raft and many opportunities to pin on rocks that have huge mounds of water piled on their upstream faces. Standing waves, capable of standing large rafts vertically, abound.

At the 1.0-foot level on the Albright Bridge gauge the first few miles of canyon are a fairly easy Class IV. The next 3 miles are Class III-III+. Then follows 3 miles of Class IV-V rapids (deep holes, large drops, tortuous channels, etc.). The last 2 miles are easy Class II. The flood of November 1985, while washing out bridges, roads, houses, schools and much else, also did a major rearranging of the many rapids on the Cheat, as well as many other West Virginia rivers. Be aware that if you have not run the Canyon since the flood, many routes and some entire rapids have disappeared and have been replaced by new ones. [Checked 1989]

*Difficulties:* The rapids in the canyon do not have obvious routes. Many resemble rats' nests, with water flowing into and around large boulders. Scouting is difficult. Due to the length of the run, extensive scouting may well turn this into a two-day trip. Experienced paddlers recommend that on the first several runs, boaters travel with others familiar with this section. Take out at the first big rapids if you have any trouble.

This river is heavily used during the spring by boaters from all over the eastern United States and many commercial rafting companies as well. On any given spring weekend you will be sharing the river with hundreds of canoes, C-1s, and kayaks and a seemingly endless parade of rafts. All this extra company should not be counted upon for any support, and if you do not stay alert you may find yourself run over by the traffic.

*Shuttle:* It is long. From Albright, take West Virginia Route 26 to Kingwood. Turn north/right onto West Virginia Route 7 to Masontown. In Masontown, turn right on the road to Bull Run. Follow the one lane dirt road down the mountain to the river. There is a bridge at Jenkinsburg and a good take-out with a short carry up to it. Find it on river right just before the junction with the Big Sandy. A number of vehicles have been vandalized at Jenkinsburg when the river traffic has been light.

*Alternate Shuttle:* Do not do it! The Valley Point Road via Rockville is much shorter, but people who have driven the road once generally do not do it a second time.

A good combination is to have one group run the Canyon and another run the Narrows. The people running the Narrows will finish first and can come to Jenkins Bridge to meet the Canyon trip.

*Gauges:* Albright Bridge gauge. This gauge should read between minus 0.5 and 5.0 feet. The Parsons gauge which is about a day upstream will probably read between 1.9 and 6.1 feet. Since the Canyon is so steep, it rises fast. There is no place for the water to spread out. The level can be influenced by storms far upstream in the Forks of the Cheat. Check the level several days running before your trip. If it is stable, or falling slowly, it should be okay. Be aware that the river rises fast and can be a nightmare at high levels. Try the Narrows if the Canyon is too high.

Note: The Albright Bridge gauge is painted on the highway bridge in Albright and should not be confused with the Albright power station gauge, which is reported by phone.

*Normal Wet Period:* No available statistics on seasons. Although this section is large, the gradient and steepness of its drops reduce the normally runnable season to early October through early July, with it often being too high during the spring runoff.

# E. Jenkins Bridge                              9.0 miles
## to Cheat Lake (Lake Lynn)

| Class | Grad | Size (Area / Volume) | Scene / Poll | Level |
|-------|------|----------------------|--------------|-------|
| III | 12/20 | Large (1,400/2,333) estimate | A/B | 0.0-4.0 Albright Bridge |

*Topographic Maps:* Valley Point (WVa), Masontown (WVa), Lake Lynn (WVa)

*County Maps:* Preston (WVa), Monongalia (WVa)

*Description:* The first section of this trip is fairly open rapids. There is maneuvering, but the course is obvious. The last 5 miles are flat as you are paddling in the backwaters of Lake Lynn. The high mountains surround the river, but do not close it in as they do upstream in the Canyon. Allow time to scout the first few rapids. [Checked 1988]

*Difficulties:* Powerboats on the lake.

*Shuttle:* From Jenkinsburg go south to Masontown, Turn right onto West Virginia Route 7. Go about 8 miles and go east on the four lane, US Route 48. Go about 6 miles, just after crossing the lake, and get off the four lane and onto County Road 857. Follow this to the old Ices Ferry Bridge.

*Gauges:* Albright Bridge gauge. This gauge should read between 0.0 and 5.0 feet. The Parsons gauge which is about a day upstream will probably read between 2.3 and 5.3 feet.

Note: The Albright Bridge gauge is painted on the highway bridge in Albright and should not be confused with the Albright power station gauge, which is reported by phone.

*Normal Wet Period:* No available statistics on seasons. Since this section is large, it should normally be runnable all year, but it may be too high from February to April.

# Big Sandy Creek

## A. Bruceton Mills to Rockville                5.8 miles
## "The Upper Big Sandy"

| Class | Grad | Size (Area/Volume) | Scene/Poll | Level |
|-------|------|--------------------|------------|-------|
| III-IV | 28/47 | Medium (200/422) | A/A | 5.8-7.0 |
| | | Rockville | | Rockville |

*Topographic Maps:* Bruceton Mills (WVa), Valley Point (WVa)

*County Maps:* Preston (WVa)

*Description:* The trip starts with 1.5 miles of flatwater and becomes progressively more difficult as one approaches Rockville. Once you pass under State Route 48 the trip is remote and pleasant. This is an intimate, isolated stream. It is very beautiful when the rhododendron blooms. It is not as difficult as the Little Sandy. [Checked 1982]

*Difficulties:* All of the Class IV rapids occur after the Little Sandy has entered. The first of these is a long slide into several hydraulics which are nearly river wide. The next rapid is a 6-foot river-wide falls which forms nasty hydraulics in the center and to the right at higher levels. Scout this, then sneak behind the rock ledge on river left at the top of the rapid. Then choose your chute. The last rapid before the bridge at Rockville is long and requires considerable maneuvering. Strainers frequently lodge here and a pin is possible. Generally, it is best to run this rapid to the right of center. This river is appropriate for expert open boaters or intermediate closed boaters.

*Shuttle:* Put in below the dam at Bruceton Mills. Take out at the bridge at Rockville. The road to Rockville is rough. Take West Virginia Route 26 to Valley Point. Turn right/west onto County Road 15. Go about 5 miles to Hudson and Mt Nebo. Turn right/north onto County Road 14. Go 0.5 miles. Turn right and then immediately left for the plunge into Rockville. Please do not block the driveways.

*Gauges:* Rockville. This gauge should read between 5.8 and 7.0 feet. This corresponds to a flow of 445 cfs to 1,120 cfs. See also comments in the Section B of this stream below.

*Normal Wet Period:* This section is normally runnable from mid February to mid April, and it does not have a season when it is too high.

## B. Rockville to Jenkins Bridge                5.1 miles
## "The Lower Big Sandy"

| Class | Grad | Size (Area/Volume) | Scene/Poll | Level |
|-------|------|--------------------|------------|-------|
| V | 81/107 | Medium (200/422) | A/A | 5.8-6.5 |
|   |        | Rockville |      | Rockville |

*Topographic Maps:* Bruceton Mills (WVa), Valley Point (WVa)

*County Maps:* Preston (WVa)

*Description:* This section is more difficult than the Tygart Gorge or Cheat Canyon and is comparable to the Upper Yough. This remote, unspoiled stream is a favorite of many local Class V paddlers, and for good reason. The rapids are technical and dramatic as the river tumbles among house-sized boulders and is punctuated by dangerous waterfalls. The scenery is unsurpassed by any river in the Monongahela watershed. The banks are choked with underbrush so that scouting is difficult, but there is an old railroad bed on the river right mountainside if a hike back to Rockville becomes necessary. [Reported 1982]

*Difficulties:* Expert boat control, a solid roll, and a companion who knows the river well are prerequisites to your first excursion here. There are at least five Class V rapids on this run. About 1.5 miles into the trip comes a tough Class IV rapid which ends in a small pool, followed immediately by an 18-foot waterfall. The next major rapid is the Zoom Flume, a 10-foot descent over a 50-foot washboard. Then Little Splat, a gloriously technical Class V rock garden. Below this lies the second major falls, Big Splat, which is a complex 25-foot drop which must be carried on the right. This is a Class VI rapid with a Class V carry on the right. After a mile of more or less continuous Class IV water one approaches First Island Rapid. This is a boulder-strewn series of 6- to 8-foot drops which is every bit as difficult as anything on the Upper Yough. The last mile of the run is a continuous Class III-IV tumble to the Cheat River.

*Shuttle:* Put in at Rockville as described in Section A. An alternative is to put in at Bruceton Mills and run the Upper Big Sandy as well, or to put in on the Little Sandy at West Virginia Route 26. These options make the trip longer, but the drive to Rockville is lengthy and rough. The take-out is the same as for the Cheat Canyon. An alternate, shorter shuttle from Rockville to Jenkinsburg via dirt roads is appropriate for rugged four-wheel-drive vehicles only.

*Gauges:* Rockville. This gauge should read between 5.8 and 6.5 feet for first time runners. This corresponds to a flow of 445 cfs to 770 cfs. An outside staff is available at Rockville under the bridge on river right. There is also a gauge under the bridge at Bruceton Mills near US Route 48. To convert a Bruceton reading to a Rockville reading multiply the Bruceton reading by 0.75 and add 5.7. The Cheat River gauges are useless since the watersheds are so far removed. The Ursina gauge on the Laurel Hill will usually be 1.7 or above when this is runnable.

*Normal Wet Period:* This section is normally runnable from mid February to mid April and does not have a season when to is normally too high. It is often available after heavy rains.

# Little Sandy Creek
# (Preston County, WVa)

## A. Hazelton to Brandonville Pike　　　　　　　　8.5 miles

*Class　Grad　　Size (Area / Volume)　　Scene / Poll　Level*
II-III　31/80　　　　　　　　　　　　　　　A / A

*Topographic Maps:* Brandonville

*County Maps:* Preston (WVa)

*Description:* The West Virginia Little Sandy (not to be confused with the Pennsylvania Little Sandy, less than 10 miles away) flows from a highland marsh near Hazelton southwest toward its confluence with the Big Sandy at Rockville. After passing through a large culvert under US Route 48 at Hazelton the creek enters a mountaintop marsh. Scarcely 20 feet wide, the stream meanders through reeds and cattails. Soon it is split into countless tiny islands, creating a maze of slow moving water. Stay with the greatest flow. The marsh offers wild birds, snags and thickets; in the summer it probably offers mosquitos. After leaving the marsh the stream begins to drop more quickly, flowing through a beautiful deciduous and hemlock forest. Here the stream is 25 feet wide, fast-moving, and shallow. The large strip mine on the left is unobtrusive; the banks are lined with rhododendron and show signs of beaver. The next several miles provide intermittent Class II+ rapids and several strainers that require evasive action. Near the end of the run the gradient increases and a few Class III rock gardens precede the Brandonville Pike take-out. [Reported 1985]

*Difficulties:* In the marsh downed trees completely block the course in several places. Since they are in slow-moving water they present little difficulty.

*Shuttle:* To reach the put-in, take the Hazelton exit from US Route 48. Cross over US Route 48 on the overpass, turn left, and drive 0.5 miles to the culverts going under US Route 48. To reach the take-out, take Bruceton exit from US Route 48, turn north onto West Virginia Route 26 to

Brandonville (1 mile). Turn right onto Brandonville Pike and drive 2.5 miles to the bridge.

*Gauges:* On the Little Sandy West Virginia Route 26 bridge paddler's gauge, 4 inches is minimum. The Bruceton gauge on nearby Big Sandy Creek will probably read above 2.0 feet.

*Normal Wet Period:* No available statistics on seasons. Since this section is tiny, it should normally be runnable only after a heavy rain or during spring snowmelt.

## B. Brandonville Pike                    2.5 miles
## to West Virginia Route 26 Bridge

*Class   Grad      Size (Area/Volume)      Scene/Poll   Level*
        18/35

*Topographic Maps:* Brandonville, Bruceton Mills

*County Maps:* Preston (WVa)

*Description:* Not reported at this time.

## C. West Virginia Route 26 Bridge        2.8 miles
## to junction with Big Sandy

*Class   Grad      Size (Area/Volume)      Scene/Poll   Level*
III-IV 32/80                              A/A-   0.5 to 2.0
                                          Route 26 bridge

*Topographic Maps:* Bruceton Mills (WVa)

*County Maps:* Preston (WVa)

*Description:* This short section of Class III water provides an alternative way to reach the Class V whitewater of the Big Sandy without having to travel the 8 miles of gravel road into Rockville. The trip begins with 0.75 miles of flatwater and then becomes progressively steeper. Several complicated 4 to 6 foot sloping ledges are separated by continuous Class II whitewater. [Checked 1988]

*Difficulties:* The action is continuous. The water is swift and shallow. The eddies are difficult to catch. Punchable hydraulics are present at the bottom of most drops. A 36" tree is now (1988) across the river in a riverwide strainer. It has been there for several years, so it will probably still be there. Portage river right.

*Shuttle:* Put in at the bridge on West Virginia Route 26, about 2 miles south of US Route 48. Intermediate boaters should take out at Rockville, or the more expert or daring can continue down the Big Sandy.

*Gauges:* There is a painted gauge on the abutment of the West Virginia Route 26 bridge. This gauge should read between 0.5 and 2.0 feet. The Big Sandy will be fairly high if the Little Sandy is runnable.

*Normal Wet Period:* No available statistics on seasons. Since this section is tiny, it should normally be runnable only after a heavy rain or during spring snowmelt.

# Fike Run & Little Sandy Creek (Fayette County)

**Five Forks to Gibbon Glade**                          4.5 miles

| Class | Grad | Size (Area/Volume) | Scene/Poll | Level |
|-------|------|--------------------|------------|-------|
| I V | 93/180 | Tiny (28/47) Gibbon Glade | A/A | |

*Topographic Maps:* Brandonville

*County Maps:* Fayette

*Description:* The first 1.4 miles are flat, quite pretty with overgrown banks (so overgrown that it is sometimes necessary to part the brush with a paddle to pass through). The stream is frequently no more than 20 to 25 feet wide, hardly ever more than 50 feet wide. Fallen trees frequently create log and brush dams; sometimes you can slide over them while still in the boat, but you must often carry around them. At this point the creek starts to drop 100 feet in the 0.6 mile until Fike Run joins Little Sandy Creek. Two drops in this section are not runnable: some water can get through, but a boat cannot. Although the shore is heavily overgrown, it is advisable to scout all drops either from the boat or on foot to be sure they are clear. In the next 0.3 mile, the creek drops another 60 feet, then levels off for a 0.2 miles before another side stream comes in from the right and the creek starts dropping again -- another 200 feet in the remaining 2 miles to the take-out. While some of the drops are quite steep (20 feet within 50 at one point), the routes are relatively clear of logs and easy to see. When the first of three bridges crosses the creek, "civilization" in the form of houses begins to intrude. The routes in these drops require very fast and sharp turns, one after another. This is a very busy, tight creek. [Reported 1986]

*Difficulties:* Trees down can completely block the creek. The steep section on Fike Run contains two impassable drops.

*Shuttle:* The route to the put-in goes past the take-out. The creek is reached by turning off State Route 381 on State Route

2005 to Gibbon Glade. A good take-out is about 100 yards before the first bridge over the creek. To get to the put-in, continue through Gibbon Glade (no signs). State Route 2005 will change to State Route 2007. At the Canaan Church (of the Brethren of Gibbon Glade) bear left onto State Route 2006. In Five Forks bear left/north onto State Route 2011. You cross the creek about 0.5 miles past Five Forks. About 400 yards past the bridge, a dirt road comes in from the right, offering a good place to park and change.

*Gauges:* Rockville. A good run was had at a reading of 8.6 feet. The creek at the take-out is fast moving and rocky; check there to see if there's enough water.

*Normal Wet Period:* No available statistics on seasons. Since this section is tiny, it should normally be runnable only after a heavy rain or during spring snowmelt.

# Shavers Fork

## A. Bemis to US 33 Bridge                14.0 miles

| Class | Grad | Size (Area/Volume) | Scene/Poll | Level |
|-------|------|--------------------|------------|-------|
| II-IV | 40/65 | Small (150/250) estimate | A/A Parsons (Shavers Fork) | |

*Topographic Maps:* Glady (WVa), Bowden (WVa), Elkins (WVa)

*County Maps:* Randolph (WVa)

*Description:* This stream drops sharply for its first few miles in fairly open, moderately heavy rapids. The last few miles are Class II rapids around many islands. See Davidson, Eister, and Davidson's *Wild Water West Virginia* for details. [Checked 1988]

## B. US 33 to Parsons                22 miles

| Class | Grad | Size (Area/Volume) | Scene/Poll | Level |
|-------|------|--------------------|------------|-------|
| I-II | 19/19 | Medium (214/553) estimate | A-B/A-B Parsons (Shavers Fork) | |

*Topographic Maps:* Elkins (WVa), Bowden (WVa), Parsons (WVa)

*County Maps:* Randolph (WVa)

*Description:* The scenery through the deep hollows is spectacular. Many rock bluffs and waterfalls line the river while the shores are studded with magnificent growths of hemlock. See Davidson, Eister, and Davidson's *Wild Water West Virginia* for details. [Checked 1985]

# Black Fork

## Hendricks to Parsons                                         3.7 miles

| Class | Grad | Size (Area/Volume) | Scene/Poll | Level |
|-------|------|--------------------|-----------|-------|
| I I | 16/26 | Medium (475/792) estimate | B/A-B | 4.0-6.0 Parsons |

*Topographic Maps:* Parsons (WVa)

*County Maps:* Tucker (WVa)

*Description:* Beginning at Hendricks the river alternates between flowing pools and open Class II which are mostly standing waves. Although it passes a four-wheel encampment and race course, the stream in general is pretty as it flows through wooded mountain sides. See Davidson, Eister, and Davidson's *Wild Water West Virginia* for details. [Checked 1985]

# Blackwater River

## North Fork Junction to Hendricks                           7 miles

| Class | Grad | Size (Area/Volume) | Scene/Poll | Level |
|-------|------|--------------------|-----------|-------|
| V-VI | 96/120 | Small (86/199) Davis | A/B | 2.5-3.5 Davis |

*Topographic Maps:* Mozark Mountain (WVa), Parsons (W Va)

*County Maps:* Tucker (WVa)

*Description:* This section of river plunges fantastically to meet the Black Fork at Hendricks. See Davidson, Eister, and Davidson's *Wild Water West Virginia* for details. [Checked 1988]

# Dry Fork

## A. Harman to Jenningston                    7 miles

| Class | Grad | Size (Area/Volume) | Scene/Poll | Level |
|-------|------|--------------------|------------|-------|
| III | 36/40 | Medium | B/A | 3.0-?? |
| | | | | Hendricks |

*Topographic Maps:* Harman (WVa)

*County Maps:* Randolph (WVa), Tucker (WVa)

*Description:* This stream flows past rural West Virginia houses, mills and farms. See Davidson, Eister, and Davidson's *Wild Water West Virginia* for details. [Checked 1988]

## B. Jenningston to Hendricks                    13.4 miles

| Class | Grad | Size (Area/Volume) | Scene/Poll | Level |
|-------|------|--------------------|------------|-------|
| III-IV | 24/31 | Medium (345/832) | A/A | 3.0-?? |
| | | Hendricks | | Hendricks |

*Topographic Maps:* Harman (WVa), Mozark Mountain (WVa)

*County Maps:* Tucker (WVa)

*Other Maps:* Monongahela National Forest Map from the US Forest Service, PO Box 1231, Elkins, West Virginia 26241

*Description:* This is generally pastoral scenery. The river is suitable for strong paddlers in open boats. While some of the rapids have some moderately difficult passages, there is always an easy passage. See Davidson, Eister, and Davidson's *Wild Water West Virginia* for details. [Checked 1989]

# Glady Fork

## Evenwood to Panther Camp Run                10.4 miles

*Class   Grad    Size (Area/Volume)    Scene/Poll   Level*
II-III   26/38        Small              A/A        3.7-??
                                                    Hendricks

*Topographic Maps:* Bowden (WVa), Harman (WVa)

*County Maps:* Randolph (WVa)

*Other Maps:* Monongahela National Forest Map from the US Forest Service, PO Box 1231, Elkins, West Virginia 26241

*Description:* There are few flat pools anywhere. The rapids are continuous but not difficult (never beyond Class III). It is a small stream with many bends and islands. This is an ideal river for intermediates who like to combine beautiful scenery with the challenge of an elementary slalom course. See  Davidson, Eister, and Davidson's *Wild Water West Virginia* for details. [Checked 1989]

# Laurel Fork

## US 33 to Jenningston                         13 miles

*Class   Grad    Size (Area/Volume)    Scene/Poll   Level*
III-IV  54/72         Small              A/A        3.7-??
                                                    Hendricks

*Topographic Maps:* Harman (WVa)

*County Maps:* Randolph (WVa), Tucker (WVa)

Description: Lots of ledges and a 12-foot unrunnable water fall. See  Davidson, Eister, and Davidson's *Wild Water West Virginia* for details. [Checked 1990]

# Tygart Valley River

The Tygart Valley River is at the limits of our range; we have included descriptions of four noncontiguous sections that are favorites of the Pittsburgh area closed boat paddlers. This river is often used as a weekend trip for groups of boaters who have mixed levels of interests and skills. Most of the interesting sections of this river are in places where the river has narrowed. This has the effect, that this river gets much more difficult as the flow increases, quicker than one would expect. More detailed descriptions of the Tygart (these sections and other sections) plus other rivers in the area can be found in Davidson, Eister, and Davidson's *Wildwater West Virginia*.

## "The Loop"                        6.5 miles
## Norton to Junior

| Class | Grad | Size (Area/Volume) | Scene/Poll | Level |
|-------|------|--------------------|-----------|-------|
| III-IV | 25/36 | | C/B | 4.0-5.0 |
| | | | | Belington |

*Topographic Maps:*   Junior (WVa)

*County Maps:*   Randolph (WVa), Barbour (WVa)

*Description:*   This section, where it can be seen from the road near the beginning and the end, is flat with some riffles. In the loop, away from the highway the Tygart becomes considerably more interesting. It has Class II to IV rapids in a beautiful, isolated, forested valley. It builds gradually to the Twin Giants rapid in the middle of the run and then gradually gentles. The Twin Giants rapid is significantly more difficult and different in character from the other rapids on the river. This rapid is marked from well upstream by rows of house size boulders on the left shore and in the center. See Davidson, Eister, and Davidson's *Wild Water West Virginia* for details. [Reported 1988]

# "The Gorge"                                    11 miles
## Belington to mouth of Buckhannon

| Class | Grad | Size (Area/Volume) | Scene/Poll | Level |
|-------|------|--------------------|------------|-------|
| IV-V | 37/65 | Medium (408/814) | A/B | 2.5-6.8 |
|       |       | Belington |          | Belington |

*Topographic Maps:*  Belington (WVa), Audra (WVa)

*County Maps:*  Barbour (WVa)

*Description:*  This is the Tygart at its most spectacular. The river drops over huge boulders and ledges through an isolated gorge. It begins quietly as it leaves Belington and remains flat for 3 miles before the rapids start. "Keyhole", two ledges, and "Hard Tongue Falls" begin the real fun. The rapids closely follow each other to the junction with the Middle Fork. In the 2 miles below the Middle Fork, the Tygart increases to its most difficult, but saves many play spots for the remainder of the trip to the mouth of the Buckhannon. See Davidson, Eister, and Davidson's *Wild Water West Virginia* for details. [Reported 1988]

# "The Arden Section"                              8 miles
## 2 miles above Arden to Big Cove Run

| Class | Grad | Size (Area/Volume) | Scene/Poll | Level |
|-------|------|--------------------|------------|-------|
| V | 27/39 | Medium (916/1,926) | C/B | 2.5-4.5 |
|   |       | Philippi |          | Philippi |

*Topographic Maps:*  Philippi (WVa), Nestorville (WVa)

*County Maps:*  Barbour (WVa)

*Description:*  This is another big water section of the Tygart River. Here the river is broad, in a steep-walled, wooded valley. The rapids are generally more open and less technical than in the upper gorge, but every bit as big. These wide rapids provide many routes among the powerful currents. There are big waves, ledges, holes, two major waterfalls and two known dangerous undercuts. The road turns away and the Tygart is isolated from below Teter Creek to the access at Big Cove Run in the reservoir. The final mile or two may be pooled or may have ugly mud slopes, depending on water level in the reservoir. See Davidson, Eister, and Davidson's *Wild Water West Virginia* for details. [Reported 1988]

## Valley Falls Section                    0.5 miles

| Class | Grad | Size (Area/Volume) | Scene/Poll | Level |
|-------|------|--------------------|-----------|-------|
| V I | 40/40 | Large | A/A | |

*Topographic Maps:* Fairmont East (WVa)

*County Maps:* Taylor (WVa), Marion (WVa)

*Description*  When there is enough rain or if Graffton Dam is releasing water, this section consists of two waterfalls with lethal hydraulics and Class VI rapids.

During the summer, when everything else is too low this short stretch is a great place to practice running waterfalls and technical maneuvering. There is an 8-foot and a 14-foot falls and four Class IV-V rapids, all terminating in quiet pools. Those considering running the river down to Hammond should read Davidson, Eister and Davidson's *Wild Water West Virginia* for details. [Reported 1988]

# Middle Fork River

## A. Laurel Fork to Audra State Park          5 miles

| Class | Grad | Size (Area/Volume) | Scene/Poll | Level |
|-------|------|--------------------|-----------|-------|
| III | 26/40 | Small | A/B | 3.5-6.0 |
| | | | | Audra State Park |

*Topographic Maps:*  Ellamore (WVa), Audra (WVa)

*County Maps:*  Upshur (WVa), Barbour (WVa)

*Description:*  This is a great option if you want an easier trip while others run the Class IV-V Middle Fork. This starts as a beautiful, flat stream in a narrow, isolated valley with a few riverside cottages. The river gradually builds in difficulty from Class I to Class III. Take out above the bridge in Audra State Park. Below here the difficulty increases significantly. See Davidson, Eister, and Davidson's *Wild Water West Virginia* for details. [Reported 1988]

## B. Audra State Park                          6 miles
## to junction with Tygart River

| Class | Grad | Size (Area/Volume) | Scene/Poll | Level |
|-------|------|--------------------|-----------|-------|
| IV | 65/120 | Small | A/A | 3.5-5.0 |
| | | | | Audra State Park |

*Topographic Maps:*  Audra (WVa)

*County Maps:*  Upshur (WVa), Barbour (WVa)

*Description*  The Middle Fork is an exciting, continuous, technical challenge which contrasts sharply with the drops and pools of the heavier, pushy Tygart Gorge. Only the first 2.5 miles of this run are actually on the Middle Fork, which joins the Tygart in the midst of the Gorge. There is no access here, so boaters must paddle to the mouth of the Buckhannon. Most boaters enter the Gorge by way of the Middle Fork instead of at Belington at high levels; the shuttle is shorter. See Davidson, Eister, and Davidson's *Wild Water West Virginia* for details. [Reported 1988]

# Miscellaneous Rivers

# Lake Erie Shoreline

Lake Erie provides Pennsylvania's only coastal waters. Most of the shoreline is private property or state park, so it is best to plan with public campsites and access areas in mind, allowing sufficient time to go from point to point. Most of the shoreline is undeveloped, remaining in a wild natural condition with erosion ridges running down its multicolored clay banks. Signs of civilization can be seen on top of the steep cliffs which rise from the water's edge. There are only two public campgrounds with lake frontage along the entire Pennsylvania shoreline.

Canoe travel is best done in July through the first half of August. The water is still too cold in June and from mid-August onward storms and wind-whipped waves can last several days at a time, causing a lot of down time for small craft. The lake can turn up its waves on short notice. Waves have been recorded 12 to 15 feet high in bad storms. It is not unusual to see waves 3 to 5 feet. On the other hand it can be flat as a pancake. Check the weather before going. If small craft warnings are posted, find some place inland or try the lagoon system in Presque Isle State Park. It's handy to carry a battery-powered weather radio to get up-to-the-minute reports on lake weather.

The Coast Guard requires a PFD for each person in the canoe. It also requires a signalling device (whistle) for each craft. It's a good idea to fly a bicycle flag to improve your visibility to power boaters. In addition, a white light visible through 360 degrees (i.e., in all directions) is required for night travel. A Pennsylvania State Park boat permit is needed for launching or landing in Presque Isle State Park.

Canoes should be a minimum of 17 feet long and have plenty of freeboard. Become proficient in open-water rescue before venturing far from good shoreline. You may be far from shore, or the shoreline may offer no place to stand at the base of the cliffs.

We have described these sections assuming you will paddle from west to east, the direction of the prevailing wind. If, when you paddle, the wind is from the east, you will probably want to start your trip from the described take-out points.

# A. Conneaut, Ohio to Walnut Creek          18.5 miles

*Class   Grad      Size (Area/Volume)      Scene/Poll   Level*
  A       Lake         Huge                   B/A

*Topographic Maps:* Conneaut (Ohio), East Springfield, Fairview SW, Fairview, Swanville

*County Maps:* Ashtabula (Ohio), Erie

*Description:* [Checked 1985]

*Difficulties:* High cliffs descend to the lake, often directly to the water without any shoreline. Do not attempt to pass the cliff areas shown on the topographic maps if the wave action is picking up. When the lake is turbulent, there is no shoreline to stand on along the base of the cliffs if you should swamp the canoe. Stay clear of the cement walls around Trout Run Marina and jetties sloping into the lake. Exercise caution at Walnut Creek inlet.

*Shuttle:* Put in at the municipal pier in Conneaut. If your car will be there more than a day, the local police department should be notified and a float plan should be filed with them. Pennsylvania maintains a public launch site at the mouth of Walnut Creek. Virginia's Beach Campground is at the 6.5 mile point, just before Crooked Creek.

*Gauge:* Not needed

*Normal Wet Period:* All year. During the winter the lake will be frozen. During Spring and Fall, storms and high winds are always a possibility.

## B. Walnut Creek to Erie public dock          12-15 miles
depending on choice of route in bay

| Class | Grad | Size (Area / Volume) | Scene / Poll | Level |
|-------|------|----------------------|--------------|-------|
| A | Lake | Huge | A / A | |

*Topographic Maps:* Swanville, Erie North

*County Maps:* Erie

*Description:* Presque Isle State Park juts out into the lake and curls east along the shore to form a bay. One can paddle the outside of the curl in the main lake, or portage across the arm and paddle in the bay. A description of Presque Isle State Park can be obtained from Presque Isle State Park, Department of Environmental Resources, Erie, Pennsylvania. [Checked 1985]

*Difficulties:* Exercise caution before attempting to paddle across the main inlet from the tip of Presque Isle to the main shore. It is a 500 ft crossing. Expect to wait it out until wave action settles down.

*Shuttle:* Put in at Walnut Creek access area. There is a public campground (Beachcomber Campground) just past Waldameer Park which is near the west end of Presque Isle where it joins the shore. Continue to the east end of Pettinato Beach, Presque Isle State Park. This is the official (1985) portage route between the lake and the bay. There is a food concession and restroom at this point. The State Park Bathing Beach runs the entire length of Presque Isle peninsula. Therefore it is not permitted to beach or launch a canoe at any point other than Pettinato Beach or the marinas. It is a one third mile carry along a path to Marina Lake. From here you can either go east along the south side of Presque Isle and across the bay to the Erie Public Dock, or west past the Erie Yacht Club and eastward to the Erie Public Dock. The crossing of the bay requires that the entrance to the bay be calm so the decision should be based on the winds and weather. If you elect the south side of Presque Isle see the description of Presque Isle trip elsewhere in this guide. It is best to take out on the leeward side of the dock. An intermediate take-out is at Pettinato Beach.

*Gauge:* Not needed

*Normal Wet Period:* All year. During the winter the lake will be frozen. During Spring and Fall, storms and high winds are always a possibility.

## C.  Erie public dock to Ripley NY                21 miles

| Class | Grad | Size (Area/Volume) | Scene/Poll | Level |
|-------|------|--------------------|-----------|-------|
| A     | Lake | Huge               | B/C       |       |

*Topographic Maps:* Erie North, Harborcreek, North East

*County Maps:* Erie, Chautauqua (NY)

*Description:* [Checked 1985]

*Difficulties:* On approach to the inlet between the Bay and Lake Erie, tie up at the first inlet light tower and walk out on jetty to check the wave action in Lake Erie. If it is too turbulent, portage at this point and launch again at Lampe's Marina. Caution: the cliffs east of the marina have no shoreline to stand on in event of a swamping, so do not attempt passage if wave action is too rough. The water in this area shows signs of pollution. It is best not to be closer to the cliffs than the "slop line" in the water (this is the point where the backwash from the cliffs meets the incoming waves off the lake). The area of easiest paddling is approximately 25 yards from shore.

*Shuttle:* Put in at the public dock in Erie. The take-out point is at Lakeside Campground just over the New York border. A fee is charged for use of the launch area. Intermediate public access can be had at Eight Mile Creek and Sixteen Mile Creek.

*Gauge:* Not needed

*Normal Wet Period:* All year. During the winter the lake will be frozen. During Spring and Fall, storms and high winds are always a possibility.

# Presque Isle State Park

## Grave Yard Pond to Grave Yard Pond          4.0 miles

| Class | Grad | Size (Area/Volume) | Scene/Pol | Level |
|-------|------|--------------------|-----------|-------|
| A     | lake | Huge               | A/A       |       |

*Topographic Maps:* Erie North

*County Maps:* Erie

*Other Maps:* The Western Pennsylvania Conservancy has a more detailed write-up of this section.

*Description:* The Presque Isle Peninsula is designated a National Natural Landmark. Canoeing on the park's inland lagoon system is an enjoyable way to see some of the diverse habitats that are present on the landward side of the Isle. The lagoon system is really a series of ponds that were linked by a dredging project in the 1930's. This area is prime habitat for many different bird species and includes about a third of the rare plant species existing in Pennsylvania. [Reported 1988]

*Difficulties:* Navigation in the ponds appears to be a problem from the maps, but this is not the case. The maze of channels shown on the map are clogged with plant life, and there are obvious cleared routes to take. If you want to get somewhere, take the widest, clearest path going in that direction. If the return is made via Presque Isle Bay rather than back through the ponds, the possibility of wind gusts and high waves should be considered. Know the weather forecast for the area as winds and storms can develop and move very quickly on the open waters of Lake Erie.

*Shuttle:* Put in at the lagoon boat launch area near the east (far) end of the peninsula. The East Boat Livery rents canoes at this launch ramp. Take out at the same place.

*Gauge:* None needed

*Normal Wet Period:* All year. During the winter the lagoon will be frozen. During Spring and Fall, storms and high winds are always a possibility.

# Conneaut Creek

## Cherry Hill to Conneaut, Ohio                     26.5 miles

| Class | Grad | Size (Area/Volume) | Scene/Poll | Level |
|-------|------|--------------------|-----------|-------|
| I | 9/15 | Small (152/253) | B/A | |
| | | Pa-Ohio border | | |

*Topographic Maps:* East Springfield, Conneaut (Ohio),
   North Kingsville (Ohio)

*County Maps:* Erie, Ashtabula (Ohio)

*Description:* This stream cuts through the glacial ridge as
it heads west to Kingsville, Ohio and then loops back to
Conneaut. Very little evidence of civilization is seen as you
travel between high shale cliffs and forested flats, through
rapids and around islands. The gradient is very evenly
distributed in many short riffles over small rocks. This all
combines to make an excellent stream for learning to canoe
easy white water. The creek above Cherry Hill is mostly
deeper water and thus flatwater paddling. About 1 mile
beyond Furnace Road you will pass under a covered bridge
on Middle Road which is now closed to traffic. [Cherry Hill
to Farmington checked 1990, Farmington to Kingsville
checked 1988]

*Difficulties:* At low levels some problem may be experienced
just below the bridge on Horton Road and again just before
reaching the bridge on Interstate 90. The Ohio Department
of Natural Resources reports the following hazards on this
stream: a broken weir dam under Center Road bridge south
of Farnham, dam only extends on left side, is runnable; two
broken weir dams about 1.0 and 1.5 miles further, portage
right, or take center chute on both; a broken weir dam at
Locust Lane Campground in Kingsville, the center chute is
open; a broken weir dam upstream of the Center Road
bridge in Conneaut, take the center chute with care; a
broken weir dam at Old Main Road bridge off of Woodworth
Road in Conneaut, the center chute is open.

*Shuttle:* The 26 miles of river has several loops and can be
divided into a number of different sections. The uppermost
put-in is at the the covered bridge on Barney Road (State

Route 3003). From Cherry Hill go one mile east on State Route 3002, then turn left/north on State Route 3003 and proceed 0.75 miles to the bridge. The Farnham take-out/put-in is on the left bank below the concrete arch bridge on Center Road. The Kingsville take-out/put-in is below the bridge on the left bank. In Conneaut proceed north from the bridge a short distance to the ball field.

| | |
|---|---|
| Cherry Hill to Farmingham | 9.5 miles |
| Farmingham to Kingsville | 7.5 miles |
| Kingsville to Conneaut | 9.5 miles |

When planning your day do not expect much push from the current unless the river is really high.

*Gauges:* Painted gauge on left/south abutment of bridge at Cherry Hill. If the creek looks floatable from the old bridge on Center Road to the new bridge upstream at US Route 7 this trip should be okay. Painted gauge on the right/north abutment of the old concrete arch bridge on Center Road at Farnham. Painted gauge on right/east abutment of the bridge at Kingsville. Minimum level for this trip is about 1.5 feet. These gauges were installed and are currently maintained by the Ohio-Penn Paddlers Canoe Club.

*Normal Wet Period:* No available statistics on seasons. Since this section is small, it should normally be runnable approximately January through April.

# Twenty Mile Creek

## South of Ripley NY to Lake Erie          10.6 miles

*Class  Grad    Size (Area/Volume)    Scene/Poll  Level*
I V    47/100      Tiny (36/60)
               mouth of creek

*Topographic Maps:* South Ripley (NY), North East

*County Maps:* Chautauqua (NY), Erie

*Description:* This is a geologically young stream, with shale walls and bottom, and evidence of active erosion and cutting. Bare shale offers good footing on the river bottom, but overlying soils coat the cliffs to make the banks slippery and hard to climb. Twenty Mile immediately enters into a canyon, but the whitewater remains tame for a couple of miles. After an hour of easy whitewater, spectacular waterfalls, and near total wilderness, the river starts to develop significant ledges, around 3 to 4 feet high. This marks the beginning of the steep section. After another ledge on a sharp left corner, Gage Gorge enters parallel to the main stream, separated from it by a thin high wall of shale. Both drop into a common pool, roar down a narrow slot barely 6 feet wide at the water line, and plunge out of sight. The slot is 100 feet long; the last drop plunges sideways into the right wall, but the approach lets you stay left until the last second and the drop deposits you into the pool below. From Gage Gorge to this point is a box canyon with no good way to portage or pull out. After the gradient lets up, the earlier pattern of small ledges and slides resumes, and there are many playing spots. A railroad on trestles with major piers in the streambed offers some interest and signifies the end of the remote canyon. The second railroad is at US Route 20 and would be very intimidating if not scouted. Between US Route 20 and the lake there are several complex, long sloped ledges. [Reported 1988]

*Difficulties:* The railroad underpass immediately upstream of the US Route 20 bridge has a paved concrete floor and a sloped chute ending in a 3-foot drop; scout it from the highway bridge before you start the run. The one mile of stream around Gage Gorge has a gradient of 100 feet/mile. Stop to scout 100 feet before Gage Gorge enters. This requires climbing a 25-foot high shale wall. The portage would be a real problem, so be sure of your party before embarking on this one.

*Shuttle:* To get to the put-in, head upstream through Ripley, New York on New York Route 76. A county road off New York Route 76 near the top of the ridge leads to the put-in. Take out at the mouth on Lake Erie or at the US Route 5 bridge near the mouth.

*Gauges:* If the shallow ledges at the put-in and small rocky rapid downstream offer some scraping, but are passable, then the level is low but acceptable.

*Normal Wet Period:* No available statistics on seasons. Since this section is tiny, it should normally be runnable only after a heavy rain or during spring snowmelt.

# Chautauqua Creek

## Lyons Road to Lake Erie                              13.1 miles

*Class   Grad     Size (Area / Volume)      Scene / Poll   Level*
III-IV   63/90                                A / A

*Topographic Maps:* Sherman (NY), Westfield (NY)

*County Maps:* Chautauqua (NY)

*Description:* This is a geologically young stream, with shale walls and bottom, and evidence of active erosion and cutting. Bare shale offers good footing on the river bottom, but overlying soils coat the cliffs to make the banks slippery and hard to climb. After a few miles the stream starts to cut into a shale canyon. The run is similar to Twenty Mile Creek except for three small water supply dams and a section of over a mile with braided channels and trees in which the route was always clear but not always deep. As you approach Westfield there are increasing signs of development and options for access. The gorge cut by the stream is known as the "Glug". [Reported 1988]

*Difficulties:* Carry around three water supply dams ranging from 6 to 10 feet in height. The second has a nasty step on a 4-foot drop and is particularly dangerous.

*Shuttle:* To get to the put-in, leave Westfield on Chestnut Street going upstream, on river left; put in on Lyons Road at an old bridge site.

*Gauges:* This stream is runnable if you can scrape by on the riffles at the put-in.

*Normal Wet Period:* No available statistics on seasons.

# Canadaway

## Hamlet/Cassadaga Road to Laona                    9.0 miles

*Class   Grad      Size (Area/Volume)      Scene/Poll   Level*
III-IV 67/100                              A/A

*Topographic Maps:* Dunkirk (NY), Cassadaga (NY),
    Hamlet (NY)

*County Maps:* Chautauqua (NY)

*Description:* The water level at the put-in is supplemented
by input from a steady influx of side streams for the first
3 miles. The start of the shale canyon is noticeable as the
stream stops meandering and is confined in the narrowing
gorge. Unlike Twenty Mile Creek and Chautauqua Creek,
which increase their gradients as they enter their canyons,
on the Canadaway the bottom drops out. A 35 foot falls
(Arkwright Falls) requires a very difficult portage (see
Difficulties) that may be problematical at high water levels.
It is followed by two more difficult ledges just as houses
come into view. The second ledge is Shumla Falls. The last
2 to 3 miles of the trip are accessible by road and contain
enjoyable chutes, rapids, and ledges. A final ledge along
New York Route 60, near the take-out, should also be
scouted. [Reported 1988]

*Difficulties:* A 35 foot falls appears just above a left corner;
the only possible carry is on the left with shale cliffs above
the falls on that side; this portage requires ropes. At low
levels it is possible to beach on a mid-river sandbar and walk
down to the take-out for this carry; at high water this could
present a serious problem. A pair of ledges that occur just
after houses come into view should be scouted and perhaps
carried, as should another ledge along New York Route 60.
A 40 foot falls under the town bridge in Laona has a nearly
impossible portage. This is downstream of the suggested
take-out.

*Shuttle:* The put-in is on New York Route 60 just outside
Cassadaga. Turn left before (not in) town. Follow this road
4 miles to the put-in between Cassadaga and Hamlet. Take
out well above the 40 foot falls that is immediately under the

town bridge in Laona. An alternate shuttle is New York Route 60 to New York Route 83. Follow New York Route 83 about 4 miles to the crossroads at Arkwright. Turn right and go 3 miles to the put-in at the bottom of the hill.

*Gauges:*

*Normal Wet Period:* No available statistics on seasons.

# Cattaraugus Creek

## A. New York 39 east of Springville          19 miles
## to Otto Road Bridge

| Class | Grad | Size (Area/Volume) | Scene/Poll | Level |
|-------|------|--------------------|-----------|--------|
| I-II  |      |                    |           | ??-3.5 |

Otto Road bridge

*Topographic Maps:* Sardinia (NY), West Valley (NY),
   Ashford Hollow (NY), Collins Center (NY)

*County Maps:* Erie (NY), Cattaraugus (NY)

*Description:* The run is Class I except for about a mile of
Class II water below the dam at US Route 219. [Reported
1988]

*Difficulties:* The only difficulty is a 30-foot dam just below
US Route 219. Carry on the right, but you will have to fight
your way up a steep mudbank.

*Shuttle:*

*Gauges:* Streamside. A reading of 3.5 feet on a gauge
painted on the Otto Road bridge provides a good high water
run.

*Normal Wet Period:* No available statistics on seasons.

## B. Otto Road Bridge to Gowanda          8.8 miles

| Class | Grad | Size (Area/Volume) | Scene/Poll | Level |
|-------|------|--------------------|-----------|--------|
| III-IV | 20/40 |                   | A/B       | ??-3.5 |

Otto Road bridge

*Topographic Maps:* Collins Center (NY), Gowanda (NY)

*County Maps:* Erie (NY), Cattaraugus (NY)

*Description:* The run builds in difficulty from Class I at Otto
Road to Class IV at Gowanda. The route drops into the

heart of the remote Zoar Valley canyon with spectacular cliffs among the scenery. The rapids have good playing holes, surfing waves, ender waves, and more. The difficulty picks up after the South Branch enters about 4 miles below Otto Road. Noteworthy are a chain of large waves with eddies on both sides, the waves trailing into a cliff on a left turn, and shallow ledges with good holes near town. Several play spots occur after a flood wall appears on river left. The final drop is the best with diagonal ledges funnelling water into a large breaking wave. There are sneak options at every drop. [Reported 1988]

*Difficulties:* Large holes above 3.5 feet on the gauge.

*Shuttle:* To find put-in take US Route 62 out of Gowanda on river right. Continue straight where US Route 62 bears left. Cross the tracks and take the Gowanda-Zoar Road to Zoar. The Zoar Valley Road follows along the river to the put-in at Otto Road bridge. Take out at railroad bridge river left upstream of US Route 62 bridge in Gowanda.

*Gauges:* Streamside. A reading of 3.5 feet on a gauge painted on the Otto Road bridge provides a good high water run.

*Normal Wet Period:* No available statistics on seasons.

# Cattaraugus Creek, South Branch

**Otto to main stem**                                    12.0 miles

*Class   Grad      Size (Area/Volume)      Scene/Poll   Level*
III-IV  33/56                              A/A          ??-3.5
                                                        Otto Road bridge

*Topographic Maps:* Cattaraugus (NY), New Albion (NY), Gowanda (NY)

*County Maps:* Cattaraugus (NY)

*Description:* The whitewater run begins 5.5 miles above the mouth at Skinner Road Ford. Access problems here require an additional 5 miles of Class I paddling with a put-in near Cattaraugus. The additional 2 miles from Otto is worthwhile, making this a 14 mile trip. There are two ledges between Otto and Cattaraugus with the next few miles to the Skinner Hollow road largely uneventful. A shale canyon starts below Skinner Hollow and a 3-4 foot ledge appears about 0.2 miles downstream. Paddlers should be aware of the falls below here, which must be portaged (see Difficulties). The falls are on a blind left corner; it's not the first blind left corner, so treat them all with extreme caution. Below the falls one rapid narrows to a 10-foot wide chute that presents no special problem. Below this you find spectacular shallow ledges, scenery, and mental relief from the strain of identifying the falls. The whitewater continues intermittently to the mouth, culminating in a series of ledges dropping 8-10 feet over 50 yards. Two miles of Cattaraugus Creek must be run to the take-out. This is the best whitewater of Zoar Canyon. See the Cattaraugus Creek write-up. [Reported 1988]

*Difficulties:* The Falls. It is a true Ohiopyle size falls on a blind left corner with *no take-out* once you have committed yourself to the left turn. A vertical cliff on the left 0.2 miles upstream may help to identify this spot, but treat every left turn with extreme caution and proceed only when you can see definite eddies on the left against a gravel shore. As you approach the corner with the falls, a smooth sheet of water moves around the corner on an apparent shallow bottom. The falls drops 25 feet with another 2-4 feet of sloping ledge on the approach. The portage is on the left; it requires rope assist to get into the lower gorge.

*Shuttle:* To reach the put-in follow North Otto Road to Otto and turn right. Put in at first bridge, or continue about 2 miles to unnamed tributary near Cattaraugus. Take out at Gowanda. See Cattaraugus trip description.

*Gauges:* Streamside. A reading of 3.5 feet on a gauge painted on the Otto Road bridge provides a good high water run.

*Normal Wet Period:* No available statistics on seasons.

# Pine Creek
# (Pa. Grand Canyon)

**Ansonia to Slate Run**                                    29.1 miles

| Class | Grad | Size (Area/Volume) | Scene/Poll | Level |
|-------|------|--------------------|-----------|----------|
| II | 15/27 | Medium (604/816) | A/A | 2.0-3.5 |
| | | Cedar Run | | Cedar Run |

*Topographic Maps:* Tiadaghton, Cedar Run, Cammal,
   Slate Run, Jersey Mills

*County Maps:* Tioga, Lycoming

*Description:* The Grand Canyon of Pennsylvania contains
some of the most outstanding scenery in the state. It is a
very popular area with canoeists and is to be studied for
inclusion in the National Wild and Scenic Rivers Act. Most
canoeing is done before Memorial Day. Pine Creek is in
north central Pennsylvania, about a 5-hour drive from
Pittsburgh. There is a commercial rafting operation on this
stream. The Ansonia-Cedar Run trip should take two days.
There are many nice camping spots in the canyon. The
scenery is wild and unpopulated above Blackwell. Other
than the campgrounds at Tiadaghton, Cedar Run, Slate
Run, and Cammal, there is little intrusion by people for the
rest of the trip. This is a good 2-3 day camping trip.
[Checked 1989]

*Difficulties:* Some whitewater experience is required. The
most difficult rapids is "Barbour's Bend", 1.75 miles from
Rail Island Run. It is a left turn with a steep mountainside
on the right. Run it on the left. There are some tricky
maneuvers to be done just below Barbour's Bend at lower
water levels. "Whiskey Flip" rapids, a few miles down (in
front of Colton Point Park), is a couple of ledges on the right
side. They are easily avoided by paddling on the left. The
rest of the stream is mostly Class I rapids with long calm
pools in between.

*Shuttle:* The put-in at Ansonia is 300 yards behind the gas
station at the concrete bridge on the one-lane paved road to
Colton Point Park. For the put-in by Rail Island Run follow

this road about 1 mile and turn left onto an unmarked dirt road. The put-in is 0.75 miles down this road at a point where the road first comes alongside the creek. The dirt road continues for 5 miles and deadends in the nonexistent town of Owassee.

The shuttle to Blackwell or Cedar Run: Go back to the one-lane road into Colton Point State Park. Take the second road to the right (dirt). Take two left turns in the heads of small runs and a third in the "Slide Island Draft" run. The next side road to the left, leading to Bradley Wales State Park, should NOT be taken. Keep left at the next two intersections. At the bottom of a long grade, you meet State Route 414. Make a sharp left to Blackwell, or keep going for Cedar Run. The take-out at Cedar Run is above the bridge on the east (river left) side of the stream. The access road goes right to the water's edge. Total road mileage is about 30 miles. This is the shortest and most scenic route, but it is also dusty.

An alternate shuttle is from Ansonia, go east across Marsh Creek on US Route 6. Turn right on State Route 362 (paved). Continue to the intersection with State Route 287 outside Wellsboro. Turn south on State Route 287 to Morris, then turn west on State Route 414 to Blackwell. The road from Morris to Blackwell parallels Babb Creek, also a canoeable stream. Below Blackwell, State Route 414 parallels Pine Creek to its junction with the Susquehanna River.

An extra 16 miles of pleasant Class I-II canoeing can be had by putting in at Galeton. Put in at the State Route 144 bridge below the dam. The shuttle via State Route 6 to Ansonia.

Any number of take-outs are possible along this section.

| | |
|---|---|
| Galeton to Ansonia | 16.0 miles |
| Ansonia to Rail Island Campsite | 11.6 miles |
| Rail Island Run Camp to Blackwell | 6.0 miles |
| Blackwell to island 1.8 miles below Slate Run | 13.3 miles |
| Island below Slate Run to Jersey Mills | 9.5 miles |

*Gauges:* Cedar Run. This gauge should read between 2.0 and 3.5 feet. Call the National Weather Service for the Susquehanna Basin. See phone number in Appendix E.

*Normal Wet Period:* This section is runnable through the middle of June.

# Susquehanna River, West Branch

## Shawville to Keating                                    54 miles

| Class | Grad | Size (Area/Volume) | Scene/Poll | Level |
|-------|------|--------------------|-----------|-------|
| I | 6/12 | Large(1,462/2,447) | A/B | 2.0-?? |
|   |      | Karthaus |  | Karthaus |
|   |      | Large(2,975/4,912) Renovo |  |  |

*Topographic Maps:* LeContes Mills, Frenchville, Karthaus, Pottersdale, Snowshoe NW, Keating.

*County Maps:* Clearfield, Centre, Clinton

*Description:* The stretch from Shawville to Keating makes an excellent canoe-camping trip. It is quite attractive with little civilization showing. There is a power plant at Shawville and a dam at Clearfield not far upstream. There is some pollution due to mine drainage and heating by the Shawville power station. [Checked 1987]

*Difficulties:* One riffle that is slightly rougher than the rest is about 6 miles upstream from Karthaus, just beyond the point where the railroad on your left turns to enter a tunnel. This is called "Moshannon Falls" by local residents.

*Shuttle:* Put-in is 0.1 miles south of Shawville on State Route 0970. To get to the take-out, take State Route 0879 towards Karthaus or Keating. Go straight through the turn off to Karthaus taking State Route 1011, a Forestry Road. The State Route number changes to 2001 at the county line and also becomes Wykoff Run Road. Continue to Sinnemahoning Creek where you cross the bridge and turn right on State Route 120. Turn right on the first road which is State Route 4002. This road first crosses the Sinnemahoning Creek. Take-out is just west of Keating, 0.25 miles upstream of the junction with the Sinnemahoning Creek. A convenient intermediate access point is Karthaus (at the railroad bridge over the mouth of Mosquito Creek). It is 21 miles upstream from Keating.

*Gauges:* Karthaus. This gauge should read at least 2.0 feet. Call National Weather Service for the Susquehanna Basin. See phone number in Appendix E.

*Normal Wet Period:* No available statistics on seasons. Since this section is large, it should normally be runnable all year, but it may be too high from February to April.

# Shenandoah River

## Millville, W. Va.                                        7 miles
## to Sandy Hook, Maryland
## "The Staircase"

| Class | Grad | Size (Area/Volume) | Scene/Poll | Level |
|-------|------|--------------------|-----------|-------|
| II-III | 10/20 | Large(3,040/2,698) | A/B | 2.0-4.0 |
|        |       | Millville          |     | Millville |

*Topographic Maps:* Charles Town (WVa), Harpers Ferry
(WVa)

*County Maps:* Jefferson (WVa)

*Description:* This is a wide, majestic river in a beautiful
and historic area. This section of the Shenandoah River
separates Virginia from West Virginia until it joins the
Potomac River (which separates Virginia from Maryland)
at Harpers Ferry. The normal run starts at the power plant
above Millville and continues from the Shenandoah into the
Potomac to Sandy Hook, Maryland. The first few miles are
flat and flowing. The first rapids come as the river narrows
to the left for a right-hand bend -- about 100 yards of Class II
rapids with a course that is easy to recognize. The river
then pools up behind a river-wide shelf, Bull Falls. This is a
4-foot drop through several channels into hydraulics and
haystacks. It is usually Class III, and should be scouted the
first time. At low levels, scouting can be done from bare
rocks in the middle of the river. At low levels it is easy to
carry the boats back to try a different chute.

Bull Falls is followed by another 100-yard descent, more
difficult than the first. As the highway bridge comes into
view, you approach the fabled "Staircase" of the
Shenandoah. This is a mile-long series of river-wide ledges,
slanting diagonally across the river from right to left. At
low to medium water levels, the space between the ledges is
just about wide enough for a canoe, so a course must be
chosen very carefully. Ferry to find a passage, drop over a
ledge, ferry for the next passage, and so forth. Shortly after
the end of the Staircase, the Shenandoah flows into the
Potomac. Harpers Ferry, laden with Civil War history, is at

the top of the bluff on your left. See the description of the "Needles" section of the Potomac for information on the Potomac below Harpers Ferry. [Checked 1982]

*Difficulties:* Bull Falls should be scouted, especially in high water, and White Horse Rapids on the Potomac (see "Needles" section) deserves respect, but the greatest potential danger is an upset in high or cold water. This river is BIG, and a spill can put you in heavy water a long way from shore.

*Shuttle:* Put in at the water intake above Millville. The Sandy Hook take-out is on the left side of the Potomac just past the highway bridge. You must carry your canoes across the C & O Canal (there is a footbridge) and a railroad track to the road.

*Gauges:* Millville. This gauge should read between 2.0 and 4.0 feet. Call the National Weather Service for the Potomac River Basin. See Appendix E for the phone number. Since this section includes a section of the Potomac, the Hancock gauge should also be checked and compared to the write-up for the Potomac.

*Normal Wet Period:* No available statistics on seasons. From the size/volume of this section, one would expect it to be runnable all year. However it is only runnable through mid July because of the rock structure, which causes the water to spread evenly throughout the channel.

# Potomac River

## Low dam above Harpers Ferry                    3 miles
## to Sandy Hook "The Needles"

| Class | Grad | Size (Area/Volume) | Scene/Poll | Level |
|-------|------|--------------------|------------|-------|
| II | 14/14 | Large | A/B | 2.0-4.0 |
|  |  |  |  | Hancock |

*Topographic Maps:* Charles Town (WVa), Harpers Ferry (WVa)

*County Maps:* Jefferson (WVa), Washington (Md)

*Description:* The "Needles" is aptly named, for getting through this section of the river is like threading a needle through the shallow areas and numerous channels. Basically, the Needles is a large number of rocks and small islands that demand a great deal of maneuvering. At medium to low levels the water is not very powerful, but at high levels a spill will leave you a long way from shore and rescue. At low water levels the channels seem to go to the right through the islands, but at medium levels there is enough water for the shorter routes to the left. Since the run is so short, you have time to beach your boats at the confluence with the Shenandoah and walk up the hill to Harpers Ferry, taking a side trip for history and ice cream. About 0.5 miles below the junction with the Shenandoah you run into White Horse rapids. This is a set of good standing waves on the left side of the river. [Checked 1982]

*Difficulties:* Beware of the wreckage of bridge girders in White Horse rapids. Beware of high water. Below the junction with the Shenandoah, the Potomac is over 300 feet wide and has an average volume on the order of 5,000 cfs. This is twice as much as the Youghiogheny at Ohiopyle. At the water levels suggested here, there are pools and islands for rescue, but at higher levels a dump means a long swim and a tough boat rescue.

*Shuttle:* Use road maps to get to the pool above the dam. Put in above the dam and carry around it on the left bank. Take out at Sandy Hook, on the left side of the river just past the highway bridge. You must carry your canoes across the C & O Canal (there is a footbridge) and a railroad track to the road.

*Gauges:* Hancock. This gauge should read between 2.0 and 4.0 feet. Call the National Weather Service for the Potomac River Basin. See Appendix E for the phone number. Levels of 5.0 feet and above are dangerous. Since this stretch includes a section of the Shenandoah, the Millville gauge should also be checked and compared to the write-up on the Shenandoah.

*Normal Wet Period:* No available statistics on seasons.

# Potomac River, North Branch

## Gormania, West Virginia to Kitzmiller, Maryland                    15.0 miles

| Class | Grad | Size (Area / Volume) | Scene / Poll | Level |
|-------|------|----------------------|--------------|-------|
| IV | 47/66 | Medium (225/452) Kitzmiller | B/C | 4.0-6.0 Kitzmiller |

*Topographic Maps:* Gorman (Md), Mount Storm (WVa), Kitzmiller (Md),

*County Maps:* Garrett (Md), Grant (WVa), Mineral (WVa)

*Description:* This reliable standard is favored by whitewater enthusiasts from the Washington and Baltimore area. The run features fairly continuous Class III and IV water with numerous ledges and an infinite number of surfing possibilities. Though polluted by mine drainage, the river valley is scenic and remote for the most part. A railroad parallels the river, which serves as the boundary between Maryland and West Virginia.

About 4 miles into the run the Stony River enters from river right and the volume increases. About 0.5 miles below this point is the first of three large river-wide ledges, which should be scouted. The remainder of the run is characterized by wave trains marred by concealed souse holes. [Checked 1985]

*Difficulties:* At higher levels this river is comparable to the New (Class V). Above 6.0 feet the river is dangerous because of recirculating holes formed by the three ledges noted above. At 6.5 feet the wave trains reach a height of 8 to 10 feet, which sounds like great fun. Unfortunately there are gigantic hydraulics buried in these wave trains that could easily recirculate a boat and/or paddler for a very long time. These holes could be avoided if you knew their location, but they can not always be spotted from upstream. At high water the action is continuous and a swim could be long and unpleasant.

If the Stony River gauge is 5 feet or higher, the Kitzmiller gauge will probably be above 6 feet. Hence, any time you run the lower Stony at higher levels you may have to paddle out via the Potomac in dangerously high water. Allow time to scout and carry.

*Shuttle:* Approximately 3.5 hours from Pittsburgh. To reach the put-in take State Route 50 to Gormania, then take a dirt road on river left, 2 miles to Steyer.

An alternate put-in is on the Stony River State Route 50 bridge. Take out in Kitzmiller, or eliminate 2 miles of tedious water by driving up river left to Shallmar, Maryland.

*Gauges:* Kitzmiller. This gauge should read between 4.0 and 6.0 feet. Call the National Weather Service for the Potomac River Basin. See Appendix E for the phone number.

*Normal Wet Period:* No available statistics on seasons. Since this section is medium-sized, it should normally be runnable approximately December through May.

# Stony River

## VEPCO Dam to US Route 50          13.6 miles
## to the North Branch Potomac

| Class | Grad | Size (Area/Volume) | Scene/Poll | Level |
|-------|------|--------------------|-----------|---------|
| IV-V  | 75/150 | Small | A/B | 4.0-6.5 |
|       |        |       |     | Kitzmiller |

*Topographic Maps:* Mt. Storm Lake (WVa), Gorman
(WVa), Mount Storm (WVa)

*County Maps:* Grant (WVa)

*Description:* This little rip-snorter should be high on every
expert boater's list. It is only available in early spring or
after very heavy rains. Flow is controlled by the power
company dam. The steep gradient and small volume
combine to produce a run that is continuous Class IV
whitewater with occasional Class V sequences. The Stony
twists and turns, and eddies are few and far between. The
river can not be effectively scouted from shore because of the
dense vegetation. Decisions must be made quickly and good
boat control is a must.

Either section alone is physically demanding; together they
make a grueling run virtually without comparison. A
distance of 22 miles may be covered in one day, if one puts in
at the VEPCO Dam, runs to the junction of the Stony with
the Potomac, then continues on to Kitzmiller, Maryland.
All of it Class IV-V. The net drop in altitude is over
1000 feet! If you decide to attempt this stunt, leave one
vehicle at the bridge on US Route 50, midway through the
run, just in case you overestimated your ability or
endurance. [Checked 1985]

*Difficulties:* The stream is small and swift and there are
numerous pinning possibilities and few rescue spots. A
single log can obstruct the entire river. One could easily
chase a boat for more than a mile before recovery. The
mountainsides are covered with dense, tangled rhododendron. Hiking out would be a nightmare. This is no
place to miss a roll! There is a Class V+ rapid which should

be scouted and/or carried about 0.25 miles from the junction
with the Potomac. It occurs after the river makes a
sweeping curve to the left.

If you run the lower section, you will probably paddle out to
Kitzmiller on the Potomac at levels higher than usually
recommended. See the section on the North Branch of the
Potomac.

In summary, this is an exciting run appropriate only for
groups of experts in closed boats. Consider it an expedition
and be prepared.

*Shuttle:* For the upper section put in at the VEPCO Dam
(Mount Storm Lake). The US Route 50 bridge is midway
through the run, an alternate put-in or take-out. There is
no good take-out at the junction with the Potomac. You will
have to paddle out at least as far as Shallmar, Maryland
which is 2 miles upstream from Kitzmiller on river left.

*Gauges:* Kitzmiller. This gauge should read between 4.0
and 6.5 feet. On river left below the US Route 50 bridge. At 4
feet it is technical, shallow rock gardens. At 6.0 feet it is
very pushy. With the Stony at 5.0 feet the Kitzmiller Gauge
on the Potomac has been measured at 6.5 feet. Paddling the
Stony at levels of 5.0 feet or over will usually mean paddling
out to Kitzmiller on the Potomac at dangerously high levels.
To obtain the gauge call the National Weather Service for the
Potomac River Basin. See Appendix E for the phone
number.

*Normal Wet Period:* No available statistics on seasons.
Since this section is medium-sized, it should normally be
runnable approximately December through May.

# Rivers of West Virginia

West Virginia contains many excellent rivers, not part of the Monongahela watershed, that are routinely run by Western Pennsylvania paddlers. These streams are described in *Wild Water West Virginia* by Davidson, Eister and Davidson. To describe them here would entail a tremendous duplication of resources, as well as exceed the intended range of this guide. The following snippets are intended to provide just a sampling of the selections available. Read Davidson, Eister and Davidson, grab your paddle, and enjoy!

### Bluestone      Class II-IV      25 miles

A spectacular narrow gorge with 200 foot cliffside waterfalls provides the scenery for more than 20 miles of continuous tumbling fun.

### Cranberry      Class III-V      13 miles

Very little, very steep, and very busy.

### Gauley (upper)  Class IV-V      16 miles

From Summerville Dam to Peters Creek this river is big, long, inaccessible, tough, dangerous, and intoxicating. All this within a steep-walled canyon.

### Gauley (lower)  Class III-V      8 miles

From Peters Creek to Swiss this river is less strenuous than the upper, but still challenging, heavy-duty whitewater.

### Greenbriar      Class I-II      43 miles

From Durbin to Cass to Marlinton is a delightful open canoe camping trip.

### Meadow (upper)  Class II-V      15 miles

There is 8 miles of flatwater followed by THE Rapids, 4 miles of unrelenting action.

### Meadow (middle) Class III-IV    5 miles

Busy run in a beautiful canyon with an easy shuttle. Resembles the Mile on the Slippery Rock Creek in Pennsylvania.

### Meadow (lower)  Class V-VI    5 miles

Super-difficult and super-dangerous with scouting and carrying often the main activities.

### New (Bluestone to Sandstone)  Class II-III    11 miles

Broad valley with wide open rapids, but watch for 6-foot Brooks Falls and 20-foot Sandstone Falls.

### New (Sandstone to Thurmond)  Class II-III    30 miles

Scenic valley, open rapids, widely spaced by pools, excellent fishing and many campsites.

### New (Gorge)    Class III-V    14 miles

The biggest whitewater in West Virginia. A powerful river with long, but open rapids and with 6-foot to 8-foot waves a dime a dozen.

### New (Dries)    Class III-IV    6 miles

This normally dry river bed (due to the water being diverted for power plant cooling) becomes an exciting run when the New's flow exceeds 10,000 cfs.

### Potomac (Main stem)    Class C-II    115 miles

Beautiful, historic, West Virginia-Maryland border. A huge river, mostly flat and flowing with widely spaced easy rapids suitable for floating and camping. At high levels very powerful and dangerous.

### Savage (in Maryland)    Class III-IV    5.5 miles

Small but fierce. Might be considered as one very very long rapid.

# Appendix A
# Western Pennsylvania Boating Lakes

Pennsylvania offers many opportunities for flatwater canoeing on lakes. This appendix lists public lakes in State Parks, Corps of Engineers projects, and other areas operated by the Department of Environmental Resources and the Fish Commission.

## Key:

*Area:*     Summer pool area is given for Corps of Engineers lakes; maximum pool area is much larger.

*Launch Ramp:*
| | |
|---|---|
| y | Launch ramp |
| ds | Canoe launch area downstream of dam only |

*Agent:*
| | |
|---|---|
| ANF | Allegheny National Forest |
| COE | US Army Corps of Engineers, with specific facilities operated by licensees and concessionaires |
| DER | Pa Department of Environmental Resources |
| PFC | Pa Fish Commission |

*Max HP:*
| | |
|---|---|
| Elec | Electric motors only |
| UNL | Unlimited horsepower, at least in some sections |
| 6 | Limited to 6-hp motors |
| 10 | Limited to 10-hp motors |

*Permit:*
| | |
|---|---|
| none | No permit requirement known |
| ovrnt | Overnight mooring permitted with permit |
| SP | Pennsylvania State Park Launch Permit |

*Camping:*
| | |
|---|---|
| y | Camping available |
| n | No camping available |

*Page no:*  Page reference number if additional description is available with river description

| Lake | State Park | Agent | Area acres | Launch Ramp | Max HP | Per-mit | Camp-ing | Page no |
|---|---|---|---|---|---|---|---|---|
| **Allegheny County** | | | | | | | | |
| **Armstrong County** | | | | | | | | |
| Crooked Creek | | COE | 350 | y | UNL | | y | 205 |
| Keystone Reservoir | | PFC | 950 | y | Elec | none | n | |
| Mahoning Creek | | COE | 280 | y | 10 | | y | 215 |
| **Beaver County** | | | | | | | | |
| Hereford Manor | | PFC | 32&47[1] | y | Elec | | n | |
| Raccoon Creek | Raccoon | DER | 101 | y | Elec | SP | y | |
| **Butler County** | | | | | | | | |
| Glade Run | | PFC | 400 | y | Elec | ovrnt | n | |
| Lake Arthur | Moraine | DER | 3,225 | y | 10 | SP | | |
| **Cambria County** | | | | | | | | |
| Duman Dam | | PFC | 20 | y | Elec | ovrnt | n | |
| Glendale | Prince Gallitzin | DER | 1,640 | y | 6 | SP | y | |
| **Centre County** | | | | | | | | |
| Blanchard Res. | Bald Eagle | DER | 1,730 | y | UNL | SP | y | |
| Black Moshannon | Black Moshannon | DER | 250 | y | Elec | SP | y | |
| Colyer | | PFC | 77 | y | Elec | | n | |
| Poe Valley | Poe Valley | DER | 25 | y | Elec | ovrnt | y | |

[1] Hereford Manor contains two separate lakes.

| Lake | State Park | Agent | Area acres | Launch Ramp | Max HP | Permit | Camping | Page no |
|---|---|---|---|---|---|---|---|---|
| **Clarion County** | | | | | | | | |
| Kahle | See Venango County | | | | | | | |
| **Clearfield County** | | | | | | | | |
| Curwensville Res. | Curwensville | DER | 790 | y | UNL | SP | | |
| Parker Dam | Parker Dam | DER | 20 | y | Elec | SP | y | |
| **Crawford County** | | | | | | | | |
| Drake's Mill Dam | | PFC | 53 | y | | none | n | |
| Pymatuning | Pymatuning | DER | 14,500 | y | 10 | SP | y | |
| Tamarack | | PFC | 562 | y | Elec | ovrnt | n | |
| Woodcock Creek | | COE | 333 | y | 10 | | y | |
| **Elk County** | | | | | | | | |
| E. Br. Clarion Res. | Elk | DER | 1,160 | y | UNL | SP | y | |
| **Erie County** | | | | | | | | |
| Eaton Reservoir | | PFC | 246 | y | Elec | none | n | |
| Erie | Presque Isle | DER | huge | y | UNL | SP | | 390 |
| Union City Res. | | COE | dry[1] | n | | | n | 262 |

[1] Union City Reservoir is the only dry-bed reservoir in the Pittsburgh District. The normal flows pass unimpeded so that it has no pool area.

| Lake | State Park | Agent | Area acres | Launch Ramp | Max HP | Per- mit | Camp- ing | Page no |
|---|---|---|---|---|---|---|---|---|
| **Fayette County** | | | | | | | | |
| Dunlap Creek Res. | | PFC | 8 | | | | | |
| Greenlick Reservoir | | PFC | 100 | | | | | |
| Virgin Run | | PFC | 35 | y | no power | | | |
| Youghiogheny River | | COE | 2,840 | y | UNL | | y | 307 |
| **Forest County** | | | | | | | | |
| Tionesta | | COE | 480 | y | UNL | | y | 284 |
| **Greene County** | | | | | | | | |
| Ryerson | Ryerson Station | DER | 64 | y | Elec | SP | y | |
| **Indiana County** | | | | | | | | |
| Conemaugh | See Westmoreland County | | | | | | | |
| Hemlock | | PFC | 59 | y | Elec | | n | |
| Mahoning Creek | See Armstrong County | | | | | | | |
| Yellow Creek | Yellow Creek | DER | 720 | y | 10 | SP | n | |
| **Jefferson County** | | | | | | | | |
| Cloe Reservoir | | PFC | 29 | y | Elec | ovrnt | n | |
| Kyle Reservoir | | PFC | 155 | y | Elec | ovrnt | n | |
| Mahoning Creek | See Armstrong County | | | | | | | |
| **Lawrence County** | | | | | | | | |
| Bessemer | | PFC | 28 | y | Elec | | n | |

| Lake | State Park | Agent | Area acres | Launch Ramp | Max HP | Per-mit | Camp-ing | Page no |
|---|---|---|---|---|---|---|---|---|
| **Mercer County** | | | | | | | | |
| Lake Wilhelm | Maurice Goddard | DER | 1,440 | y | 10 | SP | n | |
| Shenango | | COE | 3,560 | y | UNL | y | y | |
| **Portage County (Ohio)** | | | | | | | | |
| Berlin | | COE | 3,590 | y | UNL | | y | |
| Michael J. Kirwan | | COE | 2,650 | y | UNL | | y | |
| **Somerset County** | | | | | | | | |
| Cranberry Glade | | PFC | 112 | y | Elec | ovrnt | n | |
| High Point | | PFC | 342 | y | Elec | ovrnt | n | |
| Laurel | Laurel Hill | DER | 65 | y | Elec | SP | y | |
| Somerset | | PFC | 253 | y | Elec | ovrnt | n | |
| Youghiogheny River | See Fayette County | | | | | | | |
| **Taylor County (WVa)** | | | | | | | | |
| Tygart River | | COE | 1,750 | y | UNL | | y | |
| **Trumbull County (Ohio)** | | | | | | | | |
| Mosquito Creek | | COE | 7,850 | y | UNL | | y | |
| **Venango County** | | | | | | | | |
| Kahle | | PFC | 150 | y | Elec | | n | |
| **Warren County** | | | | | | | | |
| Chapman | Chapman | DER | 68 | y | Elec | SP | y | |
| Allegheny Res (Kinzua Dam) | | ANF | 12,080 | y | UNL | | y | 141 |

| Lake | State Park | Agent | Area acres | Launch Ramp | Max HP | Per-mit | Camp-ing | Page no |
|------|-----------|-------|-----------|-------------|--------|---------|----------|---------|
| **Washington County** | | | | | | | | |
| Canonsburg | | PFC | 75 | y | Elec | ovrnt | n | |
| Dutch Fork | | PFC | 91 | y | Elec | ovrnt | n | |
| **Westmoreland County** | | | | | | | | |
| Conemaugh | | COE | 500 | ds | | | | 168 |
| Donegal | | PFC | 90 | y | Elec | ovrnt | n | |
| Keystone | Keystone | DER | 78 | y | Elec | SP | y | |
| Loyalhanna | | COE | 400 | y | UNL | | y | |

# Appendix B
# Canoeing Associations

The American Canoe Association (ACA) is the major national organization that supports canoeing. The annual dues to this association are $20.00/year (1990). For information write to American Canoe Association, PO Box 1190, Newington, Virginia 22122. (703) 550-7495.

The American Whitewater Affiliation (AWA) is for canoeists interested in white-water canoeing. Dues include a bimonthly magazine with articles on trips, races, techniques, equipment, etc. For a membership application, write AWA, PO Box 85, Phoenicia, New York 12464. (914) 688-5569.

The United States Canoe Association newsletter is of interest to canoeists interested in racing and in cruising. Individual memberships are $4.00/year. Most of the membership is currently in the Midwest. Send for information from E. H. Wahl, 1818 Kensington Blvd., Fort Wayne, Indiana 46805.

The American Rivers Conservation Council supports the preservation of free flowing rivers. Their primary activity is lobbying Congress. They publish a citizens guide to the National Wild and Scenic Rivers System, and a quarterly newsletter. Send donations to American Rivers Conservation Council, 323 Pennsylvania Avenue, S.E., Washington DC 20003.

# Appendix C
# Local Canoeing Groups and Schools

American Youth Hostels, Pittsburgh Council runs a training program all summer. One-day paddling schools are offered for beginners and intermediates in both canoes and kayaks. Contact AYH for details and schedules (412) 362-8181, on Thursday evenings only. AYH meets every Thursday evening at 8:30 in the Pittsburgh Council Headquarters located behind the Pittsburgh Center for the Arts at the corner of 5th Avenue and Shady Avenue, 6300 Fifth Avenue, Pittsburgh, Pennsylvania 15232.

The Three Rivers Paddling Club provides two weekend training clinics per year for members. A clinic is held in June on Slippery Rock Creek, with the summer clinic being held on the Youghiogheny at Ohiopyle. Both clinics offer instruction for canoes and kayaks from beginner to advanced levels. TRPC meets on the 2nd Tuesday of each month at 7:30 PM at the Pittsburgh Garden Center behind the Pittsburgh Center for the Arts at the corner of 5th Avenue and Shady Avenue. For membership information write Three Rivers Paddling Club, 304 Hilltop Drive, Lower Burrell, Pennsylvania 15068. (412) 335-8324.

Sylvan Canoe Club is a private, family-oriented canoe club founded in 1904. The club is located on the Allegheny River. Canoes, small sailboats and rowing shells can be launched from the concrete ramp and large wooden floating dock. The four-acre scenic grounds and large two-story building provide a pleasant place to relax. The building includes rest rooms, large dining area, and ground level storage for 80 canoes and kayaks. Membership at $220 annually is limited and there is generally a waiting list. Contact Sylvan Canoe Club, 132 Arch Street, Verona, Pennsylvania 15147.

The Pittsburgh Chapter of the American Red Cross, (412) 263-3100, conducts classes in flat-water canoeing and in sail canoeing for groups of reasonable size at their camp on the northwest end of Pymatuning Lake from late spring through early fall. Instruction and use of camping facilities are free.

The following list of potential contacts and canoe clubs was current as of January 1989. Some are very active clubs with a large membership and facilities, other are just a group of people who meet to go canoeing or other outdoor activities. Please let the editors know of your experience.

| | | |
|---|---|---|
| Allegheny Canoe Club | 755 W Spring Street | Titusville,Pa 16354 |
| Bens Creek Canoe Club | PO Box 2 | Johnstown,Pa 15907 |
| Doug Gibson | RD #2 PO Box 266 | Pittsfield, Pa 16340 |
| Explorer Post 65 | 22 Caralpa Place | Pittsburgh, Pa 15228 |
| Fort Pitt Paddlers | 1401 Maple Dr, Apt #8 | Pittsburgh, Pa 15227 |
| Fox Chapel Canoe Club | 610 Squaw Run Road | Pittsburgh, Pa 15238 |
| IUP Outing Club | Indiana Univ | Indiana, Pa 15701 |
| Keystone River Runners | RD #6, Box 359 | Indiana, Pa 15701 |
| Oil City Canoe Club | Route 62, Road 2 | Oil City, Pa 16301 |
| Penn Hills Whitewater | 12200 Garland Dr | Pittsburgh, Pa 15235 |
| Raystown Canoe Club | Box 112 | Everett, Pa 15537 |
| Outing Club | Slippery Rock Univ | Slippery Rock,Pa 16057 |
| Sylvan Canoe Club | 132 Arch Street | Verona, Pa 15147 |
| W Pa Paddle Sport | Box 8857 | Pittsburgh, Pa 15221 |

# Appendix D
# Sources of River Information

When this guide was first developed, sources of information about specific river runs were scarce and highly informal. In more recent years, many guides have reached formal publication. Coverage has increased, and multiple guides in different styles are available in some areas.

This guide covers the portions of Western Pennsylvania and northern West Virginia in which streams flow toward the Ohio River or Lake Erie. A few favorite streams just outside this area are included, and coverage is lighter in the southern portion of the Cheat River basin.

## Western Pennsylvania Canoeing

The US Army Corps of Engineers controls several major rivers and lakes in the Corps' Pittsburgh District. They supply free maps of their major lakes (Berlin, Conemaugh River, Crooked Creek, East Branch Clarion River, Loyalhanna, Mahoning Creek, Michael J. Kirwan, Shenango River, Tygart, Union City, Woodcock Creek, and Youghiogheny River), free pamphlets about the locks and dams on the major rivers, and (not free, but $6.00 each) detailed navigation maps of the Ohio, Allegheny, and Monongahela Rivers. Order from:

US Army Engineer District, Pittsburgh
Corps of Engineers
Federal Building
1000 Liberty Avenue
Pittsburgh, Pennsylvania 15222

The Western Pennsylvania Conservancy provides maps with lists of access sites for the Allegheny and Clarion rivers. They also have narrative trip write-ups for several other area canoe trips  Single copies are free to Conservancy members. Contact:

Western Pennsylvania Conservancy
316 Fourth Avenue
Pittsburgh, Pennsylvania 15222

# Canoeing in the Surrounding Areas

The Pennsylvania Fish Commission publishes wall charts, pamphlets, and books. Although most of their material is directed at fisherfolk and power boaters, some is pertinent to canoeing. These include pamphlets on canoe safety and PFDs and a booklet called *Paddle Pennsylvania*. The latter includes write-ups on sections of eight of the rivers included in this guide. A list and order form are available from:

> Pennsylvania Fish Commission
> Publications Section, PO Box 1673
> Harrisburg, Pennsylvania  17105-1673

A new edition of the Penn State Outing Club's guide to rivers of Central Pennsylvania is scheduled to appear in 1989. Contact:

> Stream Guide
> Penn State Outing Club
> 4 Intramural Building
> University Park, Pennsylvania  16802

Eastern and Central Pennsylvania streams are covered by Ed Gertler's *Keystone Canoeing - A guide to Eastern Pennsylvania* published by Seneca Press, 530 Ashford Road, Silver Springs, Maryland.

West Virginia streams are covered in *Wildwater West Virginia*, by Davidson, Eister, and Davidson in two volumes. *Volume I -- The Northern Streams* covers northern West Virginia, including the Cheat and Potomac basins. *Volume II -- The Southern Streams* covers southern West Virginia, including the New, Gauley, and Greenbriar basins. These are published by Menasha Press, PO Box 59257, Birmingham, Alabama.

Maryland streams are well covered in a new (1989) edition of Ed Gertler's *Maryland and Delaware Canoe Trails - A Paddlers Guide to Rivers of the Oldline and First State*, published by Seneca Press, 530 Ashford Road, Silver Springs, Maryland.

Virginia streams are covered by *Virginia Whitewater*, by H Roger Corbett, published in 1988 by Seneca Press, 530 Ashford Road, Silver Springs, Maryland.

Ohio streams are covered by the *Canoeing Guide to Streams of Ohio* by Combs and Gillion in two volumes (North and South). These volumes were out of print in the spring of 1989 and the editors have received mixed reports on the progress of the revisions.

A number of guidebooks cover several (sometimes many) states but include only a few of the most popular rivers in each region. A good example of this sort of guide is *Appalachian Whitewater*, in three volumes. *Volume II -- the Central Mountains*, by Grove, Kirby, Walbridge, Eister, Davidson, and Davidson, covers Virginia, West Virginia, Delaware, Maryland, and Pennsylvania. Coverage in Western Pennsylvania includes portions of the Youghiogheny, Slippery Rock, Dark Shade, Shade, Stony, and Pine Creek (Tioga Co).

## Safety

*River Rescue* by Les Bechdel and Slim Ray covers rescue techniques that are useful to all canoeists as well as some procedures that require special equipment and/or might be necessary in only extreme circumstances. It is published by Appalachian Mountain Club, Boston, Massachusetts.

## Maps

The best detailed maps are topographic maps. The standard US Geological Survey 7.5 minute maps cover an area of about 10 by 20 miles at a scale of 1:24,000. The USGS now also offers county maps created from mosaics of the 7.5 minute maps, reduced to a scale of 1:50,000. Some counties take two maps. Both 7.5 minute quads and county maps are available at local map shops or quality book stores. The Hillman Library at the University of Pittsburgh has a complete set of topographic maps, and a copy machine. These maps can be obtained by mail from Distribution Section, US Geological Survey, 1200 South Eads Street, Arlington, Virginia  22202. Each 7.5 minute map costs $2.50, each county map $4.00 (Winter 1990). A 50 percent discount is available on orders of $500 or more. Since it typically takes 10 to 15 of the 7.5 minute maps to cover a county, the modest loss of detail is offset by the substantial price saving on the county map. An index map for each state is available free. These maps are particularly useful for locating back roads for put-ins and take-outs. They should be considered essential on any trip where the possibility of having to walk out exists. Bear in mind, that these maps are not revised very often and roads may have been created and/or destroyed since the last map revision. If you have never really used topographic maps before, be sure and request the two free booklets. *Topographic Map Symbols,* and *Topographic Maps: Silent Guides for Outdoorsman.*

The local county road maps are another good map set of maps to have. These are generally available free at the local courthouse. A booklet of county road maps is available for $11.90 (Winter 1988) from County Maps, Puetz Place, Lyndon Station, Wisconsin 53944. Order the *Pennsylvania County Maps.*

A book of reduced size topographic maps called *Pennsylvania Atlas and Gazetteer* is published by DeLorome Mapping Company, PO Box 298, Freeport Maine 04032. It is also available at many outdoor stores. Note that the State Route numbers in the second edition of this booklet have the old numbers. The third edition (1990) has been updated to match the road signs.

Maps of the lakes maintained by the Army Corps of Engineers are available from the Pittsburgh District Office, Federal Building, Pittsburgh, Pa 15222. Maps of lakes controlled by the Pennsylvania Fish Commission are available from them at PO Box 1673, Harrisburg, Pa 17120. The maps show the lake area, surrounding highways and local roads, and developed recreation sites, such as launching sites, and picnic areas.

Maps of wildlife refuges under federal protection are available form the Fish and Wildlife Service, Division of Wildlife Refuges, Department of the Interior, Room 2343, Washington DC 20204. In the United States there are over 400 wildlife refuges and more than 10,000 wetland areas

State Park maps are available at park headquarters, or at some of the bulletin boards on the park grounds.

# Magazines

The following magazines are those that the editors know about.   We suggest you check your local newsstand or library to see if they are of interest to you.

*Canoe*   published 12 times per year for $30.00.   Order from *Canoe* Magazine PO Box 10748, Des Moines, Iowa 50349.

*Canoe Sport Journal*   published 6 times a year for $15.00. Order from The Tanis Group, PO Box 697, Fallbrook, California 92028.

*River Runner*   published 6 times a year for $15.00. Order from The Tanis Group, PO Box 697, Fallbrook, California 92028.

## Other Facets of Pennsylvania Rivers

A narrative history of the Youghiogheny river, *Youghiogheny: Appalachian River*, by Tim Palmer is published by the University of Pittsburgh Press and is available in many bookstores.

A history of canal development in Pennsylvania, *The Amazing Pennsylvania Canals*, was written by William H. Shank and published by the American Canal and Transportation Center, York, Pennsylvania

A history of the Sandy-Beaver Canal, along with other information about the early and mid 1800s can be found in *The Sandy and Beaver Canal* by R. Max Gard and William H. Vodery, Jr. and published by East Liverpool Historical Society, East Liverpool, Ohio.

A survey of Pennsylvania's covered bridges has been published as *The Covered Bridges of Pennsylvania: A Guide* by Susan M. Zacher published by the Pennsylvania Historical and Museum Commission.   Pennsylvania is noted for its covered bridges, and a canoe is the best way to visit some of them.

Effects of changing water level at the former Ohiopyle gauge on the Youghiogheny River ( downstream side of pier on former bridge). The upper picture was at normal levels (3 feet on the Confluence gauge), the lower picture at near-flood level (over 10 feet on the Confluence gauge). Note the increased turbulence and the bridge pier's resistance to the water flow in the lower picture.

# Appendix E
# Sources of Gauge Information

## Western Pennsylvania

NOAA Weather Radio, which broadcasts weather information 24 hours a day, also broadcasts river gauge information between the hours of 9:00 AM and 1:30 PM. This report includes the same list of gauges that is available from the Weather Bureau telephone recording (see next source). The whitewater gauges alternate with the major river gauges on about a 5 minute cycle. A radio which gets just the weather frequencies costs about $15 and is also useful for getting current weather reports. Pittsburgh cable TV also carries this station on one of its channels.

Weather Bureau and River Forecast, Federal Building, Pittsburgh, Pennsylvania 15222. Telephone (412) 644-2890. From about noon, through the night, till about 7:30 AM, gauge readings are given by a tape recording.

US Army Corps of Engineers, Pittsburgh District Office, 2129 Federal Building, Pittsburgh, Pennsylvania 15222. Open 8:00 AM to 4:30 PM weekdays, Saturday and Sunday until noon. (412) 644-6847. Territory includes all water flowing past New Martinsville, West Virginia via the Ohio River. A number of gauges are now transmitting their information via satellite every four hours. The most recent reading can be obtained by calling the above number.

US Geological Survey, Pittsburgh Office, 1917 Federal Building, Pittsburgh, Pennsylvania, 15222. Open 7:30 AM to 4:00 PM weekdays, Telephone (412) 644-2865. Their territory includes the portions of the Ohio River and Lake Erie watersheds within Pennsylvania.

Several streamside gauges can be called directly. Some voice their data while other give the water depth in a coded form. These gauges operate 24-hours a day. Most of them are battery powered and are used by local emergency personnel as well as the Corps of Engineers. If calls from canoeists interfere with access by the intended users, the phone numbers will be changed. If you come across one of these phone numbers, please be circumspect about using it.

When a coded gauge answers, the first extended beep is an alert signal. The second beep series is water depth in feet, the third series is tenths of feet, and the fourth and final series is hundreds of feet. There can be up to nine beeps in each series or an extended beep for zero.

## West Virginia and Potomac Basin

US Army Corps of Engineers, PO Box 1715, Baltimore, Maryland 21203. Territory includes the Potomac River System. They have a recording for discharges from the Savage River Dam and Bloomington Dam (Randolph Lake) on the North Branch of the Potomac River. (301) 962-7687

A recording of levels in the Potomac and Rapahannock River Basins, including also some levels in the Cheat and Youghiogheny basins, is available 24 hours a day at (202) 899-7378.

US Geological Survey, 3303 New Federal Building, Charleston, West Virginia, 25301. Telephone (304) 343-6181, ext 310 or 311. Territory includes the New River and most of the rest of West Virginia (including the North Fork of the South Branch of the Potomac).

For the North Fork of the South Branch of the Potomac call Elkins, West Virginia (304) 636-1538 for the gauge 16 miles west of Petersburg.

## Central and Eastern Pennsylvania

In Central Pennsylvania the River Forecast Service gives gauges for the Susquehanna River Basin call (717) 234-6812; in the evening this provides a recording of water levels in the Susquehanna Basin, including Pine Creek (Grand Canyon of Pennsylvania).

U.S. Geological Survey, Water Resource Division, Federal Building, PO Box 1107, Harrisburg, Pennsylvania 17108.

# Appendix F
# Gauge Readings and Water Levels

The amount of water in a river has a major effect on the success of your canoe trip. At low runnable levels you may have to maneuver quite precisely to avoid rocks. This can be a lot of fun, but you'll be busier than on a float trip. Medium levels are often easiest, with enough water to cover the rocks but not so much as to be pushy. High runnable levels offer stronger current and bigger waves.

However, rivers are not always runnable. If you attempt to run a river that is too low, you may wind up wading or scraping for yards or even miles. At the other extreme, your trip on a river that is too high may turn into a frantic chase after floating people and equipment or even into a salvage operation. Furthermore, a river that is much too high can be dangerous because of high waves, debris, and shoreline hazards. The introduction illustrates this at two locations near Ohiopyle at low and very high water levels.

To help you decide whether the river you want to run is at a suitable level, this guide suggests good water levels or good seasons for running each of the trips.

This appendix explains how to get the information you need about river levels and how to interpret the information once you have it. We begin with ways to avoid thinking about gauge readings. Next we describe gauges useful to canoeists, factors that affect water levels, and the kinds of water level information we provide. This leads to strategies for using this information to select a river. Finally we give some nitty-gritty details about the sources of information used in preparing this guide and precise meanings of phases used to described water levels.

## What Do You Really Need to Know about Water Levels?

You don't actually have to know anything about water levels and gauges to have a lot of fun canoeing. You can, for example, run the Youghiogheny every weekend; it's virtually never too low, and if it's too high someone will probably let you know. Alternatively, you can arrange your trip with an outfitter; the outfitter probably specializes in a few rivers in one region and knows which ones make the best trips at any given time. Another option is to join a canoe club and let the leader decide--but when you become a leader, you'll need to select the river.

Even though you can paddle happily for years without paying any attention to river levels, learning a little about gauges and levels will pay off. You'll have more variety, and perhaps even more fun, if you learn a little about how rivers behave and what the weather, the season, the gauge readings, and the river itself are telling you about conditions on any particular day.

The easiest way to use water levels in your selection of rivers is to compare gauge readings from the sources listed in Appendix E to the levels recommended in the river write-ups. The most convenient sources of gauge readings are the 24-hour recorded messages. The first time you call a gauge recording, the readings will seem to go by quickly, but with a little practice you'll be able to pick out the information you need. For gauge readings not available on a recording, you can call one of the other sources. Select the gauges you need before you call and be prepared to ask, for example, "May I have today's gauge readings for Markleton on the Casselman and Confluence on the Youghiogheny, please?" If you are offered a choice of "flow" and "stage" readings, ask for "stage" (the stage is the gauge height, or level). The folks who supply gauge readings are expert hydrologists, but few of them paddle. They are very helpful with basic gauge information, but it isn't reasonable to ask them to interpret the information specifically for canoeing.

Another useful source of information is the river itself. When you arrive at the river bank, check to see whether the water appears to be out of its normal channel, unusually swift, or full of debris. Also, check the stream write-up to see if it mentions a "streamside" gauge. These gauges are usually references to physical features at the put-in or take-out such as large boulders, scales painted on bridges, or the number of bricks above waterline at a particular place. If you run the same rivers frequently, get familiar with the way they look at the put-in and take-out, then ask yourself each trip whether anything looks unusual.

## Determining Water Levels

Suppose, though, that you want to lead canoe trips or run some rivers other than the few most popular ones. You'll need to get accurate information or make educated guesses about water levels in order to decide whether the river you have in mind is at a runnable level the day you decide to go. When gauges are available, their readings provide good indicators of current water levels. Write-ups on individual rivers tell you what information you need, and Appendix E tells you where to get it.

Canoeists use both formal and informal gauges. Formal gauges are installed by organizations such as the US Geological Survey, the Corps of Engineers, or a hydroelectric company. Informal gauges may be marks on bridge piers or references to physical features at the river. The information you want from a gauge is the amount of water flowing in the river, but this is expressed in different ways by different gauges. We'll consider formal and informal gauges separately.

### *Formal gauges*

The National Weather Service, the Corps of Engineers, the US Geological Survey, and various hydroelectric companies maintain gauges for purposes such as water level prediction, water quality determination, and historical records. The National Weather Service uses this and other data for flood prediction. In the past, data for most of the gauges was collected only weekly or monthly. Over the past few years the Corps of Engineers, which regulates outflow from reservoirs, has developed a system for satellite reporting from the gauges. They now receive reports from over 100 gauges every few hours. As a result, timely information from many more locations than ever before is now available to the paddling community. The Geological Survey archives the data for historical purposes, producing an annual report with full records from the major gauges. This makes it possible to determine historical patterns of water levels and to get levels for particular dates in the past. This information is important for establishing the runnable levels reported in this guide.

A gauge reading tells you how high the river is. The reading is usually expressed as the gauge height in feet, or the height of the water surface above an arbitrary reference point. This is called the *stage* or *level*. The level is an indirect indicator of the amount of water flowing in the river, which is usually expressed in cubic feet per second (cfs). The relation between the level and the flow depends on the shape of the river bottom at the gauge and the speed of the water. This isn't a simple relation; it is determined for each river and expressed as a *stage-discharge relation*, also called a *rating chart* or *rating table*.

For example, Figure F-1 gives the rating charts for several gauges in the Beaver River basin at levels from 1.0 to 7.0 feet.

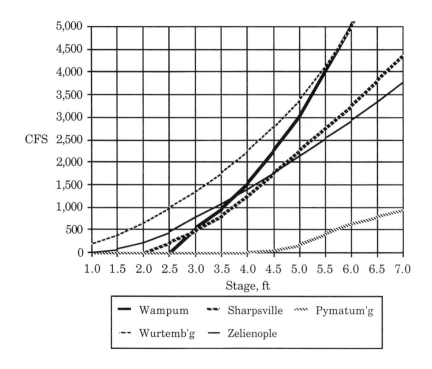

Figure F-1: Rating charts for Beaver River Basin

The actual ratings continue up into flood levels but should be of little interest to the canoeist. The curves have different shapes because these rivers have different bottom profiles and gradients at the gauges. In addition, the minimum runnable levels differ. The streams become runnable with different volumes of water because their river beds accommodate different normal flows.

This particular group of gauges illustrates the general rule that the zero point on a gauge is arbitrary: Pymatuning, which has the smallest volume, has the highest gauge reading for the minimum runnable level. Runnable levels for these streams are:

| River | Gauge | Minimum Level | Minimum CFS |
|---|---|---|---|
| Beaver R | Wampum | 3.5 | 980 |
| Shenango R | Sharpsville | 2.6 | 280 |
| Shenango R | Pymatuning Outflow | 4.6 | 66 |
| Slippery Rock Ck | Wurtemburg | 1.0-1.5 | 185-375 |
| Connoquenessing Ck | Zelienople | 1.6 | 1155 |

If the river at the gauge is much wider than it is over most of the trip, a small rise in the level at the gauge can translate to a large increase in level, turbulence, and difficulty in the rapids. Conversely, if the gauge is at a narrow location the character of the river will be relatively insensitive to small changes in gauge reading. For example, Slippery Rock Creek near McConnells Mill gauge is 50 to 75 feet wide; however, some of the rapids within the next mile downstream have passages no more than 15 to 20 feet wide. Two or three inches more water at the mill can raise the level in the Triple Drop by most of a foot.

The write-up of each stream for which we have formal gauge information gives runnable levels and the corresponding flows. In addition, abbreviated rating tables for several of our most popular streams are given at the end of this appendix.

### Informal gauges

Not all canoeable streams have formal gauges. Even when they do, formal gauges often cannot be read at the river. As a result, we have tried to identify informal ways to determine whether a stream is at a runnable level.

Some formal gauges have outside scales that can be read on site. Other rivers have gauges painted on retaining walls or bridge piers. They are usually, but not always, calibrated in feet. For example, Stony Creek is gauged by a scale (marked in feet) painted on the center pier of the State Route 403 bridge in Hollsopple. Similarly, a painted gauge on the Beaver Grade Road bridge provides information for Montour Run. On the other hand, the gauge at Van on East Sandy Creek has marks about 4 inches apart with Roman numerals V and X labelling the fifth and tenth marks (it's runnable above the third mark, or "III"). Painted gauges such as these are sometimes called "Carter gauges" after the informal gauges established in Virginia by Randy Carter in the 1960s. Although Carter's gauges were calibrated so that a reading of zero corresponded to the minimum canoeable level, that custom has, regrettably, failed to reach western Pennsylvania.

Another convenient kind of reference is often provided by a bridge pier or retaining wall constructed from brick or stone. These structures can be used as gauges by counting the number of rows of bricks or stones showing *above* the waterline. For example, the Casselman River's minimum level of 2.0 ft at Markleton corresponds to about "11 bricks" on the right pier of the Ft Hill bridge; the high level of 3.5 ft at Markleton corresponds to about "3 bricks" at Ft Hill. A formal gauge is not available for Cowanshannock Creek, but the write-up recommends 5.5 to 4.5 blocks at the State Route 85 bridge. Similarly, the lower section of Sandy Creek is runnable with 8 blocks showing and "real fun" with 7.5 to 5.5 blocks showing on the State Route 965 bridge abutment. Note that when a gauge is expressed as "6 bricks" or "4 blocks", *smaller* numbers correspond to *higher* water--as the water rises it covers more bricks and decreases the number that remain showing.

Sometimes a particular section of a stream that's visible from the road gives a good indication of overall conditions. Also, prominent objects near the waterline can also be used as gauges. Here are some of the physical references used as gauges in this guide:

- On Sandy Lick Creek, the riffle at Brookville (the take-out) is one of the shallowest spots on the run; if this is passable you have enough water.

- The upper section of Turtle Creek is runnable when a drainpipe near a particular bridge is partly under water.

- One section of Buffalo Creek in Washington County is runnable when you can paddle over a certain low-water bridge.

- The "Connie's Challenge" section of Connoquenessing Creek is high for open boats when the rock in the middle of Calgon ledge is under water.

When you run a river, pay attention to how it looks at the put-in and the take-out. Look carefully at permanent objects near the waterline. Then you'll have a reference for future trips. Some of these references simply can't be described in writing: there is a tree root at the put-in for Buffalo Creek (Armstrong County) that the editors use as a gauge but have never managed to identify to anyone else except by standing on the bank and pointing at it.

In addition to checking the level of the water, check the overall condition of the river. Look at the color of the water (chocolate brown water is often high, clear water is often low). Observe the relation of the vegetation line to the water line (vegetation under water often means the stream is high, while an expanse of rocks along the shoreline sometimes means it's low). Look at vegetation near the water line; if the water has recently been higher, grass and weeds may be flattened toward downstream. Soon you'll be able to say with confidence, "It looks high today," or, "It has been high, but it's falling." These rules are not infallible. For example, the Youghiogheny at Confluence is just downstream from the Youghiogheny Lake dam. Water released from the dam is usually clear, so the water at Confluence can be both quite high and quite clear.

## Factors that Affect Water Levels

You are not always fortunate enough to have a gauge on the river you are interested in. Even then, gauge readings from nearby rivers can provide a general picture of water levels in the area. Further, if you are trying to predict conditions a few days in advance certain generalizations can help you make educated guesses even if specific gauge information or runnable levels are not available.

Water levels are affected by seasons, weather, terrain, and human uses. The combination of these cause tremendous fluctuations of water level through the year. This is illustrated by the behavior of the Casselman River at Markleton for water year 1988 (October 1987 through September 1988).

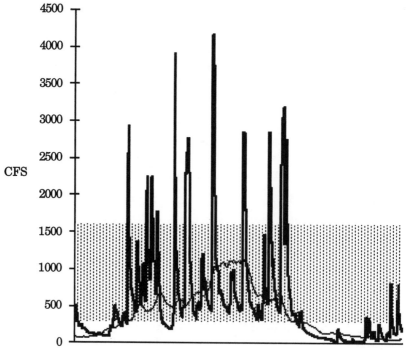

Figure F-2: Water Year 1988 and median flows of Casselman River

Figure F-2 shows the daily mean flows for that year (heavy line) together with the recommended runnable levels (2.0 to 3.5 feet or 190-1630 cfs, the shaded area) and the weekly rolling average of median daily flows for the 49-year period 1923-1972 (the light line), which is an indication of seasonal change.

Water year 1988 saw no floods. Periodic rains from December to May frequently brought the stream above runnable levels. In mid-June a widespread drought brought the stream well below runnable; it didn't recover until September. The mean daily flow for the year was 558 cfs, well below the 68-year mean of 660 cfs; nevertheless the river was high enough to run on 202 days (55% of the year, as compared to 52% in a normal year) and it was above the maximum recommended level on 23 days (6% of the year, as compared to 8% in a normal year).

### Seasons and water levels

Generally speaking, Western Pennsylvania rivers run above their mean annual flow in February, March, and April; as a result, the runnable season for smaller rivers is late winter through mid-spring.  Rivers generally fall steadily through May and June, often with a sharp drop in June. They reach summer levels in June or July and continue to drop slowly through September before beginning to recover in late October.  The normal high-season flow is about 50% higher than the mean annual flow.  The variation in flow (cfs) from low season to high season is typically a factor of 10 to 20.  In comparison, the variation in flow from low runnable to high runnable on a canoeable stream is typically only a factor of 3 to 8.

The Casselman River has a fairly typical normal season, which is shown as the light line in Figure F-2.  The "normal" level for each day of the year is the median of the daily flows for that day over a period of half a century.  We have smoothed this data with a weekly rolling average. Since this is the median value, the actual flow on that day will be higher in about half the years and lower in about half the years.  Figure F-2 shows actual flows for water year 1988 that are both above and below median flows.

Because of seasonal fluctuations like these, many rivers have seasons for which they can normally be expected to be up.  Some also have seasons for which they can normally be expected to be too high.  For example, the lower section of Little Beaver Creek is normally up from late November to late June but normally too high from mid March to early April.  Similarly, Slippery Rock Creek from Eckert Bridge to Harris Bridge is normally up from early November to early July but normally too high from early March to early April. Although these two streams can be run at various times from July through October--usually after a day or two of rain--you should not assume that they will be runnable on a typical weekend.

## Weather and water levels

Although the normal flow of our rivers varies with the seasons, much larger variations are caused from day to day by runoff from rainfall and snowmelt. This variation is the major source of the fluctuations in actual flow in Figure F-2. The highest daily discharge of the year (in cfs) is often several hundred times as large as the lowest. For example, in water year 1988 (October 1987-September 1988) the following ranges were observed:

| River | Gauge | Maximum | | | Minimum | | | Ratio of |
|---|---|---|---|---|---|---|---|---|
| | | Flow | Lev | Date | Flow | Lev | Date | Flows |
| Oil Ck | Rouseville | 3420 | 6.1 | 4/4 | 47 | 0.6 | 8/22 | 73 |
| Clarion R | Cooksburg | 7000 | 7.6 | 11/30 | 290 | 2.2 | 7/14 | 24 |
| Redbank Ck | St Charles | 5110 | 8.4 | 2/4 | 30 | 2.2 | 8/16 | 170 |
| Crooked Ck | Idaho | 4550 | 9.0 | 2/2 | 17 | 2.2 | 8/15 | 268 |
| Blacklick | Josephine | 4950 | 7.0 | 2/2 | 32 | 2.9 | 8/14 | 155 |
| Loyalhanna | Kingston | 3060 | 6.5 | 2/2 | 9 | 1.2 | 7/18 | 333 |
| S Fk Ten Mile | Jefferson | 3800 | 8.3 | 2/2 | 1 | 0.6 | 8/18 | 3801 |
| Casselman | Markleton | 4160 | 5.2 | 3/4 | 22 | 0.8 | 8/12 | 189 |
| Laurel Hill | Ursina | 2050 | 3.5 | 3/4 | 3 | 0.6 | 7/10 | 661 |
| Connoquenes'g | Zelienople | 4320 | 7.6 | 2/2 | 24 | 1.1 | 7/16 | 180 |
| Slippery Rock | Wurtemburg | 2550 | 4.3 | 2/4 | 44 | 1.0 | 7/17 | 58 |

Runoff from rainfall or snowmelt first affects the small headwater streams. As it flows down these tributaries into larger creeks, the larger creeks rise too. It takes several hours for the surge of water to reach the main rivers, and by this time the headwater streams have often started falling. For example, during the high water of November 1987, the peak flow occurred at Wilcox on the West Branch Clarion at 4 PM on November 29; it peaked 60 miles downstream at Cooksburg, on the main stem, 15 hours later (at 7AM on November 30).

The rise and fall can easily take place within a single day. For example, in early September of 1989, Slippery Rock and Connoquenessing Creeks were at low summer levels, which are well below runnable. The night of September 7, two to three inches of rain fell in parts of the headwaters of these two creeks. Figure F-3 shows the water levels on both creeks at four-hour intervals on September 8 and 9. As measured at the Wurtemburg gauge, the Slippery Rock rose briskly between 4:00 AM and 8:00 AM, then fell in several stages, falling to low runnable levels by the evening of September 9. The continuous record at Wurtemburg correlates well with the three available readings at McConnells Mill.  The rainfall reached the headwaters of the Connoquenessing sometime after it reached the Slippery Rock basin; as a result, the Connoquenessing rose and fell about 12 hours after the Slippery Rock.

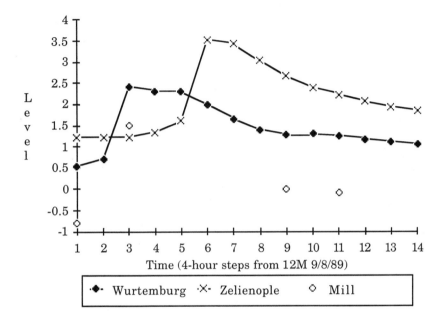

Figure F-3: High levels after heavy rain

River levels depend on the amount of rainfall as well as its timing.  The average annual rainfall varies across the state, as does the average runoff that results from that rainfall. Figure F-4 shows the historical patterns of rainfall and runoff.

The effects of seasons and weather can complement or cancel each other.  The tiniest streams require rainfall in addition to seasonal flow, and even large rivers can be too low during a dry spell in late summer.

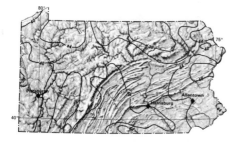

lines of equal
average annual
precipitation
interval 4 inches

Figure F-4a: Precipitation in Pennsylvania

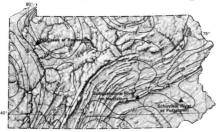

lines of equal
average annual
runoff in inches,
variable interval

Figure F-4b: Runoff in Pennsylvania

## *Terrain and water levels*

Local geography affects the way a stream responds to
rainfall.  Streams in smaller watersheds rise and fall soon
after a rain, especially if they are in narrow, steep valleys.
For example, Laurel Hill Creek and Buffalo Creek in
Armstrong County have watersheds of comparable area
(121 square miles at Ursina and 137 square miles at
Freeport, respectively).  The Laurel Hill is runnable about
20% of the year, compared to 40% for the Buffalo.  The
Laurel Hill's steeper valley combines with its larger
gradient (40 feet/mile for the Laurel Hill, 10 feet/mile for the
Buffalo) to bring the stream up and down faster than the
Buffalo.

Small streams run together to form larger streams, which
carry more water throughout the year; these larger streams
respond more slowly to rainfall because the water takes a
few hours to get downstream from the tributaries.  Since
they receive water from a wider area they usually have
higher flows throughout the year and their runnable
seasons are correspondingly longer.  For example, the
Youghiogheny River at Confluence draws water from three
major and several minor tributaries.  The Youghiogheny

itself is at least high enough to run during most of the year, partly because of its large watershed area and partly because Youghiogheny Dam just upstream from Confluence moderates the flow.  It is, however, often too high from early January to mid May.  The Casselman River, next largest in size, is runnable in its lower reaches about half the year (early December to early June).  The Laurel Hill Creek watershed is a third the size of the Casselman's; the Laurel Hill is runnable less than a quarter of the year, and it is only reliably up from early March to mid-April. Youghiogheny Lake is used for flood control as well as recreation; its contribution is to regulate the flow of the river below Confluence (see Figure F-5); the lake decouples upstream weather from downstream levels. You can't predict when the smallest of the canoeable tributaries, such as Whites Creek and Coxes Creek, will be up--you just have to catch them after very heavy rain when the other creeks are too high.

Another effect of terrain is that wide, shallow rivers require more water (as measured by flow in cfs) than narrow, deep rivers.  For example, Slippery Rock Creek violates the usual rule of thumb that downstream reaches of a stream are usually runnable at lower gauge readings than upstream reaches.  From McConnells Mill to Harris Bridge the Slippery Rock runs through a deep gorge and the creek is quite narrow.  It's runnable here with a flow as low as 155 cfs (0.9 at Wurtemburg or about minus 0.3 at McConnells Mill).  After Harris Bridge, however, the stream gets much wider.  From Harris Bridge to Wurtemburg, the wide shallow stretches are too low to float a boat below flows of about 375 cfs (1.5 at Wurtemburg or about 0.2 at McConnells Mill).

### Human use

Natural runoff patterns can be disturbed by reservoirs or industrial use.  The most common of these in Western Pennsylvania are lakes and reservoirs, especially those which include flood control, low-flow water quality, and hydroelectric power among their major purposes.

Our flood control lakes have two major effects on the flow downstream from the dam: they retain runoff after a rain in order to decrease the peak flow downstream, and they save water for release in the dry season, thereby lengthening the effective runnable season.  Rivers that benefit from such extended seasons include the Youghiogheny below Confluence, Mahoning Creek below Mahoning Dam, the Shenango River below Pymatuning Lake, the Clarion River (partially controlled by East Branch Lake), and, of course, the Allegheny River below Kinzua Dam.  The segment of a river between a flood-control dam and the next large tributary downstream will often be an exception to the rule that rivers rise shortly after a rain as the dam holds back runoff until the downstream tributaries have had a chance to drain.

This pattern is illustrated in Figure F-5, which shows the flows at Markleton on the Casselman and at Youghiogheny Dam and Confluence on the Youghiogheny River for the two-week period from February 29 to March 13, 1988.

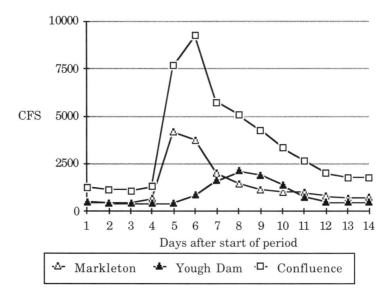

Figure F-5: The Youghiogheny and its tributaries

On the fourth day of this period the rivers in the area rose. The flow from the Casselman (augmented by the Laurel Hill, which enters the Casselman below Markleton) brought up the Youghiogheny at Confluence.  The Casselman peaked on the fifth day, the Youghiogheny at Confluence on the sixth.  The runoff from upper reaches of the

Youghiogheny was held in Youghiogheny Lake and released on the seventh through tenth days, after the uncontrolled tributaries dropped.

Hydroelectric plants often run when demand for electricity is high; this can cause substantial variations from hour to hour in the flow downstream from the plant. Water use in other kinds of plants can also create variations in flow: for example, the Keystone power plant can divert as much as 30 cfs (7% of mean flow) from Crooked Creek near Idaho, mine pumpage causes diurnal fluctuations at low flow in Mahoning Creek above Punxsutawney, and Bethlehem Steel plants and city water supplies along the Little Conemaugh River divert unspecified amounts.

## Kinds of River Level Information in This Guide

This guide provides a variety of information that can help you determine water levels. This section lists the information provided in river write-ups. The section below on nitty-gritty details explains precisely how this information is defined.

*Size of river:* Rivers are classified as tiny, small, medium, large, and huge based on the mean annual flow. When the mean flow is not available it is estimated from the drainage area. The header for each river section includes size, area, and mean flow.

*Recommended water levels:* When reports from people who have paddled the river are available, we show the range of reported runnable levels. Whenever possible, we use a formal gauge that is on the river being described and reasonably close to the section. When this is not possible, we refer to an informal gauge or to another gauge in the area (for example, Rouseville on Oil Creek is used for several streams). The recommended levels appear in the header and in the *Gauges* section of the write-up. For rivers up to Class III in difficulty, runnable levels are recommended with open canoes in mind. For rivers of Class IV difficulty and above, levels are selected for closed boaters. Runnable levels for closed boats are generally higher at both ends of the range.

*Flows that correspond to runnable levels:* This provides an indication of the absolute size of the river at the gauge site. Also the river stages (water levels) reported for a given flow can change with time. The flow is an indication of runnability that is less likely to change with time. When the information is available, the *Gauges* section includes the flows that correspond to the runnable levels. When reports on runnable levels are not available, we sometimes give the gauge reading that corresponds to the mean annual flow and some hints about how to interpret it (see below).

*Correlations between gauges:* In a few cases the *Gauges* section includes correlations between formal and informal gauges or between two nearby gauges. These are given as scatter plots of observed readings.

*Normal runnable season:* When historical data is available, this section of the write-up reports the portion of the year the median flow is greater than the minimum runnable flow. Sometimes a "too-high" season can also be determined from historical data. We also report the fraction of the year the actual flow exceeds the minimum and maximum runnable levels, when this data is available. If data is not available, we estimate the season based on the size of the river. This information helps you guess which part of the year you're likely to be able to run the river of your choice or how much rain will be required to make a river runnable during the current season.

# Where River Level Information Comes From

This section presents detailed explanation of our sources of data and how we use them to derive information.

### Sources of information

Information on water levels and seasons has been derived in part from the following resources:

* *Pennsylvania Gazetteer of Streams.* Commonwealth of Pennsylvania, Department of Environmental Resources, Water Resources Bulletin No. 6, 1971. This reference lists streams, shows the relation of tributaries to main streams, and gives the drainage area of each stream at its mouth.

• *Low Flow Characteristics of Pennsylvania Streams.* Commonwealth of Pennsylvania, Department of Environmental Resources, Water Resources Bulletin No. 12, 1977. This reference gives basic data on formal gauges, including the exact location, drainage area at the gauge, mean annual flow, and man-made regulation of flow. It also tabulates the duration of daily flow (a table that shows the percentage of the time that various flows (in cfs) are equalled or exceeded).

• *Water Resources Data--Pennsylvania--Water Year 1988, Volume 3.* US Geological Survey Water-data Report PA-88-3. This reference is published annually for all states with the obvious changes of title and report number. It contains historical data giving specifications of gauges and flows on each day of the year.

• *Selected Streamflow Experience Graphs for Southwestern Pennsylvania.* US Geological Survey Open-File Report (Greater Pittsburgh Regional Studies), April 1976. This is a collection of duration hydrograph plots, or graphs showing the how often the river has run at various flows over a period of several decades.

### Size of river

The size of a river is determined by the area of its watershed (drainage basin) and by its mean annual flow:

| Size | Area (sq mi) | Mean Flow (cfs) |
|---|---|---|
| Tiny | less than 60 | less than 100 |
| Small | 60-180 | 100-300 |
| Medium | 180-1,200 | 300-2,000 |
| Large | 1,200-6,000 | 2,000-10,000 |
| Huge | more than 6,000 | more than 10,000 |

The area at the mouth of a river is given in the *Gazetteer*; areas at other points are given in *Low-Flow Characteristics of Pennsylvania Streams* and in the annual report *Water Resources Data--Pennsylvania*. Where precise data is not available the area is estimated, taking account of the contributions of major tributaries. Statistically, the mean annual flow is strongly correlated with the drainage area. The correlation clearly depends on the mean annual rainfall and runoff (see Figure F-4). Figure F-6 shows the correlation for the area covered by this guide; a good estimate is

mean flow in cfs = 5 / 3 x (drainage area in square miles)

Mean annual flows at gauged locations are taken from *Low-Flow Characteristics of Pennsylvania Streams*; flows at other points are estimated with the above formula.

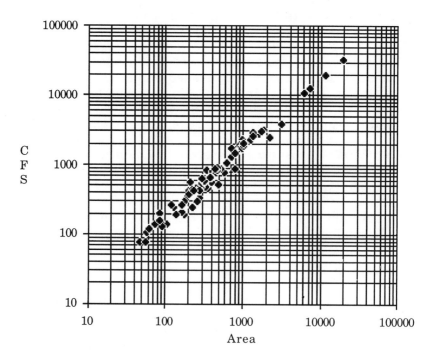

Figure F-6: Mean flow and drainage area

### Recommended water levels

As we noted at the beginning, the amount of water in your river on the day you run it has a major effect on the kind of trip you have.  Descriptions such as "low" and "high" are somewhat subjective.  Closed-boat paddlers and rafters can handle higher, more turbulent water than can open canoeists.  Different paddlers also have different tastes about maneuvering and large waves.  In addition, the physical structure of a river affects the way the river changes with water level.  As a result, the determination of low and high water  must ultimately be made individually for each river.

Recommended water levels are based on reports from paddlers. Two kinds of reports are useful. The report, "we ran Rushin' River from Startsville to Endbridge at a level of 6.0 on the HowHigh gauge and found it high but runnable" gives us a direct report. The report, "we ran Rushin' River from Startsville to Endbridge on August 13, 1985 and found it low but runnable" is at least as good; we can consult the annual report *Water Resources Data--Pennsylvania* for water year 1985 to discover that the flow at HowHigh was 570 cfs on that date, which corresponds to a level of 3.5 feet. Note that this means we can get useful level information from your old canoeing logs.

When recommended levels aren't available but a mean annual flow is, we give the gauge reading for the mean flow and a hint about whether runnable levels are most likely to be above or below that level (this hint is based on river size, as described below). The data indicates that the typical river is higher than its mean annual flow about 30% of the time.

### Flows that correspond to runnable levels

The relation between flow and level is determined individually for each river as described above and illustrated in Figure F-1. The current rating tables were made available to us through the courtesy of the US Army Corps of Engineers and the US Geological Survey. Since the profile of the river bed at a gauge site can change, old gauge readings may be misleading. This has happened at several of the gauges used in this guide:

| River | Gauge | Difference at runnable levels |
|---|---|---|
| Loyalhanna Ck | Kingston | 1.5 higher in 1989 than in 1975 |
| Crooked Ck | Idaho | 1.5 higher in 1989 than in 1975 |
| Blacklick Ck | Josephine | 0.4 lower  in 1989 than is 1975 |
| Casselman R | Markleton | 0.2 higher in 1989 than in 1975 |
| Laurel Hill Ck | Ursina | 0.2 lower  in 1989 than in 1975 |

Where possible we have corrected the recommended levels. Because of this problem, canoeing trip reports with dates are somewhat more useful than reports that give levels alone. If we have the date of the trip, we can look up the flow on that date and see what level it corresponds to now.

## Correlations between gauges

In several cases we provide correlations between gauges, often to calibrate an informal gauge against a formal one. These are usually based on notes collected by individuals.

## Normal runnable season

The report *Selected Streamflow Experience Graphs for Southwestern Pennsylvania* provides the median flow for each day of the year over a period of several decades for a number of rivers. For these rivers, the normal runnable season is defined as the period when the median daily flow exceeds the minimum runnable level. Sometimes a season when the median daily flow exceeds the maximum runnable level can also be identified. The fraction of the year the river is above the minimum or maximum runnable level is determined by converting the level to a flow and comparing it to the Duration of Daily Flow tables in *Low Flow Characteristics of Pennsylvania Streams*.

The runnable season of a river depends substantially on its size. Even if it is not possible to determine a normal season from historical data about a particular river, certain generalizations about the relation between size and season offer guidance about when to expect that river to be up:

| Size | How Often OK | Too High | Normal Season | Relation of Runnable Level to Mean Flow |
|---|---|---|---|---|
| Tiny | 0%-20% | rarely | after lots of rain | runnable level much higher than mean |
| Small | 15%-35% | 0%-10% | Jan-Apr | runnable level at least as high as mean, or higher |
| Medium | 30%-65% | 5%-25% | Dec-May | mean level is probably okay, perhaps a bit high |
| Large | 60%-95% | 25%-40% | all year (high in Jan-Apr) | mean is probably near maximum runnable level |
| Huge | mostly | 35%- ? | often high | always runnable, often too high |

The high-season flow (the median daily flow during the high season) is usually about 50% higher than the mean annual flow.

# Definitions of Phrases Used for Gauges and Levels

This section gives definitions for phrases used in the guide to describe water levels. We illustrate typical gauge descriptions with the hypothetical example of Rushin' River (which has a gauge at HowHigh) and Swift Creek, a tributary of Rushin' River with no gauge of its own.

### Formal gauge on the river

In the write-up of Rushin' River: *"The HowHigh gauge should read between 3.0 and 6.0 feet. This corresponds to a flow of 500 cfs to 900 cfs."* This phrase is used when the gauge is on the river being described and close enough to the section to provide a good indication of level. The flow in cfs is included to provide an absolute indication of size that is comparable between rivers; flows in different years are comparable even if the calibration of the gauge has changed. The flow in cfs is at the gauge; the actual size of the river on sections several miles upstream or downstream from the gauge will be smaller or larger, respectively. Sometimes we also indicate differences in the character of the river at different levels.

The Corps of Engineers' satellite reporting system has made current information available for more gauges. As a result we can get good data from some gauges that were formerly not helpful for making paddling decisions. These include Zelienople (formerly Hazen) on Connoquenessing Creek, Wurtemburg on Slippery Rock Creek, Rouseville on Oil Creek, Moffatts Mills on Raccoon Creek, and Jefferson on Ten Mile Creek. A gauge at Freeport on Buffalo Creek should soon join this list. We have also identified some gauges that should provide better indications than the ones previously used. For example, Grantsville should provide a better indicator than Markleton for levels on the Casselman above Garrett; Grantsville is between 0 and 24 miles from any part of this section whereas Markleton is between 14 and 38 miles away. Also, Idaho was previously used as a general indicator of levels in the area, but it is substantially controlled by the lake that provides cooling water to the Keystone power plant and its rating chart has changed substantially.

## No formal gauge on this river, formal gauge on nearby river

In the write-up of Swift Creek: *"The HowHigh gauge on nearby Rushin' River will probably read between 5.0 and 7.3."* This form is used when the gauge is on a nearby river or at a distant point on the same river. Since the gauge will be affected by factors remote from the section of interest, it is a less reliable indicator than a nearby gauge. It will be least reliable when local rainfall has been recent and irregular; it will be most reliable during seasonal runoff (no recent rain) and when rainfall has been gentle and uniform in the area.

## Formal gauge on the river but no information on runnable levels

In the write-up of Rushin' River: *"We do not have enough information to report runnable levels on this section. A reading of 3.5 on the HowHigh gauge corresponds to the mean flow of 570 cfs. Since this is a medium-sized river, we speculate that the river will be runnable at 3.5 feet and may be on the high side of runnable at that level."* The interpretation is based on the size of the river and the information in the table above, namely, "We speculate that ..."

Tiny: *"... a much higher level than 3.5 will be required for the river to be runnable."*

Small: *"...the runnable level will be at least 3.5 and perhaps more."*

Medium: *"... the river will be runnable at 3.5 and may be on the high side of runnable at that level."*

Large: *"... the river is runnable most of the year; at 3.5 it may be too high."*

Huge: *"...the river is almost always runnable but is often too high."*

This description is simply a guess; the editors will appreciate reports on actual runnable levels.

### Streamside gauge

When a good streamside gauge is available, its description and interpretation are included.  We may give a streamside gauge even if there is a formal gauge, because the current reading for a formal gauge is not always available and local heavy rains can cause flash flooding with little warning.

## Definitions of phrases used for normal wet seasons

This section gives definitions for phrases used in the guide to describe normal runnable seasons.

### Formal gauge with streamflow experience graphs

In the write-up of Rushin' River: *"This section is normally runnable from late November to early June, except it is normally too high from early March to early April."*  A description of this form is based on comparing the runnable levels to a streamflow experience graph.  The months when the median daily flow exceeds the minimum runnable flow is the runnable season; the months when the median daily flow exceeds the maximum runnable flow is the season during which it is normally too high.  For some streams the median daily flow never exceeds one of these thresholds; in this case we say there is no normal runnable season or no period during which it is normally too high.  Note that on any given day any particular creek may be much higher or lower than its median level for that day--this information is useful for advance planning or for estimating the effects of recent weather, not for absolute prediction.

### Formal gauge with daily flow duration statistics

In the write-up of Rushin' River: *"The HowHigh gauge is above 3.0 feet 55% of the time and above 6.0 feet 15% of the time."*  This phrase indicates that without regard to normal seasons, Rushin' River is runnable over half the time and that it's too high often enough to be worth thinking about.  This information will help you make educated guesses about the combined effects of seasons and recent weather:  The lower the chance (percentage) that the stream is above some level, the more likely it is to need rain during the spring or very heavy rain during the summer to bring it above that level.

### No available statistics on seasons

If no specific seasonal information is available for this stream, we estimate the season by analogy to other streams of comparable size:

Tiny: *"Since this section is tiny, it should normally be runnable only after a heavy rain or during spring snowmelt."*

Small: *"Since this section is small, it should normally be runnable approximately January through April."*

Medium: *"Since this section is medium-sized, it should normally be runnable approximately December through May."*

Large: *"Since this section is large, it should normally be runnable all year, but it may be too high from February to April."*

Huge: *"Since this is a huge river, it should be runnable all year. However, it will be too high whenever the river is reported as too high for recreational boating."*

### Dam controlled stream

If the stream is substantially or completely dam-controlled, the description of normal seasons will indicate the effect this has on the stream.  Dams, especially if they are operated for flood control or water quality improvement, often extend the runnable season of the river downstream from the dam. This happens in two ways.  First, when high runoff is retained by the dam the highest flows and their durations-- and hence the too-high season--are reduced.  Second, when the retained water is later released, the lower flows are increased and the too-low season may thereby be shortened.

The history of water levels on the Clarion River at the East Branch Dam illustrate this moderation of flows to reduce both high season and low season.  Figure F-7 shows the "mean exceedance" levels for the East Branch Clarion River at the outflow of the dam, northeast of Glen Hazel.  The dashed line shows the levels before the construction of the East Branch Dam, the solid line shows the levels after construction of the dam, and the shaded area shows roughly the runnable levels (70 cfs is reported as minimum, 500 cfs is estimated maximum).  Before construction of the dam, the flow exceeded 500 cfs about 5% of the time but after the dam began operating the flow exceeded 500 cfs less than 2% of the time.  At the other end of the range, before the dam was built the stream was runnable--above 70 cfs--about 55% of the time but afterward the flow was above 70 cfs nearly 60% of the time.

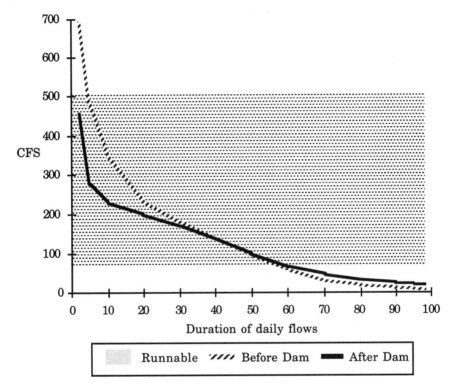

Figure F-7: Moderation of Flow at East Branch Clarion Dam

## Sample Rating Tables

The next two pages give rating tables for streams of interest.  They are current as of spring 1989 but are subject to change as the rivers change.  All these gauges are reported via satellite to the Corps of Engineers  Many of them are also included on the Weather Bureau telephone recording.

| River | Gauge | Area | Mean | 1.0 | 1.5 | 2.0 | 2.5 |
|---|---|---|---|---|---|---|---|
| Allegheny | Franklin | 5982 | 10550 | - | - | 790 | 1,640 |
| Allegheny | Parker | 7671 | 13550 | - | 2,000 | 3,200 | 4,600 |
| Allegheny | Warren | | | 100 | 450 | 1,000 | 1,690 |
| Beaver | Beaver Falls | 3106 | 3758 | - | - | - | - |
| Beaver | Wampum | 2235 | 2494 | - | - | - | - |
| Big Sandy | Rockville | 200 | 422 | - | - | - | - |
| Blacklick | Josephine | 195 | 370 | - | - | - | - |
| Buckhannon | Buckhannon | | | - | - | - | - |
| Buffalo | Freeport | 137 | 194 | 17 | 85 | 220 | 445 |
| Casselman | Markleton | 382 | 661 | 45 | 133 | 290 | 570 |
| Cheat | Parsons | 718 | 1697 | - | 26 | 102 | 255 |
| Clarion | Cooksburg | 807 | 1462 | - | - | 240 | 450 |
| Clarion | Piney Dam | 951 | 1787 | - | 49 | 149 | 310 |
| Clarion | Ridgway | 303 | 591 | - | - | - | 135 |
| Conemaugh | Seward | 715 | 1281 | - | - | 130 | 450 |
| Conemaugh | Tunnelton | 1358 | 2882 | - | - | 50 | 260 |
| Connoquens'g | Zelienople | 356 | 466 | 16 | 93 | 231 | 446 |
| Crooked Ck | Idaho | 191 | 295 | - | - | - | 45 |
| Dry Fork | Hendricks | 345 | 832 | - | 0 | 3 | 23 |
| E Br Clarion | E Br Outflow | 73 | 138 | - | 22 | 70 | 156 |
| French Ck | Meadville | | | 80 | 250 | 520 | 870 |
| Kiskiminetas | Vandergrift | 1825 | 3106 | - | - | - | - |
| L Mahoning | McCormick | 87 | 153 | - | 10 | 37 | 87 |
| Laurel Hill | Ursina | 121 | 266 | 32 | 190 | 520 | 1,020 |
| Little Beaver | E Liverpool | 496 | 514 | - | - | 36 | 95 |
| Loyalhanna | Kingston | 172 | 303 | - | 19 | 59 | 135 |
| Mahoning | Mahon'g Dam | 344 | 601 | - | 36 | 117 | 265 |
| Mahoning | Punxsutawney | 158 | 277 | 36 | 99 | 230 | 420 |
| Oil Ck | Rouseville | 300 | 538 | - | - | 135 | 300 |
| Redbank | St Charles | 528 | 873 | - | - | - | 100 |
| S Fk Ten Mile | Jefferson | 201 | 180 | 8 | 60 | 160 | 278 |
| Shenango | Pymatuning | 167 | 208 | - | - | - | - |
| Shenango | Sharpsville | 584 | 761 | - | - | - | 236 |
| Slippery Rock | Wurtemburg | 398 | 572 | 185 | 375 | 650 | 990 |
| Stony | Ferndale | 451 | 771 | - | - | 34 | 113 |
| Tionesta | Lynch | 233 | 426 | 63 | 200 | 420 | 680 |
| Tionesta | Tionesta Dam | 479 | 891 | 143 | 270 | 435 | 650 |
| Tygart Valley | Belington | 408 | 814 | - | - | 6 | 46 |
| Tygart Valley | Philippi | 916 | 1926 | 7 | 52 | 155 | 320 |
| W Br Clarion | Wilcox | 63 | 126 | - | 32 | 125 | 255 |
| Youghiogheny | Confluence | 1029 | 2005 | - | 380 | 670 | 1,040 |
| Youghiogheny | Connellsville | 1326 | 2580 | - | - | 550 | 1,000 |
| Youghiogheny | Friendsville | 295 | 646 | - | - | 53 | 168 |

| 3.0 | 3.5 | 4.0 | 4.5 | 5.0 | 6.0 | 7.0 | 8.0 | 9.0 | 10.0 |
|---|---|---|---|---|---|---|---|---|---|
| 2,690 | 3,930 | 5,370 | 6,920 | 8,650 | 12,600 | 17,000 | 22,000 | 27,500 | 33,500 |
| 6,100 | 7,700 | 9,700 | 11,700 | 13,800 | 19,000 | 25,000 | 31,000 | 3,800 | 45,000 |
| 2,500 | 3,440 | 4,500 | 5,720 | 7,080 | 10,100 | 13,500 | 17,300 | 21,600 | 26,100 |
| - | 740 | 1,650 | 2,900 | 4,400 | 8,100 | 13,000 | 18,000 | 23,400 | 30,200 |
| 560 | 980 | 1,540 | 2,250 | 3,000 | 5,000 | 7,000 | 9,000 | 11,000 | 13,000 |
| 6 | 24 | 55 | 113 | 200 | 530 | 1,120 | 1,950 | 3,000 | 4,250 |
| 43 | 133 | 325 | 699 | 1,260 | 2,880 | 4,990 | 7,180 | 9,750 | 12,560 |
| - | 11 | 48 | 121 | 221 | 450 | 720 | 1,010 | 1,330 | 1,680 |
| 740 | 1,045 | 1,400 | 1,800 | 2,208 | 3,088 | 4,061 | 5,185 | 6,483 | 7,887 |
| 1,030 | 1,630 | 2,330 | 3,090 | 3,890 | 5,850 | 8,190 | 11,200 | 15,000 | 20,300 |
| 500 | 830 | 1,280 | 1,880 | 2,600 | 4,450 | 6,900 | 9,900 | 13,000 | 17,000 |
| 730 | 1,080 | 1,540 | 2,080 | 2,597 | 3,970 | 5,700 | 7,800 | 10,300 | 13,200 |
| 560 | 914 | 1,350 | 1,840 | 2,450 | 3,870 | 5,490 | 7,355 | 9,400 | 11,400 |
| 270 | 430 | 630 | 860 | 1,110 | 1,700 | 2,350 | 3,050 | 3,800 | 4,650 |
| 1,080 | 1,900 | 2,760 | 3,610 | 4,460 | 6,220 | 8,320 | 10,490 | 12,910 | 15,530 |
| 720 | 1,350 | 2,150 | 3,050 | 4,050 | 6,160 | 8,600 | 11,160 | 14,000 | 17,100 |
| 778 | 1,080 | 1,400 | 1,760 | 2,140 | 2,940 | 3,800 | 4,700 | 5,750 | 6,950 |
| 170 | 390 | 770 | 1,080 | 1,450 | 2,250 | 3,100 | 3,850 | 4,550 | 5,300 |
| 180 | 580 | 1,210 | 2,060 | 3,070 | 5,400 | 8,100 | 10,900 | 14,000 | 18,000 |
| 286 | 460 | 658 | 895 | 1,160 | 1,780 | 2,450 | | | |
| 1,280 | 1,750 | 2,220 | 2,660 | 3,100 | 3,900 | 4,800 | 5,800 | 7,000 | 8,300 |
| 410 | 700 | 1,110 | 1,600 | 2,150 | 3,370 | 4,900 | 6,700 | 8,700 | 10,800 |
| 180 | 294 | 440 | 590 | 740 | 1,060 | 1,460 | 1,920 | 2,520 | 3,210 |
| 1,520 | 2,020 | 2,520 | 3,020 | 3,650 | 4,950 | 6,250 | 7,550 | 8,850 | 10,150 |
| 195 | 355 | 565 | 840 | 1,150 | 1,930 | 2,900 | 4,011 | 5,395 | 7,007 |
| 255 | 420 | 680 | 1,040 | 1,470 | 2,500 | 3,720 | 5,280 | 7,200 | 9,500 |
| 480 | 770 | 1,120 | 1,540 | 2,020 | 3,300 | 5,300 | 7,700 | | |
| 640 | 900 | 1,200 | 1,500 | 1,850 | 2,600 | 3,500 | 4,500 | 5,600 | 6,800 |
| 550 | 890 | 1,270 | 1,750 | 2,250 | 3,360 | 4,800 | 6,620 | 8,580 | 11,100 |
| 225 | 425 | 675 | 975 | 1,305 | 2,200 | 3,240 | 4,500 | 5,900 | 7,400 |
| 433 | 617 | 837 | 1,100 | 1,380 | 2,030 | 2,810 | 3,550 | 4,350 | 5,150 |
| - | - | 11 | 51 | 180 | 640 | 940 | 1,230 | 1,480 | |
| 495 | 810 | 1,250 | 1,750 | 2,250 | 3,250 | 4,350 | 5,450 | 6,550 | 7,750 |
| 1,340 | 1,760 | 2,240 | 2,790 | 3,400 | 4,990 | 6,900 | 8,900 | 11,000 | 13,100 |
| 280 | 560 | 920 | 1,300 | 1,840 | 3,150 | 4,800 | 6,800 | 9,100 | 11,960 |
| 1,030 | 1,380 | 1,750 | 2,150 | 2,580 | 3,550 | 4,690 | 6,200 | 8,400 | 11,100 |
| 920 | 1,240 | 1,600 | 2,100 | 2,650 | 4,060 | 5,900 | 7,900 | 10,600 | |
| 180 | 410 | 675 | 950 | 1,250 | 1,910 | 2,610 | 3,400 | 4,270 | 5,270 |
| 620 | 160 | 1,620 | 2,220 | 2,820 | 4,020 | 5,221 | 6,420 | 7,650 | 8,950 |
| 415 | 615 | 840 | 1,065 | 1,310 | 1,810 | 2,480 | 3,280 | 4,260 | 5,320 |
| 1,500 | 2,100 | 2,780 | 3,610 | 4,460 | 6,350 | 8,470 | 10,890 | 13,570 | 16,570 |
| 1,620 | 2,390 | 3,300 | 4,300 | 5,300 | 7,400 | 10,200 | 13,200 | 16,200 | 19,400 |
| 451 | 918 | 1,593 | 2,500 | 3,450 | 5,597 | 7,550 | 9,685 | 11,990 | |

# Appendix G
# Help Improve this Guide

This guide is far from complete. Much more needs to be added by way of new trips, more gauge information, trip notes, corrections, and the like. For one person or a small group of people to obtain this information would be a very time-consuming task. Thus we appeal to all canoeists who use this guide to contribute their experiences and comments for inclusion in later versions.

To encourage updates, the editors will send a complimentary copy of the next edition of this canoe guide to anyone who has contributed a trip report containing new information, corrections, etc. that are used in the new edition. Send these reports to: Canoeing Guide Editor, American Youth Hostels, Pittsburgh Council, 6300 Fifth Avenue, Pittsburgh, Pennsylvania 15232.

Gauge readings are not necessary. You may give the gauge reading, if you know it, or you may just give the date and place with comments on the level, etc. The editor will then obtain the gauge reading from the appropriate source. A trip report form on the next few pages may be used; however, we will be happy to receive reports in any form. On reports describing new streams it would be desirable (but not necessary) for the reporter to write up the trip notes as he thinks they should appear so as to avoid errors of interpretation by the editor.

# Trip Report Form

River _____

Put-in _____

_____

Take-out _____

_____

Approximate number of miles by river _____

Class _____ Please reread pages 28-29 before answering.

Scenic Value                          Pollution Value

A  Natural state                      A  Good swimming
B  Pretty but nothing special         B  moderate, not offensive
C  Moderate population                C  Foul
D  Heavy population, industry

Date of Trip _____          Type of trip: tandem, solo

For pleasant canoeing was water level - Too low, low but okay, okay, high but okay, too high.

Name _____          Telephone ( __ ) _____

Address _____

City/State _____          Zip _____

How experienced a canoeist are you ? _____

_____

_____

_____

Send to :   Canoeing Guide Editor
            American Youth Hostels, Pittsburgh Council
            6300 Fifth Avenue
            Pittsburgh, Pennsylvania 15232.

River _____ (Continued)

In the space below place provide description, difficulties, and shuttle. It would be helpful if they were in the style of the existing guide, but this is not necessary.

Description of Stream _____

_____

_____

_____

_____

_____

Difficulties _____

_____

_____

_____

_____

_____

Shuttle _____

_____

_____

_____

# Trip Report Form

River _____

Put-in _____

_____

Take-out _____

_____

Approximate number of miles by river _____

Class _____ Please reread pages 28-29 before answering.

Scenic Value                    Pollution Value

A  Natural state                A  Good swimming
B  Pretty but nothing special   B  moderate, not offensive
C  Moderate population          C  Foul
D  Heavy population, industry

Date of Trip _____     Type of trip: tandem, solo

For pleasant canoeing was water level - Too low, low but
okay, okay, high but okay, too high.

Name _____     Telephone ( __ ) _____

Address _____

City/State _____ Zip _____

How experienced a canoeist are you ? _____

_____

_____

_____

Send to :  Canoeing Guide Editor
           American Youth Hostels, Pittsburgh Council
           6300 Fifth Avenue
           Pittsburgh, Pennsylvania 15232.

465

River _____ (Continued)

In the space below place provide description, difficulties, and shuttle. It would be helpful if they were in the style of the existing guide, but this is not necessary.

Description of Stream _____

_____

_____

_____

_____

_____

Difficulties _____

_____

_____

_____

_____

_____

Shuttle _____

_____

_____

_____

# Trip Logs

In order to provide more complete gauge information, we ask that you log your trips and send a copy to the editors at American Youth Hostels Inc, Pittsburgh Council, 6300 Fifth Avenue, Pittsburgh, Pennsylvania 15232. Please give the exact date (this helps us determine runnable levels and seasons) use the following evaluations of the level: too low, low but okay, okay, high but okay, too high.

| Date | River | Put-in | Take-out | Scn/Pol | Miles | Level | Comments |
|------|-------|--------|----------|---------|-------|-------|----------|
|      |       |        |          |         |       |       |          |
|      |       |        |          |         |       |       |          |
|      |       |        |          |         |       |       |          |
|      |       |        |          |         |       |       |          |
|      |       |        |          |         |       |       |          |
|      |       |        |          |         |       |       |          |
|      |       |        |          |         |       |       |          |
|      |       |        |          |         |       |       |          |
|      |       |        |          |         |       |       |          |
|      |       |        |          |         |       |       |          |

| Date | River | Put-in | Take-out | Scn/Pol | Miles | Level | Comments |
|------|-------|--------|----------|---------|-------|-------|----------|
|      |       |        |          |         |       |       |          |
|      |       |        |          |         |       |       |          |
|      |       |        |          |         |       |       |          |
|      |       |        |          |         |       |       |          |
|      |       |        |          |         |       |       |          |
|      |       |        |          |         |       |       |          |
|      |       |        |          |         |       |       |          |
|      |       |        |          |         |       |       |          |
|      |       |        |          |         |       |       |          |
|      |       |        |          |         |       |       |          |
|      |       |        |          |         |       |       |          |
|      |       |        |          |         |       |       |          |
|      |       |        |          |         |       |       |          |
|      |       |        |          |         |       |       |          |

**Membership Application**
**American Youth Hostels**
Pittsburgh Council
6300 Fifth Ave.
Pittsburgh, PA 15232

## Membership types available:

|  |  |  |
|---|---|---|
| _____ | $25 | Adult (age 18 to 54; renewals $15) |
| _____ | $10 | Youth (age 17 and under) |
| _____ | $15 | Senior Citizen (age 55 and over) |
| _____ | $35 | Family (with children under 18; renewals $25) |
| _____ | $50 | Supporting Membership |
| _____ | $100 | Sustaining Membership |
| _____ | $250 | Life (individual lifetime membership) |
| _____ | Total | Make checks payable to Pittsburgh AYH |

**Memberships are valid for 12 months from month of issue**
**Prices are subject to change after September 1, 1991**

Name_____
      (last)        (first)        (middle)

Street_____

City_____ State_____ Zip_____

Phone_____ Birthdate_____

_____
(Signature)

### Benefits of AYH Membership

- Pittsburgh Council ID card good for discounts at local bike shops and outfitters.
- North American Hostel Handbook, listing over 300 hostels in the United States and Canada.
- *The Knapsack*, National AYH travel newsletter.
- *The Golden Triangle*, Pittsburgh Council's newsletter of trips and activities.
- Open house Thursday nights at Council headquarters.
- Access to National travel programs and Leadership Training courses.